How Ireland Voted 2016

Michael Gallagher • Michael Marsh
Editors

How Ireland Voted 2016

2016

The Election that Nobody Won

palgrave
macmillan

Editors

Michael Gallagher
Professor of Comparative Politics
Trinity College Dublin
Ireland

Michael Marsh
Emeritus Professor of Political Science
Trinity College Dublin
Ireland

ISBN 978-3-319-40888-0   ISBN 978-3-319-40889-7 (eBook)
DOI 10.1007/978-3-319-40889-7

Library of Congress Control Number: 2016956809

Cover illustration: © FusionShooters

Printed on acid-free paper

This Palgrave Macmillan imprint is published by Springer Nature
The registered company is Springer International Publishing AG
The registered company address is: Gewerbestrasse 11, 6330 Cham, Switzerland

PREFACE

The 2011 election, held at a time of economic crisis generating gloom and anger in equal measure, was Ireland's 'earthquake election', witnessing change on an unprecedented scale, with Fianna Fáil, the largest party in the state continuously since 1932, losing three-quarters of its seats. A Fine Gael–Labour coalition government was elected, and most of the economic indicators improved over the next five years, though after an initial honeymoon its popularity soon started to slide.

With the election due by spring 2016 at the latest, 2015 was a year of uncertainty. The economic indicators showed impressive growth, yet most people complained that they were feeling no benefit from this, and while Fine Gael's poll ratings started to recover, Labour was flatlining at a level not much above the proverbial 'margin of error'. In the autumn there was briefly an outbreak of speculation about an immediate election, and though this did not happen it meant that the election campaign lasted, in effect, from early November 2015 until election day on 26 February 2016, even though the formal campaign, which did not begin until the dissolution of the Dáil on 3 February, was exceptionally short. Politicians and pundits alike found it difficult to predict what would happen. Perhaps the outgoing government would do as abysmally as it had in the 2014 local and European Parliament elections, or alternatively it might be grudgingly re-elected. Fianna Fáil might bounce back from its 2011 nadir, or it might slip further. Sinn Féin might become the second largest party, the anchor of a new left-wing coalition government—or, alternatively, might succumb to the same dynamic as at several previous elections, proving to have peaked in mid-term and performing below expectations on election day. And perhaps independents would do as well as the polls were saying but more probably, surely, voters would prioritise government formation when it came to the crunch of election day and much of the independent support would evaporate.

Whether things would have worked out better for the government parties if they had gone to the country in November 2015 we will never know, but they could hardly have worked out much worse. Both parties slumped in support relative to 2011, Fianna Fáil made a modest recovery, Sinn Féin consolidated third spot, and Dáil strength was scattered among seven parties and a record number of independents. The independents themselves constituted one loose alliance, another even looser alliance, a family (literally) of independents, and a few sole traders. Exactly how a government was to be formed from such a fragmented parliament was, as Flann O'Brien would put it, 'a very difficult piece of puzzledom'. The riddle was not solved until, a record 70 days later, a minority government supported by only 59 of the 158 TDs took office—for how long, no one could be sure.

This volume in the *How Ireland Voted* series, the eighth, analyses this election that nobody won. The first three chapters analyse pre-election developments. Chapter 1 narrates the history of the years leading up to the election: the high hopes with which the outgoing government had entered office, and where things went wrong. Chapter 2 assesses how fully Fine Gael and Labour had fulfilled their 2011 election pledges over the following five years, and comes up with some surprising findings. Chapter 3 examines the parties' selection of their candidates, asking whether, despite the apparent democratisation of procedures, the party centres retained or even increased their control of the process.

The next two chapters consider various aspects of the campaign. Chapter 4 analyses party strategies, identifying the key decisions and events and, based on interviews with insiders from all parties, it presents and assesses the parties' perspectives on what went right and what went wrong for them. In Chapter 5 six Dáil candidates give their personal accounts of what it was like to face the voters on doorsteps across the country and one of them also recounts a historic successful Seanad election campaign.

The next four chapters analyse different aspects of the results themselves. Chapter 6 assesses the performances of the parties, identifies possible gender bias in the betting markets, and analyses the composition of the new parliament. Chapter 7 analyses survey data to investigate the reasons why people voted as they did, tackling the apparent paradox whereby a government that could point to significant improvement in virtually all major economic indicators was rejected by the voters almost as emphatically as its predecessor, which had presided over an economic collapse. Chapter 8 analyses the impact of a high-profile change to Ireland's electoral rules: the requirement that all parties achieve a degree of gender balance among their candidates. Chapter 9 focuses on an example of Irish exceptionalism: the presence, in sizeable numbers, of independent members of parliament. It asks why independents are so popular in Ireland, and whether the presence of independent deputies should be evaluated positively or regarded as a problem for the political system.

In Chapter 10, the election of the Seanad, Ireland's upper house of parliament, is analysed. The corresponding chapter in the 2011 book in this series had the title 'The final Seanad election?', because abolition of the second chamber was in the air—yet, in a referendum in 2013, the people voted narrowly to retain it. Even so, any future Seanad election might be completely different in almost every respect due to current reform proposals, as detailed in the chapter. Chapter 11 discusses the construction of the new government, one that controls not much more than a third of the seats in the Dáil. Some believe that this heralds a 'new politics' in which policies will in effect be made on the floor of parliament, perhaps in a consensual way, while sceptics regard such expectations as naive. Finally, Chapter 12 puts the scale of recent political upheaval into a broader European context. Appendices to the book contain the election results, information on all 158 TDs and on government ministers, and other relevant background information.

At the front of the book we have included a chronology of the election campaign, and the book is illustrated throughout by a selection of photographs and campaign literature that capture the spirit of election 2016. We thank RTÉ, *The Irish Times*, merrionstreet.ie and Gerry Stronge for permission to sample their stock of photographs and reproduce some of them here. Thanks are due also to Patricia O'Callaghan of RTÉ for her help in identifying the ones we have used and pointing us towards other sources.

As always, we thank our cooperative and patient contributors, who were put under great pressure by the demands of a book being produced on a very tight schedule. We are pleased that this volume, like its three predecessors, is being published by the major international publisher Palgrave Macmillan, and in particular we would like to thank Ambra Finotello for her support for our initial proposal and Imogen Gordon Clark for her work on taking it through the production process.

Michael Gallagher and Michael Marsh
Dublin, June 2016

CONTENTS

Notes on Contributors

David Barrett is an Irish Research Council doctoral candidate in the Department of Political Science in Trinity College Dublin. His research assesses the electoral impact of internal cohesion in political parties, with a particular focus on Britain and Canada. He has also written on recent election results in Ireland and Greece.

Fiona Buckley is a lecturer in the Department of Government, University College Cork where she specialises in gender politics and Irish politics. She publishes in the area of gender and politics, and is co-editor of *Politics and Gender in Ireland: The Quest for Political Agency* (with Yvonne Galligan, Routledge 2015).

Rory Costello is a lecturer in the Department of Politics and Public Administration at the University of Limerick. His research examines legislative and electoral politics in Ireland and the EU, with a particular focus on questions of democratic representation and government performance.

David M. Farrell MRIA is the Head of Politics and International Relations at UCD. A specialist in the study of parties, elections and electoral systems, his current research is focused on the operation and outcome of the Irish Constitutional Convention, of which he was the research director.

Michael Gallagher is Professor of Comparative Politics and head of the Department of Political Science in Trinity College Dublin, Ireland.

Yvonne Galligan is Professor of Comparative Politics and Head of the School of History, Anthropology, Philosophy and Politics, Queen's University Belfast. Professor Galligan has published extensively on gender and politics, including *States of Democracy: gender and politics in the European Union* (editor, Routledge 2015).

Pat Leahy is the deputy political editor of *The Irish Times*. He holds a degree in law from UCD and was a Reuters fellow at Oxford University. He is the author of two bestselling books, *Showtime: the Inside Story of Fianna Fail in Power* and *The Price of Power: Inside Ireland's Crisis Coalition*, and has made a number of television documentaries about politics for RTE. He was previously deputy editor and political editor of *The Sunday Business Post*.

Gail McElroy is Professor in Political Science at Trinity College Dublin. Her research interests are primarily in the area of legislative and party politics. She has been actively involved in the Irish National Election study since its inception and also runs the Irish module of the Comparative Candidate Study.

Claire McGing teaches and researches in the Department of Geography, Maynooth University. She specialises in gender politics and the geography of Irish elections.

Michael Marsh is Emeritus Professor of Political Science in Trinity College University of Dublin, Ireland. He was principal investigator for the 2002, 2007 and 2011 Irish National Election Studies, co-author of *The Irish Voter* (2008) and co-editor of *The Conservative Revolution* (2016).

Gary Murphy is Professor of Politics at the School of Law and Government at Dublin City University. He has held visiting professorships at the University of North Carolina, Chapel Hill and the University of Notre Dame. He has published extensively on modern Irish politics. His latest book is *Electoral Competition in Ireland since 1987: the politics of triumph and despair* (Manchester, 2016).

Mary C. Murphy is a lecturer in politics in the Department of Government, University College Cork. She specialises in European Union and Northern Ireland politics, and the study of parliament. She is a Jean Monnet Professor and Fulbright-Schuman awardee. Mary was appointed to the Seanad Reform Working Group by An Taoiseach, Enda Kenny, in 2015.

Eoin O'Malley is senior lecturer in politics at the School of Law and Government, Dublin City University. His research focuses on cabinet government and political leadership in Ireland. He is the co-editor of *Governing Ireland: from cabinet government to delegated governance* (IPA 2012) and is preparing an edited book on Fianna Fáil.

Paul O'Neill recently completed an MA in European Politics and Governance at the University of Limerick. His research interests are in the areas of Irish and European Union legislative politics.

Theresa Reidy is a lecturer in the Department of Government at University College Cork. Her research interests lie in the areas of party politics and electoral behaviour in Ireland. She is co-editor of *Irish Political Studies*.

Jane Suiter is a senior lecturer at the DCU School of Communications and is Director of the Institute for Future Media and Journalism. She is currently working on projects around political communication on social media and populist political communication. She is co-convener of the Political Studies Association of Ireland (PSAI) specialist group Voters, Parties and Election.

Robert Thomson is Professor of Politics at the University of Strathclyde, Glasgow, UK. He previously held positions at Trinity College Dublin, and at the Universities of Groningen and Utrecht in the Netherlands. His research focuses on international comparisons of democratic representation, as well as negotiations and policymaking.

Liam Weeks is a lecturer in the Department of Government at University College Cork. He has co-authored *All Politics is Local* (Collins Press, 2009), and co-edited *Radical or Redundant. Minor Parties in Irish Politics* (History Press, 2012). His next book is *Independents in Irish Party Democracy* (Manchester, 2017).

GLOSSARY

Áras an Uactharáin, residence of the President of Ireland

ard-fheis (plural ard-fheiseanna), national conference (of a political party)

Ceann Comhairle, speaker or chairperson (of the Dáil)

Dáil Éireann, directly elected lower house of parliament to which the Irish government is answerable

Fianna Fáil, the largest party in Ireland from 1932 until 2011

Fine Gael, second largest party in Ireland from 1932 to 2011, now the largest party

Leinster House, seat of houses of parliament

Oireachtas, parliament (has two houses: Dáil and Seanad)

Seanad Éireann, indirectly elected upper house of parliament

Sinn Féin, republican party

Tánaiste, deputy prime minister

Taoiseach, prime minister

Teachta Dála (TD), Dáil deputy

Abbreviations

AAA	Anti-Austerity Alliance
EU	European Union
FF	Fianna Fáil
FG	Fine Gael
GAA	Gaelic Athletic Association
GP	Green Party
Grn	Green Party
IA	Independent Alliance
IMF	International Monetary Fund
Lab	Labour Party
MEP	Member of the European Parliament
MW	Mid-West
N	North
NAMA	National Asset Management Agency
NC	North-Central
NE	North-East
NW	North-West
PBP	People Before Profit
PDs	Progressive Democrats
PR	Proportional representation
RTÉ	Raidió Teilifís Éireann, the national broadcasting station
S	South
SC	South-Central
SD	Social Democrats
SE	South-East
SF	Sinn Féin
SRWG	Seanad Reform Working Group

STV	single transferable vote
SW	South-West
TD	Teachta Dála (member of the Dáil)
ULA	United Left Alliance

Chronology of 2016 Election Campaign

3 Feb   Taoiseach visits Áras an Uachtaráin and advises president to dissolve the 31st Dáil. The election date is set for Friday 26 February, making the formal campaign duration 23 days, one of the shortest on record.

5 Feb   The early days are dominated by discussion of the 'fiscal space' in the years ahead, a neologism coined to refer to the amount of discretionary spending that will be available to the next government on various assumptions about future economic growth. Parties accuse each other of making unrealistic assumptions and hence exaggerating the size of the spending pot that will be available, while jargon-averse commentators plead that the term 'fiscal space' be banned from the airwaves entirely for the duration of the campaign.

5 Feb   SF reiterates its call for the abolition of the non-jury Special Criminal Court, an appeal backed by civil liberties groups. On the same day, a high-profile gangland murder leads other parties to insist that a non-jury court is needed in certain cases because of the risk of jury intimidation. These parties also take the opportunity to remind the public of the case of Thomas 'Slab' Murphy of south Armagh, allegedly a former leading figure in the IRA, who was recently convicted of tax offences in the Special Criminal Court, and whom several leading figures in SF have described as 'a good republican'.

7 Feb   Michael Noonan, the Minister for Finance, announces that FG policy is to abolish the Universal Social Charge (USC),

which brings in around €4bn annually. He describes the USC as 'hated', and says that while it was needed to deal with the financial emergency, the emergency is now over. Commentators suggest that this promise risks damaging FG's painstakingly built reputation for financial prudence. Virtually all other parties also advocate either abolishing or reducing the USC, as well as proposing increases in spending, while denying that they are engaging in precisely the kind of 'auction politics' widely blamed for the economic collapse of 2008. The advice of independent economists that any discretionary expenditure be used to pay down the country's debt finds little traction with any of the parties.

9 Feb   SF launches its manifesto in the august setting of the Royal Irish Academy in Dublin, enabling its leader Gerry Adams to allude to the media's continued scepticism about his claim never to have been an IRA member by saying 'I am really glad to be in the RIA'. The manifesto, with the slogan 'For a Fair Recovery', promises to abolish the local property tax and water charges, to remove the low paid from the USC, and to increase spending on many areas, especially health, housing and education. Many of the questions from journalists focus on the party's proposal to abolish the Special Criminal Court.

Micheál Martin is asked about his party's attitude to participation in government after the election, and he appears to take care not to rule out the possibility that FF might support a minority FG government.

11 Feb   Micheál Martin launches FF election manifesto, with the slogan 'An Ireland for All'. It promises tax cuts and spending increases, but he denies that this marks a return to auction politics.

The first leaders' debate of the campaign, involving the leaders of FG, FF, Labour and SF, aired on TV3. Analysis finds it difficult to identify either a clear winner or a clear loser and there are many complaints that the participants spent too much time trying to talk over each other, making it hard for listeners to hear what anyone was saying.

12 Feb   Green Party launches its manifesto, under the theme 'Think ahead, act now'. It advocates referendums to enshrine in the constitution housing as a social right and a guarantee that water supply will remain in public ownership.

15 Feb   FG launches manifesto with the title 'Let's Keep the Recovery Going', a slogan that has already attracted criticism from those who say they have not felt any signs of a recovery.

At the halfway point of the campaign, there is consensus among commentators that the campaign so far has been inchoate and lacklustre and has failed to engage the electorate.

16 Feb   Labour launches manifesto, emphasising the need to keep the party in government in order to ensure progressive policies on social and economic issues and promising to insist on a referendum on repealing the eighth amendment to the constitution (inserted in 1983 with the intention of preventing the legalisation of abortion) if it gets back into government.

In the evening a televised seven-way leaders' debate takes place, in which the moderator is assessed to have been the best performer, though the Social Democrats' representative Stephen Donnelly is also commended for stating that his party does not favour abolishing or cutting USC given its importance as a source of government revenue. The most exciting moment occurs when a piece of paper floats from Micheál Martin's lectern onto the floor, as helpfully pointed out to him by Enda Kenny (see book cover).

18 Feb   In an RTE radio interview with Seán O'Rourke, Gerry Adams repeatedly seems unsure on details of SF's policies, especially regarding taxation or anything to do with numbers, and is generally perceived to have performed poorly.

20 Feb   At an election rally in his home town of Castlebar in County Mayo, Enda Kenny commends his government and decries the local 'whingers' who allege that nothing good is happening. When opposition parties accuse him of branding all those who are struggling in difficult economic circumstances as 'whingers', Kenny says that some people in the town 'wouldn't know sunshine if they saw it'. Only on 22 February does he apologise for his use of the term and state that he was referring to a handful of local FF members, and not to the people of the town generally.

23 Feb   Outgoing FF TD Seán Fleming says that his party is open to a coalition with Labour, and the Social Democrats and Renua as well. The party's finance spokesperson Michael McGrath says that FF might yet win more seats than FG, adding that 'The

Irish people like an underdog'—a sign of the changed times given FF's dominance of Irish politics from 1932 to 2011.

The last leaders' debate is aired on RTE; like the first one, it features the leaders of the largest four parties. Joan Burton is perceived to have given her best performance of the campaign, but there is agreement that there was no sign of any 'killer punch' or spectacular gaffe. Many pundits describe it as 'dire' and 'boring', and the occasional creaking noise made by the set seems to generate more interest than anything else. Even so, viewership figures are high, estimated at 622,000.

24 Feb   Enda Kenny, responding to criticisms of what are seen as his gaffes during the campaign, recognises that he has made mistakes during the campaign. A FG minister, Leo Varadkar, acknowledges that Kenny may not be the strongest advocate for the party in television debates: 'Enda is not going to win a debating competition but he has other strengths'.

25 Feb   FG and Labour leaders announce a transfer agreement, urging their supporters to pass on lower preferences to candidates of the other party.

26 Feb   Election day

FG publicises a letter received by Enda Kenny from David Cameron, prime minister of the UK, in which he offers Kenny his 'best wishes' for the election and adds 'Good luck!'. The *Irish Independent* reports this under the heading 'Cameron backing for Kenny on eve of election', but the following day's *Irish Examiner* reports the British Embassy in Dublin as denying that Cameron was backing Kenny and stating that he would not intervene in an election in another country.

3 Mar   At just after 8 am, the 158th and final seat in the 32nd Dáil is filled with the election of Willie Penrose in Longford–Westmeath, where there have been several recounts.

10 Mar   The 32nd Dáil meets for the first time. It elects its Ceann Comhairle (speaker), for the first time doing this by secret ballot and using the alternative vote; from a field of five candidates, Seán Ó Fearghaíl (FF) is elected. After that, four party leaders are, in succession, proposed as Taoiseach but defeated. Enda Kenny visits the president to tender his resignation but, under

the constitution, he and his government remain in office until successors are appointed.

6 Apr   After the Dáil has met and once again failed to elect a Taoiseach, Enda Kenny and Micheál Martin have their first meeting since the election. It emerges that Kenny offered FF a 'partnership' government, in which the two parties would have the same number of cabinet positions and there would also be participation by Independent TDs. The question of a 'rotating Taoiseach' (whereby the two parties would take it in turns to hold the office) was not reached.

7 Apr   FF parliamentary party meets for four hours and decides to reject the FG proposal. A couple of days later, the two parties start talks on the terms on which FF would give de facto external support to a FG minority government.

14 Apr   Dáil votes again on Taoiseach, with more or less the same results. A couple of days earlier FF said that this would be the Independents' last chance to vote for Micheál Martin as Taoiseach; if he didn't overtake Enda Kenny on this occasion, his name wouldn't go before the Dáil again. FF reiterates this position after Kenny does again win more votes than Martin.

17 Apr   Poll shows FF ahead of FG and as the largest party for the first time since autumn 2008.

         Growing speculation that Labour, which initially said it would go into opposition, might be tempted back into government with FG, though within a few days Labour rules this out.

18 Apr   Talks between FG and FF on the terms under which FF would support a FG minority government begin in the Provost's library of Trinity College Dublin.

25 Apr   Counting of votes in the Seanad election begins. The last of the 49 elected Seanad seats is filled three days later.

29 Apr   FG and FF announce that in 'the Trinity talks' they have reached an agreement on the terms on which FF will support a FG minority government, provided that FG can secure the agreement of a majority of the other TDs (i.e. excluding the FF TDs) in the Dáil, which means that, with 50 TDs of its own, FG needs to secure the support of another eight TDs.

2 May   Negotiations start between FG and Independent TDs.

6 May   FG eventually reaches agreement with sufficient Independent TDs. Enda Kenny is re-elected Taoiseach by 59 votes to 49, with

FF TDs and some others abstaining from the vote. The new cabinet, announced later in the day, consists of 12 FG TDs and three Independents. Three ministers of state (junior ministers) are also announced.

10 May   Joan Burton announces resignation as leader of Labour Party, saying 'We didn't do everything right but I believe we left Ireland a better place and I think that's the true test for any party in government'.

14 May   Lucinda Creighton announces that she is stepping down as leader of Renua Ireland.

19 May   Announcement of the remaining 15 ministers of state, making 18 in all. Three are independent TDs and the other 15 are FG TDs.

20 May   Brendan Howlin becomes new Labour leader after he is the only person to be nominated. His first press conference as leader is attended by all the party's other TDs—apart from former deputy leader Alan Kelly, who had wanted to run himself but could not persuade any other TD to second his nomination.

Seán Canney, new minister of state, admits that he and Kevin Boxer Moran tossed a coin to decide which of them should hold this position first; after 12 months, Moran will replace Canney.

27 May   Taoiseach finally announces the names of his 11 nominees to the 60-member Seanad, thus completing the composition of the Houses of the Oireachtas. It emerges that by agreement with Enda Kenny, FF leader Micheál Martin had been allowed to select three of these nominees.

LIST OF FIGURES

LIST OF TABLES

Fine Gael and Labour leaders enjoy a cuppa [Irish Times]

Fine Gael manifesto launch. Enda Kenny and Michael Noonan with deputy leader
James Reilly and Heather Humphreys [RTE]

FG Finance Minister Michael Noonan looks tired and drawn as he stands over his party's ill-fated election slogan [Irish Times]

Eyes right for FG ministers Frances Fitzgerald, Leo Varadkar and Simon Harris at press event as Enda Kenny exits left [Irish Times]

Leader Joan Burton, deputy leader Alan Kelly (left) and Brendan Howlin (right) stand up to assert Labour's message [Irish Times]

Another Labour photo-op goes wrong, as its leader Joan Burton tries to engage with the internet era [Irish Times]

FF party leader Micheál Martin explains how his party will create a fairer Ireland

'I am really glad to be in the RIA' said SF leader Gerry Adams at the launch of his party's campaign in the Royal Irish Academy [Irish Times]

Gerry Adams makes a point in characteristic mode [Irish Times]

Mary Lou McDonald and Pearse Doherty of Sinn Féin remind voters they too are against water charges [Irish Times]

FF's Director of elections Billy Kelleher unveils a hoarding telling the voters what (in FF's view) Enda Kenny really stands for [Irish Times]

The clock runs down on a Social Democrat press conference featuring its leadership troika of Róisín Shortall, Catherine Murphy and Stephen Donnelly (who left the party seven months later) [Irish Times]

Labour declares that it supports motherhood and apple pie

No right turn for SF and Joan Collins in Dublin South Central

A group of FG campaigners with colourful posters calling for tax cuts come together spontaneously in Dublin 4, and by chance the media were on hand to capture the moment. After the election, such events were seen to epitomise much that was wrong with the Dublin-centred FG campaign [Irish Times]

Clare Daly and running mate Barry Martin make themselves heard in Independents 4 Change election literature

People Before Profit literature highlights the iniquity of water charges

Boxer will Deliver: Election literature from successful independent candidate Kevin 'Boxer' Moran (Longford–Westmeath)

FG's Stephanie Regan (Dublin Bay North) makes the case for more women in politics

Canvassing down on the farm: Minister for Agriculture Simon Coveney and the Taoiseach doing what they have to do. [RTE]

Enda Kenny campaigning in Leitrim accompanied by local candidate Gerry Reynolds [Irish Times]

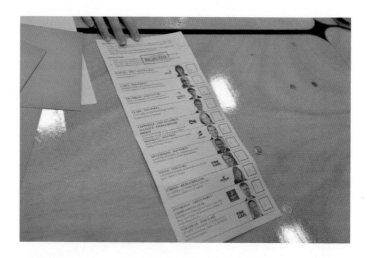

Dublin West ballot paper that was rejected because the voter wrote 'None of these' in the boxes [Irish Times]

Checking and counting the Dublin North-West ballot papers [Irish Times]

Renua Ireland leader Lucinda Creighton puts on a brave face as she arrives at the count centre for the formal announcement that she has lost her seat [Irish Times]

The Green Party wins 2 seats after 5 years in the wilderness: Eamon Ryan and Catherine Martin pose for the cameras [Irish Times]

Jubilation in Dublin 4 as Kate O'Connell (FG) secures election in Dublin Bay South, and even FF TD Jim O'Callaghan does not seem too unhappy [Irish Times]

Former Labour deputy and now independent Tommy Broughan is re-elected for a sixth consecutive term in the Dáil [Irish Times]

Newly-elected People Before Profit TDs Bríd Smith and Richard Boyd Barrett [Irish Times]

Anne Rabbitte, the first FF woman to be elected to the Dáil in East Galway, with Brigid Hogan O'Higgins (FG), who in 1957 had become the first woman ever elected in Galway [Gerry Stronge]

The Healy-Rae brothers, Michael (left) and Danny (right), meet the cameras on the first day of the new Dáil. Both were elected as independents in the Kerry constituency [RTE]

SF's Caoimhghín Ó Caoláin takes his place for his party's photocall [Irish Times]

Independents Michael Collins and Mattie McGrath talk about talks on government formation [Irish Times]

Seán Ó Fearghaíl accepts the applause as he becomes the first Ceann Comhairle (speaker of the Dáil) to be elected by secret ballot [RTE]

Independent Alliance TD Michael Fitzmaurice engaged in last-minute discussions about joining the government fold. In the end he remained outside [Irish Times]

Members of the Independent Alliance: Finian McGrath, John Halligan, Seán Canney, Shane Ross, Ross's special adviser Aisling Dunne, and Kevin 'Boxer' Moran [RTE]

Shane Ross, leader of the Independent Alliance, fields a tricky question on RTÉ News [RTE]

FF and FG negotiators in the Provost's Library in Trinity College Dublin [Trinity College]

Rural independents Michael Collins, Michael Harty, Noel Grealish and Denis Naughten in the Dáil on May 6 check their texts as the Dáil waits to see whether a government will be elected [RTE]

Enda Kenny becomes the first FG leader to win a second successive term as Taoiseach as he appears to receive two seals of office from President Michael D. Higgins [Irish Times]

The new government, which is not quite as gender-balanced as the photo attempts to make it appear, waits to enter the Dáil chamber [merrionstreet.ie]

The Background to the Election

Gary Murphy

THE END OF THE 31ST DÁIL AND THE CALLING OF THE ELECTION

At 9:32 am on Wednesday 3 February 2016, the Taoiseach Enda Kenny entered a packed Dáil chamber and without any great fanfare or ceremony announced to the gathered deputies that he was headed to Áras an Uachtaráin to advise the President to dissolve the Dáil. Wishing TDs who were not seeking re-election the best for the future and good luck to those offering themselves to the public again, Kenny was inside the chamber for all of two minutes. Leaving behind an array of disgruntled opposition deputies the Taoiseach then, in that most modern of fashions, took to Twitter to announce that the general election would be held on Friday 26 February. The strapline to his tweet was titled 'Let's Keep The Recovery Going.'[1]

While that apparently anodyne phrase would ultimately cause Fine Gael no end of trouble during the subsequent election campaign (see Chapter 4 in particular) it was, to the party's election gurus, the obvious slogan on which to run its short three-week campaign. After all Fine Gael and Enda Kenny had seen the hated 'Troika' of the European Central Bank, European Union (EU) and International Monetary Fund from the country's

G. Murphy (✉)
Dublin City University, Dublin, Ireland

© The Author(s) 2016
M. Gallagher, M. Marsh (eds.), *How Ireland Voted 2016*,
DOI 10.1007/978-3-319-40889-7_1

1

shores and were heading up a government that was presiding over a seriously impressive macroeconomic recovery. By the time the election was called Ireland was the fastest growing economy in the EU, which was no inconsiderable achievement after the grim years of austerity that had stalked the Irish landscape and its people since 2008. The trouble for the government would be that not enough people felt the micro effects of the recovery in their own lives, as would become clear during the campaign. In any event, after sending his tweet, which consisted of a video of himself outlining the issues at stake in the forthcoming campaign, Kenny met up with Tánaiste (deputy prime minister) and leader of the Labour Party Joan Burton and together they staged an extremely cumbersome-looking photo opportunity for the media throng that had gathered outside Government Buildings. Kenny quipped to Burton that 'this is not goodbye'[2] and hopped into his state car which brought him to Áras an Uachtaráin. Burton was left awkwardly alone to wave the Taoiseach off. She then made a number of brief remarks to the amassed journalists in which she expressed confidence that the government would be re-elected and that Labour, despite numerous poor opinion poll showings, would do well once the votes were cast and counted. After an extremely difficult five years in power this display of togetherness between Kenny and Burton masked considerable tensions between the parties and the leaders themselves. It had all been so different five years earlier.

On nominating Enda Kenny for Taoiseach on 9 March 2011, Fine Gael's youngest TD, the 24-year-old newly elected deputy for Wicklow Simon Harris, declared: 'Today, the period of mourning is over for Ireland. Today, we hang out our brightest colours and together, under Deputy Kenny's leadership, we move forward yet again as a nation.'[3] As a nod to both the economic catastrophe presided over by Fianna Fáil and the great lost leader of Fine Gael, Michael Collins, Harris's comments were symptomatic of the bullishness of Fine Gael as it entered office with 76 seats, the largest number it had ever received in its history.[4] It was a similar story with Labour who won a historic 37 seats in the 2011 general election, and after a brief period of negotiation the Fine Gael–Labour coalition, with the largest majority in the history of the state, duly took office on the first day of the 31st Dáil with Enda Kenny elected Taoiseach and Labour leader Éamon Gilmore Tánaiste. Government formation in 2011 was relatively simple because all budgetary decisions and indeed discussions had to be taken within parameters set by the Troika.[5]

Over the lifetime of the government both parties would suffer significant defections from their ranks and be embroiled in a number of controversies over broken election promises, cronyism and policy-making failure. The five years between elections would see politics in the Irish state become increasingly competitive. As support for both government parties fell throughout the government's tenure (see Fig. 1.1) and as Fianna Fáil appeared increasingly becalmed, the old certainties long associated with Irish politics seemed destined to disappear for ever. The rise of Sinn Féin, the formation of two new political parties—Renua and the Social Democrats—the increasing assertiveness of previously fringe left-wing groups, principally associated with opposition to water charges, and the seemingly never-ending rise of independents as political alternatives worth voting for, all made the 2016 general election the most difficult to call in modern Irish history. Notwithstanding the resilience of the traditional parties of Fianna Fáil, Fine Gael and Labour, it was clear that the combined vote for all three was going to be the lowest in the history of the state. In that context it was almost certain that as the campaign began, government formation

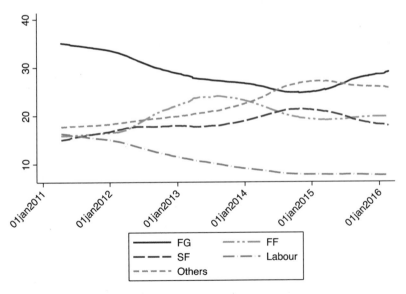

Fig. 1.1   Party support 2011–16
Note: Polling trends based on all published polls

would be extremely difficult once the votes were cast. No one, however, could have predicted how difficult.

PARTY COMPETITION

The result of the February 2011 general election effectively sundered the Irish party system.[6] Three months after the arrival of the Troika to bail out the Irish state Fianna Fáil suffered its worst ever election result, polling only 17 per cent of the first preference vote and winning a historic low 20 seats out of a possible 166. Since it first entered government in 1932 its previous worst result was 65 seats in 1954, while in the May 2007 general election it won 78 seats. Probably best described as a catch-all party since its foundation in 1926, it hovered consistently at above 40 per cent of the vote at election time only dropping to 39 per cent on two occasions, in 1992 and 1997.[7] It had a chameleon-like ability to appeal to all social classes both urban and rural.[8] Once it decided to break one of its core values and enter coalition politics in 1989 with the Progressive Democrats (PDs), Fianna Fáil's centrist appeal looked like it could enable the party to govern in perpetuity.[9] The PDs in 1989, 1997, 2002 and 2007, Labour in 1992, and the Greens in 2007 had all been persuaded to enter government with Fianna Fáil and it was also skilled at doing deals with independents. Such coalition building was based on the assumption of Fianna Fáil polling around its normal 40 per cent level thus giving it the possibility of choosing alternative coalition partners. After the party's brutal rejection in 2011 by an electorate which placed the blame almost entirely on it for the austerity that had brought misery across the state this was clearly no longer the case.

The voters in 2011 decided that the best alternative to Fianna Fáil was a Fine Gael–Labour coalition, which they regarded as the most likely to get the country out of the mire of austerity. Neither party had been in power since their 1994–97 'rainbow' coalition government with Democratic Left. The fluid nature of Irish politics in the 1990s was summed up best by the change in government during the 27th Dáil when the Fianna Fáil–Labour government collapsed in November 1994 to be replaced by the partnership of Fine Gael, Labour and Democratic Left.[10] But in 1997 that coalition was itself voted out of office to be replaced by a Fianna Fáil–PD government which would be re-elected twice, the last in 2007 with the help of the Green Party.

While Fine Gael's success in the 2011 general election might have been seen as inevitable given the collapse in support for Fianna Fáil, it was nevertheless an impressive achievement. This was all the more so given the depths to which Fine Gael had fallen just under a decade earlier in 2002 when it returned with a historically low 31 seats on just over 22 per cent of the vote and its long-term future seemed in grave doubt, particularly as by accepting coalition in 1989 Fianna Fáil opened itself up to alliances that would once have been the sole preserve of Fine Gael. A significant improvement in its fortunes in the 2007 general election where it won 20 extra seats under the leadership of Enda Kenny at least meant that Fine Gael remained relevant in Irish politics. Yet doubts within Fine Gael about Kenny's leadership saw Richard Bruton mount a 'heave' (a leadership challenge) in June 2010 which Kenny, to the surprise of many, successfully rebuffed.[11] Within nine months Kenny was Taoiseach and back in the comfortable surrounds of coalition with the Labour Party.

The result of the 2011 election was a critical juncture for the Labour Party. After a disappointing election in 2007 Labour changed leaders, with the former Democratic Left TD Éamon Gilmore taking the helm from Pat Rabbitte. Gilmore immediately went on the attack in the Dáil, aping the tactics of a previous Labour leader Dick Spring, and proved a vitriolic critic of Fianna Fáil. This culminated in March 2010 when he accused the Taoiseach Brian Cowen of 'economic treason' for signing off on the state guarantee of Anglo Irish Bank in September 2008 declaring that the decision had been made 'not in the best economic interests of the nation but in the best personal interests of those vested interests who I believe the Government was trying to protect on that occasion.'[12] Unmerciful attacks on Fianna Fáil and full-blooded opposition to austerity had led Labour to a position whereby it had a historic decision to make in 2011 on the back of its greatest electoral achievement. Labour could either go into government with its normal partner Fine Gael or it could stay outside and try to grow further from the opposition benches with a possibility of leading a government after the next election. The dominant view in Labour was that having run a campaign where it promised 'balanced' government—that is, that it would provide a check on possible Fine Gael excesses—it could not then remove itself from the responsibility to govern. Moreover most of its leading lights including Gilmore, Rabbitte and Ruairí Quinn were old enough to realise that this might well be their last chance to achieve office. In that context remaining in opposition was never really seriously considered as an option.[13] Labour serenely went into office. It would come out five years later fighting for its very survival.

Part of the reason for Labour's calamitous period in government was the increased assertiveness of left-wing opposition to the government both inside and outside Dáil Éireann. Sinn Féin was revived after the 2011 general election having increased its strength from 4 seats to 14 and it would prove to be a magnet for voices on the left who were disaffected by Labour's performance in government. Rivalling Sinn Féin for this constituency was an assorted cocktail of various left-wing groups and independents. While they had come together under the United Left Alliance banner in 2011 the inevitable split soon followed, although a revived version running under the auspices of AAA—PBP would be a serious force come the 2016 election in its attempts in particular to draw voters away from Labour. As the election loomed ever closer in late 2015 and early 2016, it was Labour that had to face the accusations of treachery and betraying working-class people from such left-wing groups. The continued popularity of former so called 'gene-pool independents'[14] from Fianna Fáil and Fine Gael (see Chapter 9) combined with the introduction of two new political parties onto the electoral stage added to the uncertainty of Irish politics during the five-year period between 2011 and 2016. By the time Enda Kenny called the election it seemed likely that Fine Gael, given the fact that it was comfortably ahead of all other parties in the polls, would win the most seats and be in the prime position to form a government. The campaign still had to be fought, however, and perhaps more than in any other election in living memory how that campaign transpired would have a significant impact on the result.

THE FINE GAEL–LABOUR COALITION 2011

While government formation in 2011 was reasonably straightforward the spoils of office proved far more contentious for a government with the largest majority in the history of the state, especially within Labour. Its deputy leader Joan Burton was highly affronted not to be appointed to an economic ministry, instead having to settle for the Department of Social Protection, and told Gilmore he 'was making a big mistake.'[15] In choosing Ruairí Quinn over Róisín Shortall Gilmore also stoked up much resentment in the parliamentary party and faced accusations of looking after the old boys who had 'muscled in' to cabinet.[16] More importantly, the hostility between Burton and Gilmore became a staple of everyday life for Labour in government and one that would have dramatic consequences after the mid-term European and local elections. For his part, Enda Kenny's choice of ministers proved much more straightforward as he combined long-term supporters Phil Hogan, James Reilly and Alan Shatter with newer blood and those who had tried to depose him in the 2010 heave such as Simon Coveney and Leo Varadkar. He also brought former deputy leader Richard Bruton back into cabinet.

While compiling their cabinet Kenny and Gilmore took two crucially important decisions. First, they decided to split the existing Department of Finance into two: a department concentrating on banking and finance led by Michael Noonan of Fine Gael as Minister for Finance, and a Department of Public Expenditure and Reform headed up by Labour's Brendan Howlin. Even more significant perhaps was the decision to create an Economic Management Council which would consist of Taoiseach, Tánaiste and the two finance ministers, supported by an array of officials and advisers. Essentially, this was a cabinet within a cabinet or as Gilmore himself described it a 'war cabinet to manage the country's financial crisis.'[17] This innovative structure had a number of advantages in that it allowed Labour an equal say in economic policy making, ensured there would be open and frank dialogue between Fine Gael and Labour, thus allowing trust to be built between the two parties, and perhaps most importantly had the support of the Troika which saw it as a sign that the incoming government was taking the economic crisis seriously.[18] If nothing else this showed that no matter what decisions it made this new coalition with its huge mandate from the people still had to seek approval from the Troika in relation to basic policy making. It was a sobering reminder of the realities of governing in bankrupt Ireland. In that context, the new government basically continued to pursue the broad parameters of the economic policy of the previous Fianna Fáil-led administration. Talk of the 'burning' of bondholders and a renegotiation of the bailout deal quickly went nowhere as it became clear that attitudes in Europe to Ireland's banking and indeed monetary crisis had, if anything, hardened after the election of the new government.

While the Economic Management Council grappled with the country's crippling debt and the unsympathetic attitude to Ireland's economic plight emanating from Brussels, normal politics resumed. The first test of the government's popularity came when the untimely death of the former Fianna Fáil Minister for Finance Brian Lenihan resulted in a by-election in Dublin West, held in October 2011. Labour, still basking in the warm afterglow of its general election success, selected as its candidate Patrick Nulty, who had been Joan Burton's running mate nine months earlier. Nulty, on the far left of the party, won the seat, becoming the first member of a government party to win a by-election in close on 30 years. Nulty's Dáil membership was, however, an unhappy one. Just six weeks after his election he voted against his government's budget in protest at expenditure cuts and immediately lost the party whip. He left the Labour Party in June 2013 and ultimately resigned his seat in March 2014 in some personal distress after admitting inappropriate use of social media from within the confines of Leinster House.

On the same day as this by-election the electorate was also asked to vote for a new President and, in referendums, on proposals to reduce the pay of judges and to allow for the Houses of the Oireachtas to conduct full inquiries and thus reverse a 2002 Supreme Court ruling that prevents such inquiries from making findings critical of individual citizens. The referendum on judges' pay proved relatively uncontroversial and was comfortably passed but that on Oireachtas inquiries was defeated. While there was widespread public support for the principle of providing inquiry powers for the Oireachtas, a majority of the electorate voted No mainly due to an ineffective Yes campaign and a belief that the proposals went too far.[19] A dramatic late intervention by eight former Attorneys General calling for a No vote was generally regarded to have been influential.

The 2011 presidential election campaign was the first in 14 years and came at the end of the widely perceived successful two-term presidency of Mary McAleese. Given the meltdown of Fianna Fáil in the general election of February 2011, Fine Gael's poor performances in previous presidential elections and the large number of potential independent candidates who expressed an interest in running for the office, it was clear that the 2011 presidential election would be a wide open affair.[20] Fine Gael and Labour, fresh from their historic triumph, targeted the presidential election as a vehicle to continue to mobilise public support and an opportunity to occupy the highest office in the land. Labour's eventual candidate Michael D. Higgins had made it clear from at least a year prior to the end of the McAleese presidency that he was interested in succeeding her. For its part, Fine Gael was very keen to win the presidency seeing it as the one blank in its political résumé. Against its leadership's wishes, however, the party chose the most partisan candidate seeking the nomination, Gay Mitchell, who, despite his electoral successes as a MEP in Dublin, was never able to gain any traction with the public and ended up being deserted in droves by core Fine Gael voters. Fianna Fáil was undecided about running a candidate at all after its disastrous outing in the general election and eventually chose not to, while SF viewed the presidency as offering yet another opportunity to make significant political inroads in the Republic. It ran veteran activist and Deputy First Minister of Northern Ireland Martin McGuinness, but his campaign floundered over his controversial IRA past and he ultimately did much more poorly than expected.

Eventually seven candidates made their way on to the ballot paper with the three party candidates being joined by independents Mary Davis, Seán Gallagher, David Norris and Dana Rosemary Scallon. A dull campaign in which party affiliation played little part was livened up considerably in the last week when Gallagher, the frontrunner in the polls, imploded in a series of three media appearances where he was unable to convincingly answer questions as to his myriad business dealings and his previous links with Fianna Fáil. On the RTÉ *Frontline* debate programme broadcast just four days before the election and featuring all seven candidates Gallagher was asked to respond to what was later discovered to be a fake tweet which stated that a man who gave Gallagher a cheque for use by Fianna Fáil would present himself at a press conference the following day. Gallagher was unable to reply to this with any certainty and then had to expend much time and energy explaining a trail of accounting errors to an audience in the studio who appeared deeply sceptical. This scepticism deepened when he gave a rather rambling response to another assertion that he had mislaid a cheque for €89,000.[21] He was unable to undo the damage in two further media interviews the following day and was ultimately beaten into second place by Higgins who received nearly 40 per cent of the first preference vote to win comfortably. In essence this was a personal victory for Higgins as those who were undecided in the last week of the campaign went with the veteran Labour politician and his call for a decent and inclusive society.

Neither Fine Gael, which polled a barely believable six per cent of the vote, nor Labour took the view that the presidential election result would have any significance as the government continued to grapple with the economic sovereignty of the state, as was wryly summed up by Ruairí Quinn writing in his diary in early January 2012: 'The Troika return today. Our debt mountain rises and I continue to worry about our future and money in this little country of ours. Keep to the knitting!'[22] Quinn had every right to worry on both the economic and political fronts. On 5 and 6 December 2011, the government introduced its first budget in two parts with Brendan Howlin outlining a range of tax increases and spending cuts to the order of €3.6 billion while Michael Noonan outlined the very narrow fiscal parameters within which the government operated.[23] The government might have changed but austerity remained and the Irish people were not pleased. Satisfaction with the government immediately plummeted falling from 36 per cent in October to 26 per cent in one poll in the immediate aftermath of the budget (see Fig. 1.2).[24] The government's honeymoon was well and truly over. Over the course of its tenure its satisfaction

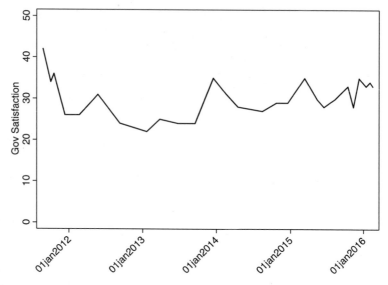

Fig. 1.2 Government satisfaction 2011–16
Note: Based on Behaviour & Attitudes polls for *The Sunday Times*

ratings would never again reach the heady heights of 36 per cent; an eloquent testimony to its difficulties in addressing austerity.

THE END OF THE TRIBUNAL ERA

In March 2011, just a month after the general election, the Moriarty tribunal established in 1997 to investigate payments to politicians published its second report in two volumes. In total it had lasted for 13 years and 6 months, ran to some 2348 pages and cost an estimated €50 million. Its main finding was that Michael Lowry as Minister for Transport, Energy and Communications 'not only influenced but delivered the result' of the awarding of the state's second mobile phone licence to the Esat Digifone Company headed up the businessman Denis O'Brien who had made direct financial contributions to both Lowry and Fine Gael.[25] The tribunal found that irregularities within the evaluation process were complemented by the 'insidious and pervasive influence' of Lowry.[26] The report was met with outright indignation by Lowry and O'Brien who rejected its findings as biased, selective and not substantiated by evidence or fact.

In welcoming the publication of the report and accepting its finding the newly installed Taoiseach stated it was another report 'reeking of fanatical greed, obsessive attachment to power, and breathtaking attempts to acquire, use and access privilege … for the sake of our democracy, and in the context of the national misery caused by weak and reckless administrations and corrupt, self-serving politicians, we must return both government and parliament to the people.'[27] Notwithstanding the findings of the tribunal and the unstinting attacks on it by Denis O'Brien, just over seven months later in early October 2011, the government had no problem with inviting him to its Global Irish Economic Forum summit as one who had an important role to play at the event aimed at building Ireland's economic recovery. It was also happy to invite him back to subsequent forums, notwithstanding some disquiet in Labour circles. The findings of the Moriarty tribunal were never allowed to get in the way of the business of doing government. In this case, economics certainly trumped politics.

The government's reaction to the final report of the Mahon tribunal into planning matters and payments, issued in March 2012, struck a similar tone.[28] Again there were outraged statements in the Dáil, with Éamon Gilmore thundering that the report was 'a chronicle of betrayal, ignominy and disgrace for the individuals it names and condemns, for the system of planning in Dublin that was foully corrupted and for the Fianna Fáil Party.'[29] Mahon's final report mostly concerned the travails of Fianna Fáil and for journalists and the general public its verdict on the bizarre nature of Bertie Ahern's finances was its most intriguing story line.[30] Yet its publication was slightly uncomfortable for the government in that it begged the question of why a year after its report nothing had been done about the findings of the Moriarty tribunal.

For its part, Fianna Fáil under the leadership of Micheál Martin reacted to the Mahon tribunal with alacrity by accusing Bertie Ahern of 'conduct unbecoming' and declaring that it would seek to expel him from the party. Fianna Fáil felt obliged to take action given that a sworn tribunal of inquiry held that a senior office holder of the party received large amounts of money of unclear origins for which he could not give any credible explanation. It ultimately accused Ahern of betraying the trust placed in him by his country and his party.[31] Ahern did not give Fianna Fáil the satisfaction of expulsion and instead resigned his membership of the party to which he had given his life's devotion. Proclaiming his innocence to the last he insisted that both Fianna Fáil and the tribunal itself had done him a great disservice.

In 2015, the Mahon tribunal began to unravel when Justice Mahon apologised to the former minister Ray Burke and a number of businessmen for finding that they had hindered and obstructed the work of the tribunal and struck out all findings that they had done so. It also reversed findings of corruption against the former Dublin city assistant manager George Redmond.[32] By that stage, however, no one in government or indeed the Irish state itself cared much about the tribunals of inquiry at all. There were far more important things to worry about.

GOVERNMENT MID-TERM WOES

On Thursday 7 November 2013, the unloved Troika made its last visit to Irish shores and a month later Ireland became the first Eurozone state to exit its rescue programme. Irish economic sovereignty was restored. This spelled good news for the government which saw its standing rise in polls taken in the immediate aftermath of the Troika's exit. Government satisfaction rose by 6 per cent to 26 in an *Irish Times/MRBI* poll and by 11 per cent to 35 in a *Sunday Times/Behaviour and Attitudes* poll.[33] But these numbers were still inherently weak and the parameters for government spending remained stringently narrow. Moreover, the Troika's insistence that a local property tax and water charges be instigated continued to remain government policy. The results of such Troika economics were to be seen to dramatic effect when the government resoundingly failed its first major electoral test in the local and European Parliament elections held on Friday 23 May 2014.

These elections were held to the backdrop of the sensational resignation of the Minister for Justice Alan Shatter on 7 May 2014. An Enda Kenny loyalist during the 2010 heave, Shatter had been involved in a number of controversies since his appointment to cabinet. A crusading and activist minister, Shatter was responsible for a number of important legislative acts relating to citizenship, personal insolvency and criminal justice amongst others. In May 2013, he criticised a number of garda (police) whistleblowers who had exposed what they claimed to be misuse by other gardaí of their discretionary power to cancel driver penalty points. He landed himself in further controversy when on the live RTÉ TV programme *Prime Time* he announced in a debate with the colourful Wexford TD and whistleblower supporter Mick Wallace that Wallace himself had been warned by gardaí for driving while using a mobile phone, but had benefited from garda discretion and thus avoided penalty points, raising the question of how he, Shatter, had obtained this supposedly confidential information.[34] In October that year the Comptroller and Auditor General published a report into the penalty points scandal which supported the claims of the whistleblowers, Maurice McCabe and John Wilson, and to compound this Shatter then gave what seemed to be misleading information to the Dáil when he claimed that the two whistleblowers involved had not cooperated with an internal Garda inquiry into the allegations; they pointed out that their cooperation had not been sought by the inquiry.[35]

The year 2014 saw matters get much worse for Shatter as the Garda Síochána Ombudsman Commission (GSOC) began to conduct a new inquiry into the penalty points allegations. In February, the *Sunday Times* ran a series of articles alleging that GSOC's offices had been bugged with highly specialised equipment and that GSOC itself believed this to be the case.[36] In March, the Garda Inspectorate published its review into the penalty points system and upheld many of the complaints of the whistleblowers, leading Shatter to eventually apologise to the two whistleblowers concerned. In the midst of all this, the government was rocked when on 25 March 2014 the Garda Commissioner Martin Callinan announced that he was to retire with immediate effect, citing the best interests of the gardaí and of his family. This led to scenes of uproar in the Dáil on the same day when accusations were made by various opposition deputies that Callinan was in fact sacked by the Taoiseach, a step that procedurally would have required the approval of the whole government.[37] A Commission of Inquiry under retired judge Nial Fennelly was established to investigate the circumstances of Callinan's resignation and the widespread recording of calls into and out of garda stations dating back to the 1980s. It reported in August 2015 and concluded that Callinan's decision to retire was effectively his own and that he could have decided otherwise. It did state, however, that the decision by the Taoiseach to send a senior civil servant, the secretary general of the Department of Justice, to Callinan's home on the night before his resignation to tell the commissioner of the government's concern over the issue of the recording of telephone conversations in garda stations was the catalyst for that decision.[38]

Alan Shatter ultimately resigned on 7 May 2014 after he had received the report of barrister Seán Guerin who was tasked with inquiring into allegations made by the garda whistleblowers in relation to penalty points. Shatter was given a copy of the report by Enda Kenny, who drew his attention to certain chapters in particular. Aware that he no longer enjoyed the Taoiseach's confidence, he tendered his resignation. Subsequently, though, he rejected the report, was critical of Guerin's decision not to interview him in relation to it and made it clear that he himself felt wronged by Kenny who would not give him the 24 hours to study the report that he had asked for.[39] In any event his resignation on the eve of the local elections did not augur well for the government.

The local elections were particularly notable in that they were held after the landmark 2014 Local Government Reform Act, which radically reduced the numbers of local authorities from 114 to 31 and the numbers of councillors from 1627 to 949.[40] Yet the dramatic nature of the changes in the numbers of local representatives and of councils themselves had little impact on the voters as these elections saw the second lowest turn-out for local elections in the history of the state at close to 52 per cent, which in effect meant that 200,000 fewer people voted in 2014 than in the previous election in 2009.[41] More than in any previous local election, debates on the economy and on austerity at the national level had specific local consequences due to the local property tax and water charges. As the government had planned to allow local authorities to use 80 per cent of the monies gathered from the local property tax, and to vary the rate of the tax by up to 15 per cent in each direction, candidates in the election began to campaign on this issue.[42] While this was contentious in and of itself, far more emotive and damaging for the government in the longer term was the whole issue of water charges with the local elections illustrating for the first time the real hostility the proposed charge had instilled in large sections of the electorate. Anti-water service charge protestors became a feature of the campaign particularly in the cities and attempted to prevent contractors from the newly created public utility Irish Water from installing water meters prior to and during the election campaign. The government parties might have expected to do well at these elections given the definite signs of an upturn in the economy, which indeed from this point onwards improved steadily (see Fig. 1.3).

Instead, the local election results were calamitous for both Fine Gael and Labour. The trouble remained the economy. While the macroeconomic indicators were clearly showing signs of improvement many people still felt little improvement in their own personal circumstance and used the ballot box to remind the governing parties of this fact. Labour was electorally devastated winning just 51 of the 949 local government seats and losing more than half of its votes and seats, and Fine Gael also sustained large losses (see Table 1.1).The local elections were always going to be difficult for Labour. Being in government had proven to be a trying experience and

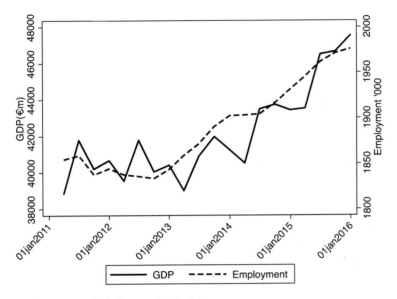

Fig. 1.3 Economic indicators 2011–16
Note: Based on data from the CSO: www.cso.ie/indicators

Table 1.1 Results of local elections, Friday 23 May 2014

Party	Seats	Change since 2009	First preference percentage	Change since 2009
Fianna Fáil	266	+49	25.3	−0.1
Fine Gael	235	−105	24.0	−8.2
Labour	51	−81	7.2	−7.5
Sinn Féin	159	105	15.3	+7.8
People Before Profit	14	+9	1.7	+0.9
Anti-Austerity Alliance	14	+10	1.2	+0.3
Greens	12	+9	1.6	−0.7
Independents	193	+71	22.5	+7.6
Others	5	−2	1.2	−0.2
Total	949		100.0	

Source: See http://electionsireland.org/results/local/2014local.cfm. Also Kavanagh, 'An end to "Civil War" politics,' p. 75 (cited in Note 44)

Note: Others refer to Workers' Party, United Left, South Kerry Independent, Workers and Unemployed Action Group and Republican Sinn Féin, all of whom won one seat. Various named other groupings were also on ballots across the state but failed to have any candidates elected

the parliamentary party had come under serious strain. While the defection from the parliamentary party by the veteran left-winger Tommy Broughan in December 2011 might have been expected, far more serious was the resignation of Róisín Shortall as minister for state in the Department of Health and from the party whip in September 2012 after a difficult relationship with the Fine Gael Minister for Health James Reilly. Three months later party chairperson Colm Keaveney resigned over cuts to respite care contained in the 2013 budget, and would later join Fianna Fáil.

Fine Gael was also suffering from its own internal difficulties. In July 2013, the Dáil passed the government's Protection of Life During Pregnancy Bill, the latest in a long line of initiatives to solve the intractable problem of abortion. However, five Fine Gael TDs were expelled from the parliamentary party for voting against it: Minister of State for European Affairs Lucinda Creighton, Terence Flanagan, Peter Mathews, Billy Timmins and Brian Walsh. Moreover, the government had rather surprisingly lost a constitutional referendum to abolish the Seanad in October 2013. Notwithstanding serious divisions about it within Fine Gael and no great enthusiasm for it in Labour, Seanad abolition became part of the programme for government. Once the referendum was called a variety of interest groups came together to campaign for its defeat. While the polls predicted abolition would succeed, 52 per cent of the voters rejected the proposition on the day on a turnout of just over 39 per cent (see also Chapter 10).[43] Although hardly a fatal blow to the government, the defeat of a referendum that was widely considered to have been a personal initiative of the Taoiseach's could hardly have inspired confidence within government.

The collapse in the government's local election support allowed three things to happen: first, Fianna Fáil made a Lazarus-like comeback from its general election calamity to become the largest party in terms of both votes and seats (see Table 1.1); second, Sinn Féin made significant inroads, trebling its seat numbers; and third, independents made startling increases to become the third largest grouping in Irish local government behind Fianna Fáil and Fine Gael. Candidates from the 'independents and others' grouping accounted for the largest share of the vote at both the local and European elections showing the volatile nature of Irish politics in the age of austerity. These trends would be closely mirrored in the 2016 general election.

At the European election there were 11 seats to be fought for in the three newly configured constituencies of Dublin, Midlands North-West and South. The independent vote held up strongly with three independents, Nessa Childers, Luke Flanagan and Marian Harkin getting elected.

Fine Gael managed to hold onto its four seats despite seeing its vote fall by seven per cent. Labour bore the brunt of the anti-government vote and lost all its three seats while Sinn Féin won three seats with its candidate Lynn Boylan topping the poll in Dublin, which augured very well for its chances in the capital at the general election. Fianna Fáil, notwithstanding the fact that it won only one seat, mainly due to poor candidate selection strategy, managed to win the largest number of votes to continue its reha-bilitation in Irish politics. It did encounter some difficulty when its peren-nial poll topper in South, Brian Crowley, decided to leave the European Parliament grouping 'Alliance of Liberals and Democrats for Europe', to which Fianna Fáil was aligned, for the more right-wing European Conservative and Reformist grouping.[44] But that was something that hap-pened in Strasbourg and to which the Irish electorate paid little atten-tion. One other notable factor in the local and European elections was the revival from near death of the Green Party. After their wipeout at the 2011 general election the Greens looked to have no future at all, but Eamon Ryan, their leader, came close to taking a European seat in Dublin and they managed to win an at least respectable 12 seats in the local elections. An RTÉ exit poll on voter issues in the local elections showed that the three main factors that influenced voter choice were discretionary medical cards, water charges and the local property tax. All would remain difficult for the government as the general election loomed ever closer.

The main casualty of these mid-term elections was the Labour leader and Tánaiste Éamon Gilmore, who resigned just four days after the vot-ers went to the polls. Feeling that he had been undermined for some time from within the party, and having led Labour to these calamitous results, Gilmore felt he had no choice but to resign. At the same time, eight members of the parliamentary party were putting down a motion of no confidence in him, which made him feel 'hurt and angry.'[45] While this heave may have been unnecessary, the fact that it was going to take place at all showed how far Labour and Gilmore had fallen from the pre-cipitous heights of their general election triumph just over three years previously. Labour's difficulties were further emphasised by the vic-tory of the Socialist candidate Ruth Coppinger in the Dublin West by-election that was held on the same day as the mid-term elections. Labour's Loraine Mulligan polled a paltry five per cent of the vote as the party's oppo-nents on the left, the Socialists and Sinn Féin, garnered close to 42 per cent between them. After defeating Alex White for the leadership of the party, Joan Burton immediately became Tánaiste and extracted her revenge on

Gilmore for not appointing her to an economic ministry back in 2011. In a meeting lasting less than three minutes she asked him for his resignation as Minister for Foreign Affairs and Trade and told him bluntly that he would not be appointed the new EU Commissioner, a job he was apparently quite keen on. And with that the man who had brought Labour to its greatest ever election triumph was summarily removed from public life; yet another victim of austerity.

OF WATER, CRONYISM AND MARRIAGE

One person who didn't leave the electoral landscape quietly was Lucinda Creighton. After making various noises about setting up a new party since her expulsion from Fine Gael, Creighton ultimately took the plunge in March 2015 and established Renua Ireland, which espoused a generally centre-right view on economic issues and a free vote on social issues such as abortion. Declaring that it did not believe that party politics in Ireland had a place for issues of conscience, Renua revealed a twenty-first century updating of the old Progressive Democrat policy of rolling back the state from the lives of Irish citizens. Creighton advocated the view that Ireland needed to build an economy for entrepreneurs across the social, private and public sectors and stated that she and her party wanted a place in government.[46] Four months later another new party, the Social Democrats, was introduced into the Irish electoral game by three independents, Stephen Donnelly, Catherine Murphy and Róisín Shortall, placing itself decidedly on the centre-left, advocating an Ireland where all citizens could play full and active lives.

But many in Ireland were now attracted to a harder left-wing politics. Following on from Ruth Coppinger's by-election victory, the hard left had another by-election triumph in Dublin South-West in October 2014 through the AAA's Paul Murphy, who basically ran on a single-issue campaign of refusal to pay water charges. The introduction of water charges had been included in the Troika agreement signed off on by the then Fianna Fáil-led government as part of the 2010 bailout deal. In July 2013, the government attempted to centralise the provision of water services throughout Ireland by establishing a semi-state company, Irish Water, under the Water Services Act 2013. Its aim was to bring the water and wastewater services of the 34 local authorities together under one national service provider and to charge for water usage. Once the company came into operation in 2014 it was met with massive public opposition.

The establishment of Irish Water was beset by difficulties from the outset. It faced accusations of being a bureaucratic quango that was spending millions of euros of taxpayers' money on excessive salaries for its management, expensive consultants and the installation of unwanted water meters. Moreover, there was confusion over whether landlords or tenants would have to pay the charges in rented properties. There was also a rather cack-handed political response to initial protests when the then Minister for the Environment Phil Hogan stated in March 2014 that those people who didn't pay the charges would have their water pressure turned down to a trickle.[47] The following month the government decided to postpone the charges until 2015 but opposition to both Irish Water and the water charges continued unabated. Hogan was appointed EU Commissioner and departed the Irish political scene in July 2014 but the controversy surrounding water charges remained for his successor, Labour's Alan Kelly, to deal with. The opposition to Irish Water manifested itself in a series of mass marches against the water charges, beginning in October 2014, which saw up to 100,000 people take to the streets. This prompted a major government climbdown on the way the charges were implemented and the introduction of a universal 'water conservation grant' which, bizarrely, was not related to usage. Paul Murphy's by-election victory had also caused a hardening of attitudes against water charges by the main opposition parties, Fianna Fáil and Sinn Féin. Fianna Fáil would ultimately seek a suspension of water charges for five years in its 2016 general election manifesto while Sinn Féin representatives declared en masse that they wouldn't pay their own water charges after having initially decided that they would. By June 2015, it was revealed that only 43 per cent of people had paid their first quarterly water bill. All this ensured that the issue of water charges would remain on the political agenda as the election neared.[48]

On the same day as Paul Murphy's victory, the independent Michael Fitzmaurice, associated with the newly elected MEP for Midlands NW Luke 'Ming' Flanagan, also won a by-election in Roscommon–Leitrim South, which was testimony to the fact that the government's electoral woes extended into rural Ireland. The government's record in by-elections was rather mixed. Fine Gael had held its seats in Meath East in March 2013 and Longford–Westmeath in May 2014 but could not in May 2015 hold on to the seat in Carlow–Kilkenny left vacant by Phil Hogan's exit to Brussels. The fact that Fine Gael lost the seat to Fianna Fáil only made matters worse with Bobby Aylward becoming the first Fianna Fáil politician to win a by-election in two decades. But governments had lost by-elections before and gone on to win general elections and this was a defeat Fine Gael could live with.

In September 2014, what should have been a far more low-key by-election on the Seanad Cultural and Education panel proved anything but as the government's candidate John McNulty became embroiled in controversy over his appointment to the board of the Irish Museum of Modern Art by the Minister for Arts, Heritage and the Gaeltacht Heather Humphreys. There seemed no plausible explanation to appoint McNulty to the museum's board, when there was not even a vacancy, except to boost his credentials for the Seanad election, given the requirement that candidates need to have some credentials relevant to the panel on which they are running (see also p. 232 in Chapter 10). Humphreys insisted that McNulty was appointed to the museum on merit, which stretched credulity as McNulty had no history of interest in modern art at all. After a number of weeks during which accusations of cronyism and political strokes flew about, McNulty in effect withdrew, by asking that government TDs and Senators not vote for him. He nevertheless received 84 of the 193 votes cast but was beaten by the independent candidate Gerard Craughwell, who was to play a significant role in the 2016 Seanad election (see p. 237 in Chapter 10).[49] It was an unedifying affair but one that Fine Gael felt it could overcome given the relative unimportance of the Seanad in the ordinary lives of Irish citizens.

One issue that was important for the lives of ordinary citizens was same-sex marriage. After the 2011 election, a Constitutional Convention had been set up: 66 citizens, 33 politicians and an independent chair examined a number of constitutional issues over successive weekends and made recommendations about whether changes should be made. In April 2014, the convention voted by 79 to 18 that the constitution should be changed to allow for civil marriage for same-sex couples. Once it had reached this decision the Fine Gael–Labour government was quickly able to agree a timetable for the referendum and it duly took place in May 2015. This was an important victory in government for the Labour Party, as its leader Éamon Gilmore had as early as June 2012 described the right of gay couples to marry as the 'civil rights issue of this generation.'[50] With cross-party support and a large civil society input the Yes campaign to allow for same-sex marriage built a wide-ranging coalition that enthused large swathes of Irish society. Ultimately, on a turnout of close to 61 per cent,

62 per cent of the people voted Yes making Ireland the first country in the world to bring in same-sex marriage by a popular vote.[51]

Yet while Labour could trumpet the passing of the referendum as a serious achievement in office, the reality of Irish politics was that as the government entered its last months the likelihood of the people rewarding it for such an initiative come the general election remained very slim indeed. Labour received no bounce whatsoever in the opinion polls in the aftermath of the same-sex marriage referendum (see Fig. 1.1). Its poll numbers were so bad that it was clear that its main aim come the election would be to minimise its losses. Ultimately it was clear that issues surrounding the economy and public services remained the key to how the general election would play out. For its part Fine Gael, having, as it saw it, righted the ship of state, decided to stress the economic recovery and how much improved things were since it came to office in 2011. The opposition concentrated on the government's failure to address shortcomings in public services. The battle lines were drawn for the election.

CONCLUSION

After a generally well-received budget in mid-October 2015, there was a flurry of journalistic and political speculation that the Taoiseach would call an election in November to take advantage of the general strength of Fine Gael in the polls and the fact that there seemed no possibility of the formation of a government that did not have a strong Fine Gael at its helm. This was especially the case as Fianna Fáil support had continued to vary between 17 and 20 per cent in national opinion polls throughout 2015, a full ten points behind Fine Gael (see Fig. 1.1). A *Sunday Business Post/ Red C* poll on 25 October showed Fine Gael up two points to 30 per cent, 10 per cent ahead of Fianna Fáil, while Labour had lost three points to fall to 7 per cent.[52] Labour was polling in single-digit figures consistently throughout 2015 in a series of polls conducted by Ipsos MRBI, Behaviour and Attitudes and Red C. Government satisfaction polls in October and November also showed the government enjoying its largest levels of satisfaction since it took office (see Fig. 1.2). If ever a time seemed appropriate for Enda Kenny to call the election it was November 2015.

Two issues seemed to have dissuaded the Taoiseach from this course of action; the continued weakness of Labour in the polls and the fact that an Oireachtas banking inquiry would fall without reporting once the Dáil was dissolved. Even before the budget was delivered it was widely reported that Tánaiste Joan Burton had reacted badly to reports of a November election and repeatedly demanded that the Taoiseach not seek a dissolution of the Dáil until at least February 2016 in order that the government could complete its term and that Labour would have more time to prepare its own campaign.[53] For Fine Gael and Enda Kenny, while there might have been some loyalty towards their government colleagues, the failure to call the election would prove to have serious consequences. The possibility that Labour would improve in three months when it had been static in the polls for so long seemed far-fetched at best and is probably better read as a postponement for as long as possible of the inevitable serious losses Labour would face.

Delaying the calling of the election on the grounds of allowing the banking inquiry to finish its business was also somewhat curious. Even though there had already been three separate reports into the banking crisis in Ireland, the government was keen to have an Oireachtas inquiry. Established in November 2014, its purpose according to its official website was to 'inquire into the reasons Ireland experienced a systemic banking crisis, including the political, economic, social, cultural, financial and behavioural factors and policies which impacted on or contributed to the crisis and the preventative reforms implemented in the wake of the crisis.'[54] Many observers, however, suspected that it would be used by the government parties to serve as a useful reminder to the electorate that Fianna Fáil was at the helm of the ship of state when the economy imploded. This view seemed strongly substantiated when the government added two members to the composition of the inquiry committee to re-establish its majority on the committee after the Seanad had originally and unexpectedly appointed two non-government members to the all-party committee. The question of a government majority on the inquiry had agitated some members of Labour in particular for a long time with minister for state and then Labour Party leadership candidate Alex White stating some five months earlier that the Taoiseach's insistence on such a majority gave 'politics a bad name'.[55] Eventually 131 witnesses gave testimony during 49 days of hearings. During these hearings it soon became evident that laying the blame for Ireland's banking crisis solely on Fianna Fáil was a charge that was unlikely to stick. Once the hearings were over the writing of the report became fractious in late 2015, and the chairperson of the inquiry Labour's Ciarán Lynch had to seek a number of extensions to its deadline for publication. Ultimately, Enda Kenny decided not to call the election in November, thus allowing the inquiry to complete its business, and it eventually reported in January 2016.

The majority report held that the decision to guarantee the banks was not taken on the single night of 29 September 2008 and that Ireland was not bounced into its bailout in November 2010. It did, however, discover through evidence from the Minister for Finance Michael Noonan that the former European Central Bank President Jean-Claude Trichet had warned him in late March 2011 that 'a bomb would go off' in Dublin's financial sector if he implemented so-called 'haircuts' on €3.7 billion worth of unsecured, unguaranteed senior debt connected with the Irish Bank Resolution Corporation, which comprised the old Anglo Irish Bank and the Irish Nationwide Building Society. This would have been considered a default by the European Central Bank and was not a risk Noonan was willing to take, so ultimately he abandoned this plan, changing a Dáil speech at literally the final hour.[56]

The consequences of this decision were serious for both parties but particularly Labour. Coming as it did when the government had just taken office, Labour could subsequently never claim Labour's way over Frankfurt's way (see p. 29). For both Labour and Fine Gael, presiding over a growing economy in the final two years of their administration could not overcome the difficulties of being in office during its first three years of ongoing austerity. The Irish public had a short memory when it came to austerity blame. As the banking inquiry could not blame Fianna Fáil uniquely for Ireland's banking and financial crisis, the electorate also decided that Fianna Fáil with its promises of better public services was worth a closer look as Enda Kenny called the election. The stage was set for the great recovery in Irish politics.

Notes

1. https://twitter.com/endakennytd/status/694822324692844544
2. *Irish Independent*, 4 February 2016.
3. *Dáil Debates* 728:1, 9 March 2011.
4. On 25 August 1922, three days after the death of Michael Collins, George Bernard Shaw wrote to Collins's sister Johanna stating: 'So tear up your mourning and hang out your brightest colours in his honour.'
5. Eoin O'Malley, 'Government formation in 2011', pp. 264–282 in Michael Gallagher and Michael Marsh (eds), *How Ireland Voted 2011: the full story of Ireland's earthquake election* (Basingstoke: Palgrave Macmillan, 2011) at pp. 271–275.

6. Peter Mair, 'The election in context', pp. 283–297 in Michael Gallagher and Michael Marsh (eds), *How Ireland Voted 2011: the full story of Ireland's earthquake election* (Basingstoke: Palgrave Macmillan, 2011).

7. Liam Weeks, 'Parties and the party system', pp. 137–167 in John Coakley and Michael Gallagher (eds), *Politics in the Republic of Ireland*, 5th edn (Abingdon: Routledge, 2010), at p. 143.

8. Gary Murphy, *Electoral Competition in Ireland since 1987: the politics of triumph and despair* (Manchester: Manchester University Press, 2016), pp. 103–105.

9. The PDs themselves were in essence a breakaway from Fianna Fáil. See Michael Laver and Audrey Arkins, 'Coalition and Fianna Fáil', pp. 192–207 in Michael Gallagher and Richard Sinnott (eds), *How Ireland Voted 1989* (Galway: PSAI Press, 1990).

10. John Garry, 'The demise of the Fianna Fáil / Labour "Partnership" government and the rise of the "Rainbow" coalition', *Irish Political Studies* 10 (1995), pp. 192–199.

11. Kevin Rafter, *The Road to Power: How Fine Gael made history* (Dublin: New Island Press, 2011), pp. 292–307.

12. *Dáil Debates* 706:1, 31 March 2010.

13. O'Malley, 'Government formation', p. 269.

14. These are independents who formerly belonged to a political party and might still be perceived to belong to the wider political 'family' based around their former party.

15. Éamon Gilmore, *Inside the Room: the untold story of Ireland's crisis government* (Dublin: Merrion Press, 2016), p. 98.

16. Pat Leahy, *The Price of Power: Inside Ireland's Crisis Coalition* (Dublin: Penguin Ireland, 2013).

17. Gilmore, *Inside the Room*, p. 103.

18. Leahy, *The Price of Power*, p. 111.

19. Michael Marsh, Jane Suiter, Theresa Reidy, *'Report on Reasons Behind Voter Behaviour in the Oireachtas Inquiry Referendum 2011'* prepared for the Department of Public Expenditure and Reform, January 2012, pp. 35–37, available at http://per.gov.ie/wp-content/uploads/OIReferendum-Report-Final-2003-corrected.pdf

20. Eoin O'Malley, 'Explaining the 2011 Irish presidential election: culture, valence, loyalty or punishment?', *Irish Political Studies*, 27:4 (2012), pp. 635–655, at p. 638.

21. Eoin O'Malley, 'The 2011 presidential election: explaining the outcome', in John Coakley and Kevin Rafter (eds), *The Irish Presidency: Power, Ceremony and Politics* (Dublin: Irish Academic Press, 2014), pp. 170–193, at p. 183.
22. John Walshe, *An Education: How an outsider became an insider and learned what really goes on in Irish government* (Dublin: Penguin Ireland, 2015), p. 86.
23. See http://budget.gov.ie/budgets/2012/Documents/Budget%20 2012%20Leaflet.pdf
24. See for instance Sunday Times/Behaviour and Attitudes Government Satisfaction Levels, *Sunday Times* (Irish edition), 18 December 2011.
25. Mr Justice Michael Moriarty, *The Moriarty Tribunal Report. Report of the Tribunal of Inquiry into Payments to Politicians and Related Matters, Part 2.* (Dublin: Stationery Office, 2011), p. 1050. Also available at http://www.moriarty-tribunal.ie
26. Ibid. See also Elaine Byrne, *Political Corruption in Ireland 1922–2010: A Crooked Harp?* (Manchester: Manchester University Press, 2012), pp. 165–166.
27. *Dáil Debates* 728:6, 29 March 2011.
28. See http://www.planningtribunal.ie/images/finalReport.pdf
29. *Dáil Debates* 760:3, 27 March 2012.
30. See Gary Murphy, The background to the election', pp. 1–28 in Michael Gallagher and Michael Marsh (eds), *How Ireland Voted 2011: the full story of Ireland's earthquake election* (Basingstoke: Palgrave Macmillan, 2011) at pp. 9–11.
31. Murphy, *Electoral Competition*, p. 98.
32. *Irish Times*, 15 January 2015.
33. See *Irish Times*, 12 December 2013; *Sunday Times* (Irish edition), 15 December 2013.
34. The main Irish broadsheet newspapers, *Irish Examiner, Irish Independent* and *Irish Times* 16, 17, 18 May 2013 all carried comprehensive coverage of these issues.
35. Again the *Irish Examiner, Irish Independent and Irish Times* all carried large accounts of these events on 3 October 2013.
36. See *Sunday Times* (Irish edition), 9 and 16 February 2014.
37. *Irish Times*, 26 March 2014.
38. *Interim Report of the Fennelly Commission of Investigation (Certain Matters relative to An Garda Síochána and other persons), p. 276, available at* http://www.taoiseach.gov.ie/eng/News/

Taoiseach's_Press_Releases/Interim_report_of_the_Fennelly_
Commission.pdf
39. See *Sunday Independent,* 22 June 2014.
40. Aodh Quinlivan, 'The 2014 local elections in the Republic of
Ireland', *Irish Political Studies,* 30:1 (2015), pp. 132–142 at p. 133.
For the background to the changes in the local election boundaries
see Gary Murphy, '"Residents are fearful that their community will
die around them": Some thoughts from inside the 2013 Local
Electoral Area Boundary Committee', *Irish Political Studies,* 30:4
(2015), pp. 555–574. The comparison between the 2009 and 2014
election results is between county and city council seats in 2009 and
Local Electoral Authority seats in 2014, disregarding the town
council seats that were abolished prior to the 2014 elections.
41. Quinlivan, 'Local elections', p. 135.
42. Ibid., p. 136.
43. Muiris MacCarthaigh and Shane Martin, 'Bicameralism in the
Republic of Ireland: the Seanad abolition referendum', *Irish
Political Studies,* 30:1(2015), pp. 121–131.
44. Adrian Kavanagh, 'An end to "civil war" politics? The radically
reshaped political landscape of post-crash Ireland', *Electoral
Studies,* 38 (2015), pp. 71–81 at p. 77.
45. Gilmore, *Inside the Room,* p. 289.
46. Murphy, *Electoral Competition,* p. 159.
47. *Irish Times,* 7 March 2014.
48. A useful chronology of the saga of Irish Water charges is provided
by Harry McGee at http://www.irishtimes.com/news/politics/
irish-water-timeline-1.2300157
49. *Irish Times,* 11 October 2014.
50. Gilmore, *Inside the Room,* p. 216.
51. On the background to, and the campaign of, the same-sex marriage referendum see Gráinne Healy, Brian Sheehan, Noel Whelan,
*Ireland Says Yes: the inside story of how the vote for marriage equality
was won* (Dublin: Merrion Press, 2015); on its importance in the
lives of ordinary citizens see Charlie Bird, *A Day in May: Real
Lives, True Stories* (Dublin: Merrion Press, 2016).
52. *Sunday Business Post,* 25 October 2015.
53. See for instance *Irish Independent, Irish Times,* 9 October 2015.
54. https://inquiries.oireachtas.ie/banking/
55. *Irish Times,* 13 June 2014.
56. *Irish Times,* 30 January 2016.

CHAPTER 2

The Fulfilment of Election Pledges by the Outgoing Government

Rory Costello, Paul O'Neill, and Robert Thomson

The government's record of fulfilling pledges that Fine Gael and Labour had made in their 2011 manifestos was one of the dominant themes of the 2016 election campaign. The Labour Party in particular came in for sustained attack on this front from opposition parties, particularly Sinn Féin. Mary Lou McDonald, the Sinn Féin deputy leader, claimed that Labour 'tore up every promise it made', and the issue was raised by party leader Gerry Adams in each of the three televised leaders' debates.[1] Sinn Féin ran a billboard campaign on 'Labour's Broken Promises', featuring an image of former Labour minister Ruairí Quinn signing a pledge not to increase university fees. Another billboard, this time from Fianna Fáil, featured a remark by Labour minister Pat Rabbitte ('isn't that what you tend to do during an election?') made in response to an accusation that the party had over-promised on the issue of child benefit (Fig. 2.1). Many political commentators attribute the collapse in support for Labour to the widespread perception that it broke many of its election promises on issues such as water charges, child benefit and health insurance.[2]

R. Costello (✉) • P. O'Neill
University of Limerick, Limerick, Ireland

R. Thomson
University of Strathclyde, Glasgow, UK

© The Author(s) 2016
M. Gallagher, M. Marsh (eds.), *How Ireland Voted 2016*,
DOI 10.1007/978-3-319-40889-7_2

27

Fig. 2.1 Billboard criticising Labour's record of election pledge fulfilment [Gavan Reilly]

Fine Gael did not escape criticism either, and was repeatedly accused of broken promises on issues such as Universal Health Insurance, burning bank bondholders and political reform. For example, Fianna Fáil leader Micheál Martin claimed that Taoiseach Enda Kenny received a 'massive mandate based on a series of promises that turned out to be lies'.[3] Fianna Fáil also ran a billboard campaign alluding to Fine Gael's failure to fulfil its pledge to 'end the scandal of patients on trolleys' (a statement that actually comes from Fine Gael's 2007 election campaign).

The view that Fine Gael and especially Labour had a poor record of pledge fulfilment was widely held in the public at large. A survey conducted as part of the Irish National Election Study 2016 found that only 38 per cent of respondents believed that Labour had done some or most of what it had promised, while 58 per cent thought that Fine Gael had delivered on some or most of its promises.

In stark contrast, the government's own assessment was that it delivered or made significant progress on 93 per cent of the commitments in the Programme for Government.[4] Senior Fine Gael and Labour cabinet members made media appearances explicitly to defend their party's record of pledge fulfilment. For instance, Fine Gael's Simon Coveney appeared on radio on 2 December 2015 to defend the party's record of fulfilment in relation to each heading in its 2011 manifesto. Labour minister Alex White appeared on radio the day before the election to argue that Labour had kept its promises, citing pledges to create jobs, to protect the vulnerable and to introduce marriage equality.

The huge disparities in these claims regarding what should be objectively verifiable information point to the difficulties in assessing pledge fulfilment. Part of the difficulty stems from the sheer number of commitments made by political parties in modern election campaigns, making a comprehensive assessment a significant undertaking. A second difficulty with assessing election pledge fulfilment is that some of the key commitments made by parties during an election campaign are too vague to be tested objectively. For example, the phrase 'Labour's way or Frankfurt's way' came to be associated with the Labour's Party campaign in 2011,[5] and was later cited by critics as an example of the party's broken promises. What exactly this phrase entails is a matter of interpretation.

This chapter has two main objectives. First, we seek to provide a systematic and impartial analysis of Fine Gael and Labour's record of election pledge fulfilment in the 2011–16 government period. To make our study as objective as possible, we consider only clear commitments made in election manifestos to carry out specific actions or to produce specific outcomes. To put the government parties' pledge fulfilment records in context, we compare them with similar data from previous government periods.

Second, we examine the extent to which pledges made by the two main opposition parties were enacted. If elections really matter in terms of shaping policy, then we should find that pledges made by parties that 'win' an election and go on to form a government are enacted in significantly greater numbers than pledges made by parties that enter opposition. While previous studies on pledge fulfilment have generally found this to be the case, it is a particularly pertinent question in light of the external constraints operating on the Irish government during this period.[6] A common refrain during the period of the EU–IMF 'bailout' was that Ireland had lost its economic sovereignty. If indeed the government had little control over economic policy, then we would not expect to find significant differences in the rates of pledge fulfilment for government and opposition parties (with the exception of opposition parties that opposed the bailout agreement outright).

The chapter proceeds as follows. We begin by describing the pledges contained in the 2011 manifestos of the main political parties, including an analysis of the relationship between these pledges. We then move on to the analysis of pledge fulfilment over the subsequent government period, and compare the rate of fulfilment with findings from similar studies on previous Irish governments. The next section examines the patterns of pledge fulfilment, identifying the types of pledges that were most likely to be fulfilled, including a separate discussion of the fulfilment of particularly prominent pledges. We then turn to the comparison of pledge fulfilment between government and opposition parties, addressing the question of whether it mattered who was in government during this period. We conclude by discussing some of the implications of our findings.

ELECTION PLEDGES MADE IN 2011

We examine pledges made by the largest four parties in the 31st Dáil: Fine Gael, Labour, Fianna Fáil and Sinn Féin. We therefore exclude a number of small parties, none of which won more than two seats in 2011. Following an established body of literature, we adopt a relatively strict definition of what counts as an election pledge.[7] Firstly, we consider only pledges that are contained in election manifestos. Parties make many policy statements over the course of an election campaign, some of which may be interpreted as election pledges, but producing a comprehensive record of these statements and determining which count as pledges is beyond the scope of this study. There are a couple of examples of high-profile commitments made by individual politicians that were not featured in the party manifesto but were probably interpreted as party pledges by the general public, such as the pledge by Labour's Ruairí Quinn not to raise the university student contribution charge.[8] We do not include these pledges in the present study, but as there are only a small number of these cases, their exclusion is very unlikely to alter our main findings.

Secondly, we consider a statement in a manifesto to be a pledge if it indicates unequivocal support for or opposition to a specific and testable action or outcome during the lifetime of the next government period. Some statements contained in manifestos are not considered pledges because they do not identify a specific action or outcome. For example, the statement 'Labour will insist on the highest standards of transparency in the operation of NAMA' is not specific enough to count as a testable pledge. Other statements are excluded because they indicate equivocal or qualified support for the action or outcome that makes it impossible to judge them objectively. Examples include the Fine Gael pledge that 'no A&E services will be withdrawn unless a demonstrably better service is put in place' or the pledge 'Labour is opposed to further fire-sales of bank assets which impose greater losses than necessary'. Still other statements are excluded because they do not refer to the relevant government period, such as the pledge 'Fine Gael will introduce Universal Health Insurance (2016–2020)'.[9] We count each pledge only once, even if it is repeated several times in the same manifesto.

There are substantial differences in the numbers of clear pledges made by different parties. Fine Gael made the most pledges (237), followed by Labour (186), Sinn Féin (167) and Fianna Fáil (129). Fianna Fáil's manifesto, which according to its introduction 'put aside the old approach of addressing every single policy', stands out as being unusually short by the party's standards; some important policy areas, such as health, were not addressed.

Not all pledges are of equal importance. For example, few people would dispute that the Fine Gael pledge to 'establish a single state-owned commercial water company—Irish Water' is more important than its pledge to 'strike a medal named after General Michael Collins'. However, assessing the significance of pledges in a systematic and objective way is problematic. The Michael Collins medal pledge notwithstanding, the vast majority of pledges we have identified could be considered to be important to some groups in society. We treat all pledges equally in most of the analysis in this chapter, but we also include a separate analysis of high-profile pledges emphasised by the media.

Table 2.1 summarises the pledges made by each party and their relationship to pledges made by other parties. We categorise a pledge as consensually related to a pledge of another party if the fulfilment of the latter would automatically mean the partial or complete fulfilment of the

Table 2.1 Relationship between pledges made by different parties in 2011

	Fine Gael	Labour	Fianna Fáil	Sinn Féin
Consensus with any party	76 (32 %)	74 (40 %)	45 (35 %)	51 (31 %)
Consensus with FG	–	50 (27 %)	26 (20 %)	30 (18 %)
Consensus with Lab	52 (22 %)	–	29 (23 %)	36 (22 %)
Consensus with FF	26 (11 %)	24 (13 %)	–	13 (11 %)
Consensus with SF	31 (13 %)	36 (19 %)	14 (11 %)	–
Programme for Govt.	104 (44 %)	87 (47 %)	20 (16 %)	20 (12 %)
Total number of pledges	237	186	129	167

former.[10] For example, the Labour pledge to 'bring about a 50 per cent increase in Dáil sitting days' and the Fianna Fáil pledge 'the Dáil will be scheduled for a normal working week for most of the year' were coded as being in consensus with one another.

Table 2.1 can be read by examining each column in turn. Of the 237 pledges made by Fine Gael, 76 (32 per cent) were in consensus with pledges made by other parties. The party that Fine Gael was most often in agreement with was Labour; 52 Fine Gael pledges (22 per cent) were in consensus with Labour pledges. Turning to Labour, a slightly larger proportion of its pledges (74/186, or 40 per cent) were positively related to pledges made by other parties, and the party that Labour was most often in agreement with was Fine Gael. For Fianna Fáil, the rate of agreement with other parties was 35 per cent, and the party that Fianna Fáil most often agreed with was Labour. Finally, for Sinn Féin too around a third of its pledges (31 per cent) were in agreement with those of other parties, and again Labour was the party it most often agreed with.

These patterns of agreement between the parties are broadly in line with the results of an analysis of the 2011 manifestos carried out by Jane Suiter and David Farrell, using a different methodology.[11] In that study, the authors found that Labour and Fine Gael had moved quite close together in terms of policy positions at the 2011 election, in anticipation of a coalition partnership. Sinn Féin, meanwhile, was found to be the most distinctive of the major parties, as it was the only one not working within the broad parameters of the agreement that the outgoing government had reached with the EU and the IMF.

The second last row in Table 2.1 shows how many of each party's pledges were included in the Programme for Government that was subsequently agreed between Fine Gael and Labour. Comparing the two government parties, Fine Gael had more pledges in the Programme for Government than Labour (104 Fine Gael pledges against 87 Labour pledges), although as a proportion of each party's pledges, Labour did marginally better on this measure. Relatively few pledges made by Fianna Fáil or Sinn Féin were contained in the Programme for Government, as we would expect; and of those that are, most duplicated pledges made by one of the government parties.

Given that the majority of pledges made by each party were not in agreement with pledges of other parties, this suggests that voters were presented with policy choices in the 2011 election. However, the choices were not necessarily clear-cut. Parties referred to different initiatives, but this does not mean they were opposed to policies proposed by their competitors. Indeed, we found very few examples of pledges that were in direct opposition to pledges made by other parties. A better test of the policy differences between the parties is found in the analysis of pledge fulfilment. If government parties that command a clear majority in the Dáil go on to enact a high proportion of pledges made by an opposition party, this suggests that the policy differences between them were not that great. We return to this issue towards the end of the chapter.

FULFILMENT OF ELECTION PLEDGES, 2011–16

For each of the 719 pledges identified in the 2011 manifestos of the four main parties, we assess whether the pledge was fully fulfilled, partially fulfilled or not fulfilled. A wide range of sources were consulted in making these assessments, including legislative acts, annual budgets, responses to Dáil questions, reports from government departments and agencies, and newspaper reports. Each pledge was assessed by a primary coder and independently cross-checked by a second coder.

Pledges are deemed to be fully fulfilled when the stated outcome or action is achieved in the manner and timeframe specified. For example, the pledge by Labour to reverse the decision of the previous government to cut the minimum wage was fully fulfilled, as the minimum wage was restored to the previous rate of €8.65 in the first budget of the new administration. Pledges are categorised as partially fulfilled if there was policy change in the direction of the pledge, but the change fell short of what was promised or did not occur in the specified timeframe. For example, Fine Gael's pledge to cut the number of TDs by 20 was partially fulfilled, as the Electoral Amendment Act passed in 2013 reduced the number of TDs by eight for the next election.

Table 2.2 presents the figures on pledge fulfilment for each of the four main parties. Looking first at the government parties, Fine Gael fully fulfilled 43 per cent (101/237) of its pledges and partially fulfilled a further 17 per cent (41/237), while Labour also fully fulfilled 43 per cent (80/186) of its pledges and partially fulfilled 19 per cent (36/186). Both parties therefore implemented a clear majority of their pledges at least partially, and the rate of fulfilment for the two parties is remarkably similar. This is a surprising finding in light of the popular perception that Labour in particular broke most of its promises.

It is possible that the negative public perception of pledge fulfilment by the government parties (especially Labour) reflects a poor record with

Table 2.2   The fulfilment of election pledges in the 2011–16 government period

	Government		Opposition	
	Fine Gael	*Labour*	*Fianna Fáil*	*Sinn Féin*
Fully fulfilled	101 (43 %)	80 (43 %)	63 (49 %)	31 (19 %)
Partially fulfilled	41 (17 %)	36 (19 %)	23 (18 %)	31 (19 %)
Not fulfilled	95 (40 %)	70 (38 %)	43 (33 %)	105 (63 %)
Total	237 (100 %)	186 (100 %)	129 (100 %)	167 (100 %)

respect to important or high-profile pledges. As discussed previously, it is difficult to make an objective assessment of a pledge's importance. Nonetheless, to provide an indication of which pledges were most prominent, we make use of a summary table produced by the *Irish Times* on the day of each party's manifesto launch in 2011, listing what the editors considered to be the main points in each manifesto.[12] Of the 14 Fine Gael pledges highlighted by the *Irish Times*, 11 (77 per cent) were at least partially fulfilled. Two of the pledges that were not fulfilled related to elements of the planned renegotiation of the EU–IMF agreement; the third was a pledge to reverse the ban on stag hunting.

Of the 13 Labour pledges selected by the *Irish Times* as noteworthy, 9 (69 per cent) were at least partially fulfilled. The four that were not fulfilled include pledges on burden-sharing with bondholders, water charges, a new trade czar, and legislation on universal care insurance. While these are certainly significant blemishes on the records of both parties, it does not fully account for the widespread perception that Labour broke more promises than Fine Gael. We return to this question in the conclusion.

Another factor to consider when assessing the record of the government parties is how well they performed in comparison to their predecessors. Fortunately, we have comparable data on pledge fulfilment from previous government periods in Ireland, collected using the same methodology.[13] Figure 2.2 compares the rate of fulfilment by Fine Gael and Labour with that of government parties from the previous three administrations. Both parties performed far better than their immediate predecessors in terms of pledge fulfilment. In contrast, the rate of pledge fulfilment by the government parties in the 1997–02 and 2002–07 periods is slightly higher than that for Fine Gael and Labour. This pattern is consistent with previous findings that pledge fulfilment is strongly influenced by economic conditions.[14] The governments that took office in 1997 and 2002 enjoyed

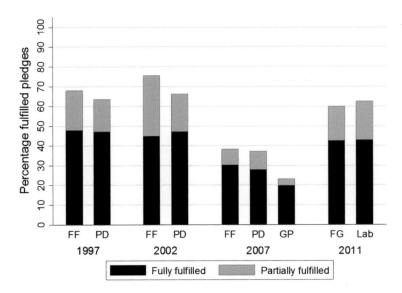

Fig. 2.2   Pledge fulfilment by government parties, 1997–16

favourable economic conditions, with average GDP growth of over 5 per cent. This is in sharp contrast to the 2007–11 period, when the economy contracted. The Fine Gael–Labour government presided over a period of modest growth during most of its term, with average annual GDP growth of just over 3 per cent.[15]

Returning to Table 2.2, we also show the pledge fulfilment rates for the main opposition parties. Here, the findings are quite surprising. While the number of Sinn Féin pledges that were enacted is relatively small (19 per cent fully fulfilled and a further 19 per cent partially fulfilled), the rate of fulfilment for Fianna Fáil pledges is actually higher than that for either of the government parties. Almost half, 49 per cent, of Fianna Fáil's pledges were fully fulfilled and a further 18 per cent were partially fulfilled. We return to explanations for this surprising finding later.

Explaining Pledge Fulfilment

Why are some pledges fulfilled and others not? Previous research identifies a number of factors that influence the chances that a promise made during a particular election is kept. There is consistent evidence that pledges made by parties that go into government are more likely to be fulfilled than pledges made by parties that enter opposition, both in Ireland and in other countries.[16] However, as we have seen, Table 2.2 shows an unusually high fulfilment rate for pledges made by the opposition party Fianna Fáil. The reasons for this are explored in the following section.

There are also differences in the likelihood of fulfilment depending on the nature of the pledge. The most obvious distinction is between pledges to bring about some change in policy and pledges to keep the status quo. Status quo pledges, such as Labour's commitment to 'maintain Irish as one of the three core compulsory Leaving Certificate subjects' are considerably easier to implement than other pledges. Only 47 of the 719 pledges we identified are status quo pledges, and they are spread relatively evenly among the parties. The vast majority of these status quo pledges (85 per cent) were fulfilled at least partially.

For government parties, previous research finds that pledges made by the senior coalition party, which delivers the Taoiseach, are significantly more likely to be fulfilled than pledges made by junior coalition parties. This finding is not replicated here. As shown in Table 2.2, Labour pledges were enacted at a similar rate to Fine Gael pledges. We do however find some differences in pledge fulfilment rates depending on whether or not the party held the relevant ministerial post. Fine Gael held 10 cabinet seats and Labour 5 throughout the period, but there was some reshuffling of portfolios half way through the government term. A total of 65 per cent (136/208) of pledges made by a party that held the relevant ministerial portfolio for the entire government period were at least partially fulfilled, compared to 57 per cent (122/215) of pledges made by parties that did not hold the relevant portfolio throughout the period.

The relationship between pledges made by different parties is an important determinant of fulfilment. Governments often prioritise policies where coalition parties are in agreement, and this is reflected in our data. Of the pledges made by a government party that were consensually related to a pledge made by their coalition partner, 75 per cent (77/102) were at least partially fulfilled, compared with 56 per cent (181/321) of other government party pledges. Agreement with one of the government parties is also an important factor in the fulfilment of opposition party pledges: 72 per cent (63/87) of opposition party pledges that were in agreement with a government party pledge were fulfilled at least partially, compared to only 41 per cent (85/209) of other opposition party pledges (most of which were made by Fianna Fáil, as discussed below). In contrast, agreement with an opposition party has no effect on the likelihood of a pledge being fulfilled, regardless of whether the pledge is made by a government or opposition party.

A related but separate factor is the Programme for Government. Pledges on which there is agreement between government parties often, though not always, make it into the Programme for Government and are therefore prioritised. However, many pledges made by only one government party were also included in the Programme. A number of opposition party pledges (40) were also included in the Programme for Government; the majority of these are pledges that were also made by one or both government parties. Inclusion in the Programme for Government has a very significant impact on the likelihood of pledge fulfilment: 78 per cent of all election pledges that were featured in the Programme for Government were fulfilled at least in part, compared to 46 per cent of other pledges.

To further test these findings, we examine the unique effect that each of these factors had on pledge fulfilment, controlling for other factors.[17] The results are summarised in Table 2.3. The figures show how the likelihood of fulfilment changes when a particular factor is present. For example, the first row of the table indicates that for pledges made by a government party, the likelihood of fulfilment increases by 12 per cent if the party goes on to hold the ministry relevant to that pledge. Each of the factors identified as important above—consensus with a government party, status quo pledges, inclusion in the Programme for Government, and (for government parties) holding the relevant ministry—are all statistically significant in the analysis reported in Table 2.3. The term 'statistically significant' in

Table 2.3 Marginal effects of variables on probability of pledge fulfilment

	Government party pledges	Opposition party pledges
Relevant ministry	+12%*	–
Programme for Government	+29%*	+34%*
Consensus with government party	+17%*	+24%*
Consensus with opposition party	+5%	–6%
Status quo pledge	+30%*	+40%*
N	423	296

*Indicates a statistically significant effect ($p < 0.05$). Figures refer to the difference in the probability of fulfilment when the relevant variable changes in value, for example, from not holding the relevant ministry to holding the relevant ministry. Other variables are held at their median values. Estimates based on logistic regression models

this context means that these differences in likelihoods of pledge fulfilment are very unlikely to have occurred just by chance.

The largest effects relate to the nature of the pledge and its inclusion in the Programme for Government. Controlling for other factors, pledges made by a government party are 29 per cent more likely to be fulfilled if they are included in the Programme for Government; and 30 per cent more likely to be fulfilled if they are status quo pledges rather than pledges for policy change. The corresponding effects for opposition party pledges are even larger: the likelihood of fulfilment increases by 34 per cent if it features in the Programme for Government, and by 40 per cent if it is a status quo pledge. The effect of consensus with a government party is also substantial. A pledge made by a government party that is in consensus with a pledge made by the other government party is 17 per cent more likely to be fulfilled. Opposition party pledges, meanwhile, are 24 per cent more likely to be enacted if they are in agreement with a pledge made by a government party.

WHAT EXPLAINS THE HIGH RATE OF FULFILMENT OF FIANNA FÁIL PLEDGES?

As reported in Table 2.2, Fianna Fáil had the highest rate of fulfilled election pledges of all the parties analysed, despite being in opposition. The explanatory factors discussed above do not fully account for this.[18] A substantial number of Fianna Fáil pledges that were not status quo pledges and were not in agreement with pledges made by government parties were enacted. This goes against the conventional wisdom that opposition parties have little or no opportunity to influence government policy in Ireland.

One reason for this surprising finding could be the small number of pledges made by Fianna Fáil. Indeed, when we look at the total number of enacted pledges as opposed to the rate of fulfilment, Fianna Fáil was far behind both Fine Gael and Labour (Table 2.2). On the other hand, the brevity of the Fianna Fáil manifesto reflects the fact that it focused on three core areas: restoring public finances (17 pledges), jobs (66 pledges) and political reform (46 pledges). As these were crucial policy areas in the context of the 2011 election, the high fulfilment rate for Fianna Fáil pledges means that many important aspects of national policy under the new administration were similar to what Fianna Fáil had proposed.

The high rate of fulfilment of Fianna Fáil pledges can only be understood in terms of the unique political and economic circumstances that shaped the 2011 election campaign and the government period that followed. Three months before the election, the government was forced to accept an €85 billion financial assistance programme from the EU and IMF, which came with significant conditions attached. To meet the requirements of the assistance package, the Fianna Fáil-led government produced a 'National Recovery Plan', setting out a series of measures designed to address the huge gap in public finances.

For the first three years of the Fine Gael–Labour government, the country was officially part of this EU–IMF programme. Both Fine Gael and Labour were committed to working within the broad terms of the bailout, although both parties wanted to renegotiate aspects of it. Only Sinn Féin opposed the bailout outright. Even after the country formally exited the programme, the government continued to be subject to regular post-programme surveillance by the EU and IMF. As the head of the IMF mission Ajai Chopra later reported, the Fine Gael–Labour government 'modified a few elements' of the National Recovery Plan, but 'the fundamental structure remained'.[19] In other words, while Fine Gael, Labour and Fianna Fáil emphasised different things in their manifestos, they were essentially committed to the same path on economic policy.

Mr Chopra's assessment is broadly supported by our evidence on pledge fulfilment. Only seven Fine Gael pledges clearly specified reversing or modifying elements of the National Recovery Plan, and most of these (4/7) were not fulfilled, including pledges on student registration fees, commercial rents, a site sale profit tax, and forced burden-sharing by bank bondholders. In contrast, Fine Gael made 18 pledges that were in line with the plan, and 16 of these were at least partially fulfilled.

Labour made slightly more pledges to reverse aspects of the National Recovery Plan (12 in total), but again in most of these cases (8/12) the policy pursued by the government was actually closer to what was in the National Recovery Plan than to what Labour had said in its manifesto. For example, Labour pledged to reduce public service numbers by 18,000 between 2011 and 2014, while the National Recovery Plan called for a reduction in public service numbers of 24,700. The actual reduction over the period was 25,400. Similarly, Labour pledges to reverse the plan on issues including the VAT rate, burden-sharing and water charges were not fulfilled.

The high level of fulfilment for Fianna Fáil pledges can be partially explained by the new government's adherence to the National Recovery Plan. One quarter of all Fianna Fáil pledges (32/129) came directly from the plan, and fulfilment was highest for these pledges (72 per cent fulfilled at least partially). These include pledges that were not specifically made by other parties in their manifestos, such as the commitment to reduce the public service pay bill to €14.7 billion by 2014 and the pledge to cap the number of Special Needs Assistants at 2011 levels. They also include pledges that were repeated by other parties, such as the commitment to reform bankruptcy legislation. Some other components of the National Recovery Plan were not mentioned by Fianna Fáil in its manifesto, such as the introduction of a local property tax, but were subsequently enacted by the new government.

In sum, the majority of opposition party pledges that were enacted were either status quo pledges, pledges that were in agreement with government party pledges, or (for Fianna Fáil) pledges that came from the National Recovery Plan. There are also some examples of opposition party pledges that do not fall into any of these categories, yet were fulfilled. For instance, Fianna Fáil proposed to introduce a secret ballot for the election of the Ceann Comhairle, and was the only party to do so. This was later recommended by the Constitutional Convention and was implemented shortly before the 2016 election.

CONCLUSION

This chapter set out to address two questions: to what extent did the government parties fulfil their election pledges in the 2011–16 period, and were pledges made by parties that entered government fulfilled in significantly greater numbers than pledges made by parties that went into opposition? We conclude by highlighting our main findings on these questions and reflecting on the implications.

As highlighted at the beginning of this chapter, much of the commentary during the campaign implied that the government parties had performed particularly poorly in terms of delivering on their promises. Our findings show that both Fine Gael and Labour fulfilled a majority (approximately 60 per cent) of their election pledges at least partially. While this means that many Fine Gael and Labour election promises were broken, these figures on fulfilment rates compare reasonably well with the fulfilment rates from earlier government periods. The gap between public perception and reality when it comes to election pledges is not unique to this election. Previous research has also found that the public tends to systematically underestimate the government record of pledge fulfilment.[20]

However, it is something of a puzzle why Labour in particular received so much criticism for broken promises during the course of the 2016 campaign. Labour did fail to deliver on some high-profile promises, but the party performed comparatively well in terms of fulfilling both high-profile pledges and its full set of pledges. It is reasonable to expect a junior party in government to have to compromise on some of its policies, yet Labour seems to have been held to a particularly high standard by other parties and the public when it came to assessing pledge fulfilment. This may also have been the case for junior partners in previous governments in Ireland, which have often performed very poorly at the subsequent election.[21]

One possible reason for the fierce criticism levelled against Labour is that smaller parties tend to be defined by their policies to a significant extent, perhaps more so than large, catch-all parties.[22] Supporters of small parties may judge their party more on the basis of its ability to deliver on election pledges (as opposed to, say, how well the economy was managed). Voters may therefore be particularly unforgiving of broken promises by small parties in government. Another plausible reason is that the public judge parties based on the tone of their election campaign rather than their specific election pledges. Arguably, Labour's 2011 campaign gave the impression that it would bring an end to austerity, which clearly is not something the public believes was achieved. Further research is needed to fully understand the negative public perception of Labour's record.

We find mixed evidence in relation to our second research question. Pledges made by the government parties were far more likely to be fulfilled than pledges made by the opposition party Sinn Féin. While the governing parties fulfilled greater *numbers* of their pledges than those of the other main opposition party, Fianna Fáil, in *percentage* terms fulfilment was highest for Fianna Fáil. The high percentage of Fianna Fáil pledges that were fulfilled is certainly a remarkable finding. In principle, the fulfilment of opposition parties' pledges can be democratically legitimate. Despite not entering government office, opposition parties often receive substantial percentages of the popular vote and their pledges may reflect policies that are popular among large parts of the electorate. In this case, however, the explanation lies in the unique circumstances in which Fianna Fáil found itself as a government party prior to 2011, and the international constraints to which the Fine Gael–Labour government was subject after 2011. The agreement that the Fianna Fáil-led government reached with the EU–IMF in November 2010, and that was honoured to a large extent by the subsequent Fine Gael–Labour government, is key to understanding the high rate of pledge fulfilment for Fianna Fáil. This agreement bound the Fine Gael–Labour government to the terms of the external assistance programme to meet the day-to-day costs of running the country. Many of Fianna Fáil's fulfilled pledges referred to elements of this agreement.

In the 2011 edition of *How Ireland Voted,* the late Peter Mair argued that Ireland is a democracy without choices:

> the election outcome, however dramatic, will have mattered little in the sense of any real mandate for action. Regardless of the vote, in other words, the path that will be followed in the coming years will be much the same.[23]

Our analysis of election pledge fulfilment broadly supports this conclusion for the 2011–16 government period, but adds more nuance. The high rate of fulfilment of pledges made by Fianna Fáil implies that government policy on many of the issues central to the 2011 election would have been essentially the same if Fianna Fáil had been in power. On many of the key issues, particularly around fiscal policy, the policies pursued by the government were not substantially different from what had been proposed by Fianna Fáil in its manifesto. Nonetheless, our analysis reveals that Fine Gael and Labour did put their own stamp on government policies despite the international constraints that bound the government. There are many examples of Fine Gael and Labour pledges that were fulfilled, and we would certainly have observed lower rates of fulfilment for Fine Gael and Labour pledges had they been in the opposition after the 2011 election. Moreover, as Ireland emerges from the economic crisis, future governments will be less constrained. It would therefore be premature to conclude that elections have lost their meaning in Ireland.

NOTES

1. 'Sinn Féin's Mary Lou McDonald launches attack on Labour at 'broken promises' billboard launch', *Irish Independent* 15 February 2016, available: http://www.independent.ie/irish-news/election-2016/news/sinn-fins-mary-lou-mcdonald-launches-attack-on-labour-at-broken-promises-billboard-launch-34454588.html (accessed 4 April 2016).

2. See, for example, Stephen Collins, 'Seismic shift sends Irish politics into new phase'. *Irish Times* 28 February 2016, available: http://www.irishtimes.com/news/politics/seismic-shift-sends-irish-politics-into-new-phase-1.2552848 (accessed 4 April 2016).
3. Micheál Martin speaking on RTE's Morning Ireland, 1 December 2015.
4. Harry McGee, 'Annual progress report ignores Coalition failures: many government promises unfulfilled despite claimed 93% success rate', *Irish Times* 12 January 2016, available: http://www.irishtimes.com/news/politics/annual-progress-report-ignores-coalition-failures-1.2493070 (accessed 4 April 2016).
5. Michael Gallagher and Michael Marsh (eds), *How Ireland Voted 2011: the full story of Ireland's earthquake election* (Basingstoke: Palgrave Macmillan, 2011), p. xx.
6. Robert Thomson and Rory Costello, 'Governing together in good and bad economic times: the fulfilment of election pledges in Ireland', *Irish Political Studies* 31:2 (2016), pp. 182–203.
7. The most recent example of this work is Robert Thomson, Terry Royed, Elin Naurin, Joaquín Artés, Rory Costello, Laurenz Ennser-Jedenastik, Mark Ferguson, Petia Kostadinova, Catherine Moury and François Pétry. 'Explaining the fulfillment of election pledges: a comparative study on the impact of government institutions.' *Annual Meeting of the American Political Science Association, Washington DC.* 2014. For a review of earlier research on pledge fulfilment see, for example, Terry J. Royed, 'Testing the mandate model in Britain and the United States: evidence from the Reagan and Thatcher Eras', *British Journal of Political Science* 26 (1996), pp. 45–80.
8. We do however include a related pledge, which was in the Labour manifesto, that the party would not re-introduce third-level fees.
9. However, we do include a Fine Gael pledge on the groundwork that would be done during the lifetime of the 2011–16 government to prepare the way for Universal Health Insurance ('FairCare will gradually dismantle the HSE and replace it with a system of Universal Health Insurance (UHI) starting in 2016... Prior to the introduction of UHI Fine Gael will introduce a series of reforms to make the system more efficient and fairer'). This pledge is coded as unfulfilled, as the Minister for Health Leo Varadkar stated in

November 2015 that preparations for UHI would be pushed back to a later government term.

10. The number of consensually related pledges between any two parties is not always the same. For example, Table 2.1 reports that there were 52 Fine Gael pledges that were in agreement with Labour pledges; while there were only 50 Labour pledges in agreement with Fine Gael pledges. This apparent discrepancy arises because some pledges are more specific than others: a broad pledge made by one party can be related to two or more specific pledges made by another party.

11. Jane Suiter and David M. Farrell, 'The parties' manifestos', pp. 29–46 in Michael Gallagher and Michael Marsh (eds), *How Ireland Voted 2011: The Full Story of Ireland's Earthquake Election* (Basingstoke: Palgrave Macmillan, 2011).

12. Harry McGee, 'Labour says plan will set state on right course', *Irish Times* 12 February 2011. Harry McGee, 'Fine Gael promises to create 100,000 jobs', *Irish Times* 16 February 2011. Note that in a couple of instances the *Irish Times* listed a pledge by one party while omitting a related pledge by the other party. For these cases, we chose to consider both pledges as 'important'.

13. Lucy Mansergh, *Do Parties Make a Difference? The Case of Governments in Ireland, 1977–1997,* PhD thesis, Trinity College Dublin, 2004; Rory Costello and Robert Thomson, 'Election pledges and their enactment in coalition governments: a comparative analysis of Ireland', *Journal of Elections, Public Opinion and Policy* 18:3 (2008), pp. 239–256.

14. Thomson and Costello, 'Governing together in good and bad economic times', pp. 193–195.

15. Figures based on data from the World Bank.

16. Thomson et al., 'Explaining the fulfillment of election pledges'.

17. We use a logistic regression model, estimated separately for government party pledges and for opposition party pledges. This type of statistical model is appropriate when the outcome to be explained can take one of two values, in our case either 'not fulfilled' or 'at least partially fulfilled'.

18. To test this, we ran the model reported in Table 2.3 on all pledges (government and opposition), and included dummy variables for each party, with Fianna Fáil as the reference category. The results

show that pledges made by Fianna Fáil were significantly more likely to be enacted than pledges made by any other party.

19. *Report of the Joint Committee of Inquiry into the Banking Crisis*, Volume 1 (Houses of the Oireachtas, 2016), p. 351.

20. Robert Thomson, 'Citizens' evaluations of the fulfillment of election pledges: evidence from Ireland', *The Journal of Politics* 73: 1 (2011), pp. 187–201.

21. See Eoin O'Malley, 'Punchbags for heavyweights? Minor parties in Irish government', *Irish Political Studies* 25:4 (2010), pp. 539–561.

22. For a discussion of the notion of catch-all parties, see André Krouwel, 'Otto Kirchheimer and the catch-all party', *West European Politics* 26:2 (2003), pp. 23–40.

23. Peter Mair, 'The election in context', pp. 283–297, in Michael Gallagher and Michael Marsh (eds), *How Ireland Voted 2011: The Full Story of Ireland's Earthquake Election* (Basingstoke: Palgrave Macmillan, 2011), p. 296.

CHAPTER 3

Candidate Selection and the Illusion of Grass-Roots Democracy

Theresa Reidy

INTRODUCTION

Speculation about the date of the 2016 election began to build after the 2014 local and European elections (see Chapters 1 and 4). All of the parties initiated preparations for their campaign strategies and a number of new parties and alliances were formally announced. For much of 2015 the possibility of an autumn election was in the air but in the end the government saw out its full term. While the 2011 election occurred in the midst of an economic and political crisis, the 2016 contest had been long anticipated and took place over a short and relatively uneventful campaign. However, the election followed a turbulent Dáil term that brought substantive movement in opinion polls (see Chapter 1). As the

I am particularly grateful to all of the political party general secretaries and strategists from the parties and alliances along with the many candidates who agreed to be interviewed for this chapter. To a person, they were generous with their time and insights. All of the data listed in the tables were sourced from candidate websites and social media pages, political parties and interviews.

T. Reidy (✉)
University College Cork, Cork, Ireland

© The Author(s) 2016
M. Gallagher, M. Marsh (eds.), *How Ireland Voted 2016*,
DOI 10.1007/978-3-319-40889-7_3

election approached, Fine Gael and Labour faced significantly reduced vote shares while Fianna Fáil was showing signs of recovery from its 2011 collapse.

The febrile political environment in 2011 led to the emergence of several new parties and groups, many of whom failed to mount a national campaign and ended up having little impact on the election. In contrast, the new parties and groupings that appeared on the general election ballot in 2016 were better organised; many of them having formed within the Dáil as splinter groups from other parties or new coalitions of non-aligned TDs. As a direct consequence of having incumbent TDs, the new parties were able to deploy some of their staff and resources to prepare for the election. They were also going into the election with incumbent TDs in a system where incumbency is a very considerable advantage. Renua, the Social Democrats and the Independent Alliance all fall into this category.

In total 551 candidates contested the election, slightly down on the all-time high of 566 at the previous election (see Table 3.1). The size of the Dáil had been reduced to 158 seats in the intervening period and boundary revisions in 2012 reduced the number of constituencies from 43 to 40. Laois had the lowest number of candidates, with just six competing for three seats, while the largest field of candidates (21) was to be found in Dublin South-West. Both Dublin Bay North and Galway West also had long ballots with 20 candidates on each. Two candidates opted to contest the election in two constituencies. With several new parties spread across the ideological spectrum, a wide choice was on offer for voters.

This chapter will document the processes through which candidates get onto the ballot. It will begin by outlining the rules that define candidate

Table 3.1 Candidate numbers by party, 1997–16

	1997	2002	2007	2011	2016
Fine Gael	90	85	91	104	88
Fianna Fáil	112	106	107	75	71
Sinn Féin	15	37	41	41	50
Green Party	26	31	44	43	40
Labour	44	46	50	68	36
AAA–PBP	–	–	–	–	31
Others	195	138	108	235	235
Total	484	463	471	566	551

selection procedures within the main political parties and some of the new groups and parties that formed before 2016. Insights into the realities of internal party competition are provided through highlighting some of the controversies that dominated the party convention season in 2015–16. In the penultimate section, the occupational backgrounds, family connections and varied political experiences of candidates are laid out in a profile of candidates in 2016.

Party selectors are important gatekeepers on the road to the ballot paper and the decisions they make shape the electoral choices presented to all voters on election day. The use of proportional representation by the single transferable vote (PR–STV) (see Appendix 4) and the long-standing tradition of non-party candidates in Ireland (see Chapter 9) mean that party selectors do not exclusively control ballot access as they do in many other countries, but nevertheless they have an especially vital role in the overall electoral process. Political parties dominate electoral competition in Ireland even though they are not mentioned in the constitution. In recent years, a growing body of legislation has developed that regulates the operation of political parties but this legislation is almost exclusively focused on their financial affairs. The internal operating structures of parties are at their own discretion. Nevertheless, there is a remarkable similarity in the rules governing candidate selection across many of the parties. In most cases, prospective candidates go before constituency-level conventions. All of the large parties operate a system of one member, one vote (OMOV) which means that each party member is entitled to vote for the candidate(s) who will contest the election in their area. The specific rules vary: Fine Gael requires that participants be members of good standing for 2 years, Fianna Fail specifies 12 months, Labour requires 6 months and PBP just 6 weeks. Some of the new small parties used interview procedures in 2016 but as their organisations grow, they anticipate moving in the direction of constituency selection conventions with OMOV.

A more inclusive approach to defining party selectorates has taken hold across established democracies.[1] This democratic contagion has spread across parties and systems and stems from the premise that providing greater participation opportunities for party members in decision making is, in normative terms, good for democracy, as well as being good practice by political parties. Once one party within a system begins to move in this direction, a diffusion effect means that pressure grows on all parties to offer wider roles for party members.

There are a number of factors that feature in each party's calculus of candidate selection and these vary depending on the size and ambitions of the party. Maximising votes and seats is the overall objective of each party but beyond this, parties also need to keep in mind a number of criteria. At each election, for parties that run more than one candidate in a constituency, achieving a good balance in the geographic location of their candidates will be a priority. Local issues and delivering for the needs of the constituency are a priority for a substantial cohort of voters, with choosing the next Taoiseach and indeed matters related to policy being decidedly secondary criteria (see Chapter 7), so this must be given due weight by the selectors. In practice, localism means that many voters have a particular propensity to support candidates who may be known to them personally, may live close by or are well versed in community issues. This 'friends and neighbours' effect is more pronounced at local elections but cannot be discounted at general elections.[2] The phenomenon is particularly acute in constituencies that span more than one county, and it has been shown over many years that voters are more likely to support a candidate from their own county.

Balancing the age and gender profile of the party ticket is an important aspect of long-term planning. Age profile is important especially as it relates to succession planning; parties will want to ensure that they have a pipeline of candidates in place for future elections. The Electoral (Political Funding) Act (2012) tied state funding of political parties to improved female gender representation. Specifically, it introduced a penalty of a 50 per cent reduction in Electoral Act funding for parties that failed to field at least 30 per cent of their candidates from both genders. The law was gender neutral but in practice, it operated as a female candidate quota owing to the low numbers of female candidates contesting general elections over the decades (see Chapter 8). The legal change meant that the selection of female candidates was centre stage in the strategy deliberations of many parties but most especially for Fine Gael and Fianna Fáil.

For large parties, the decision on the overall number of candidates that will be fielded involves convoluted discussions that draw on all of the points above as well as incumbency and projected poll position as they seek to navigate the complexities of PR–STV. PR–STV can punish parties for both over nomination and under nomination.[3] From the outside looking in, the impression can often be that these deliberations are more hocus-pocus than science but the balance is critical if parties are to maximise their seat returns. Smaller parties face different challenges.

They have to find a balance among the cost of fielding candidates, ambitions to have a candidate in each constituency to ensure that the party has a presence, and the very practical need to achieve two per cent of the national vote and thereby ensure funding of the party under the Electoral Acts.

Parties must consider many factors in their candidate decision making and as a result most parties issue precise directions, known as candidate directives, to their local organisations. Prior to 2016, geography was the most common factor with local constituency conventions often being directed to select two candidates, for example, one from the east of the constituency and one from the west. Geographic lines are usually based on local electoral area boundaries. For the 2016 election, gender became a far more prevalent criterion and many parties tasked their selectors with choosing one man and one woman. Often, the most contentious conventions in 2016 took place when party selectors were asked to choose one candidate with the stipulation that that candidate had to be a woman.

Members in good standing may have the final decision among the candidates at the selection convention but the power to set the rules of the convention lies firmly with the party elite in all of the parties. Some offer more flexibility than others but no party offers a free choice to its local organisation to decide their own strategy. The extent of the selectorate democratisation is open to debate. Party members have been given a greater say in candidate selection over the decades but the democratisation has been restricted with party elites retaining the capacity to define the decision that will be taken.

GETTING ONTO THE TICKET; RULES AND REALITY

The regulations on candidate selection are contained within the constitutions and rule books of the individual parties. There is a common core to the party rules although the practice on the ground can vary considerably both within and across parties depending on the size of the party, the extent of competition and the local environment. Each party has a national council or party elite that makes the main decisions on candidate strategy, specifically how many candidates the party will run, and where, and this group is also frequently responsible for ratifying the overall candidate slate and any individuals who proceed to the ballot without going through formal conventions. Candidate selection decisions are informed by the national position of the party in opinion polls, local factors and the list of criteria discussed in the preceding section. Decisions are made on an ad hoc, and often evolving, basis as the election approaches.

The bulk of the candidate selection work was carried out by parties during 2015. Conventions and meetings were organised at constituency level. Conventions are usually chaired by a senior party figure from outside the constituency; some parties require this in their rules but in any case the practice is established across the parties. As 2016 approached, most parties had all of the selections completed and there were just a few last minute additions in early 2016.

Four parties ran a candidate in each constituency: Fine Gael, Fianna Fáil, Sinn Féin and the Green Party. Perhaps reflecting the smaller Dáil and also the volatile opinion polls, Fine Gael, Fianna Fáil, Labour and the Greens all ran fewer candidates than they did in 2011. Growing support was a factor in the increased number of candidates fielded by both Sinn Féin and the AAA–PBP alliance. The group listed as 'Others' in Table 3.1 includes non-aligned candidates, hereafter known as Independents; candidates who contested as part of the Independent Alliance, a group of Independents who collaborated on strategy and (in the broadest of terms) policy but did not formally establish as a political party; Independents 4 Change, a group of left-wing Independents who contested under the umbrella of the party name but otherwise operated as individual candidates; and candidates from several micro parties including Direct Democracy Ireland, Fís Nua and the Catholic Democrats (the National Party). The Other category included 235 candidates, the same number as contested the election in 2011.

Fine Gael

Fine Gael was the largest party in the Dáil and also fielded the most candidates. It established a national strategy committee (NSC) which was chaired by cabinet minister Frances Fitzgerald and involved several other senior ministers. Candidate strategy was given over to a subcommittee of the NSC, which was chaired by Brian Hayes MEP, who was appointed director of elections. The subcommittee included members of the executive council, members of the parliamentary party and staff from the party. Having lost both of the architects of its 2011 successful strategy, Phil Hogan and Frank Flannery, there was some interest in whom the party would choose to craft its 2016 plan.[4]

Once the review of the party's 2014 local elections performance had been completed, the party initiated its general election planning. Formally candidate selection decisions are made by the executive council on the basis of proposals from the party leader. In practice, the party leader receives analysis and guidance from the candidate subcommittee which contributes to the recommendations that he makes to the executive council. In 2016, the director of elections and party staff were the decisive actors in the overall process. Enda Kenny had been party leader since 2002 and at the elections in 2007 and 2011, Phil Hogan and Frank Flannery oversaw the design and detail of the candidate strategies with Kenny tending not to intervene overmuch in the process. This non-interventionist approach was replicated by the party leader for 2016 but it was Brian Hayes and party staff who assumed the positions of power brokers. Recommendations on candidate decisions from the party leader to the executive council are often discussed at length by the council and their views shape overall policy but in 2016 the substantive power to shape outcomes lay with Hayes and party staff.

Two issues were to the forefront of candidate strategy in 2016: incumbency and gender. Arising from a particularly successful election in 2011, the party had to devise a strategy that accommodated a higher than usual level of incumbency. Retirements, two resignations[5] and the emergence of Renua as a splinter party from Fine Gael meant it was entering the election with 61 TDs seeking re-election. While formally the party was targeting 70 seats at an early stage in its preparations, analysts suggested that 55–60 seats would be the more likely outcome. These projections were made on the basis of the party receiving at least 30 per cent of the votes cast and taking account of the smaller Dáil of 158 seats. In this scenario, which turned out to have been overly optimistic, the party was facing a loss of 7–10 TDs from the outset.

The first step for the candidate subcommittee was to prepare an analysis of the political landscape that took account of the boundary changes and the reduction in Dáil seats. Towards the end of 2014, each constituency was asked to establish a strategy committee. The committees were tasked with conducting a full analysis of the local environment. They were required to consider how the gender quota would be implemented and to identify potential female candidates. Using the well-established management tool Strengths, Weaknesses, Opportunities and Threats (SWOT), analyses were conducted and the committees had access to local and national opinion polls conducted by party HQ. The committees were given a deadline of

February 2015 to deliver their reports to the executive council and the reports were shared with the candidate subcommittee. It turned out that the contents of many of the reports were also inadvertently shared with the media, and some unflattering evaluations of candidates, plus the accusation that the Taoiseach had not delivered sufficiently for his Mayo constituency, caused considerable embarrassment.

Incumbents must go through candidate conventions along with all other interested candidates but, as with other aspects of the electoral process, there is a significant incumbency advantage. Incumbents were predominantly male, which presented a specific challenge in light of the gender quota. Expecting a lower vote share than in 2011 and with male incumbents in many constituencies, the candidate strategy subcommittee had limited room for manoeuvre. There was an overwhelming need that new candidates, whether coming through conventions or being added centrally to the party ticket, be female. This scenario had implications for ambitious new male candidates and had to be managed especially carefully in the case of sitting male Fine Gael senators who faced greatly reduced opportunities to seek election to the Dáil. The combination of information on incumbency, gender and national and local polling research allowed the candidate committee to arrive at a preliminary plan on the overall number of candidates and gender targets.

Selection conventions began in March 2015 and all 40 constituencies were completed by October. A deliberate strategy was taken to ensure that contentious selection conventions were left close to the end of the cycle to allow the party to adapt its strategy to circumstances and to ensure that overall strategy was not derailed at any early stage. The final convention took place in the party leader's constituency of Mayo on 19 October 2015 and a further ten candidates were added after that date with the final announcements made on 15 January 2016. In total the party added 15 candidates, 6 men and 9 women. Gender was the predominant factor underpinning the female additions while geography (Longford–Westmeath) and constituency revisions (Donegal) were factors for the male additions.

Candidate selection procedures produce winners and losers and complaint and controversy follow the process at most elections. Despite Fine Gael's strategy of leaving the most difficult cases till last, the party got off to a rocky start when cabinet minister Richard Bruton failed to be selected in his Dublin Bay North constituency on 30 April 2015. The executive council had issued a directive to select two candidates, one of each gender. This resulted in the only female candidate, Stephanie Regan, securing automatic nomination. Naoise Ó Muirí, a local councillor, argued at the selection convention that delegates should select him rather than Bruton, because Bruton was certain to be added to the party ticket even if he was not selected at convention. Bruton lost out and as predicted was added to the party ticket the very next day. Most of the remaining conventions proceeded with just small local grumblings. In Cork North-Central, complaints continued for some weeks following the convention which saw just one candidate selected, incumbent TD Dara Murphy. Opinion polls were the subject of considerable dispute with differing permutations emerging on the electoral strength of Senator Colm Burke. In Galway East, a geographic directive was used to have the effect of ensuring incumbent Ciarán Cannon would be selected.

The most contentious convention was held in the Sligo–Leitrim constituency on 16 October 2015. The directive issued required that the party select a candidate from Sligo and a candidate from Leitrim; an immediate consequence of which was the de-selection of an incumbent TD given that the party had two Sligo-based TDs. Tony McLoughlin TD and former Leitrim TD Gerry Reynolds were selected at convention, meaning that John Perry, a TD and former junior minister, lost out, leading to a controversy that brewed for a number of months. After his efforts at lobbying the party leader and the executive council to add him to the ticket had failed, he mounted a legal challenge in the High Court. The case was settled by the parties in December when Fine Gael agreed to add Perry to the party ticket. The reasons why Fine Gael chose to settle the case were never fully disclosed but speculation in the media was that the party was concerned that it might lose, with the potential that decisions made in other constituencies could be unravelled just weeks before the election.

The Perry decision marked a climbdown by Fine Gael but, this decision aside, the party elite, through the candidate committee and the executive council, managed the candidate selection process very carefully, ceding little power. Local constituencies played an important role in shaping policy through their strategy reports but decisions were taken at the centre and strategy was implemented through detailed instructions on the numbers of candidates to be selected, from where and of which gender. Only after these framing rules had been put in place did local members begin to influence decisions.

Ensuring the party met the gender quota required careful management and it was a priority all the way through the process with most of the candidates added at the end of the process being female. Despite early fears that male incumbents would lose out as a direct result of the gender quota, all incumbent male TDs who sought a nomination eventually received one; relatively painlessly in the case of Bruton and through eventual legal challenge in the case of Perry. Given that it was clear from the outset that the party was managing an inevitable contraction in votes and seats, there was a view that, the Perry dispute aside, the process worked reasonably well.

Fianna Fáil

In the aftermath of the party's electoral meltdown in 2011, a process of renewal and reform was initiated. Changes to candidate selection rules and the regulations governing the election of the party leader formed part of a suite of measures agreed at the 2012 ard-fheis (annual conference). The system of OMOV was introduced for all candidate selections, replacing a delegate voting system under which each local branch was entitled to three votes at selection conventions. Discontent with the delegate system had been brewing for years and the decision to move to OMOV was informed by a general belief that it would help revitalise the branch network of the party which was reputed to have been in substantial decline even before the 2011 electoral collapse. It was anticipated that giving members a greater role in key decisions would be an attractive proposition. Party HQ believes that this was the case in practice and can point to very high turnouts at candidate selection conventions throughout 2015 even in cases where conventions were uncontested, although some strategists suggest that the use of restrictive selection directives may have left some members questioning the extent of the democratisation that had been promised under OMOV. Nevertheless, the adjustment to wider democratisation of selection processes was reasonably smooth but in common with Fine Gael, it was clear that the party elite retained a decisive influence in the process and detailed directives were used to frame decisions that were taken at local level. To some extent, the gender quota requirements strengthened the party elites' role as there was widespread, if grudging, agreement that the targets had to be met. One Fianna Fail strategist described the situation quite bluntly saying that 'party HQ always interfered in candidate selection but the gender quota gave them a legislative basis for doing it'.

The national constituencies committee (NCC) had been the main body overseeing candidate selection for decades and the party agreed a new protocol for decisions on candidate selections in 2013. Candidates were to be selected at constituency-level conventions which would be operated on the basis of guidelines issued by the NCC. The NCC retained the power to add and de-select candidates. A new NCC was established for the 2016 election. It was chaired by Michael Moynihan and included members of the Ard Comhairle, the governing body of the party, and senior party personnel. Moynihan, a TD for Cork North-West, is a close ally of party leader Micheál Martin. Martin was known to favour improving the gender profile of the party and supported the changes to party rules on candidate selection. Publicly, and behind the scenes, he supported targets set by the NCC but did not intervene directly in its work.

Fianna Fáil strategy was devised with reference to the party's improving position in the national polls, a much improved position in the local elections, and research prepared by the party headquarters, including national and local opinion polls. With just 18 incumbent TDs seeking re-election, the NCC had a great deal of scope to influence the shape of the party ticket. Electability and gender were priorities for the party. The party had specific criteria in relation to electability: it wanted its candidates to be in the frame on the first count and it assessed this to mean achieving 60 per cent of the quota (cf p. 127 below). It is difficult to determine what percentage of the vote a candidate will receive months before the election but having specific criteria allowed the party to communicate precise goals to its local organisation.

The party established the Markievicz Commission in 2014 and tasked it with developing a gender roadmap for the party. Its recommendations were influential in shaping candidate selection decisions. The NCC issued six gender-specific directives to constituencies and nine of the candidates added to the party ticket were women. As the party was coming from a particularly low base of female representatives (going into the 2016 election it had no female TDs and only one female senator), meeting the gender quota was a challenge and one that the party admitted had to be carefully managed to the very end of the process. There were occasional controversies on the way, the most significant one being a High Court challenge to the gender quota legislation by Brian Mohan, an aspiring candidate who was not selected at convention (see p. 189 below).

Apart from gender, the NCC also paid attention to longer-term planning with geographical balance and preparing a pipeline of candidates for future elections influencing the decisions made. Three candidates were run in seven constituencies, two candidates in seventeen constituencies and one candidate in sixteen constituencies. The party employed a one-candidate strategy in much of Dublin, where it had no TD going into the 2016 election.

The one-candidate decisions produced some of the controversies over the selection process with the Mohan court challenge arising from a directive that required the convention in Dublin Central to select one female candidate. This meant that Mary Fitzpatrick, as the only female aspiring candidate, was guaranteed selection. In Dublin West, David McGuinness, who had been a prominent by-election candidate for Fianna Fáil, was not successful at the selection convention and decided to contest the election as an independent, alleging that his working-class background had been used against him during the selection campaign. The party picked Jack Chambers instead, and he won a seat (see his account in Chapter 5). Questions were raised after the election about the decision to run just one candidate in a number of constituencies—Cork North-Central, Laois, Limerick City and Limerick County—with high-profile incumbents.

There was quite a bit of low key complaining about the gender issue in local media. Aoife Byrne, who contested the election in Wexford, faced criticism in the local papers from several male contenders who missed out on selection and attributed this to the gender quota legislation. Lorraine Clifford Lee was added to the Fianna Fáil ticket in Dublin Fingal by Fianna Fáil and was also subject to criticism from local party councillors who complained that she had been parachuted onto the ticket over them.

Perhaps the most high-profile convention for Fianna Fáil was in Dún Laoghaire, where former minister Mary Hanafin lost out at convention to Cormac Devlin. The build-up to the convention could be traced back to the run-up to the May 2014 local elections, when Hanafin and her Fianna Fáil running mate Kate Feeney both took seats in what was known as the Battle of Blackrock. The date of the general election convention was brought forward and party members who had been recruited by Kate Feeney were deemed ineligible to vote as they had not been members for the required 12 months. Both women lost out at the Dún Laoghaire selection convention in 2015 but Hanafin was subsequently added to the ticket amidst much local complaint.

Managing the gender profile of the candidates selected was the biggest challenge for Fianna Fáil and produced its main controversies. The NCC added sixteen candidates to the party ticket; nine of these were women and seven were men. Meeting the gender quota was a significant factor in the decisions but additions were also influenced by geography, especially in the case of constituencies where there had been substantial boundary revisions. With few incumbents, the party was able to devise a candidate strategy that met the immediate needs of the 2016 election but was influenced by party needs in the coming election cycles. Fianna Fail struggled to adapt to its collapsing support levels in 2011 and the party elite's candidate selection interventions had proved ineffective. The year 2016 marked a sea change and candidate selection was carefully guided by the NCC. Since it went on to exceed expectations in terms of seats, the party was satisfied with its overall approach.

Sinn Féin

Sinn Féin ran 50 candidates in 2016. Decisions on the numbers of candidates and election strategy are taken by the governing council of the party, the Ard Comhairle. The party has an election department which manages the process in individual constituencies, issuing convention notices and interviewing candidates. The party operates OMOV for selection decisions and the Ard Comhairle ratifies the candidates selected, as well as having the power to remove candidates. There were two phases to the candidate strategy for the 2016 election. Selection conventions were held in constituencies up to the late spring of 2015 but decisions on adding extra candidates were delayed until late in 2015 as the party developed a clearer picture of its standing in the polls and constituency research by the party was prepared. Internal polling was carried out in constituencies prior to and after selection conventions. In each case where a candidate was being added to the ticket, a second selection convention was held.

Over the years, the party had experienced few controversies and its selection processes are managed very carefully from the centre. The year 2016 marked something of a break for the party as a number of selection decisions produced disagreement and dispute. To some extent, this is a normal feature of party expansion but Sinn Féin is an unusual movement and it was quite uncomfortable at times dealing with the problems that emerged.

Controversy bedevilled the party in Cork East. Allegations of financial irregularities by local branch members and complaints by the incumbent TD Sandra McLellan that she was being undermined locally and bullied led to the party establishing an investigation led by Jonathan O'Brien TD. A number of members left the organisation, including Cllr Kieran McCarthy, who went on to contest the election as an Independent. Ultimately, Pat Buckley secured the party nomination at convention with

McLellan having announced her intention not to contest the party convention some weeks earlier.

The gender profile of the party is reasonable but the party set itself a goal of running 40 per cent women candidates and it developed a 'gender intervention process' to achieve this goal. Some constituencies were directed to select one female candidate only and in most instances where two candidates were being selected, a balanced gender directive was issued. The directives led to some differences of opinion at local level. Cathleen Carney Boud was selected in Dublin North-West, causing some local disagreement. It was also suggested in some media commentary that the selection of Louise O'Reilly in Dublin Fingal was influenced by gender. Ultimately, 36 per cent of the party's candidates were women putting it well ahead of the gender quota requirements but a little short of its own target.

The selection convention in Cork South-Central had to be run a second time after the first round resulted in a tie between the two candidates, Chris O'Leary and Donnchadh Ó Laoghaire. With more than 100 delegates voting on the second occasion, Ó Laoghaire came through and went on to take a seat for the party (see his account in Chapter 5).

Labour

Disastrous local election results combined with persistent poor opinion poll results (see Chapter 1) meant that the Labour Party was fully aware of the scale of the electoral challenge it faced. The organisational committee of the party is the main management and decision-making entity for candidate selection. The committee is a subgroup of the executive board and its members included executive board members, senior party figures and staff from party headquarters. It set about developing its candidate strategy from late 2014. It was clear from very early in the process that managing decline would be the predominant concern. As with Fine Gael, assessing the likely number of incumbent TDs who would be seeking election was the first step. Retirements, including those of Ruairí Quinn, Pat Rabbitte, Éamon Gilmore, Seán Kenny and Robert Dowds, meant that there were a few vacancies but the party still had 26 incumbent TDs and 5 senators contesting the election. In an unusual streak of luck for the party, some of the retirements occurred in constituencies where it held two seats from 2011.[6] This simplified the selection process somewhat in that it did not face selection conventions where there were two incumbent TDs.

Labour fielded just 36 candidates. The number is notable for two reasons. First, it is one less than the number of TDs the party had elected in 2011 and second, it meant the party did not contest six constituencies, a disappointing, although entirely realistic, position for a party that had just completed a five-year term in government. The party fielded two candidates in only two constituencies, Dublin South-West and Louth. In the former, there was no incumbent and the party ran two councillors with a geographic spread, while in Louth there was an incumbent TD and a senator, both of whom sought selection. Both Louth candidates had also contested the 2011 election and there was a good geographical balance between the two although relations between the two candidates were strained at times.

The organisational committee of the party decides on overall strategy and the process of candidate selection is implemented from party headquarters from where the general secretary issues a notice of convention. The numbers of candidates to be selected and any geographic or gender criteria are set down by the organisational committee. The party constitution sets out the standing orders that govern the process. OMOV has been in practice for many years in Labour. Each constituency establishes a candidate selection panel whose function is to interview potential new candidates. New candidates must be recommended to the selection convention by the candidate selection panel. Oireachtas members are not required to go through the panel process. The combination of high levels of incumbency and poor opinion poll figures contributed to a large number of the party selection conventions being uncontested. Dún Laoghaire was one of the few constituencies where a convention was contested and Cllr Carrie Smyth fought off competition from three other aspirants.

Green Party

Having lost all of its seats in the Dáil and all of its funding under the Electoral Acts in 2011 by falling just short of the two per cent threshold, the Green Party faced a substantial organisational challenge as it approached the 2016 election. The party retained one full-time staff member who contributed to the administration of the candidate selection process. Overall electoral strategy is agreed by the Election Task Force (ETF), which oversees the candidate selection process but tends not to be overly prescriptive. The ETF has wide-ranging powers including the option of adding and de-selecting candidates. Among the members of the ETF are the party leader, deputy leader, party chairman and the director of elections.

There were two core objectives to the party strategy; to provide voters with the opportunity to vote Green and to meet the two per cent threshold for securing funding. Despite running a candidate in every constituency, expectations about winning seats were modest, with leader Eamon Ryan seen as the prime contender. Selection conventions were organised locally with a requirement that the chairperson come from outside the constituency. Postal voting was provided as an option. In cases where there was no local organisation, candidates were ratified by the ETF. The ETF maintained a watchful eye on the overall gender profile of the candidates selected but the party comfortably met the quota requirements.

NEW PARTIES, GROUPS AND ALLIANCES

For many of the new parties and groups that were established in the years leading up to the election, the rules regarding candidate selection were somewhat fluid. Most of them lacked national organisational structures and established memberships. As a result, interview by party elites was a common approach adopted.

Renua Ireland

Renua Ireland was launched in March 2015 and as a new party faced a considerable organisational challenge. While it had a number of incumbent TDs and a senator, it did not have a national branch network and it issued a call for candidates through the media and its political networks. Initially, the party hoped to run a candidate in every constituency but ultimately it ran just 26 candidates.

Potential candidates who came forward went through an interview process that involved three officers from the national board of the party. This group included all of the party TDs and senators as well as the party chairman. The party estimates that it interviewed around three to six candidates in each constituency, although media commentary suggests that in the early stages of its selection process, it struggled to attract candidates and application deadlines had to be extended. In common with other parties, policy compatibility was a clear priority for the party in making decisions and this was followed by electability. But the party struggled with the electability criterion and attracting high-profile candidates. Party chairman Eddie Hobbs, a well-known figure due to his media profile, declared finally in September 2015 that he would not be

contesting the election. Throughout 2015, there was regular speculation that the party was approaching councillors to encourage them to
join the party ticket but just three councillors joined the ranks of Renua
and 65 per cent of the party's candidates were new candidates with no
previous political experience. The party had a female leader in Lucinda
Creighton and attracted a reasonable cohort of female candidates from
an early stage. Towards the end of the process, gender became a more
significant criterion but the party did not experience any notable difficulties in meeting the target.

Renua faced problems throughout its selection process as candidates
stepped away from it before the election was called. Desmond Hayes in
Limerick City opted to stand as an Independent when he was included
on the tax defaulters' list by the Revenue Commissioners. Jack and Jill
Foundation founder Jonathan Irwin, who had been due to contest in
Kildare South, withdrew for health reasons, and somewhat more contro-
versially, Mary Smyth left the party to run as an Independent following her
declaration that the Vatican was 'the Anti-Christ'. In all, five candidates
withdrew. While the party leadership characterised some of the candidate
selection difficulties as teething problems and to be expected in a party
in its political infancy, Renua's experience points to the challenges facing
any new party entering the political arena. Renua struggled to identify
its niche in the political marketplace. Given its origins (see pp. 16 and 18
above), it was constantly required to address questions about abortion in
debates, and with no national branch network found it difficult to attract
high calibre, electable candidates.

Social Democrats

The Social Democrats operate a horizontal leadership structure. The three
TDs who founded the party and who were seen as joint leaders oversaw
the candidate selection process and all other aspects of election strategy.
The party approached a number of candidates and also used the media to
encourage interested individuals to contact the party leadership. From the
outset, the leaders emphasised that the quality of the candidates was their
essential priority. Indeed, they stressed that policy compatibility was the
primary criterion that guided the selection process. Practical elements such
as the costs of contesting an election and previous electoral experience also
featured in the decision making. Decisions were made on a consensus basis
by the three joint leaders.

Ensuring the party complied with the gender quota legislation was a variable in the overall strategy but the party easily achieved this, ending up with the highest percentage of female candidates of the main parties at 43 per cent. There was some speculation that the party ran a small number of paper candidates who put little effort into their campaigns. The party rejects this, but party strategists pointed to financial struggles, a problem shared with other small parties, as it sought to establish a party network and structure in the absence of state funding. The costs of the campaign fell heavily on the individual candidates. Just one candidate withdrew from the election: Jerry Warnock, a Longford-based councillor.

The Social Democrats formed in July 2015 and thus had less than a year to prepare for the election. In contrast to Renua, the party established itself clearly on the centre left and supportive of the Nordic model—although it must be said the party emphasised the higher public spending aspects of the Nordic model far more than the higher taxation elements and, reflecting the realpolitik of the politicisation of water charges, the Social Democrats also opposed these. However, like Renua, the Social Democrats struggled to attract high-profile candidates from within and without the political environment. Early speculation that Senators Katherine Zappone and Averil Power might join came to nothing. The three joint leaders were re-elected but no other candidate came through. While the candidate selection process operated relatively smoothly, the overall strategy was not particularly successful.

AAA–PBP Alliance

AAA–PBP was registered as a political party but its national organisational structure had been developed through two previously distinct parties, the Socialist Party and PBP, which in 2011 had stood jointly as the United Left Alliance (ULA). To a great extent, candidate selection was operated through the original party networks. There was a co-ordinating committee drawn from the two parties which liaised on overarching issues (such as gender) but candidate strategies were developed and deployed within the original party structures. Strategists from both AAA and PBP spoke of their individual selection processes as being relatively flexible and informal. Both groups had seen their numbers grow over the period from 2014 and point to the water charges protests as having had a particularly strong mobilisation impact.

Each party held meetings at constituency level to select candidates. An open call for candidates was issued in advance of the meetings. Both parties have a central register of members and all members present at conventions are entitled to vote. However, there were only a small number of contested conventions with many of the parties' councillors being selected by consensus. The candidates chosen included a mix of those who had long-standing associations with the parties and new candidates who had been mobilised by the recession and opposition to what the parties termed 'austerity politics'.

The two-party alliance fielded a total of 31 candidates; it had a one-candidate strategy in 21 constituencies and ran 2 candidates in 5 constituencies. The decision to add a second candidate in Dublin South-West was taken after the Jobstown protest;[7] a second convention was held, and following a contest, Sandra Fay of the AAA was added to the ticket. In Wicklow there were two PBP candidates, while in the other three cases, two candidates emerged as a product of the separate organisational structures. Some efforts to co-ordinate candidate strategy were attempted on the ground but with two essentially separate parties in operation, ultimately both sides proceeded with their own plans. Candidates did attest to high levels of cooperation where two candidates were contesting, with reciprocal calls for transfers issued along with more practical assistance.

Independents 4 Change

Although Independents 4 Change was formally registered as a political party, it essentially operated as a decentralised group of independents. The party was established by Mick Wallace TD and it ran candidates in local electoral areas in Wexford in 2014. Independent TDs Mick Wallace, Joan Collins, Clare Daly (both elected in 2011 for the ULA) and Tommy Broughan (elected in 2011 for Labour) opted to contest the election under the Independents 4 Change banner. Clare Daly was joined on the ballot by Barry Martin, a councillor in her constituency with whom she had a long working relationship. However, the party did not engage in a centralised strategy to select further candidates.

Independent Alliance

The Independent Alliance did not register as a political party. The group was established by five Independent TDs; Michael Fitzmaurice, Tom

Fleming, John Halligan, Finian McGrath and Shane Ross[8] and Senators
Gerard Craughwell and Feargal Quinn. In a group charter, it outlined ten
principles and priorities but it did not devise a constitution or rule book.

The alliance issued a call for candidates and interviews were held to
make selections. The interview panels consisted of the founding TDs
and most attended all of the panels. Candidates were required to sign up
to the group charter and electability was the crucial issue for the group.
Interviews involved some discussion of the candidate's background and
the group reported that while there were robust discussions, decisions in
all cases were taken on a consensus basis. As the group was not registered
as a political party, it was not bound by the gender quota legislation but
nevertheless gender was a factor in the decision making. The group ran 21
candidates, with 24 per cent of those being female. For the most part, the
group operated a one-candidate strategy but for geographical reasons, it
had three candidates in Longford–Westmeath and two in Louth, although
it admitted that this was not a satisfactory approach for future contests.
On balance, the Independent Alliance reported that candidate selection
needed a lot of time but the process was smooth.

CANDIDATE PROFILES: STILL WAITING FOR THE REVOLUTION

All of the parties and alliances were concerned with the electability of their
candidates but what that means in practice is understudied. A study of
selectors in the British Labour Party from the early 1980s confirmed that
party members are also primarily motivated by getting their candidates
elected.[9] Voter preferences for the background characteristics of candidates have received some attention with research from the UK suggesting that education levels and geographic proximity between voters and
the candidate's place of residence do matter.[10] Much less is known about
the specific preferences of party selectors. Throughout 2015, as selection
conventions were taking place and Independent candidates were declaring
their intentions to contest elections, the gender quota legislation led to a
low-key but persistent debate about whether voters had adequate choice
from both the party and non-party ranks. The provision of choice for voters was an important part of the pro-gender quota argument but it also
led to discussions about the need to provide a more diverse social class
and ethnic mix of candidates at elections. In this section, the political and
professional profiles of the candidates are examined.

Table 3.2   Occupational backgrounds of candidates, 2016

Occupation	FG	FF	SF	GP	Lab	AAA–PBP	RI	SD	Oth	Total (%)	Total (N)
Farmer	13	11	2	0	3	0	8	0	5	6	33
Commerce	24	21	10	18	8	0	31	29	22	19	105
Higher professional	16	21	2	13	22	3	31	7	10	13	72
Lower professional	20	20	14	30	36	26	15	43	14	20	109
Non-manual employee	14	32	10	22	23	8	14	17	18	99	
Manual employee	1	3	10	0	3	13	0	0	11	6	34
Other	7	10	28	30	6	35	8	7	21	17	95
Unknown	1	0	2	0	0	0	0	0	1	1	4
Total (%)	100	100	100	100	100	100	100	100	100	100	
N	88	71	50	40	36	31	26	14	195		551

Note: Figures within each party are expressed in percentages and the total *N* for candidates and occupations are included and listed in italics in the end column and the end row

The occupational profiles of candidates are set out in Table 3.2, which uses the classification system employed in the *How Ireland Voted* book series since 1987. Occupations are subdivided into seven categories. Farmers are included first. Commerce includes business people, the self-employed, financial consultants and auctioneers. Higher professional includes barristers and doctors while lower professional is mainly composed of teachers, nurses and social workers. Non-manual includes secretaries, sales persons, public sector employees and trade union officials while manual employee covers occupations such as tradespersons and manufacturing workers. The 'other' category is the most varied and includes students, the unemployed, retired persons, full-time activists and occupations as varying as carers, film and documentary makers and in 2016 even a professional surfer. Candidates are classified according to their occupation prior to entering full-time politics.

To a large extent, the occupation profiles across the different parties and groups accord with long-established expectations. But the data in Table 3.2 also reveal a degree of change compared with previous elections, a reflection of the more varied parties and groups contesting the election. The percentage of famers contesting elections continues to decline but the highest concentration of farmers is still to be found in

Fianna Fáil and Fine Gael. These parties also have a large proportion of candidates coming from business backgrounds although the party with the highest overall proportion of candidates with a business background is Renua, with almost a third of its candidates in this category. Again this aligns with expectations as the party professes a strong pro-business and low taxation policy platform.

The professions have long contributed large numbers of candidates. The Labour Party has the overall highest proportion of candidates from the professions with 58 per cent in this category but all of the parties attract candidates with professional backgrounds, although the figure is lowest for the more left-leaning parties of Sinn Féin and AAA–PBP. Left-wing parties and groups attract a higher number of candidates from manual background: ten per cent or more for Sinn Féin, AAA–PBP and those in the Other category. Overall, though, the category manual employee produces a low number of candidates but in an important indicator of change in Irish politics, the percentage of manual employees equals that of farmers in 2016.

The number of non-manual employees contesting the election has jumped sharply from 7 per cent in 2011 to 18 per cent in 2016. The category non-manual employee includes a number of trade unionists and again as might be expected these are largely to be found in left-wing parties. The arts were well represented with quite a few candidates listing their occupations as artists, film and documentary makers and even a tattoo artist. There is evidence from recent UK elections that a growing number of candidates have direct professional experience working in parliament or for political parties. This trend is also evident in Ireland and there was a notable increase in the number of parliamentary assistants who contested the election. At least seven candidates had worked in the Oireachtas as parliamentary assistants while a further two had worked in supporting roles for MEPs in the European Parliament, with one former ministerial adviser as well.

Political pathways into national elections are of interest as they give insights into the experience of the candidates and lead to discussions about incumbency and the duration of political careers. A total of 145 outgoing TDs and 20 senators sought re-election. Confirming the importance of local government experience as a pipeline into national politics, the data reveal that 155 councillors contested the election. All parties selected councillors, with Fianna Fáil and Sinn Féin having the highest percentages (see Table 3.3). 'Others' provided the single biggest number of councillors seeking election and they accounted for 26 per cent of the candidates contesting in this diverse group. At 117, the number of new candidates was lower than in 2011. Delving into the detail of this group reveals that a small but significant proportion had been politicised in the anti-water charges protests and this movement provided their pathway into politics. The smaller parties did bring some new candidates into the political arena and this is especially the case for Renua and AAA–PBP.

Table 3.3 gives data on candidates under their current political affiliations, but examination of the political backgrounds of candidates also reveals some fluidity in party membership. Party switching had always been considered fairly rare in Irish politics. The presence of new parties, some of whom had splintered from other parties, means that there is now a significant group of candidates who have previously contested elections under a different affiliation. Broadly, there are three patterns in evidence. Candidates have moved from one party to another; this group includes many Renua and Social Democrat candidates. Formerly Independent candidates have joined parties, and again Renua and the Social Democrats provide several examples. The last group remains the largest, the so-called 'gene pool': these are candidates who were at one time party candidates and who now contest the election as Independents. This latter phenomenon had been largely confined to the two big parties and the fragmented

Table 3.3   Political experience of candidates, 2016

Party	TD	Senator	Cllr	Previous electoral experience	New candidate	Total
Fine Gael	69	3	17	5	6	100
Fianna Fáil	25	6	53	6	10	100
Sinn Féin	24	6	56	4	10	100
Green Party	0	0	17	50	33	100
Labour	72	14	11	3	0	100
AAA–PBP	10	0	26	26	38	100
Renua	11	4	12	8	65	100
Social Democrats	21	7	14	29	29	100
Other	10	1	26	35	28	
Total	*145*	*20*	*155*	*114*	*117*	*551*

Note: Political experience figures are expressed as percentages within each party while the total figure for each category is included in the final row of the table and listed in italics. Previous electoral experience refers to candidates who were not public representatives when selected but had previously contested elections at either local, Seanad, Dáil or European level.
A new candidate is defined as a person with no previous experience as a candidate in an election.

Table 3.4   Gender and family links of candidates, 2016

Party	Total	Women	%	Family link	%
Fine Gael	88	27	30.7	26	29.5
Fianna Fáil	71	22	31.0	25	35.2
Sinn Féin	50	18	36.0	7	14.0
Green Party	40	14	35.0	2	5.0
Labour	36	13	36.1	11	30.6
AAA–PBP	31	13	41.9	1	3.2
Renua	26	8	30.8	4	15.4
Social Democrats	14	6	42.9	0	0
Other	195	41	21.0	14	7.2
Total	551	162	29.4	90	16.3

Note: Family link in politics is defined as where a family relation has held, or holds, office at either local or national level

hard left until recent elections but it is now in evidence across the spectrum, with a growing list of defections from Labour and Sinn Féin.

Turning to the personal characteristics of the candidates, Table 3.4 outlines the gender profile and family political background of the candidates. Family background includes parent, aunt, uncle, brother or sister and added to this classification group for 2016 is spouse. A more detailed evaluation of the gender dynamics of candidate selection is provided in Chapter 8 so all that need be noted here is that 2016 marked a significant transformation in the gender profile of candidates. All of the main parties reached the 30 per cent quota, and the legislation clearly had a pull effect on the Other group, as there was a notable increase from 9 per cent in 2011 to 21 per cent.

The political dynasty shows no sign of abating from politics in Ireland. The number of candidates with a family member in politics increased in 2016. Prior to the abolition of the dual mandate (under which a TD or senator could simultaneously hold a council position) in 2004, it was unusual to have family members serving in politics at the same time but quite a few of the candidates in the 2016 election have family members serving at various levels of politics and indeed contesting the same election. Family links are particularly strong in Fine Gael and Fianna Fáil. Many of these connections are very well known and include Fine Gael party leader and Taoiseach Enda Kenny, whose father was a TD before him and whose brother is a councillor in Mayo, while in Fianna Fáil those with prominent connections include Éamon Ó Cuív (grandson of a former Taoiseach) and Seán Haughey (son of a former Taoiseach and grandson of another former Taoiseach).

The outcome of the election brought considerable discussion of the nature of the differences between Fine Gael and Fianna Fáil, with much emphasis on their historical origins and cultural evolution. The details presented here on the professional and political backgrounds of their candidates suggest that the two parties have more in common with each other than with any of the other parties in the system. They are most likely to field candidates with a farming background, they draw heavily from commercial and professional backgrounds, and manual employees are under-represented in both. Meeting the gender quota required careful management in both parties and was achieved with some reluctance by grass-roots members. Lastly, many candidates from both parties have family connections in politics, in part reflecting the fact that these are old political parties, but it is a common feature across the two.

CONCLUSION

2011–16 provided a turbulent Dáil term. The early years of crisis management gave way to political disaffection and eventually widespread street protests against water charges. New parties and alliances emerged and voters were presented with new and varied political choices resulting in a diverse and dramatically different new Dáil.

Candidate selection processes are about routes into the political system. The year 2016 brought new emphasis on gender as the financial penalties associated with the gender quota loomed large over the parties. In many ways, the requirement for parties to meet specific gender targets facilitated the party centre exerting even more control over selection processes than at previous elections. Tensions between the centre and local parts of the organisation are ubiquitous when it comes to candidate selection but in 2016 the centre usually won out as grass-roots members understood fully that failure to reach the gender quota would bring a severe financial penalty. The use of prescriptive convention directives limited the scope of the decisions to be made by party selectorates. High turnouts were reported by many parties at conventions but if the decision-making contribution of members remains restricted, this may have an impact on their enthusiasm and engagement in the longer term.

Fine Gael and Labour were forced to manage large numbers of incumbent TDs chasing a diminishing vote and inevitable losses. In contrast, Fianna Fáil, Sinn Féin and the Green Party entered the election preparing for growth. The new parties and movements organised their candidate processes in quite similar ways and indicate intent to move towards more democratic procedures as they develop local structures. As ever, the 'Other' category brought the greatest variety to the political environment in terms of occupation and political background.

There are a number of notable points that must be made about the profiles of the candidates in 2016. Candidates from non-manual and manual employee backgrounds are becoming more prevalent. The professions still dominate but not as acutely as in the past. Overall, the percentage of candidates from farming and commercial backgrounds has declined. These trends are consistent with the change in overall candidate numbers from different parties. Fianna Fáil and Fine Gael, which are more likely to draw farmers, business people and professionals, ran fewer candidates in 2016 while Sinn Féin and AAA–PBP, which select non-manual and manual employees more heavily, ran their largest numbers yet. Candidates are displaying greater levels of mobility in their political affiliations and the nature of family connections in politics is also changing. The pattern of parent–child inheritance is still present but there are many siblings and spouses now holding political office at the same time.

NOTES

1. A detailed examination of the democratisation of candidate selection processes is provided in Lars Bille, 'Democratising a democratic procedure: myth or reality, candidate selection in west European parties 1960–1990', *Party Politics*, 7: 3 (2001), pp. 363–380.
2. The complexities of this phenomenon are discussed in Maciej A. Gorecki and Michael Marsh, 'Not just "friends and neighbours": Canvassing, geographic proximity and voter choice', *European Journal of Political Research* 51: 5 (2012), pp. 563–582.
3. This point is developed in considerable detail in Michael Gallagher, 'Candidate selection in Ireland: the impact of the electoral system', *British Journal of Political Science* 10:4 (1980), pp. 489–503.
4. Phil Hogan was appointed to the European Commission in 2014 and Frank Flannery became estranged from the party following widespread publicity about some of the activities of Rehab, the company he had led for many years.
5. Seán Conlan resigned from the party and contested the election as an Independent while Brian Walsh resigned his seat in the Dáil and did not contest the election owing to ill health.

6. Pat Rabbitte, Ruairí Quinn and Seán Kenny are all examples of expected retirements. In the case of Robert Dowds, he expressed the view that the party could retain only one of its two seats in Dublin Mid-West, and his retirement had more of an involuntary aspect to it.

7. The Jobstown protest took place on 15 November 2014. An incident occurred during which Tánaiste Joan Burton was detained in her car, which was prevented from leaving an event for a number of hours. Paul Murphy TD of the AAA was involved in the incident, which was subsequently the subject of criminal prosecutions.

8. Tom Fleming TD was initially involved but subsequently decided against contesting the election.

9. John Bochel and David Denver, 'Candidate selection in the Labour Party: what the selectors seek', *British Journal of Political Science* 13: 1 (1983), pp. 45–69.

10. Rosie Campbell and Philip Cowley, 'What voters want: reactions to candidate characteristics in a survey experiment', *Political Studies* 62 (2014), pp. 745–765.

CHAPTER 4

Campaign Strategies: How the Campaign Was Won and Lost

Pat Leahy

The political landscape as Ireland approached its 2016 general election was almost unrecognisable from the stolid certainties that characterised much of the country's history. In recent decades even the rise of new actors such as the Progressive Democrats (PDs) and the Greens had not entirely disrupted the old two-and-a-half-party system; in some respects, they actually reinforced it. By 2016, however, all had changed utterly. The behemoth that was Fianna Fáil was a shadow of its former self. Labour had surged in 2011, but then fallen away and now the party faced a showdown with voters that some party members feared could destroy it as a viable political entity, such were the levels of public antipathy towards its candidates. Fine Gael had replaced Fianna Fáil as the largest party, but approached the election not confident in its new status, but wondering how it could best contain inevitable losses. It waited, increasingly impatiently, for an anticipated recovery in its fortunes to arrive. Momentum was with the

This chapter relies heavily on the author's own coverage of the campaign in *The Sunday Business Post*, and subsequent to the election in *The Irish Times*. Further sources include a series of background interviews with politicians and campaign staff in all parties. Where possible, sources have been cited.

P. Leahy (✉)
Irish Times, Dublin, Ireland

© The Author(s) 2016
M. Gallagher, M. Marsh (eds.), *How Ireland Voted 2016*,
DOI 10.1007/978-3-319-40889-7_4

insurgent forces: independents of all stripes, the radical left, Sinn Féin (SF) and a scattering of new parties and groups that came together in the year before the election. Never had Ireland's politics looked so fractured and uncertain.

So how did the parties approach the general election with this volatile and unfamiliar backdrop? What were the campaign strategies adopted by them and how did they seek to appeal to voters in a political marketplace that had changed beyond recognition?

FINE GAEL

Fine Gael approached the general election from an unfamiliar starting point: from government, not opposition; as the largest party, not the challenger; and as the favourite, not the underdog. Nonetheless, the general structure of its approach was consciously similar to the elections of 2007 and 2011. Although the party had suffered a heavy defeat in the local and European elections of 2014 (see p. 14 above), party chiefs were not unduly worried. These were, they concluded, the customary trials of the biggest party, governing during a time of austerity. It was to be expected. If the economy recovered and the political strategy was right, it was something from which they could recover. 'I wouldn't say we were spooked,' says a senior party figure. 'Spooked would be a bit strong. We anticipated a wallop and it was worse than we expected.' The local elections had a lower level of turnout, and voters were answering a different question to that asked at a general election, Fine Gael reasoned. Anecdotally, party insiders were hearing that a lot of their natural voters had stayed at home. They were pretty confident that those voters could be won back. So they drew on the lessons of the 2007 and 2011 general election campaigns, rather than obsessing in detail over the 2014 mid-terms.

Six months after the June wallop, in December 2014, senior officials and politicians met in the Shelbourne Hotel on St Stephen's Green in Dublin to begin the organisational preparations for the next general election. A national strategy committee was set up, chaired by Minister for Justice Frances Fitzgerald. It had four 'strands,' or sub-committees: organisational, chaired by deputy leader James Reilly; candidate selection, chaired by MEP Brian Hayes (see Chapter 3); communications, chaired by health minister Leo Varadkar; and the policy group, headed by agriculture minister Simon Coveney. Each was assigned teams of party staffers, people from the national organisation and backbenchers. Aside from the politicians, the most important figures were, as ever, the general secretary Tom Curran, long-term party adviser Mark Mortell, a senior public relations executive with Fleishman Hilliard, the Taoiseach's chief of staff Mark Kennelly, and his chief policy adviser Andrew McDowell. The goal was to have the campaign ready to go by the end of the following summer. The Taoiseach could make up his mind then when he wanted to have the election.

In order to craft an election message that they hoped would resonate with their target voters, Fine Gael strategists looked at masses of research findings and data. As the largest and best-resourced party this material was both broad and deep, including quantitative polls (both published and private), qualitative work through focus groups and constant feedback from the public and members. The findings of commissioned research were kept to a limited group. 'We researched it to death,' says one strategist.[1]

Strong themes were obvious from the beginning. The success in creating jobs—the 'jobs-led recovery'—was a core Fine Gael strength, they judged. In addition both their own polls and regular polling by Red C for *The Sunday Business Post* found that strong majorities of the public believed that the country was 'on the right track'—frequently a harbinger of electoral fortune for an incumbent government. Albeit that Fine Gael's own polling numbers were pretty anaemic, they believed that the underlying dynamic demonstrated strong potential for growth in the party's support if the then nascent economic recovery strengthened. Analysis from the party's US political consultants, Greenberg Quinlan Rosner Research, amplified this hope into an expectation. Backroom people, TDs, ministers, journalists: they all dropped the old Clintonian slogan—'It's the economy, stupid'—into practically every conversation.[2] It became an unshakeable dogma, and ultimately it prevented Fine Gael from properly analysing its own flaws.

As 2015 progressed the economic recovery, and consequent strengthening of the public finances, meant that that austerity ceased to be the central fact of Irish politics. In fact, the 2015 budget (delivered in October 2014) had been mildly expansionary, moving from a planned €2 billion in cuts and extra taxes to a giveaway of €1 billion. This was, in part, a fiscal gamble necessitated by the coalition's political weakness. At that point, the government could not have sustained another austerity budget. Fiscally, it paid off—the following year saw the economy take off like a rocket. Politically, its impact would turn out rather differently.

The rapidly changing fiscal and economic situation dominated Fine Gael's thinking during the crucial months of 2015 when it was deciding its campaign strategy and the central principles of its political marketing. As the recovery took hold, with its obvious benchmarks of job creation, falling unemployment, rising incomes and returning consumer confidence, the party was sure that the single most important issue in voters' minds would be protecting this recovery. The vehicle to convey its offering on this point would be the 'stability vs chaos' narrative, contrasting Fine Gael's successful management of the economy with, variously, the disastrous record of Fianna Fáil, the dangerously radical solutions offered by the far left and Sinn Féin, and the uncertainty of the independents.

'The proposition we offered was continuity,' says Mark Mortell,[3] perhaps the party's most important political and communications strategist. That continuity found its purest expression in the slogan 'Let's keep the recovery going.' It was all entirely coherent and strongly supported by all the research, Fine Gael strategists felt. After the toughest years in the economic and social history of the country, there was no way that people would put at risk the hard-won recovery by handing the country over to the 'people who wrecked it' or to 'the people who would wreck it'. Would they?

The Tory Example

There was another event that Fine Gael election strategists were watching closely in the first half of 2015. David Cameron's Conservative Party was seeking re-election after five years of coalition with the Liberal Democrats, five years that had seen brutal austerity policies followed by a strong economic recovery. Facing them were their old rivals in Labour, who had overseen a massive economic crash when in office, and a strongly anti-austerity and nationalist fringe which sensed it was on the brink of an historic breakthrough. The Tories campaigned against them on a platform of 'chaos vs stability'. The Fine Gael backroom staff didn't have to look very hard to see the parallels.

But Fine Gael did more than observe from afar. When Cameron returned with a shock majority, Fine Gael's interest in the Tory campaign turned into a desire to emulate its success. Senior Fine Gael staffers travelled to London to pore over the entrails of the Conservatives' victory and speak to the people who made it happen. They hired as consultants the people who had run a highly effective digital campaign for the Tories, Craig Elder and Tom Edmonds, who came to Dublin to give a two-day seminar to Fine Gael staffers. Taoiseach Enda Kenny also told his staff about advice that Cameron had passed on to him. They will come to you halfway through the campaign and say that you have to change the message, that it's not working, that you have to change tack, Cameron told Kenny. That's when you have to stick to your guns. Have faith. It will work. It will turn around.[4] Kenny took the advice to heart.

How influential was the Tory example? To what extent did Fine Gael attempt to mirror the successful Conservative campaign? Fine Gael nowadays plays down the Tory comparisons. In fairness, the party played them down at the time when they were reported. But given that Tory is a byword for evil among many Irish voters, there was a powerful incentive for Fine Gael to pooh-pooh the notion that it was following a Tory playbook, even if it was. It would have left it open to attack by its rivals—something that indeed happened repeatedly throughout the campaign, by Fianna Fáil, Sinn Féin and the radical left. But it is true that the people who designed and implemented the Fine Gael campaign at a leadership level were hugely encouraged by the success of the Tory campaign. It convinced them that the economy was the right message, and that ultimately, if they stuck to it, enough of their voters would come home.

Their enthusiasm even convinced many people in the Labour Party that the Tory victory meant that the Irish coalition could be returned if it stayed the course, kept its message strong and consistent, and stuck together. Privately some senior Labour people worried that the example of the Liberal Democrats, rather than the Tories, was the appropriate one. So it would prove to be.

The parallels between the campaigns of the Tories and Fine Gael were obvious. The narrative of chaos versus stability was a common one; requiring both parties to seek to instil fear in voters about the consequences of not returning them to government. For the Tories, it was the Scottish Nationalists; for Fine Gael, it was Sinn Féin and the independents. Both delighted in excoriating their main rivals—Fianna Fáil and the British Labour Party—for their record on managing the economy. ('All our data,' says one senior Fine Gael figure, 'showed us that people were not forgiving Fianna Fáil.'[5]) Both made the economy absolutely central to their message. The Tories' strategist Jim Messina (hired after working for Barack Obama) used to tell them that 'Any day not talking about the economy is a day wasted.' More than one Fine Gaeler took to saying the same thing. Fine Gael even used the exact phrase used by the Tories, 'Long Term Economic Plan.' Weighing it up after the event, it seems fair to say that the success of the Tory campaign had a profound influence on how Fine Gael prepared for, planned and executed its electoral campaign.

By the end of the summer, Fine Gael was more or less where it wanted to be. Candidate selection was not yet complete, but it could be completed pretty quickly if necessary (see Chapter 3). The main themes, strategies and messages were in place; the logistics underway. The campaign was largely in a box, ready to be taken out. The only thing that remained was for the Taoiseach to name the day. That became quite a saga.

Fianna Fáil

'Nobody is interested in anything you are saying.' It was a long time since anyone had said that to a Fianna Fáil ard-fheis, but when the British academic and student of the Conservative Party Tim Bale spoke to Fianna Fáil delegates at the party's gathering in the spring of 2012, they hung on his every word with a sort of horrified fascination.[6] It was just a year after the organisation's Golgotha, when the party lost more than 50 seats, reducing its parliamentary representation to a wispy shadow of its former might. Bale gave it to them straight, outlining the depths of the crisis into which the party had sunk, and the long road back that lay ahead of them. To the surprise of many observers, the assembled faithful gave him a standing ovation. 'He got us,' says the party's general secretary Seán Dorgan.[7]

Four years later, as the party prepared for a general election campaign that would mark its return to the front line of Irish politics, party chiefs traced the beginning of the recovery to that 2012 ard-fheis. Bale's advice wasn't the only thing that Fianna Fáil took away from that weekend, of course. The party introduced a one-member-one-vote system for candidate selection (see p. 56 above), and changed its rules to require a special ard-fheis to approve any future coalition deal. More importantly, the 3000 enthusiastic delegates—many of them young (though many of them old too; not many in the middle, from what the present author recalls)—provided audible and visible evidence that the party was not, after all, going to fade away.

The party had achieved a significant milestone in the local and European elections in 2014, regaining its position as the largest party of local government and pipping Fine Gael in its share of the vote (see p. 15). Party strategists knew they had a long way to go but it gave them something to work with. It also gave them a new field of candidates. And for the first time since the 1997 election, Fianna Fáil did not have the distraction of being in government while preparing for the election. Government has advantages for campaigners—but also disadvantages. For one thing, it's sometimes unclear who is in charge—Government Buildings, or party headquarters? The more Fianna Fáil looked at Fine Gael, the more it thought its rivals might be suffering from that problem. Not having its senior people concerned with running a government, Fianna Fáil was able to focus totally on the election.

Election preparations had formally begun at the start of 2015, and by the time of the party's ard-fheis in April of that year it had settled on the slogan 'An Ireland for all'—a signpost towards the party's increasing orientation towards a more social democratic stance, with a greater emphasis on investment in public services, especially health. This was less a product of the focus groups—the party simply didn't have the money any more for extensive research—but rather sprung from the incessant canvassing of its leader Micheál Martin. He would return to Dublin and meet his senior staff on Tuesday mornings, telling them that the public were talking about waiting lists and class sizes. Nobody was talking about tax cuts. It also chimed with Martin's own centre-left instincts.

'It all came down to core positioning and messaging,' says one of Fianna Fáil's senior strategists.[8] 'And the core positioning was decided in the summer of 2012—it was the fairness agenda.' The centre ground politically, with a social democratic viewpoint, was where Fianna Fáil decided it wanted to fight the election. 'People are basically social democratic and we thought that the fairness of the recovery would be a central issue,' the Fianna Fáil strategist says.

Where Fine Gael was focused on the macroeconomic figures, Fianna Fáil was focused on less-noticed polling results which showed that people believed that the recovery was unevenly felt, with many people believing that the government was accentuating inequality. A position targeting the 'unfairness' of the government's application of austerity measures, rather than austerity in itself, became the dominant theme in the large amount of policy documents and speeches put out in 2012–15. Its positioning in the election was not a last-minute decision but a long-term call. Fianna Fáil was a party of 20 TDs with few effective media performers and a willingness to air every internal argument in public, so the public could be forgiven for having missed this—but nonetheless, Martin's centre-left positioning of Fianna Fáil was the core theme of all of his major speeches in this period.

The Fianna Fáil team was buoyed by another trend it noticed. Though it had nothing like the resources that it used to be able to devote to private polling in the constituencies, it began sampling some key constituencies in 2014. What it found was that the Fine Gael vote was tumbling—the local elections were not an aberration, a once-off lashing out at the government after which things would revert to a more normal equilibrium. It saw the Fine Gael vote falling down towards 20 per cent, and lower in some of them. The patchy nature of the polling meant that Fianna Fáil strategists didn't have enough data to build a reliable national picture. But they knew something was going on.

As 2015 went on, the trend strengthened. Places such as Cork North-West, Cork South-West, Waterford, Meath West, Mayo, Kerry—the polls didn't necessarily show Fianna Fáil would pick up seats, but they did show that Fine Gael would lose them. By the summer of 2015, Fianna Fáil had a firm fix on lots of constituencies where seats were in play and it was in a position to take them. 'So strategically, we needed to frame the contest as Fianna Fáil vs Fine Gael,' says Seán Dorgan.[9] That would be the next phase.

Sinn Féin

As Sinn Féin prepared for the general election of 2016, the party's future seemed to throb with potential for growth in the South. The 2011 general election had been a breakthrough, bringing Gerry Adams into southern politics and more than tripling the party's Dáil representation. As austerity remade the political landscape in Ireland for the three years after 2011, Sinn Féin seemed poised to benefit politically more than anyone. Some opinion polls suggested that Sinn Féin could become the largest party in the next Dáil. Most polls regularly said that the party could at least overcome Fianna Fáil as the second largest.

Yet there were difficulties too. Stories from his past bedevilled the party leader, leading at one stage to his arrest and detention for questioning by the Police Service of Northern Ireland for possible involvement in the abduction and murder of Jean McConville in Belfast in 1972. A controversy over sexual abuse in the republican movement—policed by its own shadowy security corps—pitted the Adams version of the past against those of articulate and angry victims, one of whom, Máiría Cahill, was made a senator by the Labour Party in November 2015.

Sinn Féin also faced a significant challenge on its left by parties of the radical left. And as time went on, the economic trends of 2015 began to run against the party that had defined itself in the 31st Dáil by its opposition to austerity. Having muscled itself into the public debate as the largest and loudest opponents of austerity, Sinn Féin was doubling down on that bet in the forthcoming election—just as austerity was ceasing to be the central fact of political life in Ireland.

Sinn Féin's basic strategy was to present itself as an alternative to the 'establishment' parties of Fianna Fáil, Fine Gael and Labour. The message was hammered home at every opportunity, not least by the party leader during the television debates when he repeatedly referred to the other parties in the collective—'You people,' 'You over there,' 'the three amigos' and so on—often gesturing with his hands to emphasise that 'they' were together, but he and his party were different. 'They' were for the 'elite'; Sinn Féin was for the people. Fine Gael, Fianna Fáil and Labour were for the few; Sinn Féin for the many. It was good, knockabout, traditional populist stuff. The central theme was 'fairness'. Fairness is a word politicians love, partly because of the warm, fuzzy feelings it arouses in their audiences. But also because it can mean anything that they want it to mean.

But Sinn Féin strategists were aware that they needed more than windy slogans. They were acutely aware of media scrutiny of Sinn Féin policies, believing (with some cause) that much of the media was as unnerved by their rise as the rest of the southern establishment.[10] Party strategists sought to bolster their case with a series of policy documents.

The fairness theme was central to a stream of policy documents that gushed from the party throughout 2015. They sketched out a policy approach that was in many respects conventionally left wing—taxes would increase for the wealthy, and the proceeds would be spent on massive investment in public services including healthcare, childcare, education, housing, disabilities and so on. Sinn Féin's analysis of the electorate concluded that about 50–60 per cent of voters constituted its target market, so at one level the policy documents represented a plan for a significant transfer of resources from the people who didn't vote Sinn Féin to the people who did; from the people who would never support it, to the people who might.

By the beginning of 2015, Sinn Féin had come to an even more important decision about its political future. Such is its level of discipline that it is not always evident that Sinn Féin is a party which has more than one opinion on any issue. However, the issue of how it would approach coalition in the post-election landscape led to a lively and lengthy internal debate. Some argued for keeping options open—essentially admitting to the possibility of a coalition deal with either Fianna Fáil or Fine Gael. Others believed that the party had to firmly rule out such a role. This would allow the party to maintain a distinctive campaigning message on the left, but would effectively rule it out of government. To that extent, it was a two-election strategy: it meant eschewing the possibility of government in 2016, but seeking to make it a reality—at the head of a left-wing government—in 2021. It hoped for a Fianna Fáil–Fine Gael coalition, turning the leadership of the opposition over to Sinn Féin. The March party conference in Derry sealed the decision that had already been reached by the party's leadership: it would take the second option, ruling out coalition with either of the big parties and setting its sights on leading a left-wing government.

There were a few strands that came together to make the decision on coalition. It recognised that the party's southern membership, particularly in urban areas, tended to be younger and more ideologically left wing than its northern wing. It also believed that the electoral competition for the party was primarily on the left. This was brought home to the party in stark terms when it lost a by-election in Dublin SW—natural territory for the party—in October 2014 to Paul Murphy of the AAA, in a campaign fought largely on the subject of water charges (see p. 18). Following Murphy's victory, Sinn Féin TDs did a U-turn on their personal approach to water charges, pledging that contrary to previous assurances that they would obey the law, they would not now pay their charges. They would stand in 'solidarity' with the non-payers in their constituencies; they would also try to win their votes back from the radical left-wing parties. A way to do that was not by contemplating coalition with the 'austerity alliance' of Fianna Fáil, Fine Gael and Labour.

There was another factor that was important, too. Gerry Adams had been leader of Sinn Féin since 1983. And while his retirement has been predicted and wished for (usually by the party's many opponents in the media) many times in recent years, it is true that they will eventually be right. He was 67 at the time of the election, and there was a general recognition that Adams would retire in the not too distant future. It would be difficult to overstate the extent to which the party is the creation of Adams and his long-time collaborator Martin McGuinness. And difficult too to overstate the challenge faced by the party in replacing him—not so much in the Dáil bearpit, or even in southern politics generally, but in the role he plays in maintaining the unity and coherence of the party's northern and southern wings. That transition, reasoned some strategists, might best be managed in opposition, rather than in the full glare of government.

LABOUR

Labour had responded to the drubbing in the 2014 local and European elections with a change of leader, following the resignation of Éamon Gilmore and a predictably easy victory for Joan Burton in the contest that followed (see p. 17). But as the leadership election had made clear, nobody really had any ideas for a new political strategy for Labour. Burton simply promised to do what Gilmore had been doing better than he had. Labour's basic belief remained that if the economy recovered, smart politics and clever positioning could return the party to government. It had always been a strategy based as much on hope as anything else. As one party strategist told the present writer as far back as 2011, 'If the economy recovers, we'll be re-elected. If it doesn't, we'll all have much bigger problems than how many votes Labour gets.' By 2015, the economy was well in recovery, but Labour was headed in the opposite direction.

In contrast to Fine Gael's relatively breezy self-confidence despite the mid-term gutting, Labour knew that the local election results presented it with a preview of an existential crisis. The locals, says one party strategist, were a good guide—their baseline expectation. An election strategy group was established in early 2015. Its most important members were Derek McDowell, a former TD and finance spokesman, general secretary Brian McDowell, political advisers Ed Brophy (the Tánaiste's chief of staff), Ronan O'Brien and Ronan Farren, communications minister Alex White and Galway TD Derek Nolan. Others came and went. Pretty early in its deliberations, the group came to a conclusion that would govern their whole approach to the election. 'We figured our only path back was: re-elect the government,' says one of their number.

Like Fine Gael, they were hugely influenced by the course of the British general election that May. 'The Lib Dems tried to disown what the government had done, and it backfired on them,' says Ed Brophy. 'We thought, we should stay close to Fine Gael. We would also get transfers from them.'[11] Moreover, Labour believed that Fine Gael's 'stability vs chaos' narrative would dominate the campaign, and reckoned that within that, their struggle would be 'to make ourselves relevant'. Like everyone else, they expected the Fine Gael vote to increase as the election neared, and that gave them the idea of offering 'balance'—offering the voters not just stability, but a stability that was marked by social democratic values, rather than the more conservative version associated with Fine Gael. 'We would bring our fairness to their stability,' Brophy recalls.

Labour's strategy was informed by a large piece of research that pollsters Red C had done for the party, which 'pushed us a bit to the left'. It depicted a country that was concerned not only about recovery, but also about what sort of society the recovery would enable. Their target voters were as concerned by public services as they were about tax cuts (though they liked those too). They even put a name and a location on the voters they needed to win back: Ashbourne Annie—a hard-pressed mum in a commuter town near Dublin, she was looking for a break—on USC, on childcare, on her mortgage. But she also wanted her kids' school to be resourced, and the local playground fixed. She understood that the economy needed to be strong to provide the resources for these things, but she wished she didn't have to haul so much of the weight. Labour thought they could convince her they were on her side—that they would not only provide the stability of a robust economy, but also the balance of investment in public services. It was a delicate piece of positioning, but they reckoned they could pull it off.

INDEPENDENTS AND SMALLER PARTIES

One of the effects of the economic crash and the subsequent age of austerity across Europe has been a desperate search for new political alternatives. In different countries insurgent parties—of the extreme on both right and left—have rushed in to fill the void created by the collapse of popular support for the parties that voters have blamed for the crash. Syriza in Greece, Podemos in Spain, the Five Star Movement in Italy, the Front National in France, Alternative für Deutschland in Germany—almost every European country has seen some incarnation of the desire for a different politics, and different politicians. This is not a new phenomenon, with even the most basic reading of history showing how economically traumatic times lead to major changes in political support—sometimes taking a sinister turn.

In Ireland it has been a little different. The same desire for an alternative was certainly evident before the 2016 general election—but it was widely diffused between different alternatives, all claiming to be offering something different, something radical, something new. All were standing on a platform of change. By the end of 2015, it was possible to identify five different elements.

1. The Independent Alliance

The Alliance was a group of Independent TDs, councillors and would-be candidates put together largely by TDs Shane Ross, Finian McGrath and Michael Fitzmaurice. It published a statement of 'policy principles'—a broad range of statements so general as to be largely meaningless but which were clearly animated by a belief in political reform. Given the subsequent participation in government of some of its TDs, it is worth enumerating them:

(a) Strip politicians of power to make appointments.
(b) Radical revival of rural Ireland, save declining communities.
(c) No party whip. Revolutionary, not token, reform in workings of Dáil Éireann.
(d) Bankers: If no reform, no privatisation.
(e) Women: remove all obstacles to achieving full potential.
(f) The vulnerable: Absolute protection of old, sick and disabled.
(g) Challenge Brussels: Stop endless kowtowing to Europe.
(h) Small business: Stimulate and support to create jobs.
(i) All insiders in public life or guardians of public money must be held accountable.
(j) Equal rights: Opportunity and access to justice for all regardless of gender, creed or age.

2. Renua

The former Fine Gael TD and junior minister Lucinda Creighton headed a new party, Renua Ireland, which was launched with great fanfare in March of 2015. Creighton had left Fine Gael—or, to be more accurate—had been drummed out for her opposition to abortion legislation in 2013, along with TDs Billy Timmins and Terence Flanagan who were to join her in the new party (see p. 16). Renua attracted support from prospective candidates and—initially at least—interest from the media for whom Creighton's articulate and combative personality always made for good copy. In some ways, the party positioned itself as the heirs to the political tradition of the Progressive Democrats (PDs)—pro-business, pro-tax cuts, determined to control public spending. Its signal policy was a promise of a flat tax, and it heavily marketed Creighton as the face of the party.

3. The Radical Left

The 31st Dáil saw a breakthrough for the radicals of the Socialist Party—also operating under the banner of the AAA and the PBP Alliance.

They campaigned against austerity in the Dáil and on the streets, and were especially prominent in the campaign against water charges, which garnered them significant publicity in the media. As a result they played an outsize role in the national political debate, especially in the pre-campaign period before broadcasting rules applied, relative to their actual support. They were heavily dependent on a small number of prominent TDs such as Paul Murphy and Richard Boyd Barrett to convey their message, and their electoral success depended less on an appetite for their revolutionary politics than from having strong candidates with a record of local activism.

4. Independent Independents

Independent TDs and candidates remain an unusual and immensely significant part of Irish politics (see Chapter 9). They varied from typical local independent candidates, focussed almost exclusively on the needs of the constituency, to maverick independents like Mick Wallace in Wexford who devoted their time to national issues. It was Wallace's proud boast that he did not attend funerals in his constituency, though it could hardly be said that this was typical amongst his independent colleagues. Whatever their ideological background—if any was discernible—they all ran stressing their independence from parties. At a time of unprecedented alienation from the political system for many voters, to be an independent was a virtue in itself.

5. The Greens

After a wipeout in the election of 2011, the Green Party lost most of its leading figures, most of its staff and many of its activists. However, under the former minister Eamon Ryan, they regrouped and had some success in the local elections of 2014, electing 12 councillors across the country which gave the party a basis from which to launch a general election campaign. Ryan himself had polled strongly in the European elections of that year in the Dublin constituency, and was tipped to regain a Dáil seat. The party hoped that its traditional ability to attract transfers would return, and stressed the challenge of climate change and the need for sustainable economic renewal in its pitch to voters.

The Campaign

The Autumn Refusal

Before the election, there was the election that wasn't. Returning after the August break, Fine Gael began to consider an autumn election in earnest. Taoiseach Enda Kenny had been toying with the idea for months and, though he had always said that the government would serve its full term, he had begun to create some wriggle room for himself. Background briefings to journalists suggested that a November election was looming large in his considerations. The budget was scheduled for mid-October. Truncated finance and social welfare bills could be rushed through the Oireachtas in the week afterwards. A brisk three-week campaign promised a mid-November election. Michael Noonan was strongly in favour of it, and the most important figures in Fine Gael's backroom team—Mark Mortell, Andrew McDowell and Mark Kennelly—became convinced that a dash to the country gave them the best chance of returning to government with a working (if diminished) majority.

Kenny himself was afraid that a winter crisis in accident and emergency units would focus debate on public services rather than on the economy, where Fine Gael had, he believed, an unassailable advantage. Others counselled caution. The polls were nowhere near where they needed to be, but the emerging trend was towards Fine Gael. Let it continue, they said. Wait for the budget to make an impact on people's personal financial circumstances. But Kenny was edging towards November. Suddenly, as Labour realised he was serious, there was panic in the ranks of the smaller party. Languishing in the polls, Labour believed that going to the country before Christmas would be a disaster for it. At least another few months gave it time to recover. Labour's view was always that if it was to stage a rally, it would be late. It wanted as much time as possible. Joan Burton made it clear, publicly and privately, that Labour would regard an early election as effectively being double-crossed. Eventually, Kenny backed down. A 2016 poll it would be.

The Great Giveaway

The Taoiseach was expected to call the election on Tuesday, 2 February. But instead, the day began with a row between himself and Burton over participation in the televised election debates. Kenny cancelled a joint press conference. Instead, when the Taoiseach left Government Buildings for Áras an Uachtaráin the following morning after a hasty announcement to the Dáil in which he failed to actually name the date for the election, there was an awkward photocall between the two leaders, but no press conference (see pp. 1–2). Burton was left forlornly alone on the steps of her offices. It set the tone for what was to come.

Fine Gael's opening press conference of the campaign a few hours later, in the Alexander Hotel on Fenian Street in Dublin's city centre, down the road from the Taoiseach's apartment, was a confused and clumsily managed affair. Journalists, party activists and supporters jostled for space; the presiding press officer announced that only three questions would be taken, immediately raising the hackles of the assembled press corps. Politicians may not like reporters, but the smarter ones know that in a campaign they need them. Worse was to come. Kenny bungled his answers to questions on fiscal policy, insisting: 'I'm not going to get into economic jargon here, because the vast majority of people don't understand.' His opponents were quick to voice their suspicions that it was actually him who didn't understand it. It was an avoidable misstep and there were plenty more to come. It only got worse over the next few days. By the end of the week, Fine Gael's 'fiscal space'—its estimation of the resources available to the next government for tax cuts and new spending—had shrunk from €12 billion to €10 billion. Instead of tapping into a mood of cautious optimism, the scale of promises in the Fine Gael plan harked back to the spendthrift era of the 2007 general election. Fine Gael TDs said it appalled supporters who had expected prudence.[12]

There was a view within Fine Gael that their match-winner would be Minister for Finance Michael Noonan, hailed within his party as the man who saved the Irish economy. Noonan actively cultivated a 'wise old owl' persona for the duration of the government, and the Fine Gael grassroots swooned with admiration for him. The general public appeared less impressed. In addition, Noonan—who was 72 at the time of the election and has had bouts of ill health in recent years, including a spell in hospital at Christmas—was not the energetic campaigner of old. He looked tired and drawn for much of the campaign. Noonan has had an amazingly productive final act in a long political career, and he was—with Brendan Howlin—the most important minister in the outgoing government. But an election-winner he was not.

In fact, the biggest misjudgement of the Fine Gael campaign was its economic message. The government was never going to be liked, but not even its opponents could dispute that Ireland's economy had recovered strongly under its watch. However, Fine Gael undermined its own economic credibility by an extended series of promises—steadily leaked in the months before the election—of tax cuts and spending increases. For young families, there would be free visits to the doctor for under-12s, a second free pre-school year and paternity leave from September 2016. For older people, there was a €3 increase in the pension and a Christmas bonus. For public servants, there was the Lansdowne Road Agreement to partly restore pay cuts. For low-paid workers, there was the rise in the minimum wage to €9.15 per hour (from €8.65). For everyone, there was the abolition of the USC. Inheritance taxes were to be slashed. Thousands more teachers, doctors, nurses and gardaí would be employed. Some 200,000 new jobs would be created. On and on it went. You can run a campaign based around the idea of responsible and prudent economic management, or you can run it around the notion of 'you've never had it so good.' But you can't do both at the same time.

Gangland Intervention

The election campaign was only in its third day when a group of heavily armed criminals, dressed in Garda-style uniforms, murdered David Byrne, a figure in Dublin's gangland, at the weigh-in of a boxing bout at the Regency Hotel in Drumcondra on the north side of Dublin. It was quickly followed by the retaliatory killing of taxi driver Eddie Hutch, a brother of the well-known gangland figure Gerry 'The Monk' Hutch.

There might only have been three gangland murders in 2015, compared to 22 in 2010, but that did not matter. It was an opportunity for Fine Gael to play its traditional law and order card, but instead the government was on the back foot, accused of underfunding the Garda Síochána. Minister for Justice Frances Fitzgerald initially stated that funding was not an issue and then announced a new armed Garda unit for Dublin, and found another €5 million to pay for tens of thousands of hours of garda overtime. This seeming contradiction was rapidly and extensively exploited by other parties. The funerals of David Byrne and Eddie Hutch passed off without incident, but the issue of crime was placed firmly on the agenda for a full week of the campaign.

The Indo versus Sinn Féin

Sinn Féin's campaign was also faltering and stop-start, with support in the polls gradually falling away over the course of the three weeks rather than increasing. This was the same dynamic experienced by the party in 2011.

Its leader frequently found himself under pressure, especially on economic matters. It is hard to escape the conclusion that whatever Gerry Adams's importance to maintaining the coherence of the organisation across the North–South divide, he is a serious electoral liability in Dáil elections. The party remains publicly adamant that Adams is an asset. 'We don't think Gerry did us any harm. The number one request from all the constituencies is to get Gerry in. He's box office and he creates a buzz there,' one of its strategists said afterwards.[13] However, that is harder and harder to believe from the outside. Another way of looking at it would be that Adams plays brilliantly to Sinn Féin's base but actively turns off the new voters the party needs to reach the potential implied in pre-election polling.

As well as several gaffes by Adams in the course of the campaign, Sinn Féin also had to contend with the outright hostility of the country's largest newspaper group, Independent News & Media. Day after day, the Indo titles warned their readers about the dangers posed by Sinn Féin, and while party figures tend to laugh it off, insisting that such hostility only galvanises their core supporters, election campaigns are mostly about winning over undecided voters. No party wants the type of coverage that Sinn Féin got from the *Independent.*

Though Sinn Féin spent the entire campaign attacking the government in harsh and sometimes personal terms, the party's principal target was not the government parties, or even Fianna Fáil. Rather, it was fighting the left-wing independents and small parties for the votes of the disaffected, disillusioned masses of voters, many of them in mainly working-class areas of towns and cities where the predominant political mood is one of hostility to the establishment parties—and especially Labour. In fact, the mood towards Labour among some voters in these areas surpassed mere hostility.

The Return of Fianna Fáil

Gerry Adams was happy to use the debates to paint himself as the sole representative of anti-establishment voters, repeatedly drawing attention to similarities between 'these three'—Fine Gael, Fianna Fáil and Labour. He might have had a point—but a bigger point was that a Fianna Fáil pronounced as being near extinction in 2011 appeared in Lazarus-like good health in 2016. The Fianna Fáil campaign was a skilful magnification of the differences between itself and Fine Gael, which allowed Micheál Martin to pose as a candidate of change, but change of a safe and unthreatening sort.

The success of Fianna Fáil's campaign was twofold: an effective ground war which quietly got on with the business of maximising votes and the return from them, and a national media campaign that managed to get the tone right and, crucially for the often chronically indisciplined party, kept to it. The party leader was a significant asset, clearly the most effective of all the party leaders, and the party cleverly structured its campaign around him. Its posters told the tale: big Micheál, small Fianna Fáil. A party leader hasn't been as influential in a campaign since 1997.

Almost all post-campaign analysis suffers from the flaw of believing that everything the winners did worked, while nothing the losers did worked. The truth is usually more complex. But Martin's tight-knit campaign team—led by party general secretary Seán Dorgan, his deputy Darragh McShea, Martin's chief of staff Deirdre Gillane, communications chief Pat McParland and strategist Peter MacDonagh, with morning meetings chaired by former general secretary Martin Mackin—succeeded in the key areas where Fine Gael failed. Crucially, they read the public mood accurately. Party Campaign Manager Billy Kelleher, a TD for Cork North-Central, having signed off on strategy, performed the role of morale officer and cheerleader—sending out daily messages to the organisation throwing digs at Fine Gael and pollsters in equal measure. Fianna Fáil understood that depth of public disaffection with the government and the desire for a change, and it designed and implemented a campaign that turned that into political advantage for Fianna Fáil candidates. After the carnage of 2011, it was an extraordinary turnaround.

Labour's Loss

Éamon Gilmore warned Labour, when he brought the party into this government, that they would pay a heavy price. He can hardly have imagined it would be so unbearable. The Labour strategy required Fine Gael to be cruising back to government with poll ratings in the low-to-mid-30s. This would have enabled the party to argue that the choice facing voters was who should be Fine Gael's coalition partner.

There were even some in the party who voiced the view that the election campaign should be about whether Fine Gael should have an overall majority, or should govern with a partner. Siptu boss Jack O'Connor expressed just this view before Christmas. That he wasn't laughed out of it demonstrated the extent to which much of the pre-campaign discourse was based around the notion that a Fine Gael surge during the campaign was inevitable. Had this actually happened, Labour's strategy (based around the idea of 'balance') might have worked. As it happened, voters figured that if they didn't like Fine Gael, they just wouldn't vote for it—rather than choosing Labour to accompany it back to government to keep an eye on it.

Enda's Gaffes

As he had done in the campaigns of 2007 and 2011, Enda Kenny finished badly in 2016. In the debates he failed to move beyond pre-cooked soundbites and never looked at ease. At a rally in Mayo during the last weekend of the campaign, he declared that Castlebar had 'all-Ireland champion whingers' who were never happy with anything. Not all gaffes or controversies matter—this did because it provided a window on the strategic flaw in Fine Gael's message. That it took two days to 'clarify' the statement was a signal of a campaign focused on implementing a pre-agreed strategy and failing to respond to events. Fianna Fáil could not believe its luck. One of its election staffers went as far as to quote Talleyrand: 'it is worse than a crime, it is a mistake.'[14]

So Why Did Fine Gael Lose?

The Tories won in 2015 because they successfully established the idea that there had been an abrupt change in the government's approach when they came to power. (Actually, the British Labour Party collaborated in this.) Voters—or enough of them in the right places, at any rate—came to accept that this was what had led to a strong economic recovery. Fine Gael and Labour made mighty efforts to establish a similar belief in Ireland, but it simply didn't work, partly because voters believed that fiscal and economic policy had not changed much when the coalition came to office. People didn't believe that Fine Gael and Labour were solely responsible for the economic recovery, and so they didn't believe that the country would go to hell in a handbasket without them. This was a little unfair. It is true that Fine Gael and Labour had simply followed existing policy—largely mandated by the EU–ECB–IMF Troika (see Chapter 1)—but their success in stabilising the public finances undoubtedly paved the way for economy growth. They oversold it, though, and it hurt their own case. Voters liked the stability idea, but they didn't buy the notion that there would be chaos without the coalition.

There was another flaw in the economic narrative. Large numbers of people believed that the recovery, as it progressed through 2015 and 2016, was unevenly and unfairly distributed. This was partly helped by media coverage—particularly on the national broadcaster RTÉ which sometimes tended to concentrate on the negative stories of those left behind rather than the positive news of job creation and returned emigrants, much to the coalition's fury—and the perception that the recovery was unfair began to dig into the public consciousness. Equally, for the majority of people who did not feel better off in their personal affairs (see p. 169), a constant trumpeting of how good things were reinforced the idea of being 'left behind.' When the recovery is felt to be unfair the slogan 'Keeping the recovery going' becomes a less compelling argument.

There were other reasons behind Fine Gael's disaster. Ireland is simply different from the UK. It is not a binary system. Voters have other options. In this case, they had the option of Fianna Fáil and Independents. The electoral system facilitates more choice. But fundamentally, Fine Gael and Labour severely damaged their own economic credibility. In doing so, they destroyed their own strongest card. They were never likely to be loved; they were having difficulty being believed. But they could have got more out of being respected for their ability to manage the economy.

Months before the election during a series of frank conversations with a senior figure in government, the present writer suggested that it was clear that having presided over a remarkable economic recovery, the government was now going to use some of the proceeds of that growth to buy the election. After the required denials that the two parties would even contemplate such a thing, the person admitted simply and honestly: 'Of course we are going to try to buy the election. But we will buy it as prudently as we can.' But people weren't selling.

THE CHANGE ELECTION

Halfway through the campaign, the Fine Gael strategist crouched over his cup of coffee. It was week two, and his party's message was faltering. The first week had been a disaster. The second week wasn't shaping up to be any better. The polls were going into reverse. But the leadership of Fine Gael's campaign wasn't rattled; it had faith in its strategy, faith in its message. This faith was based in one simple judgement. The adviser, one of the most respected figures in the political firmament, explained with certainty in his voice. 'Look—this is not a change election,' he said, with some conviction.

It was a fundamental misjudgement, and from it flowed the failure of the Fine Gael campaign. It turns out that it was a 'change election' after all. For all the fun that political figures had at the pundits' and pollsters' expense when the results became clear—and perhaps they were entitled to it—none of the parties anticipated the result either. The record of the Irish electorate in swinging decisively in the final stages of a campaign, to the consternation of everyone on count day, remains intact. A change election, then, but a very Irish one—resulting in cautious change. Indeed, in an environment where public disdain for politicians is at an all-time high, where people simultaneously expect government to solve problems, while believing them incapable of doing anything right, perhaps every election is a change election.

Notes

1. Interview with author.
2. The phrase, correctly 'The economy, stupid', was used within the 1992 Clinton campaign as a means of keeping a diverse and expanding campaign team from being distracted from core messages. Since then it has been used as a shorthand for the need for campaigns to be focused on fundamentals. See: Michael Kelly, 'The 1992 campaign: the Democrats—Clinton and Bush compete to be champion of change; Democrat fights perceptions of Bush gain,' *New York Times*, 31 October 1992.
3. Author's campaign notes.
4. Author's campaign notes.
5. Interview with author.
6. Stephen O'Brien, 'Fianna Fáil's long march back to power', *The Times* 14 January 14 2016; http://www.thetimes.co.uk/tto/irishnews/opinion/article4664799.ece
7. Dorgan, interview with author.
8. Interview with author.
9. Dorgan, interview with author.
10. Private information.
11. Brophy, interview with author.
12. Author's campaign notes.
13. Author's campaign notes.

14. The great survivor of the French revolutionary and Napoleonic eras was referencing Napoleon's battlefield trial and execution of the Duke of Enghien in 1804 for treason. (The quote is also often attributed to Joseph Fouché, the long-time police minister of the era.) In Irish political terms, being caught calling the people of your own town 'whingers' is a misdemeanour of similar status.

CHAPTER 5

On the Campaign Trail

*Peter Burke, Jack Chambers, Donnchadh Ó Laoghaire,
Alex White, Maureen O'Sullivan, and Grace O'Sullivan*

PETER BURKE (FINE GAEL, LONGFORD–WESTMEATH)

Peter Burke stood unsuccessfully for the Dáil in 2007 and 2011, finishing as runner-up on the latter occasion. In 2009, while in his mid-twenties, he was elected to Westmeath County Council, becoming chair of the council in 2012, and he was re-elected in 2014 with over 1,000 first preferences. He is a graduate of NUI Galway and worked as a chartered accountant in Mullingar for ten years before his election to the Dáil in February 2016.

After a very difficult local election for Fine Gael nationally in 2014 the focus quickly turned to the next general election and when that might be.

P. Burke • J. Chambers • D.Ó. Laoghaire • M. O'Sullivan
Dáil Éireann, Dublin, Ireland

A. White
Dublin, Ireland

G. O'Sullivan
Seanad Éireann, Dublin, Ireland

© The Author(s) 2016
M. Gallagher, M. Marsh (eds.), *How Ireland Voted 2016*,
DOI 10.1007/978-3-319-40889-7_5

I had run in the 2011 general election and finished third on the first count, with 6629 first preference votes, in the four-seat constituency of Longford–Westmeath. I had come through a very difficult local election campaign with a very strong performance. In view of my past electoral record and holding the office of the Cathaoirleach of Westmeath County Council and Mayor of Mullingar, and indeed having been very unlucky not to have been elected in the previous Dáil election, I was quietly confident I would be on the Fine Gael general election ticket. However, midway through 2015 the constituency executive of Fine Gael announced that the convention for Longford–Westmeath should be held by June and so the wheels were set in motion for Monday, 29 June in the Mullingar Park Hotel. I set about a plan to meet all the members of the party where I put my strong case forward. I devoted most of May and June travelling around the constituency meeting the membership of the party.

However, due to the dawn of the gender quota system, rumours that a directive would be issued by Fine Gael HQ to run two candidates were gathering pace. I felt very strongly that I should ignore such rumours and keep my campaign on track and this was to prove a very wise decision.

It was going to be a very difficult selection convention, in fact the most difficult for Fine Gael nationally. The history of the constituency suggested three candidates always contested for Fine Gael based in the three distinctive geographical areas of Longford, Athlone and Mullingar. I finished my campaign on the Sunday before the convention and I remember getting word that evening that Deputy Bernard Durkan was to be dispatched by HQ to chair the convention.

On the Monday evening of the convention meeting many members flooded into the Park Hotel and the concern was telling among all, irrespective of which candidate they supported, that a two-candidate strategy was going to be embarked upon. As the convention got under way, three candidates were duly proposed and seconded and the moment of truth finally came. The convention hall erupted with anger when the directive was read out to select two candidates of whom one must be a woman. This effectively ensured Deputy Gabrielle McFadden was automatically selected and a vote would ensue between myself and Deputy James Bannon who is based in County Longford.

Despite the huge anger displayed among those present and threats that the convention would be abandoned, a vote took place and I lost out by the minimum possible margin. There were two recounts and it was early morning when the result was finally announced. The constituency immediately responded and letters calling for my addition were dispatched to Fine Gael HQ and concerted lobbying was carried out by elected councillors in the constituency. All the Fine Gael elected representatives in the constituency were very clear in conversations with Fine Gael HQ that we must have a three-candidate strategy. Finally, in mid-November, news came through that I was to be added. My wife was expecting our first baby in December so some planning took place and the hard yards were left until January. Sure enough baby Leo arrived on the 9th of December.

When January finally arrived, I started canvassing immediately and took leave of absence from my employment in Stephens Cooke & Associates. As we went further into January, news arrived that the constituency would be divided into three geographical areas based on population. The Longford candidate was allocated County Longford to canvass and Westmeath was split in two based on population between the Westmeath candidates. The Director of Elections for Fine Gael enforced same.

I enjoyed the canvass and I found meeting people on the canvass was the best way to engage with the electorate and secure support. It is also important to get your message out through local media. In my constituency there are a number of local newspapers and two provincial radio stations, and I would acknowledge it can be more difficult for Dublin-based candidates to get their message across in the media as it is mostly national. I also used social media, namely Twitter and Facebook, which can be very effective but no substitute for a face-to-face meeting if possible. This is exactly how I ran my campaign. Matt Shaw based in Mullingar was my campaign manager and, with a very effective team based in North Westmeath, we organised a canvass schedule together with a series of campaign events. We decided to have a campaign launch the weekend before the election was called and this allowed us to put up posters advertising the event in advance whilst not breaking the law in any way as we were advertising a public event in my home town. It was a huge success and a large crowd from all over the constituency attended on the night and Mairéad McGuinness MEP did the official launch. For early January the canvass was either me on my own or in the rural areas with a local person. No big groups were sent out until the campaign launch was concluded and essentially that was the spring board. We got news after the launch that we had secured an excellent and highly visible election office on the Market Square in the centre of Mullingar and this assisted what was a very visible campaign.

It was a very short general election campaign and one of the most memorable points related to how personal it became regarding some other candidates, culminating in a member of the clergy releasing a video uploaded to Facebook making personal attacks on candidates. It was my understanding that members of the clergy did not get involved in electioneering so this came as a surprise. The campaign national was also very presidential in tone where the leaders of each political party were the main focus as opposed to the whole party and key spokespersons. There were more live debates than ever before between the leaders of each party, which maybe encouraged this.

My campaign manager and the director of elections took up the role of dealing with Fine Gael HQ as I was busy on the canvass and responding to queries. I had a strong understanding of the issues in the constituency and had worked hard locally as a public representative on the local council together with working with the business community in my role as a chartered accountant.

All these factors played a part in deciding the election and I would say general election campaigns are becoming more local as opposed to being weighted in favour of candidates who have a national perspective on issues. This in turn has facilitated the election of a number of Independents elected on micro-local issues. You learn lessons from every campaign and next time around I intend to utilise social media and my personal website more as you can reach a lot of people in the constituency through these channels in a short space of time.

The final leg of the campaign was a six-day siege at Keenagh, where the votes were counted. There was a count in 1965 that lasted six days in the same constituency and the election count of 2016 equalled that. As the tallies were coming in on Saturday morning, I was performing strongly in my own area and topping the poll in my home boxes. I got notice of the final tally sometime after lunch on Saturday and that settled my nerves, 5681 first preference votes was my final first count, and I travelled down to the count centre on Saturday evening.

A number of recounts were called but having finished third on the first count, the same position I finished in the 2011 general election ironically, I was reasonably secure of being elected. The result finally came in the early hours of Thursday morning and Longford–Westmeath was the final count to be concluded for the 32nd Dáil. I was delighted and my campaign team was very excited and it was a huge honour and privilege to be elected to the 32nd Dáil. I look forward to the challenge ahead.

JACK CHAMBERS (FIANNA FÁIL, DUBLIN WEST)

Jack Chambers was elected to Dáil Éireann on his first attempt in February 2016 in the Dublin West constituency, regaining the seat held by the late Brian Lenihan and becoming the youngest TD in the 32nd Dáil. He previously served as Deputy Mayor of Fingal County Council and topped the poll in the Castleknock/Blanchardstown ward in the 2014 local elections. He holds an honours degree in Law and Political Science from Trinity College and has studied Medicine at the Royal College of Surgeons of Ireland (RCSI).

On 25 February 2015, I was selected as the candidate in the Dublin West constituency with a comprehensive endorsement by the Fianna Fáil membership in the constituency, where I won the convention by a margin of 2:1. It was one year before the general election and nearly one year after my election as a member of Fingal County Council.

It was also two years since my appointment as a Fianna Fáil Local Area Representative and it was four years after the 2011 general election in which the late Brian Lenihan delivered the only success for Fianna Fáil in the capital when he retained his seat in the Dublin West constituency. I was honoured and thrilled to take up the mantle to try and regain the seat held by a man who inspired my own interest in politics from a young age. I recall the days and nights when I canvassed in the general election in 2011 where I listened to stories of emigration, unemployment, deprivation, trauma and hopelessness.

There was growing disillusionment with politics, politicians and the political system and there was an appetite for an injection of new ideas and a fresh, energetic quality of representation. Fianna Fáil leader Micheál Martin initiated a series of internal party reforms to bring about the democratisation of the organisation, with a system of one member one vote introduced. He travelled the country to all villages, towns and cities not only listening to party members but also listening to communities and their problems and challenges. This process of reconnection resulted in the appointment of Local Area Representatives in a multiplicity of areas as a platform for Fianna Fáil to reconnect with our local communities after our drubbing at the 2011 general election.[1] It was clear locally that the people whose stories I had listened to in 2011 had suffered more in the intervening years, despite the great white hope that was the Fine Gael–Labour government.

I always had a keen interest in politics, representation and public service after graduating with a degree in Law and Political Science from Trinity College. When I entered politics, I was studying Medicine in RCSI and I took the plunge after my appointment as an Area Representative. I began an intensive canvass from day one which has not diminished or subsided since I attained my current position as a TD.

Politics is the business of people and a cardinal rule is that you must be grounded in people and their issues both locally and nationally. The dichotomy at the doors in 2011 reinforced my approach that no politician can blame their party or anyone else. Personal responsibility for the result and the outcome are key, and consistent activism absolutely necessary.

In the aftermath of the selection convention in February 2015, I brought together members from different areas and drew on their experiences, background and perspective on how this election could be won and how we could regain the Fianna Fáil seat in Dublin West. Fianna Fáil, at the time, was in the high teens in the polls nationally and lower in Dublin—similar to the 2011 election result.

There was a bizarre obsession with polls in the year before the general election. The complexity of the Irish political system is well researched and having studied the multiplicity of factors that contribute to voter choice in my time in Trinity, I told all activists and people involved in our campaign to ignore all polls. A Dublin West picture cannot be extrapolated from any national poll, whether Fianna Fáil are up, down or unchanged. We set a rule that our barometer for support was doors, not polls. We set about our campaign in the year before the election and had a well-crafted plan incorporating the geographical spread of the constituency.

Dublin West is one of the most competitive constituencies in the country and in this election I faced two government ministers, in the then Tánaiste and Labour leader Joan Burton and Leo Varadkar of Fine Gael. Both were high-profile candidates, locally and nationally, with regular media appearances and constituency visits. They were joined by two incumbents from the Socialist Party/AAA, Joe Higgins and Ruth Coppinger. Joe Higgins was retiring from electoral politics and placed his full weight behind Ruth Coppinger for this election. His retirement created a lacuna to regain the seat. Paul Donnelly from Sinn Féin had performed well in previous elections so I knew he also had a good chance of taking a seat.

The constituency changed from 2011, with the Swords and North County area going back to the newly configured Dublin Fingal. The Navan Road area, previously in Dublin Central, was added to the constituency. Having been elected in the Castleknock/Blanchardstown Ward, I set about the delicate task of reinforcing and building on my core support but also growing support in both the Mulhuddart and Navan Road areas which had not been in my electoral area in the local elections.

I was elected as Deputy Mayor of Fingal in the summer of 2015 and that resulted in enhanced exposure and local profile in all areas. It was a definite bonus as I prepared for the upcoming general election. I had reopened the late Brian Lenihan's constituency office and ran regular clinics to complement an active canvass whilst also meeting community groups from all areas. We continued to implement our plan of connecting with all communities over the year and whilst uncertainty built regarding the possibility of an early general election in November, we knew we were ready. Fianna Fáil helped build my national profile with some appearances at press events and national interviews as well as asking me to do the warm up speech for Micheál Martin at the party ard-fheis in April 2015.

Polls changed and fluctuated but the response on the door gradually improved. Some of the other parties had delivered leaflets and conducted public meetings but there was very little substantive and direct political activity in the months preceding the election. As the election approached, people were told about the recovery by politicians, but this was not tangible for many in the world around them. Communities remained similar to the period of crisis in 2011 and indeed many people's lives were relatively worse.

Crises in crime, healthcare and housing were the main issues exercising the minds of voters in the Dublin West constituency. Fianna Fáil's manifesto and commitment of returning to our roots in communities and building better public services, whilst giving reciprocity for the taxes people pay, was resonating with people and the policies complemented candidates throughout the country who were active in their communities.

The election campaign itself was an intensification and a focused conclusion on what had been a consistent period of effort by the whole campaign team for the preceding year. A constituency poll was procured and published on the front page of the *Irish Independent* with the headline saying Joan Burton would lose her seat with seats for the other four contenders from Fine Gael, Sinn Féin, Fianna Fáil, AAA. I was worried. On the day it was published, I attended the Fianna Fáil manifesto launch with some of my colleagues and people were commenting on the poll. We had good momentum on the ground but up to now it had been under the radar.

That's how we wanted to keep it, but the poll changed all that. I recall Micheál Martin saying to me at the launch to keep going and not to let it distract me or the team. I reminded the team that evening about our cardinal rule: 'Ignore the polls. The doors are our measure. We needed to push through the line'.

There were many who had advised increased presence on social media. I was always sceptical of its centralised function and focus that was constantly being reported in mainstream media. For me, it is no more than a cog in the wheel. Nothing beats meeting people and actively representing and articulating their issues and concerns. We posted intermittently on Facebook and less so on Twitter but, whilst it is a platform of engagement for some of the electorate that you wouldn't otherwise meet on the doorstep, it does not replace real interaction and engagement. When reflecting on the campaign I feel one story highlights the detachment of the outgoing government and the return of Fianna Fáil as a force of the community and the people.

Canvassers from three parties had gathered at a shopping centre to go about their separate canvasses one evening when men armed with machetes raided the local Spar shop. The staff inside were understandably terrorised by the ordeal. The burglars escaped on foot and one of my canvassers chased after them. He tried anxiously to ring the emergency services but was left waiting ten minutes before he got through to them. He reacted furiously and was shocked at the series of events at the local shop. A government minister in attendance told the media afterwards: 'Unfortunately, burglaries affect every area of the country in recent years and I'm just glad no-one was hurt or harmed'. The reaction attempted to neutralise the incident and in my view it symbolised the normalisation of a two-tier Ireland and a true detachment from communities and their issues by the outgoing government.

On the day of the count I was cautiously optimistic. I listened to radio coverage and was texted key box results from the tally by the Director of Elections, Donal Foley. I asked for certain boxes in the three electoral areas of the constituency and I was certain we had done it. I arrived at the count centre and I was there for the announcement of the first count and was thrilled with the result of 6917 first preference votes. It meant I was in second place behind Leo Varadkar.

I went on to take the third seat behind Ruth Coppinger, and ahead of the then Tánaiste Joan Burton, with a total of 8315 votes. It was a great honour to regain the seat in such a competitive and high-profile field. We stuck to our plan from day one and grounded ourselves in people and the communities.

Donnchadh Ó Laoghaire (Sinn Féin, Cork South-Central)

Donnchadh Ó Laoghaire was elected to Cork County Council in 2014, representing the Ballincollig–Carrigaline local electoral area. From Togher, he is a graduate in Law from University College Cork and a former National Organiser of Ógra Shinn Féin, as well as having served a number of terms on the Sinn Féin Ard Chomhairle (national executive). His candidacy in the four-seat Cork South-Central constituency was the first time he had stood for the Dáil. Since the election he has been appointed party spokesperson on Children and Youth Affairs.

'You're on 18 per cent' my Press Officer Darren O'Keeffe had said to me. This was in a Millward Brown poll for the *Independent*, due out in the following day's paper. The news came as something of a surprise, we hadn't anticipated any constituency-based opinion polls, none publicly released anyway.

At that stage, most of the predictions were calling it as 2 Fine Gael and 2 Fianna Fáil. But that suited us fine, we wanted people to know we were in with a chance, that it was worth voting for us, and that it would be competitive, but that it would take absolutely every vote. Suddenly we were going from being under the radar, to being talked up to take one of the first two seats. Aside from a fear of complacency among our own supporters about the possibility of taking a seat in the constituency for the first time, I feared a creep of votes towards other candidates, assuming I was safe.

And in any event, it didn't quite fit. We knew the reaction was good, we had a sense of what it might materialise as on the day, but it just didn't feel as strong as 18 per cent.

'Candidatitus' can do funny things to a person's thinking. All I could do was think of the giant target that would be painted on our backs over the last 10–11 days, particularly by Fine Gael, who looked like losing a seat. And perhaps for the first time, I felt the pressure of the seat being ours to lose, rather than ours to win.

In many ways, there probably wasn't much we could do. Fine Gael would make some interventions, surely, but we had to be careful not to lose our focus. Nor was there really any danger of our activists getting complacent. Plenty of them had been around the block a few times. We knew perfectly well that we weren't going to be topping the poll. There was nothing for it, only to carry on. Keep knocking on doors, keep leafleting, keep getting press releases out, keep making calls and writing letters. Drive on till the finish.

In many ways, our campaign was a lengthy one, and something of a slow burner. Having been selected in May 2015, we set about planning, building my profile as a candidate, and indeed canvassing and leafleting.

The constituency was already being billed as 'The Constituency of Death'. And not without reason, it was definitely challenging. Five relatively high-profile TDs: Fine Gael Agriculture Minister Simon Coveney, Fianna Fáil leader Micheál Martin and Finance spokesperson Michael McGrath, Chairman of the Oireachtas Health Committee Jerry Buttimer of Fine Gael, and Chairman of the Banking Enquiry, Labour's Ciarán Lynch.

Add to that the fact that the constituency was losing a seat, going from five to four. Although likely to be the next strongest competitor, having to deprive two sitting TDs of their seats meant that I was up against it.

Despite an early start, it was frustrating in the early months of the campaign; although voters were happy to meet us, and we got a warm reception, you could tell that they just weren't in an election mind frame as yet. It was difficult to gauge. Likewise, despite considerable efforts, it was difficult to develop my profile as a candidate; the media will often, naturally, favour an incumbent for comment on issues, particularly where they have such a high profile as enjoyed by our local TDs.

Those early months felt a bit like a phoney war, grinding out marginal advances, in the knowledge that really the big effort was to come when the ball was thrown in and people's minds began to concentrate. It is a totally different dynamic, when you are engaging and persuading people who are in the process of making their minds up.

It was towards the end of autumn before it really began to generate momentum. It's difficult to firmly put my finger on what changed, but I think the fevered, and perhaps somewhat hysterical, speculation on an early election, lent itself to a change of gear.

At the same time, it was essential that if an early election was to happen, that we were ready, so fundraising and preparation of productions, such as literature and, crucially, posters, were done. We had the canvass for the last six weeks, and postering and leafleting meticulously planned.

And our messaging. We were determined to be as positive as possible, talking about the possibility of a progressive government, focused on investment in public services, particularly health and childcare, and solving the housing crisis. We also emphasised that I was the candidate best positioned to offer real change for Cork, to upset the hegemony of Fianna Fáil, Fine Gael, and Labour that had dominated politics in Cork SC for so long.

So by the time the prospect of a pre-Christmas election had drifted away, we were essentially ready for the real intense campaign.

We drew our breath to some extent over Christmas, in anticipation of the intense work that would be required once January hit. I had best man duties on New Year's eve, for my next door neighbour and lifelong friend, Leonard Keating, so that took my mind off politics for a few days. In fairness to Lenny, he more than repaid the best man duties with postering and leafleting duties subsequently!

Come 3 January we were out on the road again, and from there on, there was no let up. The numbers on the canvass and leafleting increased all the time, and momentum generated more momentum.

January also saw the Vincent Browne debate.[2] Given my position as the scrappy insurgent, I always felt this was an opportunity to mark myself out as a serious contender. All the more so now that Cork SC's debate was happening within the white heat of the real campaign.

But I came away from that Vincent Browne debate, frankly, a bit deflated. I had felt that I hadn't made the impression I had needed to make. Not a complete disaster, but a big missed opportunity. The debate had largely centred on the five sitting TDs, the first time Vincent had had all the sitting TDs in a constituency together, and Vincent revelled in it. It was hard for the rest of us to get a word in edgeways.

Thankfully, the response to the programme did not reflect my own analysis. Recognition improved significantly, and more and more, I began to be seen as a viable candidate.

The last ten days, as we began to tire, and as I stressed over how accurate or not the opinion poll was, were exhausting. I was by now, personally at least, running on fumes. The most difficult thing in some ways wasn't the constant canvassing, that's tiring, but you just get on to autopilot. It's when you stop and sit down, but still have to find the energy to follow up on issues from the canvass, or coordinate plans with my Director of Elections, Eolan Ryng, and make plans, when you are practically ready to conk off, that's where it really gets tiring.

It amazed me the lengths people were willing to go to, the time they were willing to put in and the efforts they were willing to make. An old friend, and a Sinn Féin member, Dave Collins had emigrated to London a few years before. He travelled home a week out, just to help out with a weekend's canvassing, in Lehenaghbeg and Glasheen. But although not having planned it, he travelled home for the count as well, feeling like he couldn't have missed it. Countless people made efforts that at times left me speechless. I learned what it really means to be indebted during the campaign.

Feedback on the doors was very strong and improving, including areas where our support hadn't previously been as strong. The canvass is one of the most tangible ways in politics of gauging people's attitudes, and gauging your own support. Although no two doors are the same either, and you never know the struggle a family faces behind any given door.

It was obvious from an early stage that the government had got their strategy totally wrong, that they were listening to too narrow a category of people. The issues people wanted to talk about, aside from the very local, which is always a factor, were a million miles removed from tax cuts.

Water was a massive issue, because of the huge mobilisation in many communities against the water charges. The southside of Cork City was the first place to see protests outside housing estates, with Ashbrook Heights in Togher.

But not just water. People knew public services were cut to the bone. People knew our hospitals were under unbelievable strain and needed investment. Many people had stories of frustration, and deep fury, at how they, or relatives of theirs, had been treated by the healthcare system, whether waiting inordinate lengths of time for a procedure or treatment, or losing a medical card.

You could see it right down to things like housing maintenance, an issue, so far as I can see, getting very little attention nationally. Cash-strapped councils are just unable to keep up with it, and there are some older estates where every second house had a complaint, guttering or windows and doors that need replacing, damp and cold, and the kind of damp with walls covered in mould and you could see and feel the drips. The other side of the housing crisis that you don't really hear people talking about is overcrowding. So, many, many houses with three generations under the one roof, not out of choice, and all the stress and frustration that that causes. And of course, homelessness. I met people who had relatives in the Travelodge, Edel House, or other emergency accommodation, desperate for help, and just so disconsolate that their lives had come to this.

Against that backdrop, the calls for tax cuts, as a higher priority than health or housing, just infuriated people. As did the complacency of 'Keep the recovery going'. As the campaign went on, the government failed to respond adequately to the backlash. The writing was on the wall.

At 9:40 pm on Friday 26 February, having gone around the polling stations checking turnout, and coordinating with our Get out the Vote operation, I finished as I had the last three elections. I checked the stations at Togher Girls and Boys School, where I voted myself, and walked in to the Deanrock Bar next door, for a quiet pint with a friend or two. All and sundry wished good luck.

There is a certain relief to knowing you can do more, that it is decided. The count would bring its own stress, but that could wait for morning.

In the event, after being a few hundred votes ahead on the first count, the elimination of Mick Finn and Lorna Bogue sealed it, as the transfers we had hoped for, materialised and pushed us just far enough ahead, indeed, to our surprise, ahead not only of Jerry Buttimer, but also ahead of Simon Coveney. In concession and congratulation, both men were gentlemen, for which I was grateful.

I was lifted aloft by a sea of supporters, family and friends. The emotion is the most remarkable mix of not only jubilation, satisfaction, but also relief; an awful lot of people have put their faith in you, and you become determined to justify their faith. It really was the greatest honour of my life, and a very proud day for my family, as well as neighbours and friends.

But a thing that will always stick with me, is that, in ways, there were others it meant more to.

People who had worked the ground for Sinn Féin in Cork, 20, 25 years ago, who had stood for Sinn Féin, when it was neither fashionable nor profitable, far from it. Some of them probably never imagined they would see the day. It meant the world to them, and it was their victory, just as much as it was mine. We built on their work.

And for our voters, it was a sign that their vote could count, that they could upset the established order, and that their vote could influence change. Only time will tell, if this current, new dispensation in the Dáil, is merely a hiatus, or the beginning of a new era and dynamic in Irish politics, but I certainly feel that for many parts of Irish society, the desire for change, and the desire to influence that change themselves, has never been stronger in my lifetime.

ALEX WHITE (LABOUR, DUBLIN RATHDOWN)

Alex White was Minister for Communications, Energy and Natural Resources in the Fine Gael/ Labour coalition, having been appointed in the July 2014 reshuffle. He was previously Minister of State in the Dept of Health, and chair of the Oireachtas Finance Committee. He was elected as Labour TD for Dublin South in 2011, having served in Seanad Éireann from 2007, and as a member of South Dublin County Council from 2004. Alex White is a Senior Counsel, and has practised as a barrister since 1994, prior to which he was a current affairs producer with RTE.

Although a relative latecomer to electoral politics (I was 45 when elected as a councillor in 2004), the 2016 general election was my fourth outing as a Dáil candidate in eight and a half years. The most high profile of these was undoubtedly the 2009 by-election, when RTÉ's George Lee ran away with the contest, collecting some 53 per cent of the vote. I came in second then with almost 20 per cent, and learned later that I had two-thirds of the winner's second preferences (a footnote, perhaps, but one that tells a certain Labour story).

There was one critical difference in 2016 though, and I think this difference was decisive from my point of view. In 2012, the Constituency Commission had recommended radical changes, as a consequence of which Dublin South (S), a five-seat constituency in 2011, was reduced to a three-seat constituency and renamed Dublin Rathdown. Knocklyon, Rathfarnham and Ballyboden—my original political base—were to be incorporated into an enlarged Dublin South-West (SW).

I had a difficult decision to make in the summer of 2012. Would I move to Dublin SW where Labour had two sitting TDs (Pat Rabbitte and Éamonn Maloney), or would I run in the newly created Dublin Rathdown, which after all still comprised two-thirds of the Dublin S electorate that had put me into Dáil Éireann in 2011. Would I 'go west', or would I stay?

Two key factors influenced my decision. Firstly, Pat Rabbitte was clear that he would likely stand again in SW. In fairness, it was early days, and one could hardly expect a senior minister in a crisis government to say otherwise. But I felt he was quite clear in his mind, and I also thought that even if Pat became less certain, or changed his mind, the party (under then leader Éamon Gilmore) would want big vote-getters on the ballot paper in 2016, and would pressure him.

The second factor weighing on my mind was the express support and urging of the Labour organisation in Dublin Rathdown. The key people there were very keen that I should stay. This was important to me, especially since my original emergence as a Dáil candidate had ruffled more than a few feathers. Relations, although largely repaired, hadn't always been universally happy in Dublin S Labour. Despite all this, people were now saying—please stay, we'll win the seat! That, of course, was 2012.

I came to the conclusion, considering all the various factors, that I had as good a chance of winning a single Labour seat in the new three-seater as I had of winning a second Labour seat in the five-seater, not that I felt either prospect was remotely certain. So with a heavy heart, I closed the office in Rathfarnham, and opened a new one in Churchtown—in the same building, co-incidentally, that Séamus Brennan had occupied with such remarkable electoral success for so many years.

Indeed the enduring success of the late Séamus Brennan (and his fellow Fianna Fáil TD Tom Kitt) almost defined Dublin S, electorally at least, for a generation. Regarded with some justification also as a Fine Gael stronghold (the constituency once had three Fine Gael representatives in the Dáil), Dublin S has only occasionally returned Labour to the Dáil, and then only for one term at a time. The Greens too have had intermittent success here, often alternating with Labour. In many ways, Dublin S has long reflected broader national electoral trends, though with the distinction of having returned more 'liberal' Fine Gael TDs, and Fianna Fáil figures adept at accommodating themselves to the social and liberal agenda.

With the boundary changes of 2012, the constituency's middle-class profile was, if anything, accentuated. There is no significant working-class component, and relatively few local authority estates in Dublin Rathdown. As is the case with urban and suburban constituencies generally, there is no unifying characteristic that gives us an identity such as would be the case in a county, or even a multi-county constituency. That said, there is a high level of 'social capital', especially around sports organisations. The success of GAA (Gaelic Athletic Association) clubs such as Ballinteer St. John's and Kilmacud Crokes speaks to a keen sense of identity, flowing from the county allegiances of those who have come to live in the area since the 1950s. It's not all private schools and rugby here.

As we embarked on the campaign for my re-election, I think we gave ourselves an even chance of winning the seat. We expected that Shane Ross would be at or near a quota. We thought that Fine Gael would come in strong, but that they could not reasonably expect to take two seats. Mary White (Fianna Fáil) had a good campaign, but we didn't think she would win a seat. We thought Peter Mathews wouldn't feature in the final shake-out, and that while Sinn Féin would do well, they were not a real prospect here. The main imponderable was how well the Green candidate would do. We felt that if we could get enough of the 'pro-government' vote (in addition to the core Labour vote) we would have a margin ahead of the Green.

Labour and Fine Gael had agreed on a vote transfer pact designed to solidify a combined presentation to the electorate: 're-elect the government'. Of course this made sense in many ways, but if it went wrong, Labour could expect to suffer more than was already likely to be the case. In Dublin Rathdown, we knew there was a sizeable level of support for re-electing the government. So in addition to holding the Labour base vote (which we put at about 10 per cent) we sought to attract pro-government votes based on my reputation as an effective minister with a strong media profile.

As the campaign progressed, we made slow but steady progress on this strategy, or so we felt. It was difficult. Austerity fatigue was widespread. The impact of the economic crash was and is still being felt. Some of the losses people suffered in pensions, for example, may never be recovered. But the support was there for the government; we just needed some of it to come to me.

Although we will never know for sure, I think we shed votes during the course of the campaign. Indifferent performances in the leaders' debates marginalised us in a crowded and ill-tempered campaign, and we never seemed to cut through with a distinctive Labour message beyond the call to re-elect the government. That strategy was only ever going to work for us if it was combined with a strong campaign that emphasised Labour's separate identity and programme. We also needed to be far more aggressive in responding to the 'broken promises' attack line of our opponents, a line that was cheerfully echoed as a given in the broadcast media.

The battle within Fine Gael in Dublin Rathdown played out badly—for them and for me. In the closing hours of the campaign, a letter went out to key areas, co-signed by Enda Kenny and Brian Hayes, urging first preference votes for Josepha Madigan, and second preferences for Alan Shatter. This was stated to be the best way of securing the re-election of the government.

No one could expect Fine Gael to do anything other than look for votes for themselves, even if it was clear at this stage that there was no hope of two seats for that party, and that I was the better prospect for a second government seat. This had been our repeated message on the doorsteps, but a leaflet with the authority of the Taoiseach could only have the effect of reversing that narrative.

But it got worse. When Alan Shatter saw the Kenny/Hayes move he was enraged, and followed up with his own missive, telling voters that their No. 1 vote (for him) was vital, and that people should give Madigan No. 2 (naturally), and me No. 3. All this achieved was to consolidate the government vote around Fine Gael, but not in anything like sufficient numbers to win two seats. It effectively told anxious pro-government voters to give White their No. 3 vote, putting paid to any chance that the eventual impressive vote of 40 per cent for the government parties would deliver any more than a single seat.

Meanwhile, at the other end of the contest, Sinn Féin issued their own attack leaflet—'Alex White's real record in cabinet', attributing various social welfare and other cuts to me personally. The intended effect was to communicate an anyone-but-White message to Sinn Féin voters, ensuring that their transfers broke 4:1 between myself and Catherine Martin, the Green candidate.

So instead of having a decent margin ahead of the Green, I was level with her on the first count (actually 74 votes behind), and had no hope of surviving the Sinn Féin elimination.

My 9.8 per cent vote was one of our best performances nationally, but it was far from sufficient in this reduced three-seater, especially with the loss of Rathfarnham. The benefit of hindsight might tempt one to conclude I should have run in SW. But to change constituencies at the last minute (once Pat Rabbitte announced his retirement) would certainly have attracted criticism, and it would have meant facing into a campaign in a constituency where I had no connection at all with most of the electorate. Inevitably, too, it would have caused internal problems in the party organisation there. So, I think it was right to stick with the original decision.

Reflecting on the campaign now, it was a huge effort. We had a strong canvassing team, 70 people or more. We were first up with our posters. We were visible in the shopping centres. We went everywhere for votes. We did well on social media. I wasn't on national media much until the last couple of days, but my exposure had been extensive in recent years.

There was little or no personal hostility towards me. But in truth, the party brand was a negative. It was striking how often people would respond well initially, recognising me favourably, but would visibly turn sour when they realised I was Labour.

But I am Labour and proud. I take my own part of the responsibility for what happened in the election. I do so with sadness and disappointment at the outcome, but with real hope for the future. There is a place in Irish politics, and in the Dáil, for a centre-left party, one that is prepared to serve in government in the right circumstances.

I intend now to help re-build the party for the challenges and opportunities that lie ahead.

Grace O'Sullivan (Green Party, Seanad Election Candidate)

Grace O'Sullivan is a long-time environmental campaigner and worked for Greenpeace for almost twenty years. In 1985 she was a member of the crew of the Rainbow Warrior when it was bombed by the French secret service in Auckland, New Zealand. In February 2016 she stood for the Green party in the Waterford constituency, receiving 2,237 first preferences, the seventh highest of any Green candidate in the country, before going on to stand successfully in the Seanad election. In 1981 she was the first woman to become Ireland's national surfing champion.

I entered political life as a complete stranger to the process of running for election; as such I've had a fairly steep learning curve over the past two years. Before being convinced by Eamon Ryan to run in Ireland South in the European Parliament election of 2014, I had never contested any form of elected office. I was surrounded by politics, you could say—I spent many years actively campaigning with Greenpeace in Amsterdam, including several stints at sea; my sister is an elected Councillor on Waterford City and County Council—but I had never truly got involved with electioneering, least of all on my own behalf.

So coming off the back of a really successful attempt at becoming an MEP in 2014, and a short-but-intense run at the Dáil in February 2016, I expected the Seanad election to be a cooler, more measured, less stressful experience than the manic sprints those two previous contests proved to be. I was wrong!

In many ways my election to the 25th Seanad was an improbable success. I'm the first successful Green Party candidate at a Seanad general election in the party's 35-year history, and was not expected to win a seat. Coming into this election the Green Party had 12 elected councillors nationwide, and 2 recently elected TDs—not a large pool of votes to work from.

It also took some convincing for me to run. I had voted to retain the Seanad in the October 2013 referendum, but like so many No voters at that time, I voted not to retain the institution as it was designed, but for it to realise its full potential in the future. Becoming a member of an institution I saw as flawed and unrepresentative, through an electoral process that itself is closed-off and dominated by party elites, could be seen as hypocritical by some. In deciding to run, I had to make it clear publicly, and in all the conversations I had with potential supporters, that reform had to be an overriding goal of my time as a senator, if lucky enough to be elected.

Once the decision to contest was made, the task itself seemed daunting. I soon lost any assumptions of the Seanad electoral process being less intense than other elections. I immediately benefited, however, from the experienced hands of Roderic O'Gorman, the Green Party Chairman and a councillor in Fingal, and Patrick Costello, a Dublin city councillor. Together we set out to achieve what we thought of as an unlikely goal, but one we were very much willing to give our best efforts towards.

I also had the benefit of running for a party that was newly energised. The Greens had just achieved the rare feat of returning to the Dáil after losing all their seats in 2011. The party had been through almost ten years of extremely tense, often heart-breaking times. The year 2009 had seen the wipeout of councillors; 2011 cleaned out all TDs and senators. For those committed to the Green Party it was a very tough time. To make the situation worse, the vote in 2011 fell just below the 2 per cent necessary for any form of state financing. As corporate donations are not accepted by the party, this meant five years of relying on a small stream of personal donations and a huge amount of personal commitment and volunteerism, not least on the part of Eamon Ryan, but also several other key people.

The party had to fight hard in these circumstances in the 2014 elections, the first I contested as a Green. In the European elections, the party attained 4.9 per cent of the first preference vote, up by 3 per cent on 2009. Eamon Ryan came extremely close to winning a seat in Dublin, receiving

44,000 first preferences. This election proved there was a pulse in the party and an appetite amongst the electorate for Green policy and vision.

There was some cautious hope, therefore, going into the tough Dáil election in 2016—and that hope firmly rested on Eamon Ryan taking a seat in Dublin Bay South and others polling well enough to push the party over the 2 per cent nationwide first preference vote. In the event, Eamon wasn't to be the first Green elected to the Dáil on 26 February—Catherine Martin took the honour in Dublin Rathdown and was joined by him the next day. With two TDs, the election exceeded expectations and set up a 'fair wind' at our backs for the forthcoming Seanad election.

It was in this context that the party's National Executive Committee (NEC) opted to go for an internal contest to select a candidate to contest the Seanad election. My background working at sea, my experience advocating on behalf of coastal communities, my many years of environmental campaigning with Greenpeace, my work as an educational specialist with the Heritage Council, and my involvement in setting up a marine tourism business meant I had the experience and qualifications for a run on the Agricultural Panel, and I was selected by the NEC to run.

The 11-seat Agricultural Panel was also realistically the one I had the best chance of winning a seat on. My nomination to run as an 'inside' candidate was facilitated by the Labour Party and Sinn Féin, in addition to Catherine and Eamon's signatures.[3]

With the nomination secure, the business of vote canvassing and alliance-building got under way. This process is not normally one that is reported in great detail by the media, and is held at some remove from the public, so not many people are aware of the intensity of the horse-trading that must take place. This is especially true for small parties and independents. Indeed it was widely reported that at no Seanad election since 1973 (until this year) had an independent been elected to a vocational panel—such is the level of control that established political parties have had over the whole process. Very rarely have senators from small parties been elected in this way.

We faced intense competition. Like us, the newly established Social Democrats were fielding a very capable candidate on the Agricultural Panel in the form of Jennifer Whitmore, whom I knew. We knew that they would have to pursue the same strategy as us, targeting a lot of the same Independent councillors for their number 1 vote and working with other parties to trade preferences.

Many members of the Green Party, old and new, mobilised to help my campaign. Some veteran members campaigned actively on my behalf. Roderic, Patrick and I contacted hundreds of councillors by phone, and met very many in person. Each conversation had to be more than just a perfunctory transaction; we had to make the genuine effort to make a connection with each councillor we spoke with. And in so many cases, often to my surprise, we did. I recall one conversation in which the councillor spent several minutes breathlessly upbraiding me about the Greens never having made any kind of contact with him, before going on to have a very productive exchange and finishing with the promise of a number 1.

As with canvassing door-to-door in a Dáil election, any answer other than a solid commitment for a number 1 vote should be treated with caution. Even where a genuine connection was made over the phone or in person, it didn't often end with solid support. Councillors, having run for election themselves, tend to have the intelligence not to divulge their voting intentions straight away. So right down to count day, we had no clear picture of the true level of support I could rely on. This was true of most other candidates, too.

The count for the Agriculture Panel took place on the second day of the count, so I'd had the opportunity to watch the Cultural & Educational Panel being counted to get some understanding of the procedure. Roderic and I were initially disappointed with the 48 first preferences we received, as we did not think that it would be enough to see me through. However, as the counts progressed and I was picking up decent transfers, it also became clear that being on the 'inside' panel was playing hugely to my advantage. At least four senators had to be elected from this panel, and when Jennifer Whitmore was eliminated, there were only four remaining candidates from the inside panel left, including myself. However, I still had to wait a few hours for the actual declaration. As I waited, I recall walking passed an experienced Fianna Fáil operative who was saying to his colleague 'Jaysus, yer wan from the Greens is going to do it'. And like that, I was elected to the 25th Seanad, the first Green Party candidate elected in this way.

I write this on the same day the new Seanad is meeting for the first time—8 June 2016—and I'm happy to say that my first action as an elected Senator is to co-sponsor a major piece of reforming legislation. It goes without saying that I sincerely hope that the account of the election I've just written is among the last accounts in *How Ireland Voted* that will describe such an unrepresentative, closed process. The legislation I have joined my colleagues in bringing forward draws on the Manning Report[4] and seeks to bring in wide-scale reforms of the House that will open up the electoral process as wide as is currently possible under the constitution. Unfortunately, it's highly likely that the 25th Seanad will not last a complete five-year term, so the timescale to bring about change is small. Nevertheless, there is overwhelming support for radical reform and it is something I will devote all of my energies towards achieving.

Maureen O'Sullivan (Independent, Dublin Central)

Maureen O'Sullivan is a full-time public representative who was previously a secondary school teacher and guidance counsellor in north Dublin. She was a long-time member of the political organisation of Tony Gregory, who was an Independent TD for the area from 1982 until his death in 2009. In 2016 she was in seventh place on the first count in Dublin Central and received 1,900 first preferences (8 per cent of the votes) – the lowest first preference vote with which any candidate in the country was elected, taking a seat due to the high numbers of transfers she received from other candidates.

My first experience of electioneering came in 1979—the first election the late Tony Gregory stood in as an Independent candidate for the North Inner City. I had met him a few years before as we were both involved in voluntary work in the area—he with communities and me with young people. He asked would I support him in that local election, which I did, and that was the start of me and election campaigns. There were 14 in all with Tony, both general and local; the last one was the general election in 2007. He died in January 2009 and that brought me into standing in elections as the candidate, as opposed to supporting the candidate. I have been in three elections—the first in 2009 was the by-election caused by Tony's death, the second was the general election in 2011, the third was the general election of February 2016. Each campaign election has been coloured by and determined by the experience I had with Tony in those 14 elections.

The constituency of Dublin Central was changed as a result of the work of the constituency commission; it went from being a four-seat constituency to three seats. So that was the first major challenge, as one (and maybe more than one) of the four sitting TDs would lose a seat, so I was certainly not taking being re-elected for granted. I knew it was going to be difficult especially as the other TDs were quite high profile—a deputy leader of a political party, a cabinet minister, a former junior minister—the latter having been around a long time. There was also a candidate with a recent high profile as he was Lord Mayor of Dublin and he too had been around a long time. There was the challenge from Fianna Fáil; the constituency had been the home of the very high-profile Bertie Ahern and Fianna Fáil were determined to get a seat. They had none at all in Dublin after the death of Brian Lenihan. And there were other up and coming candidates. It would be a crowded field and only three seats. So, while I didn't feel it would be hopeless I knew it was going to be a major challenge and struggle.

I was pragmatic enough, having learned from Tony, to commission a poll about 6 months before the election was due. If the result from the poll, and I know they are not always to be totally relied on, had been negative I would have considered not standing again. However, the poll was optimistic enough showing that I had a chance. I shared the results with my group, known as The Gregory Group; we discussed it and also faced the idea and possibility that we would not keep the seat. I was prepared to stand. The consensus was to stand, to put everything into the campaign and run the campaign as we always did, twice already with me and all those times with Tony, in a dignified, good-humoured way. And we did. So the selection process was smooth for me.

We opted for the three-week campaign, meeting every evening at 6.30 but also mornings and afternoons. The one advantage of the constituency being reduced to three seats meant it was also a smaller constituency. We lost huge areas in Drumcondra, Glasnevin, Navan Road, Pelletstown. So, we did door-to-door canvassing—every door was knocked on. We had a detailed leaflet outlining some of the work I had been doing, issues I had been pursuing, meetings and groups I had been attending. There was also a card which was dropped into houses either before or after the door-to-door canvass. Dublin Central has a very significant number of gated communities—apartments and estates that make it difficult to canvass door-to-door. So the leaflet was posted to those. There were some 'meet the candidates' meetings but not as many as other times. I didn't do after-masses or shopping centres. There were a number of media appearances and I appeared on any programme I was invited on to—radio and television.

I do believe my website and use of social media were significant and that was probably the biggest difference for me from the two previous campaigns where I had not used social media. I had been supporting the Patrick O'Connell campaign which had brought me to Barcelona FC and I had a lovely message of support from them. And because of that work, Irish soccer legend Paddy Mulligan and Irish rugby legend Ollie Campbell endorsed my campaign. Like every campaign there were hiccups and difficulties but we kept our cool and our dignity, not getting involved in some of the petty issues that arose. I used posters, some from the previous campaigns, some new and some were 'as Gaeilge'. I have to say I generally enjoy canvassing. I like chatting with people, hearing their views and it is always great to meet people who remember Tony and want to talk about him. There will always be some negative reaction but on the whole we were very well received. We made very conscious efforts to engage on the preference issue so those who said they were voting for X candidate or Y candidate we asked for their number 2 or next highest preference and that paid off—to put it mildly!

My personal result initially, in terms of first preference votes, was disappointing. I was way down the field; so much so that the media had me written off from early afternoon. So I spent those hours from the tally and the first count experiencing a sense of loss. Obviously, I was disappointed and not just for myself but for the group. I came in to the count centre around 5, did an interview, as I had been asked, with Sorcha Ní Riada for TG4[5] and then went home to prepare for the group coming to my house for a drink and food. A few had stayed at the count—always interested in the numbers and transfers. At home, I had decided not to watch anything political—I would catch up on Sunday. I was unaware that those at the count centre were in touch with those in the house who then became aware that I was not out of the race yet but no one wanted to tell me—in case it would be a double disappointment.

Just before 10 we got the word that the contest for the last seat was down to two candidates, one of whom was me, and the suggestion was made that I should go back over to the count; at that stage, I might have been coming back over to concede defeat. I was at the traffic lights in Ballsbridge when I got a phone call asking where I was as I was about to be re-elected!!! Sweet to get messages and texts from journalists apologising for writing me off! Back on with Sorcha and this time congratulations instead of commiserations. Someone said if I were a race horse, I could be called 'Slow starter, strong finisher'.

I think that while I was not the first choice for many in the constituency there was enough recognition and respect to feature high in the transfers. And respect for the various issues I have been involved in during my time in the Dáil and also in the extensive voluntary work I had been doing all my life. I am not sure if any other person was elected coming from so far down after the first count. Having been re-elected would I do anything differently? Why? I believe social media will be increasingly more and more important but I would also always canvass door-to-door, going back to those where there was no answer.

Notes

1. In areas where it had no elected councillors or deputies after the 2011 election setback, Fianna Fáil appointed a number of 'local area representatives' to act as quasi-councillors.
2. Vincent Browne is a well-known journalist and broadcaster who, in the months before the election, organised debates in each of the 40 constituencies between the declared candidates. These debates were broadcast on the TV3 channel.
3. For an overview of the Seanad election system, including the significance of the distinction between 'inside' and 'outside' candidates, see pp. 231–2.
4. For the Manning Report, see Chapter 10, pp. 247–9.
5. The Irish-language television station.

CHAPTER 6

The Results Analysed: The Aftershocks Continue

Michael Gallagher

The 2011 election could reasonably be termed Ireland's 'earthquake election' because of the profound upheaval it delivered to the party system. The 2016 election in some ways marked a move back towards pre-2011 normality with the two traditional main parties reclaiming their places at the head of the pack, but in other ways it represented a further shift towards something different. If not exactly another earthquake, then the 2016 election was certainly a case of the aftershocks continuing. In this chapter, we analyse vote shifts and seat gains and losses, assess the performances of the parties, draw inferences from the pattern of vote transfers and assess the utility of the betting market as a results predictor. Finally, we analyse the composition of the new Dáil.

Votes, Seats and Candidates

A move back towards familiar ground was represented by the significant growth in support for Fianna Fáil, which was not far away from reclaiming its traditional pole position, and the drop in support for Fine Gael, whose 2016 level of support was much closer to its post-1982 norm than

M. Gallagher (✉)
Trinity College Dublin, Dublin, Ireland

© The Author(s) 2016
M. Gallagher, M. Marsh (eds.), *How Ireland Voted 2016*,
DOI 10.1007/978-3-319-40889-7_6

the 2011 peak was. The precipitate fall in Labour support could also be seen in this light, its 2016 support level being much closer to its historic average than its 2011 level was. Part of the very high level of volatility displayed at the election (see Chapter 12, especially Table 12.1) was due simply to the tide that had flowed in at the 2011 election ebbing in 2016.

However, in other ways, the 2016 result definitely did not mark any kind of return to pre-2011 normality. This is most evident in the historically low levels of support for the traditional parties and the concomitant high levels of fragmentation. Fianna Fáil and Fine Gael together, which have averaged around 72 per cent of the votes over the period since 1923 and won over 84 per cent of the votes as recently as 1982, now, for the first time ever, received the support of fewer than half of all voters. These two parties plus Labour, the three constant features of the party system, also dropped to a new nadir, just 56 per cent, compared with a long-term average of 84 per cent and a percentage in the 90s at all elections in the period 1965–82. The largest party, on this occasion Fine Gael, won just 26 per cent of the votes; only once previously had the largest party received fewer than 36 per cent of the votes, that being in June 1927, when Fine Gael's forerunner Cumann na nGaedheal achieved a plurality of votes with just 27 per cent.

This greater scatter of votes and seats among parties is captured by the concept of fragmentation, and specifically by the measure of 'the effective number of parties' devised by Laakso and Taagepera.[1] By this measure, the effective number of parties at electoral level (based on the distribution of votes) was 6.57 and the effective number at parliamentary level (based on the distribution of seats) was 4.93. Both of these are new records, the previous peaks, both from June 1927, being 5.73 and 4.85, respectively. This is broadly comparable to the picture in a number of European countries known for relatively high levels of fragmentation such as Denmark, Estonia, Finland, Latvia and Switzerland, and is very similar to the situation at recent elections in some post-communist countries such as Bulgaria, Moldova and Serbia. It also bears some resemblance to the pattern at Ireland's European Parliament (EP) elections, especially that of 2014. This 'Balkanisation' of the party system, and the absence of any party within striking distance of an overall majority, had obvious implications for the process of government formation, as discussed in detail in Chapter 11.

There was considerable geographical variation in the shape of the party system produced, especially between Dublin and the rest of the country.

Outside Dublin, Fine Gael and Fianna Fáil together won 54 per cent of the votes, but in the capital they received only 38 per cent. In three Dublin constituencies, all predominantly working class, they received fewer than 30 per cent of the votes between them, and in only one (the relatively prosperous Dun Laoghaire) did they reach 50 per cent. In the rest of the country, they exceeded 60 per cent in ten constituencies, though reached 70 per cent in only one, Mayo, which has a long tradition of above-average support for the two main parties.[2] Similarly, whereas outside Dublin they won 65 per cent of the seats, in the capital they took only 44 per cent. Fragmentation was especially high in some Dublin constituencies (8.94 in Dublin Bay North [N], 7.41 in Dublin South-Central [SC]) and in only one constituency, Mayo again, was it below 3, a clear sign of how far Ireland has moved from the old two-and-a-half party system.

The number of candidates, at 551, was the second highest ever, just below the peak of 2011 and, given that the size of the Dáil had been reduced by eight seats, this represented an even higher ratio of candidates to seats. Fianna Fáil, Fine Gael and Labour between them reduced their candidate numbers by 52, but Sinn Féin's nominations were up, a number of new parties appeared, and there were numerous independents and representatives of smaller groups.

As at every election, most candidates' campaigns ended in disappointment. A plurality failed to reach the level of support required to qualify for reimbursement of expenses, and over a quarter (145) received less than 1000 first preferences. The ratio of votes to members of parliament remains low by comparative standards, around 13,600 to 1, one reason for the strong links between TDs (members of the Dáil) and their constituents in Ireland. The median number of first preferences with which a TD was elected was around 7800; only two candidates received more votes than this without being elected, while at the other end of the scale 13 candidates were elected with fewer than 5000 first preferences, the lowest of all being the 1990 received by Maureen O'Sullivan in Dublin Central (see her account in Chapter 5). As in 2011, the tipping point for success lay in the band between 0.5 and 0.6 Droop quotas (for explanation of the Droop quota, see Appendix 4, p. 309). Around half (56 per cent) of those whose first preference total fell within this band were elected. In contrast, only 23 per cent of those whose first preferences amounted to between 0.4 and 0.5 of the quota (and just two of the 335 with less than this) were elected, while 88 per cent of those with between 0.6 and 0.7 of the quota (and 90 of the 93 with more than this) were elected.

Normally, the higher a candidate's position on the political greasy pole, the better they fare: cabinet ministers do best, non-ministerial incumbent TDs less well, senators and county councillors less well still, and those without any elective status worst of all.[3] That pattern was disrupted in 2011 by the intensity of the ire directed at the outgoing government, as a result of which those cabinet and junior ministers who did not prudently retire actually fared less well than other TDs. In 2016, cabinet ministers returned to their usual position as the most successful group, though two (James Reilly and Alex White) were defeated, but junior ministers did not do as well as non-ministerial TDs; eight, five from Labour and three from Fine Gael, were defeated against only seven who were re-elected. Among senators and councillors, only a minority were elected, but candidates in these categories fared far better than those with no elected status, among whom the great majority did not qualify for reimbursement of expenses (see Table 6.1). Only two such candidates, Dr. Michael Harty (Ind) in Clare and Louise O'Reilly (Sinn Féin) in Dublin Fingal, were elected. As in 2011, it is clear that even if many voters wanted different faces in the Dáil, they wanted those to be known and reasonably familiar faces rather than brand new ones.

Recent Irish elections have displayed a growing disparity between party vote shares (based on first preferences) and party seat shares. The 2002 election produced the highest level of disproportionality seen to that date, and this figure was exceeded in 2011, when Fine Gael won 76 seats and Fianna Fáil only 20, against the 60 and 30 that would have been proportionate to those parties' respective first preference vote shares. The 2016 outcome was more proportional than either of those two cases, with a score of 5.62 on the widely used least squares index. This is still the fifth highest level of disproportionality ever produced at an Irish election, reflecting the over-representation of the largest two parties: Fine Gael and Fianna Fáil, with a fraction under 50 per cent of the votes between them, received 59 per cent of the 157 contested seats, while all parties, groups and candidates who each received fewer than 4 per cent of the votes won 30 per cent of the votes collectively but only 22 per cent of the seats. However, the 2016 disproportionality figure was very similar to the level seen at some previous elections such as those of 1943, 1944, 1948, 1969, 1987 or 2007, and is comparable to levels typical of Europe's middle-ranking countries on this measure such as the Czech Republic, Poland, Portugal or Spain. The over-representation of the larger parties is not surprising given the high degree of fragmentation and in particular the significant number of votes cast for candidates with little or no chance

Table 6.1 Fate of candidates at 2016 election

	Number	Average vote	Average Droop quotas	% elected	% not elected but qualifying for reimbursement of expenses	% not qualifying for reimbursement of expenses
All candidates	551	3871	0.36	28	30	42
Fine Gael	88	6184	0.57	58	35	9
Fianna Fáil	71	7315	0.67	62	35	3
Sinn Féin	50	5906	0.56	46	52	2
Labour	36	3914	0.37	19	61	19
Green Party	40	1450	0.14	5	18	77
AAA–PBP	31	2715	0.26	19	23	58
Soc Dems	14	4578	0.47	21	57	21
Renua	26	1790	0.17	0	27	73
Others	195	1950	0.18	12	16	72
Cabinet minister	15	7889	0.78	87	13	0
Junior minister	15	6760	0.60	47	53	0
Non-ministerial TD	115	7229	0.67	67	29	4
Senator	20	4931	0.45	35	40	25
County councillor	155	4497	0.42	31	51	18
Former TD	5	6370	0.60	60	40	0
None of the above	226	1125	0.10	1	15	84
Male	389	4115	0.38	31	28	41
Female	162	3285	0.32	22	35	44

Note: Candidates qualify for reimbursement of campaign expenses, up to a specified limit, provided their vote total at some stage of the count reaches a quarter of the Droop quota (for explanation of the Droop quota, see Appendix 4). Voting figures refer to first preference votes. 'County councillor' refers to those candidates who at the time of the election were members of a county or city council. 'Former TD' category is applied only to those former TDs with no current elected status.

of election: candidates with fewer than 2000 first preferences collectively received almost 8 per cent of the total votes or, to look at it another way, candidates whose first preferences amounted to less than a quarter of a quota collectively won over 12 per cent of the votes. Their 'share' of the seats was inevitably going to be taken by candidates who started from a stronger position, benefiting the larger parties.

Finally, we should note that turnout was down on the 2011 figure, perhaps not surprisingly given the high levels of anger present in 2011. It fell to 65 per cent (valid votes as a percentage of electorate), and the number of votes cast dropped by almost 90,000. Turnout has been in the band from 62 per cent to 69 per cent at every election since the late 1980s, and the 2016 election was not exceptional in that regard. There is considerable scepticism about the accuracy of the electoral register, which is widely believed to contain the names of many people who should not be there because they have emigrated, moved away or died, so it would be unwise to attach too much weight to moderate movements in the recorded level of turnout.

Party Performances

Much as in 2011, the headline story was of calamitous losses for the two government parties and gains for everyone else. There were a few differences, most notably that, as the subtitle of the book spells out, nobody really 'won' the election. The main government party this time, Fine Gael, did not lose votes on quite the same scale as Fianna Fáil had in 2011, and it retained its position as the country's largest party. In addition, while all of the opposition parties recorded gains, none of them made anything like the advances that both Fine Gael and Labour did in 2011, and several of them had cause to be disappointed with their performance, though they were reluctant to admit this (see Table 6.2).

Fine Gael

Fine Gael maintained its position as the largest party in the country, and its leader Enda Kenny became the first Fine Gael Taoiseach to be re-elected to a second consecutive term. That was more or less where the good news ended for Fine Gael, though, as the party did worse than almost anyone had expected. The severity of its setback was to some extent overshadowed by Labour's even more spectacular collapse, but the figures are stark.

Table 6.2   Result of 2016 election, with changes since 2011

	% vote	Change since 2011	Seats	Change since 2011	% seats
Fine Gael	25.5	−10.6	49	−27	31.2
Fianna Fáil	24.3	+6.9	44	+25	28.0
Sinn Féin	13.8	+3.9	23	+9	14.6
Labour	6.6	−12.8	7	−30	4.5
AAA–PBP	3.9	+1.2	6	+1	3.8
Social Democrats	3.0	+3.0	3	+3	1.9
Green Party	2.7	+0.9	2	+2	1.3
Renua	2.2	+2.2	0	0	0.0
Independents and others	17.8	+5.3	23	+9	14.6
Total	100.0	0	157	−8	100.0

Note: For detailed results, see Appendix 1. Table refers to contested seats; Fine Gael also won the one uncontested seat (automatic re-election of Ceann Comhairle), giving it 50 seats out of 158 in the 32nd Dáil. For AAA–PBP the 2011 comparator is the ULA, although three of the five TDs elected for the ULA in 2011 were re-elected in 2016 under different labels

Fine Gael won just 26 per cent of the votes, almost 11 points down on its 2011 performance. It lost all the vote gains it made in 2011, and in fact over the entire period going back to 1951 Fine Gael has only twice (in 1992 and 2002) won a lower share of the votes than it did in 2016. Due to generally good vote management (see later section) and the advantage that usually accrues to the larger party, Fine Gael was somewhat over-represented in relation to its votes, but even at that its total of 50 left it only 6 seats ahead of Fianna Fáil, in contrast to the 56-seat gap between the two in 2011. Its loss of 26 seats is the largest inter-election loss it has ever sustained.

Fine Gael lost votes in every region of the country, but it fared worst in rural areas (the large-scale redrawing of constituency boundaries between the two elections makes detailed constituency-by-constituency comparison impossible). It lost almost 12 per cent of the votes outside Dublin, but in the capital, where it remains comfortably the strongest party, its vote dropped by only 7 per cent. It won at least one seat in every Dublin constituency, even in Dublin North-West (NW), where it had last won a seat in 1992. Only in the most middle-class Dublin constituencies (Dublin Bay South [S], Dublin Rathdown and Dun Laoghaire) did its vote exceed 30 per cent, while in the least middle-class ones (Dublin Central, Dublin NW and Dublin SC) it attracted fewer than 15 per cent of the votes. Its comparatively modest vote losses in Dublin may reflect the lack of appealing alternatives for erstwhile Fine Gael voters, given that they were unlikely to switch to Sinn Féin, the AAA–PBP or left-wing independents. Outside Dublin, though, the independents on offer were more acceptable to former Fine Gael voters, and in a number of constituencies (Cork South-West [SW], Galway East [E] and Longford–Westmeath) Independent TDs directly took a seat from Fine Gael. The government's legalisation of abortion in certain limited circumstances in 2013 prompted protests from anti-abortion groups, and at mass rallies opponents pledged never to vote for Fine Gael again. The possibility that this cost the party votes in rural areas, where attitudes on this issue are more conservative, is consistent with its larger losses in rural areas, but there is no sign that the party suffered a particular loss of anti-abortion support in 2016. According to the 2016 RTÉ exit poll, the attitudes towards abortion of those who voted for Fine Gael in 2011 and those who voted for it in 2016 were almost identical; on a 10-point scale, where 0 is the most conservative position and 10 the most liberal, the party's 2011 supporters averaged 5.76 and its 2016 supporters averaged 5.84.[4] Moreover, only 2 per cent of those sampled by the poll declared abortion to be the most important issue.

Nationwide, Fine Gael undoubtedly lost some votes to Fianna Fáil, hardly surprising given the 2011 plea of Fine Gael's then director of elections Phil Hogan to Fianna Fáil voters to 'lend' Fine Gael their vote for that one election. In 2016, some of these votes returned to their natural home. Fine Gael's anti-Downsian abandonment of the centre ground,[5] by promising tax cuts that simply firmed up its support among the better off who were intending to vote for the party anyway, handed this terrain to Fianna Fáil, which took full advantage. As a result, Fine Gael not only lost votes but also the profile of its support base had a markedly sharper middle-class bias than in 2011 (see Chapter 7).

Altogether 21 Fine Gael TDs were defeated, on top of the 6 who retired and the 5 who had left Fine Gael between the 2011 and 2016 elections. The party was left without any representation in two constituencies: Roscommon–Galway and, more surprisingly, Tipperary, which with its plethora of large farmers seems to present the ideal demographic base for the party. On the positive side, it had eight new and relatively young TDs elected, four of them female. With just a few additional votes it could have taken seven additional seats (it came particularly close in Dublin SW, Limerick City and Longford–Westmeath), though it is true that a loss of just a few votes would have cost it five seats, its most marginal seats being Dublin

Bay S, Louth and Wexford. After the 2011 election, Fine Gael appeared to have a real chance of becoming the dominant party in the Irish party system, building a cross-class support base and establishing itself as the main actor in most governments, but its 2016 performance brought its aspirations back down to earth.

Fianna Fáil

After the 1989 election, a fresh-faced 28-year-old Micheál Martin took his place as a new backbencher in the Fianna Fáil parliamentary party. The mood in the party was chastened, as for the fifth election in a row Fianna Fáil had failed to win an overall majority; it received a disappointing 44 per cent of the votes and won only 77 seats, a performance that weakened the position of leader Charles J. Haughey to the point where only by breaking with his party's previously unequivocal opposition to the notion of participation in a coalition government was he able to remain as leader for a few more years. Three years later, things got even worse. While Martin himself was comfortably re-elected at the 1992 election, the party's vote slipped further to a calamitous 39 per cent, the first time it had dipped below 40 per cent since the 1920s, and with only 68 seats its leader Albert Reynolds was compelled to agree a 'partnership' government with Labour that gave the smaller party more cabinet seats than any junior coalition partner had had before. Both Haughey and Reynolds would have raised a quizzical eyebrow to learn that one of their little-known backbenchers would practically be doing a lap of honour and be hailed as a saviour a quarter of century later after leading the party into an election where it received 24 per cent of the votes and won 44 seats. That this was exactly how Fianna Fáil's election result was received reflected how far expectations had changed following the collapse of the party's support in 2011.

Compared with the party's losses in 2011, when its support level more than halved, its gains in 2016 could be seen as less than stellar: it picked up around one additional vote for every three it had won in 2011 and was still about 20 percentage points below its normal level during the 1932–2007 period. Its seat gains were altogether more impressive, as it more than doubled its Dáil representation despite a slight reduction in the size of the Dáil. It achieved this partly by a more adroit and hard-nosed candidate strategy, matching its numbers of candidates to its expected level of support and being prepared to ruffle some local feathers if necessary (see Chapters 3 and 4), but the main reason for its gaining so many additional seats despite an only modest increase in its votes was simply that it had been hugely under-represented in 2011.[6] On that occasion, based on its first preference votes, the party would have earned 30 seats on a proportional basis instead of the 20 it actually won, so even without winning any extra votes the party could reasonably have expected to gain ten or so seats in 2016. If seats were awarded to parties based solely on the number of votes they win nationally, Fianna Fáil would have advanced from 30 seats in 2011 to 38 seats in 2016, an altogether less dramatic advance than that from 20 to 44. In that sense the 2011 debacle had a silver lining, making the 2016 performance look all the better.

There is still a major difference between the party's performance in the capital and in the rest of the country. Outside Dublin, Fianna Fáil was the strongest party, taking 27 per cent of the votes and winning exactly a third of the seats (38 out of 114). It was the largest party in 15 of the 29 constituencies, compared with none in 2011, and won at least one seat in all of these constituencies, taking two seats in nine of them. In two constituencies (Kildare N and Sligo–Leitrim), it advanced from no seats in 2011 to two in 2016. While there are still areas of weakness—there were five constituencies where it received fewer than 20 per cent of the votes—the party could be well satisfied with its performance outside the capital. In Dublin, though, things were different. Its vote advanced only marginally, from 12 per cent to 15 per cent, and in only one Dublin constituency did it even reach 20 per cent of the votes. It won six of the 44 seats in Dublin, giving it some presence there after the death in June 2011 of Brian Lenihan had left it without any TDs in Dublin, but Dublin remains a problem area for the party.

Overall, Fianna Fáil was understandably very pleased with its performance. After the 2011 election, it found itself 56 seats behind Fine Gael and only just ahead of Sinn Féin. For much of the period between the two elections, the party was not showing any growth in the polls over its 2011 level, and it risked being made irrelevant as Fine Gael and Sinn Féin seemed to be tacitly colluding in framing the election as a choice between a Fine Gael-led government or a Sinn Féin-led government. In that context, its performance in 2016 could hardly have been better. It took full advantage of Fine Gael's abandonment of the centre ground, closed the gap with Fine Gael to just six seats, and won almost twice as many seats as Sinn Féin. The party remains a long way short of its pre-2008 dominant position within the party system, but it remains a significant force and some of the less restrained rhetoric from its opponents in 2011, such as 'devouring the Fianna Fáil carcass' or 'dancing on Fianna Fáil's grave', greatly under-estimated its resilience.

Sinn Féin

For Sinn Féin, the 2016 election outcome might seem to be one of pretty much unalloyed success. The party won only four seats in 2007, advanced to 14 in 2011 and made further impressive gains in 2016, finishing with 23 seats in a smaller Dáil. Having had less than half as many TDs as Labour in 2007 and 2011, it now has over three times as many as Labour, and the Fine Gael-led minority government with external 'facilitation' by Fianna Fáil that was put together after the election (see Chapter 11) left Sinn Féin as potentially the dominant voice on the opposition benches. Unlike the AAA–PBP, a rival on the left of the political spectrum, its support is not confined to the major urban areas; its support ranges between 11 per cent and 16 per cent in the four regions (see Table A1.2). Eleven of its seats were won in urban constituencies in Cork, Dublin, Limerick and Waterford, with a further five in border constituencies, but it also saw new TDs elected in predominantly rural constituencies such as Carlow–Kilkenny, Cork E and Offaly. Most of its new TDs had stood for the party in both 2007 and 2011, gradually building up a base, and all but one were either councillors or senators. Its twelve new TDs included five women, building on its 2014 EP election success when three of its four MEPs elected on the island were female, which along with the relative youthfulness of all its new TDs enables the party to convey an image far removed from the whiff of cordite still hanging around some of its veteran figures. Its new TDs include Eoin Ó Broin, described as 'a leading Sinn Féin strategist', in Dublin MW; Carol Nolan in Offaly, who is completing a PhD at NUI Galway; and Donnchadh Ó Laoghaire, a law graduate from University College Cork (see his account in Chapter 5).[7]

All that said, Sinn Féin's performance was decidedly at the lower end of expectations. Its eventual vote share of 14 per cent was well below its poll standings at times during the inter-election period; it averaged 19 per cent in inter-election polls, it stood at 20 per cent or more in 51 of the 137 inter-election polls, and on two occasions, in October 2014 and February 2015, polls recorded its support at 26 per cent (see Fig. 1.1).[8] In contrast, its 2016 election vote marks only an incremental improvement over its 2011 level of 10 per cent. In this, its performance mirrored that of the 2011 presidential election, when its candidate Martin McGuinness also received just under 14 per cent of the votes having appeared during the campaign to be doing much better than this. With Labour's vote share dropping by 13 per cent, Sinn Féin would have been expected to grow by more than it did. In 2016, Sinn Féin had strong expectations of making seat gains that did not materialise: at least two and possibly three seats in Donegal, second seats in Cavan–Monaghan, Dublin SC and Dublin SW, and seats in Dublin Bay S, Dublin W, Galway W, Longford–Westmeath, Mayo and Wexford. On the positive side, the party came close to winning four of these seats (in Donegal, Dublin W, Longford–Westmeath and Wexford), while only one of its own seats, that in Offaly, was narrowly won. In these and other constituencies, the party can realistically believe that 'one more push' would take it up to or beyond the 30-seat mark, but its opponents would prefer to believe that the party's rather anti-climactic result may mean that it has peaked, a perception reinforced by an unexpected drop in the Sinn Féin vote in the Northern Ireland Assembly elections in early May 2016.

Labour

The wrath of the electorate is felt by at least one party at most elections. In 1997, Labour was first in the firing line, dropping 9 percentage points and losing 16 seats; in 2002, Fine Gael lost 23 seats and some doubted whether it had a future; and in 2011, Fianna Fáil lost a staggering 58 seats and its share of the votes fell by 24 percentage points. In 2016, once again Labour's number was up. It lost two-thirds of its 2011 support, falling from over 19 per cent to below 7 per cent, and lost over four-fifths of its seats, plummeting from 37 to just 7. This was near enough the party's worst ever result; it won a slightly smaller vote share (though more seats) in both 1933 and 1987, and the same number of seats, seven, in 1932, though in a slightly smaller Dáil and with a higher vote share. This low point was all the more painful because it followed the party's record high at the previous election, which owed partly to its lacerating criticisms of the Fianna Fáil-led government's spending cuts and tax increases. When Labour in government implemented policies not so very different from those against which it had inveighed while in opposition, this caused a degree of dissatisfaction among its erstwhile supporters; having sown the wind in 2011, it reaped the whirlwind in 2016.

Labour's gains and losses tend to be magnified in Dublin, and so it was on this occasion. In 2011, its share of the vote had advanced by 15 points compared with 9 across the country as a whole, and in 2016 its strength in Dublin fell back by 21 points (from 29 per cent to 9 per cent) compared with 13 per cent in the whole country. In 2011, it had exceeded 20 per cent of the votes in 20 constituencies, but in 2016 its strongest performance was only 15 per cent (Dublin W) and it reached 10 per cent of the votes in just eight constituencies. Of the 37 Labour TDs elected in 2011, 4 had left the party by the time of the election (2 became Independents, 1 co-founded the Social Democrats, 1 joined Fianna Fáil), and a further 7 stood down, leaving just 26 incumbents seeking re-election, of whom 19 were defeated. At least the party was not decapitated, as both its leader Joan Burton and deputy leader Alan Kelly were re-elected, along with its most senior minister (and soon-to-be leader) Brendan Howlin, another cabinet minister Jan O'Sullivan, and a junior minister with leadership ambitions, Seán Sherlock. The disadvantage of this, though, was that its case in the months after the election had to be made by the leading figures in the government that had been rejected, whereas in 2011 the departure of most of Fianna Fáil's ministers not only removed the most unpopular figures from the scene but also opened the way for new faces.

As usual when a party does very badly, it is possible to make an argument that it will not survive much longer. The case for Labour's demise would point not just to its record-low support levels but also to the unprecedented degree of competition it now faces on the left of the spectrum, an area of policy space that until recently it had more or less to itself. Now it lags well behind Sinn Féin, which has over three times its seat numbers, and unlike other parties to have overtaken Labour in the past is well implanted and not a 'flash' party. Labour is also a target for the AAA–PBP, whose election literature declared that it wants 'to replace the Labour Party'. On the more moderate left, the Social Democrats, on their first outing, won nearly half as many votes as Labour, and some have speculated about Labour's possibly having to merge with this smaller party into some kind of new 'Progressive Alliance' relying more upon middle-class public sector workers than upon the traditional working class. Moreover, whereas in the past, the trade unions constituted a kind of bedrock for Labour that ensured it would not fade away like such past actors as the Farmers Party, National Centre Party, Clann na Talmhan, Clann na Poblachta or the Progressive Democrats (each of which outpolled Labour at one election) no matter how bad any short-term setback might be, these days the union movement's loyalties are decidedly split and the leaders of some unions that still back Labour have come under pressure from more militant members to break the link with the party. Even so, both Fianna Fáil post-2011 and Fine Gael post-1987 have shown that a party with a history going back decades has a resilience that inures it against most shocks. Labour was the fourth-placed party in the 2016 election, but while it is usually third, and attained the silver medal position in 2016, being fourth is not a new experience; it occupied this position also in 1923, 1933, 1944, 1948 and 1987. The challenges facing the party are considerable, but given the high volatility displayed at recent elections the prospect of a return to the party's 'normal' level of around 10 per cent is far from unrealistic.

Anti-Austerity Alliance–People Before Profit

The AAA–PBP, which came into being in autumn 2015 as an alliance of two small left-wing groups, won almost 4 per cent of the votes and elected six TDs, just one fewer than Labour. It outpolled Labour in Dublin and in Cork City, though was much weaker in rural areas than in the cities. Besides the seats it won, it was not far off additional seats in Dublin Bay N and Limerick City. Of its six TDs, only one, Richard Boyd Barrett, had been elected for the left-wing alliance put together for the 2011 election, which was named the United Left Alliance (ULA). Two of the others, Paul Murphy and Ruth Coppinger, had become TDs during the lifetime of the 31st Dáil by winning by-elections, while the other three were first-time TDs with a strong local council base built up over a number of years. The ULA disintegrated after the 2011 election, with the Socialist Party/ AAA withdrawing in January 2013. At the 2016 election, three of its other four TDs (apart from Boyd Barrett) were re-elected, but as independents. The two component parts of the alliance ran against each other in only three constituencies, and their overall vote totals were almost identical. However, each retained its separate identity, and indeed they disagreed over whether to sign up to the 'Right 2 Change' platform that centred on opposition to water charges. PBP did so but the AAA refused to follow suit because of Sinn Féin's participation and that party's refusal to rule out absolutely the possibility of coalition with Fianna Fáil, Fine Gael or Labour. The fissiparous nature of past left-wing alliances suggests that, even if its most prominent figures are around for many years to come, the AAA–PBP alliance itself may not be a long-lasting feature of the political landscape.

Others

Three smaller parties also won more than 2 per cent of the votes, the threshold for qualifying for public finance. Of these, the Social Democrats fared best. Their three incumbents were re-elected, each of them heading the poll and exceeding the quota on first preferences. The party came close to winning a fourth seat through Gary Gannon in Dublin Central. Moreover, whereas most candidates of all the other smaller groups polled poorly, only a fifth of the Social Democrats' candidates failed to qualify for reimbursement of expenses (Table 6.1). On average, each Social Democrat candidate won more votes than the average Labour candidate. The Social Democrat label was evidently worth something in its own right. In their first election, as already noted, the Social Democrats won half as many votes as Labour with its 100-year history. That said, each member of its leadership troika was a high-profile TD and would have polled strongly as an Independent; indeed, the RTÉ exit poll found that 78 per cent of Social Democrat voters said the candidate was more important than the party in determining how they cast their first preference vote, a higher figure than for any other party except Renua (see further discussion of this in Chapter 7). Unlike, say, the Progressive Democrats in 1987, the Social Democrat label in 2016 did not secure the election of anyone who would not have been elected anyway. The party started well, but sustaining an initial momentum has proved too difficult for many smaller parties in the past, and the departure of joint leader Stephen Donnelly in September 2016 emphasised the challenge involved in creating a new party.

The Green Party won six seats at the elections of 2002 and 2007, but its presence in government when the Irish economy went over the edge of the cliff in 2008 cost it dearly and it lost all its seats in 2011. Given the party's reliance on a broad outlook concerned with the environment, the continued relevance of concerns about climate change and the existence of comparable parties in pretty much every other European country, most observers expected the party to remain in existence and to make some kind of comeback, whereas small parties whose appeal is dependent on a few high-profile individuals are less likely to survive such a setback. The Greens showed that they were neither gone nor forgotten when their leader Eamon Ryan narrowly missed taking a seat in Dublin at the May 2014 EP elections, and the green shoots of recovery were unmistakeable in 2016. The party won two seats in adjacent constituencies in the well-heeled suburbs of south Dublin, both Ryan and deputy leader Catherine Martin winning a good first preference vote and proving themselves to be very transfer-friendly, long a characteristic of Green candidates.

As in 2011, the party ran a candidate in every constituency in order to boost its chances of reaching the 2 per cent threshold needed to qualify for public funding. Whereas other parties have a pool of candidates prepared to build up their strength over a period of time, the archetypal Green candidate is a first-time (and last-time) contestant who has no hope of being elected to the Dáil, or even qualifying for reimbursement of expenses, and no intention of making the commitment needed to become a councillor. Of the party's forty candidates, only seven had stood in 2011; on past form, most of the others are likely to disappear from the lists at the next election and be succeeded by a fresh batch of sacrificial lambs. A higher proportion of Green candidates than of any other group's candidates failed to reach the level to qualify for reimbursement of expenses, and only eight of the forty even managed to attract as many as 2000 first preferences. Still, the cumulative effect of their support was that the party exceeded the 2 per cent threshold that it had narrowly failed to reach in 2011, and thus qualified for public funding, putting an end to five years of operation on a financial shoestring.

The future of these two parties certainly looks brighter than that of Renua Ireland. The party's leadership came, as outlined in Chapter 1, from four Fine Gael Oireachtas members who lost the party whip in the summer of 2013 because they voted against government legislation that legalised abortion in certain restrictive circumstances. Having procrastinated about forming a party and seeming to test the water with proto-party names such as 'Reform Alliance' or 'Reboot Ireland', Renua Ireland was finally launched in March 2015. In its keenness to avoid being labelled as a single-issue anti-abortion party, though, it played down the salience of this issue, and indeed its 74-page election manifesto made no mention of it at all, not even through coded references such as 'protection of life'. This dogged insistence on avoiding the issue that, more than any other, seemed to galvanise potential supporters was reflected in a very disappointing electoral performance. All of its outgoing TDs, including party leader Lucinda Creighton, who just a few years earlier had been seen as a possible future leader of Fine Gael and Taoiseach, lost their seats, and only one other candidate, John Leahy in Laois, came anywhere close to election. Seventeen of its 26 candidates polled fewer than 2000 first preferences and only seven qualified for reimbursement of election expenses as, in contrast to the position with the Social Democrats, the 'Renua Ireland' label did not seem to confer any electoral benefit. In the immediate aftermath of the election, the party bravely declared that it would learn from the setback and remain in the fray, but it would be a surprise if Renua was anything more than a footnote to accounts of early twenty-first-century Irish political history.

A number of other smaller groups also ran candidates: Direct Democracy Ireland, which favours the introduction of citizen-initiated referendums, ran 19 candidates, but only 1 gathered even as many as 1000 first preferences; the Workers Party, which last had a TD elected in 1989, ran five candidates, who received just over 3000 votes between them; three candidates stood for the Catholic Democrats, opposed to any liberalisation of laws on abortion, but none reached even 700 first preferences; and the Communist Party of Ireland ran just one candidate, choosing to stand in Cork North-West, perhaps the most conservative constituency in the country, where it received precisely 185 first preference votes.

Finally, as always in Irish elections, there were a large number of independent candidates and a record number of independent TDs, a remarkable 23 in all. One in every six votes was cast for an independent candidate. As discussed in more detail in Chapter 9, for many voters the very notion of an independent candidate, who promises to prioritise the interests of the constituency rather than of a party, is innately appealing, even if critics are inclined to raise the objection that parties provide some answer, even if an imperfect one, to the collective action problem whereas independents provide none. Within the independents, there were several distinct groups. The only one to secure official recognition and hence have its name on the ballot paper was 'Independents 4 Change', which ran just five candidates, four of them incumbent TDs; one had been elected in 2011 for Labour, two for the ULA, and one as an independent. All four incumbents were re-elected. Twenty-one independents formed an informal grouping, that deliberately had no policy platform, known as the 'Independent Alliance', led by the patrician south Dublin TD Shane Ross, whose photograph appeared on the election literature of many candidates in the alliance. It started with four incumbents, all of whom were re-elected, and they were joined by two newcomers. The other 13 independent TDs were sole traders, though 2 of these, the Healy-Rae brothers in Kerry, stood as a team and won so many votes that had they run a third family member they might have succeeded in having all 3 elected (see Chapter 9 for a fuller account).

Most independent candidates had never stood for a party, but some had, and indeed a few had been party TDs before jumping ship and flying under the flag of independence. Many years ago, Peter Mair concluded that candidates elected for a party who subsequently stand as independents discover that 'there is not much life outside party'.[9] In the years since then, though, a number of former party TDs have thrived as independents (see Chapter 9). In 2016, it was noticeable that almost all of the six TDs who abandoned Fine Gael did indeed fare poorly: Seán Conlan and

Peter Mathews both failed even to qualify for reimbursement of expenses, and the three TDs who formed Renua (Lucinda Creighton, Terence Flanagan and Billy Timmins) also lost their seats, leaving just one, Denis Naughten, who was re-elected. Those who left Labour did rather better: two—Tommy Broughan as an independent and Róisín Shortall of the Social Democrats—were re-elected, while in contrast Éamonn Maloney polled very poorly and Colm Keaveney, who took the unusual though not unprecedented step of switching from Labour to Fianna Fáil, also lost his seat. Abandoning a party, even one suffering a loss of popularity, is a high-risk strategy.

VOTE MANAGEMENT AND INTRA-PARTY COMPETITION

How many seats a party wins in any given constituency is determined primarily by how many votes its candidates win, but sometimes it can also be affected by how these votes are distributed among the candidates. If a party is aiming for, say, two seats, then it has the best chance of achieving this if its two leading candidates have, as near as possible, the same number of votes. Specifically, they should have the same number of votes on the final count, not necessarily in first preferences; if one candidate is less transfer-friendly than the other, for example because his or her base is in a geographically peripheral part of the constituency, then it is best if that candidate starts some way ahead of his or her running mate, who will catch up during the course of the count by receiving more transfers. Parties are best advised not simply to give their candidates free rein and hope for the best; rather, they estimate, based on constituency polling or on more impressionistic methods, the relative strengths of their candidates and try to 'manage' the votes. Typically, this takes the form of 'dividing' the constituency among the candidates, awarding each one sole canvassing rights within each area, and/or requesting voters in different parts of the constituency to rank the party's candidates in a specific order. For example, in the Clontarf area of the Dublin Bay N constituency, Fine Gael asked voters to give their first preference to Naoise Ó Muirí and their second preference to incumbent minister Richard Bruton (see Fig. 6.1). In 2011, Fine Gael had won a number of seats due to excellent management of its votes.[10]

Vote management is not a simple top-down process. For one thing, given the increasing fluidity of voting intentions, parties may well not have the detailed street-level knowledge needed to be sure how many votes they should try to channel or in what direction. Moreover, attempts to

AN IMPORTANT MESSAGE
TO GOVERNMENT SUPPORTERS
FROM BRIAN HAYES MEP
Fine Gael National Director of Elections

FINE GAEL ★

Dear Clontarf voter,

May I first take the opportunity to thank you for the courtesy and support you have shown to our candidates and their canvassing teams over the last number of weeks.

If the Government is to be re-elected it is vital that Fine Gael secures two seats in Dublin Bay North. Recent opinion poll research has shown that we can do this, but that we will need to manage our vote.

I am appealing to all supporters of the Government parties in the Clontarf area to vote

NUMBER 1 Naoise Ó MUIRÍ, to vote **NUMBER 2 Richard BRUTON**, and to vote **NUMBER 3 Stephanie REGAN**.

★ FINE GAEL	BRUTON, Richard (Fine Gael)		2
★ FINE GAEL	Ó MUIRÍ, Naoise (Fine Gael)		1
★ FINE GAEL	REGAN, Stephanie (Fine Gael)		3

Brian Hayes
National Director of Elections

Enda Kenny TD
An Taoiseach

LET'S KEEP THE RECOVERY GOING

THIS IS AN OFFICIALLY AUTHORISED VOTER REQUEST ISSUED BY THE FINE GAEL DIRECTOR OF ELECTIONS IN DUBLIN BAY NORTH
For confirmation, please telephone Fine Gael HQ at 619 8444
Published by Kerry Walsh, Director of Elections, 96 Brookdene, Clontarf, Dublin 3. Printed by Fine Gael, 51 Upper Mount Street, D02 W924.

FINE GAEL ★

Fig. 6.1 Dublin Bay North Fine Gael vote management leaflet

manage the vote may well run into local resistance. Any candidate, especially an incumbent TD, who is asked by party head office to allow some of his or her support to be redirected to a running mate can be expected to be less than enthusiastic, given the risk that they will forfeit so many votes that they simply end up losing the seat to their weaker running mate. The relationship between running mates, indeed, is usually one of superficial amity that scarcely conceals intense rivalry. While all party material issued by one candidate is expected to make some mention of any running mate(s), this requirement is typically met in the most minimal fashion possible. In Galway E, a reporter noted that while Fianna Fáil TD Colm Keaveney's posters did indeed contain a mention of running mate Anne Rabbitte, 'you'd need the eyesight of a hawk to spot it'.[11]

Sometimes this rivalry reaches the public domain, as occurred in a couple of Dublin constituencies. In Dublin Fingal, canvassers for the two Fianna Fáil candidates encountered each other in a housing estate in Portmarnock and an 'altercation' ensued, following which one of the candidates stated that members of her campaign team felt 'intimidated' and 'shaken' by the 'bad language' directed at them (*Irish Independent* 24 February 2016). In the adjacent Dublin Bay North constituency, it was the Fine Gael 'team' that displayed signs of discord. The only woman among the three candidates, Stephanie Regan, complained about the vote management scheme that asked some party supporters to switch from the front runner Richard Bruton to Naoise Ó Muirí, as described above, effectively cutting her out of the picture. She claimed that this strategy was decided 'on the basis of a falsified poll, which is entirely at variance with the response that I and my team are receiving on the doorsteps' (thejournal.ie, 22 February 2016), and in response she issued a leaflet (see Plates section p. xli) asking rhetorically 'What's wrong with Irish women?' and describing herself and Bruton as constituting 'the winning team', with no mention of Ó Muirí. In the event, Fine Gael polled much more poorly than expected here and Bruton was the sole Fine Gael candidate elected.

Good vote management by Fine Gael contributed to the party's significant seat bonus, winning 31 per cent of the seats with 26 per cent of the votes. In Louth, for example, the party won two of the five seats with fewer than 20 per cent of the votes, while in Dublin Bay South it won 30 per cent of the votes and two of the four seats and in Meath East it won just 35 per cent of the votes but two of the three seats. Its vote management also contributed to the winning of a seat in Clare, Limerick County, Wexford, and perhaps Dun Laoghaire. On the other hand, suboptimal vote management meant it missed out on seats in Cavan–Monaghan, Cork East, Dublin SW, Limerick City, Longford–Westmeath and Mayo, though in most of these cases the votes were already fairly well balanced between the party's candidates and would have needed to be balanced almost perfectly for the additional seat to have been won.

Good vote management by Fianna Fáil earned that party an additional seat in Cavan–Monaghan and Mayo, but these were outweighed by seats forfeited through poor or imperfect vote management in Clare, Offaly, Wexford and probably Cork East. The case of Offaly was particularly blatant: its leading candidate received over 12,300 first preferences and the second candidate only 3394, and on the final count the weaker candidate missed a seat by a mere 170 votes, with his running mate around 2300 votes ahead of him. Fianna Fáil was also guilty of an error rarely made by parties, namely under-nomination. Perhaps because it erred by over-nominating in 2011, it ran only one candidate in several constituencies where its eventual vote would have justified two, and in one of these cases, Limerick City, it might well have won an additional seat had it run a second candidate and managed its votes well. Sinn Féin has little experience south of the border in having to manage a vote, not having had a realistic chance of winning two seats in a constituency before 2016. In Donegal on this occasion, though, it had a very good chance of doing this, but its ambition overleapt itself and, in an Icarus-like bid to win three seats, it ran three candidates, won far fewer votes than it had expected, failed to manage these votes well between the two leading candidates, and ended up with just one TD, actually losing a seat compared with 2011.

VOTE TRANSFERS

The electoral system of proportional representation by the single transferable vote (PR-STV) invites voters to rank candidates in order of their preference, and during the counting process votes are transferred from elected or eliminated candidates to continuing candidates in accordance with the preferences marked by the voter (see Appendix 4 for an explanation of the electoral system). By analysing the flow of vote transfers between candidates, we can draw inferences about the way in which voters see the political world, in terms of which parties supporters of one party feel warmer or cooler towards.

Of course, not all voters are thinking in party terms at all; as we will see in Chapter 7, for many voters their choice is based primarily upon candidate factors, and party affiliations of candidates may be secondary or even irrelevant. Survey evidence shows that party identification has been steadily declining since the 1970s,[12] and one reflection of this is a decline in parties' internal transfer solidarity. This is measured by calculating the proportion of transfers that pass from one candidate of a party to other candidates of the same party in situations where the latter are available to receive transfers. These are sometimes termed 'non-terminal transfers', as distinct from terminal transfers, which are transfers from a candidate who has no running mates still in the count.

When it comes to intra-party transfer solidarity, both major parties displayed their lowest level ever, a manifestation of weakening party identification, a blurring of the lines of competition within the party system, and a wider range than usual of party choices. Fianna Fáil used to have the highest levels of internal solidarity: prior to the 1980s, over 80 per cent of transfers from one Fianna Fáil candidate passed to another Fianna Fáil candidate when one was available to receive transfers. This figure dropped to a then-record low of 62 per cent in 2002, fell further to 58 per cent in 2011 and, as Table 6.3 shows, plumbed new depths in 2016, when little more than half of non-terminal Fianna Fáil transfers remained within the party fold. In four cases, the internal transfer rate was below 50 per cent. These occurred in Longford–Westmeath (37 per cent), and Kerry, Tipperary and Sligo–Leitrim (all in the range 45–50 per cent); all of them large rural constituencies where geographical considerations could be expected to rival or surpass party loyalties in a context of loosening of party allegiances. Fine Gael's internal solidarity also declined, falling below 60 per cent for the first time ever. Its range was large, from a mere 31 per cent in Cork E to 80 per cent or more in three cases. A stronger internal transfer might have given the party additional seats in Dublin SW, Longford–Westmeath and Sligo–Leitrim. Sinn Féin, in contrast, achieved the kind of internal transfer solidarity characteristic of the major parties in earlier decades. Its lowest internal transfer was 67 per cent (Sligo–Leitrim), which is well above the overall level for both Fianna Fáil and Fine Gael, while in Donegal the elimination of its third-placed candidate produced a transfer rate of 89 per cent to the other two candidates.

Analysis of inter-party terminal transfers shows only a few strong relationships. Two of these were between the government parties. Most terminal Fine Gael transfers went to Labour when the latter had a candidate available to receive transfers, though there were only two such cases. More meaningful is the figure for transfers in the other direction: 55 per cent of terminal Labour transfers, compared with only 38 per cent in 2011, went

Table 6.3 Transfer patterns at 2016 election (%)

From	Available	N cases	FF	FG	Lab	SF	AAA–PBP
Internal solidarity							
FF	FF	19	54.7				
FG	FG	24		58.6			
SF	SF	9				75.7	
Lab	Lab	2			35.3		
AAA–PBP	AAA–PBP	4					62.9
Inter-party terminal transfers							
FG	Lab	2			58.0		
FG	FF, Lab	2	26.5		58.0		
FF	FG, Lab	12		27.4	15.6		
FF	FG, SF	14		29.4		14.8	
SF	AAA–PBP	3					61.0
SF	FF, Lab	11	18.3		11.3		
Lab	FG	18		55.5			
Lab	FG, SF	8		55.2		8.0	
AAA–PBP	SF	18				31.7	
Grn	FF, FG	19	12.0	20.1			
Grn	FG, SF	20		20.0		10.9	
Soc Dems	FF, FG	8	9.8	17.2			
Soc Dems	Lab, SF	10			17.8	10.7	
Renua	FF, FG	16	23.2	24.8			
Others	FF, FG	81	18.3	16.0			

Note: The 'Available' column shows those parties that had candidates available in each case to receive transfers. 'Inter-party' transfers refer only to terminal transfers, in other words to cases where the party whose votes were being distributed had no candidates of its own left in the count. Figures for other parties are not given since these would be meaningless in the absence of information as to the number of cases in which these parties had a candidate available to receive transfers. The cases analysed exclude surpluses that were based on the distribution of a package of votes from a candidate of another party

to Fine Gael candidates when the latter were available to receive transfers. This could be taken as an endorsement from Labour voters of a continuation of the Fine Gael–Labour coalition, though given the collapse in the Labour vote since 2011 a more realistic interpretation would be that 'support for a continuation of the coalition with Fine Gael' was one of the defining characteristics of that minority of 2011 Labour supporters who stuck with the party in 2016. These voters strongly preferred Fine Gael to Sinn Féin when they had a choice between the two. Transfers between Labour and Fine Gael flowed at levels comparable with those for internal transfers for each party. The only other figure above 50 per cent in Table 6.3 is that for terminal transfers from Sinn Féin to the AAA–PBP, though this is based on very few cases. The flow of transfers in the other direction was not so strong, largely because of the plethora of left-wing independents available to receive transfers and not because significant numbers of AAA–PBP transfers went to the established parties.

Based on analysis of vote transfers, we could construct a preference matrix of the Irish party system in 2016. This would show a Fine Gael–Labour group confronting a Sinn Féin–AAA–PBP group, with little mutual empathy between them. Supporters of the Greens and the Social Democrats are closer to the first group than the second because of their antipathy towards Sinn Féin, while Fianna Fáil supporters rank Sinn Féin behind Fine Gael but ahead of Labour. Generally, Sinn Féin retains its position as the least appealing party for many voters and as such the least likely to receive their transfers, while Labour, the most transfer-attractive party in 2011, vied with Sinn Féin in 2016 for the position of least transfer-attractive. As in 2011, Fianna Fáil and Sinn Féin were the biggest losers from the impact of transfers, though in Fianna Fáil's case on a much smaller scale than in 2011, when it lost ten seats due to being transfer-toxic. Six Independent TDs owed their election to being more transfer-attractive than a party rival, but this apart the flow of transfers between candidates and parties made little difference to the seat numbers achieved by any party (see Table 6.4).

THE BETTING MARKET AS RESULTS PREDICTOR

Opinion polls are the standard basis for results predictions but after their perceived failure in the 2015 UK election, when they had pointed to the Conservatives and Labour being neck and neck only for the former to achieve a 6-point lead on election day,[13] polls were treated with some caution at the 2016 election. An alternative source of information on what is likely to happen is the betting market, which these days offers odds on most aspects of elections, including the number of seats each party will win, the composition of the next government, the identity of the next Taoiseach and Tánaiste, and the fate of every individual candidate.

In terms of the seat shares of the parties, the betting market did not perform particularly well. Fine Gael's seat tally was consistently over-predicted, standing at 58.5 at the start of the campaign, dropping to a low of 51.5 for a few days in the last week of the campaign following some poor opinion poll figures, but rising again to 55.5 by election day, com-

Table 6.4   Constituencies where inter-party transfers affected the outcome

Constituency	Seat won by	At the expense of	Due to transfers from
Carlow–Kilkenny	Pat Deering FG	Jennifer M–O'Connor FF	Lab
Donegal	Thomas Pringle Ind	Pádraig MacLochlainn SF	Ind
Dublin Bay N	Tommy Broughan Ind	Aodhán Ó Riordáin Lab	AAA–PBP
	Finian McGrath Ind	Aodhán Ó Riordáin Lab	AAA–PBP
Dublin Central	Maureen O'Sullivan Ind	Gary Gannon SD	FF, Ind
Dublin NW	Noel Rock FG	Paul McAuliffe FF	Lab
Dub Rathdown	Catherine Martin Grn	Alan Shatter FG	SF, FF
Dublin SC	Bríd Smith AAA–PBP	Catherine Ardagh FF	SD, SF
Dublin SW	Katherine Zappone Ind	Anne-Marie Dempsey FG	AAA–PBP, Ind
Galway W	Catherine Connolly Ind	Trevor Ó Clochartaigh SF	Lab, SD, FF
Limerick City	Maurice Quinlivan SF	Kieran O'Donnell FG	AAA–PBP
	Jan O'Sullivan Lab	Kieran O'Donnell FG	SD, AAA–PBP
Longfd–Wmeath	Willie Penrose Lab	Paul Hogan SF	FG
Sligo–Leitrim	Éamon Scanlon FF	Gerry Reynolds FG	SF

Note: The counterfactual scenario is one where the votes transferred from the party or parties in the final column went equally to the two candidates in the previous columns, in which case the candidate in the third column would have taken the seat

pared with the 50 the party actually won.[14] Similarly, Fianna Fáil's total was under-predicted; it started at 33.5 and rose only to 38.5 on election day, well below the 44 the party won. For Sinn Féin the market was steady (in the range 23.5–25.5) and reasonably accurate, finishing at 25.5 against an actual total of 23. Labour was predicted best of all, the predicted total declining gently over the course of the campaign from an initial 10.5 to 7.5 by election day, 7 being the number the party won. Overall, though, the predicted totals for each party tended to fluctuate in response to opinion polls and, as an earlier study concluded, there is no sign that the betting markets constituted an independent repository of wisdom as opposed to simply reflecting trends reported by opinion polls.[15]

Most people with an interest in politics could make a reasonable estimate of the overall seat totals that might be won by each party, but not everyone would have much knowledge of the specific candidates likely to emerge victorious from each constituency. The betting market in effect generates a perceived probability for each candidate,[16] so if the market is distilling genuine expertise then it constitutes a valuable guide to what is likely to happen.

On the whole, the constituency betting markets can be assessed as having proved fairly reliable guides to the eventual outcome. The correlation between candidates' perceived probabilities of election and the share of the constituency quota that they won was a very strong one (r = 0.887); in other words, the better a candidate's chances according to the betting market, the higher the share of votes the candidate won on 26 February. This relationship changes little if we confine the analysis to the candidates of the eight main parties (r = 0.863, n = 353) or to those candidates receiving first preferences amounting to at least a fifth of a quota (r = 0.795, n = 324). This is confirmed in the 'Average Droop quotas' column of Table 6.5, illustrating the strong relationship between the perceived probability of election and the share of first preference votes won.

This particular betting market, though, is not directly concerned with the number of votes a candidate receives but simply with the yes/no issue of whether they are elected. Here, again, there is a strong relationship between the expectation generated by the betting market and the outcome, with none of those given a likelihood of less than 10 per cent being elected compared with 94 per cent of those given at least a 90 per cent chance. The best value, according to the '% elected' column, was to be

Table 6.5   Fate of candidates 2016, by probability assigned by betting market

Betting market perceived likelihood of election	Elected	Not elected but qualifying for reimbursement of expenses	Not qualifying for reimbursement of expenses	% elected	Average Droop quotas	N
<0.101	0	52	191	0	0.11	243
0.101–0.2	1	36	7	2.3	0.31	44
0.201–0.3	4	19	1	16.7	0.40	24
0.301–0.4	8	13	3	33.3	0.42	24
0.401–0.5	8	8	0	50.0	0.53	16
0.501–0.6	10	9	0	52.6	0.55	19
0.601–0.7	17	10	0	63.0	0.59	27
0.701–0.8	12	7	0	63.2	0.58	19
0.801–0.9	24	8	0	75.0	0.66	32
0.901–1	73	3	0	93.6	0.88	76
All	157	165	229	30.0	0.36	524

Note: Betting market odds from paddypower.com. Probabilities based on odds offered on 25 February 2016, the day before election day, not taking account of overround, that is, the bookmakers' margin, the amount by which the sum of probabilities of the options exceeds 1. The 27 candidates for whom no odds were offered are excluded. All but 1 of these 27 candidates received fewer than 1000 first preferences and none qualified for reimbursement of expenses.

found among those candidates in the 0.4–0.5 band, where 50 per cent were elected, whereas in some other bands (0.1–0.2, 0.2–0.3, 0.7–0.8 and 0.8–0.9) the proportion elected was outside the band and in each case below the lower limit of the band.

The betting market was not infallible. Some very short-priced candidates were unsuccessful: Paul Donnelly (Sinn Féin, Dublin West, 1–100), Jimmy Deenihan (FG, Kerry, 1–25), Pádraig MacLochlainn (Sinn Féin, Donegal, 1–10), Chris Andrews (Sinn Féin, Dublin Bay S, 1–9) and Tom Hayes (FG, Tipperary, 1–9). Some others with a perceived low probability of success were elected: Hildegarde Naughton (FG, Galway W, 7–1), Niamh Smyth (FF, Cavan–Monaghan, 10–3), Carol Nolan (Sinn Féin, Offaly, 10–3), Lisa Chambers (FF, Mayo, 5–2) and Peter Burke (FG, Longford–Westmeath, 5–2). Eight of the twelve longest-priced winners were women while only one of the twelve shortest-priced losers was a woman, perhaps an indication of a systematic under-estimation of the appeal of strong female candidates (a hint of gender bias in the betting market), and indeed the separate market on the likely number of female TDs elected under-predicted this figure.

Despite these errors, though, the constituency betting markets can be seen as having provided a valuable and generally accurate guide to the likely outcome. For anyone who knows nothing about the competition in a particular constituency, looking at the betting market is akin to, and much more easily achieved than, having a briefing by a local expert or being shown the findings of a constituency poll. Like those methods, examining the betting market cannot be relied upon as a completely accurate guide as to what will happen when the votes are counted, but it undoubtedly distils, and hence conveys, informed opinion.

THE MEMBERS OF THE 32ND DÁIL

Turnover and Experience

The 2011 election had produced record levels of turnover, with only a minority of TDs having belonged to the previous Dáil. The 2016 election represented a settling down in this regard, with a return to less extreme, though still higher than average, levels of turnover. Twenty outgoing TDs did not contest the election, 13 of them from the government parties.[17] The decision of Ruairí Quinn, a former minister and Labour leader from 1997 to 2002, to stand down meant that this was the first campaign since 1969 in which residents of Sandymount were not treated to the sound of

Manfred Mann's 'The Mighty Quinn' coming from a loudspeaker strapped to a car roof. Other notable retirees included Éamon Gilmore, who was Tánaiste and Labour leader until the summer of 2014; Joe Higgins, who flew the flag as the lone representative in the Dáil of the Socialist Party for many years; Michael Kitt, who had first entered the Dáil in March 1975, even before Enda Kenny; and Pat Rabbitte, another former Labour leader and minister. A further 48 TDs were defeated and, remarkably, only one of these, Sinn Féin's Pádraig MacLochlainn, had not been elected for either Fine Gael or Labour in 2011; 40 TDs from the two government parties lost their seats, and there were a further seven TDs originally elected for one of these parties who now ran and lost under a different label. Only four of these incumbent defeats (three in Fine Gael and one in Fianna Fáil) were intra-party defeats, that is, cases where an incumbent was replaced by a running mate. With the Dáil's size having been reduced from 166 to 158, this meant that the election returned 60 deputies who did not belong to the previous Dáil. A third of the TDs in the 32nd Dáil (52 out of 158) are first-time deputies, and they were joined by eight former TDs regaining their seats after an absence and by 98 incumbents securing re-election.

Only 30 of these TDs had been first elected in the last century, with Taoiseach Enda Kenny the only survivor from the 1970s. For his first 18 months as a TD, Kenny sat in the same chamber as Paddy Smith, who had been a TD continuously since 1923, creating a link between the 32nd Dáil and the earliest years of the state. A further 11 TDs were first elected in the 1980s, but in all only 45 TDs were first elected before 2006, meaning that the great majority of TDs have less than ten years' Dáil experience. The median TD was first elected as recently as 2011, this exceptional situation reflecting the large influx of first-time TDs at two successive elections. The sheer newness of most TDs and the paucity of 'old hands' who socialise first-termers into prevailing norms makes it more likely that deputies will behave in ways that previous generations of parliamentarians would have regarded disapprovingly as transgressive.

Routes to the Dáil

A local government background has right from the start of the independent Irish state been the first career step for aspiring TDs, and this was true a fortiori in 2016. Of the 52 new TDs, all but 4 had previously been county or city councillors, and all but 6 were councillors at the time of the election. Of these six, four were senators, leaving just two who had never held a representative position. These were Michael Harty, elected in Clare as an independent on a platform of protecting health services, and Louise O'Reilly, elected for Sinn Féin in Dublin Fingal, and, even though she did not live in the constituency, in which Dublin airport is situated, she was well known there as a result of having worked as a trade unionist representing Aer Lingus workers.[18] In all, 130 of the 158 TDs (82 per cent) were councillors before they became TDs; a further 6 reversed the sequence, leaving just 22 (14 per cent) who have never been councillors. The public may occasionally want different representatives, but the profile of the new names usually bears a strong resemblance to that of the departing ones.

Traditionally, the other useful attribute on the CV has been having a relative who served as a TD, and this remains significant. Thirty TDs (19 per cent of the total) are related to one or more present or former TDs who preceded them into the Dáil, and on a subjective judgement this contributed significantly to the initial election of all but five of these. By far the most common familial link is from father to son, which accounts for 17 of the electorally significant 25 connections, and there are also 5 brothers, 1 daughter, 1 nephew, and 1 cousin.

Backgrounds of Deputies

The most striking difference between the 32nd Dáil and all of its predecessors is that 22 per cent of its members are women; a low figure for many parliaments, but a record for Ireland (see Chapter 8 for full analysis). Occupationally, as in most recent Dála, a little under half of all TDs are professionals. TDs with a 'commercial' background (mainly running a small, often a family, business) are atypically strong for a modern parliament, making up a little over a fifth of all TDs; they constitute around a quarter or more of the TDs of Fine Gael, Fianna Fáil and independents. The proportion of farmers, which had declined steadily in recent Dála, rose slightly in 2016 to 10 per cent of the total; 14 of the 94 TDs representing either Fine Gael or Fianna Fáil are farmers. Data on education is incomplete at the time of writing, but it appears that a small majority of TDs in the 32nd Dáil have a university degree.

The average age of TDs is 50 years, with independents being the oldest at 58 on average and the small but hardy band of Labour TDs not far behind at 57.[19] The largest three parties have very similar mean ages at 48 or 49 years. Almost a quarter of Dáil members were 60 or over at the time of the election, though only three (Michael Noonan, Seán Barrett and

Bernard Durkan, all from Fine Gael) were over 70. At the other end of the scale, only six were under 30, the two youngest being Jack Chambers and Donnchadh Ó Laoghaire (see Chapter 5 for their personal accounts). The route to becoming a TD usually lies via an apprenticeship at local government level, as mentioned above, but once this platform is established TDs typically do not have to endure unsuccessful Dáil campaigns before being elected. Most TDs in the 32nd Dáil (94, or 59 per cent) were elected the first time they stood for the Dáil, and only 34 TDs sustained more than one defeat before being first elected. This is particularly true of the two main parties: 70 per cent of Fine Gael and Fianna Fáil TDs were elected on their first Dáil candidacy, compared with only 44 per cent of other TDs, who usually have to build a party base over time as well as a personal one.

CONCLUSION

Over 30 years ago, Reif and Schmitt introduced the notion of a 'second-order election', one at which there was less at stake than in a first-order election, which was primarily about electing a government. National parliamentary elections were first-order elections, and EP elections, local elections, by-elections and (where applicable) regional elections were all examples of second-order elections. At second-order elections, Reif and Schmitt argued, we would see, inter alia, brighter prospects for small and new political parties and a loss of votes by government parties. At first-order elections, most voters feel constrained to choose among the feasible government options, and so they vote instrumentally, with the conscious aim of trying to bring about the best outcome, rather than with their heart. At second-order elections, though, they feel free to indulge themselves by voting expressively, voting in line with their 'real' preferences, so to speak, because they do not have to bother taking government formation into consideration.[20]

Since the inception of EP elections in 1979, the Irish experience has conformed well to these expectations, with smaller parties and independents doing better than at Dáil elections and government parties characteristically sustaining midterm setbacks. In this context, the striking feature of the 2016 Dáil election result is that it looks very much like the result of an EP election. For many voters, quite evidently, the election was not about electing a government, as they cast their vote for candidates or parties that either had no wish to be in government at all or were prepared to enter government only in circumstances that were very unlikely to materialise.

The level of elective fragmentation, in other words the dispersal of votes among different parties and groups, seen in the 2016 election was exactly the same as that manifested at the 2014 EP election. Irish voters, in short, are behaving, or at least behaved in February 2016, at first-order elections just like voters typically behave at second-order elections, with obvious implications for the process of government formation, as is discussed in Chapter 11. Before we come to that, though, in the next chapter we probe the motivations of voters more deeply by examining survey evidence on voting behaviour at the 2016 election.

Notes

1. Markku Laakso and Rein Taagepera, '"Effective" number of parties: a measure with application to west Europe', *Comparative Political Studies* 12:1 (1979), pp. 3–27. The intuitive meaning of a figure such as 6.57 is that the party system is as fragmented as if there are 6.57 equal-sized parties. The calculation is based on treating each independent candidate as a separate unit, except when Independents ran under a common label such as 'Independents 4 Change'.

2. Michael Gallagher, 'Politics in Mayo 1922–2013', pp. 757–780 in Gerard Moran and Nollaig Ó Muráile (eds), *Mayo: history and society* (Dublin: Geography Publications, 2014), pp. 768–769.

3. For the advantage to incumbents, see Paul Redmond and John Regan, 'Incumbency advantage in a proportional electoral system: a regression discontinuity analysis of Irish elections', *European Journal of Political Economy* 38 (2015), pp. 244–256.

4. Ian McShane and Martha Fanning, *RTE Behaviour & Attitudes 2016 General Election Exit Poll report*, pp. 83, 84. For details of the poll see Chapter 7, note 1, p. 182 below.

5. In *An Economic Theory of Democracy* (New York: Harper and Row, 1957), Anthony Downs outlined the logic whereby each party will try to position itself at the point on the left–right spectrum where it will maximise its votes, which usually entails moving towards the centre rather than away from it.

6. Michael Gallagher, 'Ireland's earthquake election: analysis of the results', pp. 139–171 in Michael Gallagher and Michael Marsh (eds), *How Ireland Voted 2011: the full story of Ireland's earthquake election* (Basingstoke: Palgrave Macmillan, 2011), pp. 152–156.

7. Noel Whelan with Kathryn Marsh, *The Tallyman's Campaign Handbook: election 2016* (Dublin: Liffey Press, 2016), pp. 167, 305, 111.

8. Figures supplied by Michael Marsh.

9. Peter Mair, *The Changing Irish Party System: organisation, ideology and electoral competition* (New York: St Martin's Press, 1987), pp. 67–68.

10. Gallagher, 'Ireland's earthquake election', p. 158.

11. Tony Galvin, 'Together again – sharing lamp posts but not parties', *Tuam Herald* 10 February 2016, p. 18.

12. Stephen Quinlan, 'Identity formation and political generations: age, cohort and period effects in Irish elections', pp. 255–275 in Johan A. Elkink and David M. Farrell (eds), *The Act of Voting: identities, institutions and locale* (London: Routledge, 2016), p. 259.

13. Philip Cowley and Dennis Kavanagh, *The British General Election of 2015* (Basingstoke: Palgrave Macmillan, 2016), Chapter 9.

14. All odds from www.paddypower.com. The seat figure quoted here is the break-even point, which Fine Gael was seen to have as much chance of exceeding as falling below. Thus, on election day, the bookmaker offered the same odds (5–6) that Fine Gael would win more than 55.5 seats as that it would win fewer than 55.5.

15. Michael Gallagher, 'The election as horse race: betting and the election', pp. 148–166 in Michael Gallagher and Michael Marsh (eds), *How Ireland Voted 2007: the full story of Ireland's general election* (Basingstoke: Palgrave Macmillan, 2008).

16. To be precise, the betting market examined here, that on www.paddypower.com, offered odds for 524 of the 551 candidates. The other 27 were presumably the object of no interest from potential punters, and indeed they all fared poorly; none of them qualified for reimbursement of expenses, and only one even received more than 1000 first preferences. The odds used for analysis are those on 25 February, the last day before polling day; by election day itself, a market existed on only 22 of the 40 constituencies. Probabilities are based on the raw odds offered, not adjusting for the overround, that is, the amount by which the sum of probabilities of the options exceeds 1.

17. This figure includes Fine Gael TD Brian Walsh, who resigned his seat less than three weeks before the Dáil was dissolved.

18. Whelan, *Tallyman's Campaign Handbook*, p. 160.
19. Analysis of age based on the 151 TDs whose birth date is known; see Appendix 5 for details.
20. Karlheinz Reif and Hermann Schmitt, 'Nine second-order national elections – a conceptual framework for the analysis of European election results', *European Journal of Political Research* 8:1 (1980), pp. 3–44, at pp. 9–10.

CHAPTER 7

Voting Behaviour: Continuing De-alignment

Michael Marsh and Gail McElroy

As we saw in the previous chapter, this election was notable once again for the size of the swing against the governing parties. As in 2011, the incumbents lost very heavily at the polls, and unlike the 1970s and 1980s, when all governments 'lost' elections without suffering huge losses, the scale of the defeat was again massive. The collapse of Fianna Fáil in 2011 was hardly a surprise given the scale of economic collapse, but the Fine Gael–Labour defeat this time is more unexpected given the extent of the economic recovery. The electorate is, clearly, in an unforgiving mood, and it now seems easier to win support at one election than to keep it at the next one. While 2011 might have been the first step towards a realignment of Irish politics, 2016 suggested that it was rather a sign of de-alignment with voters abandoning their old partisan affiliations and failing to find new ones. The scale of volatility indicates that there is now little binding voters to particular parties. However, there was also no shortage of new parties and new candidates looking to establish themselves and with the growth of Sinn Féin, AAA–PBP, the Social Democrats and some left-wing independents there was arguably a shift on the left to more radical alternatives. Some have viewed this as evidence for a clearer left–right, class-structured politics: a realignment of sorts.

M. Marsh (✉) • G. McElroy
Trinity College Dublin, Dublin, Ireland

© The Author(s) 2016
M. Gallagher, M. Marsh (eds.), *How Ireland Voted 2016*,
DOI 10.1007/978-3-319-40889-7_7

We start this exploration of voting behaviour by looking at the change in individual party choices from 2011 to 2016. We do this by using data from the RTÉ Exit poll in which respondents were asked not only how they had voted in 2016 but also to recall how they voted in 2011.[1] It is generally accepted that such recall of past vote is often inaccurate and can be biased by current voting intentions. Certainly, such data underestimate the amount of change that has taken place as voters confuse their current vote with that from five years ago, but nonetheless it does give a reasonable guide to the pattern of change. In this data, it would seem that more people recall voting Fianna Fáil in 2011 than actually did so, and many fewer recall voting Labour than must have done so, but this is to be expected as for many, a vote for Labour in 2011 would have been an unusual choice, while many who would normally have voted Fianna Fáil could not bring themselves to support that party at that time.[2]

Table 7.1 shows the scale of the turnover in vote between 2011 and 2016 with the data weighted to conform to the actual election result. As we might have expected, Fianna Fáil and Sinn Féin hung on to most of their 2011 voters, with more than three quarters of those voting for Fianna Fáil and Sinn Féin in 2011 voting for the same party in 2016. But Fine Gael and Labour suffered big losses. Fine Gael votes primarily leaked away to Fianna Fáil (14 per cent) and to independents (8 per cent), while Labour voters went to independents (12 per cent), Fine Gael (12 per cent) and Sinn Féin (11 per cent), with just over a third of Labour's 2011 support staying true (36 per cent). But even Fianna Fáil and Sinn Féin, despite growing, lost almost a quarter of their 2011 voters, in the case of Fianna Fáil to independents and Sinn Féin to independents and minor parties. More surprisingly again, independents retained over half of their voters, although this figure may obscure some change within that group as voters may have switched the individual independent they voted for. Those who went outside of the traditional party system in 2011 tended to stay there in 2016. These figures for change, as said above, almost certainly underestimate actual volatility, as voters' ability to recall how they voted five years after the event is imperfect. Bearing this in mind and ignoring those who said they did not vote or could not remember, we find that only 58 per cent voted the same way in 2016 as in 2011. This figure does not seem high. It compares with 72 per cent for the five-year period 1997–2002, 70 per cent for 2002–07, and just 52 per cent 2007–11, based on previous exit polls.[3] Volatility appears to be a very clear feature of Irish elections in the past decade (cf Table 12.1).

Table 7.1 Voting change 2011–16

2016 vote	Recalled vote choice in 2011							
	Fine Gael	Fianna Fáil	Sinn Féin	Labour	Independent	Socialist/ ULA/PBP	Green	Others
Fine Gael	55	6	2	12	7	0	12	30
Fianna Fáil	14	76	3	6	8	12	2	11
Sinn Féin	5	4	77	11	7	9	4	9
Labour	5	1	1	36	4	0	4	9
Independents	8	5	6	12	40	11	6	15
Ind. Alliance	5	2	2	3	12	0	0	0
AAA–PBP	1	1	6	7	7	47	5	8
Social Democrats	2	1	1	6	7	7	11	8
Greens	2	1	1	3	3	6	48	0
Renua	3	2	0	2	1	3	6	5
Others	0	1	1	2	4	5	2	5
Total	100	100	100	100	100	100	100	100

Source: RTÉ Exit poll. *N* = 3404

Note: Data weighted to conform to actual turnout and party support in 2016. Cell entries are percentages. Excludes those who could not remember or did not vote in 2011

Excludes those who could not remember or did not vote

The major contribution to the high levels of volatility in the years 2007–11 was the collapse in the Fianna Fáil vote in 2011 and with that party still far from restored to its normal status, these erstwhile Fianna Fáil voters arguably contribute to the ongoing uncertainty. Fortunately, one of the polling companies, RED C, has continued to ask respondents how they voted in 2007, which allows the exploration of the impact of this Fianna Fáil implosion on voter volatility. While the 2007 election is now long in the past, we can have some confidence in the data, as the profile in the samples is very close to the profile of actual voters in 2007, with 42 per cent recalling a Fianna Fáil vote and 25 per cent a Fine Gael one. Table 7.2 shows the behaviour of 2007 Fianna Fáil voters in the elections of 2011 and 2016. Only about a half of them stayed with the choice made in 2011, and most of these chose Fianna Fáil, with the rest changing yet again. Of the 29 per cent of former Fianna Fáil voters 'loaned' to Fine Gael in 2011, only a third (just under 10 per cent of the total electorate) stayed with Fine Gael, and less than a third returned to Fianna Fáil in 2016. The remainder stayed away, taking refuge with different parties, in particular independents. By 2016, the main choice of former Fianna Fáil voters who did not go back to Fianna Fáil was for independents and others, arguably a halfway house, and not even so far away if the independent was from a Fianna Fáil gene pool, as so many are. Certainly few voted for substantial rival parties, with only a quarter voting Fine Gael, Labour or Sinn Féin in 2016. The collapse of Fianna Fáil clearly contributed significantly to overall volatility, but it is not the full story. Even if we ignore these voters, volatility was still very significant, with only 60 per cent of those who voted in 2007 (excluding Fianna Fáil voters) reporting the same choice in 2011 and 2016. This is still an overestimate since 'others' are treated as a single group here.

Table 7.2   Vote choice in 2011 and 2016 of those voting Fianna Fáil in 2007

| | Vote 2011 | | | | | Total |
	Fianna Fáil	Fine Gael	Labour	Sinn Féin	Others	
Vote 2016						
Fianna Fáil	35	9	2	0	2	50
Fine Gael	3	10	1	0	1	15
Labour	1	1	1	0	0	3
Sinn Féin	2	2	1	3	1	9
Others	6	7	3	1	6	23
Total	47	29	8	4	10	100

Source: Data from RED C polls in February 2016. $N = 1188$

Note: Cell entries are percentages of those who recalled voting Fianna Fáil in 2007

It is clear that much of this change in vote choice is accounted for by events in the lifetime of the government, well before the start of the campaign. By 2014, as we saw in Chapter 1, support for both governing parties was well down on 2011 in both the local and European elections, and the final general election results were in fact very close to those of the local elections of 2014. However, we might have expected some recovery by the governing parties come election time, not least because the financial context was much better, the 2016 budget was more generous, and the campaign against water charges was no longer mobilising the same large numbers witnessed in 2014. In fact polls at the end of 2015 and early in 2016 put Fine Gael close to 30 per cent with Labour at 8 per cent, but this seems to have been a peak, as Fine Gael, Labour and Sinn Féin all appear to have lost support in the last few weeks of the election campaign, to the benefit of Fianna Fáil and 'Others' (see Chapter 4). According to the RTÉ Exit poll (see Table 7.3), almost 60 per cent of voters reported that they only made up their mind who to support during the campaign, with 15 per cent deciding on the day and 21 per cent in the last week. This is comparable to the situation in 2011, when 64 per cent decided during the campaign, but even in 2007 over 50 per cent claimed to decide during the campaign. Even treating these figures with the caution they deserve, there clearly was substantial uncertainty for significant numbers of voters as to how to cast their ballot as the election approached; so it is hardly surprising if there was a shift in support to the benefit of some parties in the last few weeks.

Looking at time of decision across the parties supported on the day, we can see that those who decided later were much more likely to vote for independents and minor parties, and much less likely to support Sinn Féin. Early deciders were twice as likely to vote for Sinn Féin as those making up their mind in the last days; and they were almost half as likely to support 'Others'.

Table 7.3   Time of decision 1997–2016

	1997	2002	2007	2011	2016
Day of the election, or day before	12	10	13	20	15
Week of election	15	14	17	21	21
2–3 weeks before	25	30	22	23	23
Before election called	48	46	48	36	41
Total	100	100	100	100	100

RTÉ Exit polls 1997–2016

This suggests Sinn Féin is not effective at picking up 'floating voters', and also provides an explanation for the decline in its support over the campaign. There is no obvious sign of a boost to Fianna Fáil from late deciders, or losses by Fine Gael in any consistent pattern across the campaign. Not surprisingly, those who reported that they had voted differently in 2011 from 2016 were more likely to decide during the campaign but even so, almost 50 per cent of those sticking with Fine Gael and Fianna Fáil decided to do so during the campaign, while just over 50 per cent of those staying with Labour and independents also did so. This is perhaps a surprisingly low figure for independents, and illustrates that this choice should no longer be seen as a one-off protest vote, if it ever was. Sinn Féin stands out here with just one in three of its 2011 voters who stayed with the party in 2016 making that decision during the course of the campaign.

Before moving on to look at the motivations for choice, it is worth looking at the age profile of support for different parties. A striking point here is that the old party system still dominates (if less strongly) among those over 35, almost 60 per cent of whom voted for Fine Gael, Fianna Fáil or Labour. Among voters under 30, Fine Gael is a little less popular, but Fianna Fáil support is much lower, just 16 per cent. But Sinn Féin equals Fine Gael among those under 35 and is in fact the most popular party with those under 30. Support for the rest is also higher, at 37 per cent compared with 29 per cent among those 35 and over. At present, the choices of those under 35 have relatively little impact on the overall results. While those under 35 make up 30 per cent of the electorate (according to figures from the Central Statistics Office (CSO)), they are only 20 per cent of voters (according to the RTÉ Exit poll), suggesting turnout is much lower in this age group.[4]

It is hard to know whether this pattern has much significance for the future. On the one hand, it could be argued that Sinn Féin's support will strengthen, as it keeps winning younger voters and those already supporting the party will continue to do so. Similarly, it might be considered that Fianna Fáil's weakness among younger voters—largely a legacy of the economic collapse—will continue to be a problem for the party, as the generation that reached voting age around the time of the crisis will distrust that party for the foreseeable future. Yet it may also be that voters do become more conservative with age, and will come to find the older parties more attractive. Younger voters were more likely to leave Labour and Fianna Fáil but were marginally more likely to stay with Sinn Féin. Overall, they were only slightly more likely to change their party from 2011 to 2016 in comparison to those over 35.

CLASS VOTING

While the growth in voter volatility is undeniable, is there a systematic demographic patterning to this vote switching? Do we see an emerging and new class basis to voting behaviour in Ireland? The relatively poor performance of the traditional parties, and particularly the two located in the centre of the political spectrum, with their origins in the civil war divisions almost a century ago, raised the prospect not just of political de-alignment but of some political realignment. There has long been a call in some quarters for political contestation to follow the sort of left versus right pattern so common in the rest of Europe. The presence of two centre-right parties that provided the bases of alternative governments inhibited this, particularly as the Labour Party was a government partner for Fine Gael normally, but also in 1993–94 for Fianna Fáil. Austerity, and the vacancy left by Fianna Fáil's collapse in 2011, perhaps could have created an impetus for a more class-based politics. Certainly Sinn Féin's rhetoric, and even more so that of the AAA–PBP alliance, manifested class war themes and most opposition groupings contrasted themselves with the pro-banker, pro-big business government, a government that did not work in the interest of ordinary Irish people.

There is quite distinct class-based voting evident in the 2016 general election. Table 7.4 shows middle- and working-class voting, and that of farmers, all based on the conventional market research categories for

Table 7.4 Class and voting behaviour

	Middle class	Working class	Farmers
Fianna Fail	22	26	25
Fine Gael	30	18	41
Labour	8	6	3
Sinn Féin	9	20	4
Rest	31	30	27
Total	100	100	100
Independent Alliance	5	4	7
Independents	10	14	13
AAA–PBP	4	5	1
Soc Dems	5	4	*
Greens	4	2	1
Renua	3	2	1

Source: RTÉ Exit poll. N = 4283

Note: Data weighted to conform to actual turnout and party support in 2016. *less than 0.5 per cent but greater than zero

classifying voters into social classes.[5] There are some distinctive profiles, most notably for Sinn Féin, which was twice as successful among working-class voters as it was among middle-class ones. In fact, that party won only 5 per cent of votes among the higher non-manual, professional and business grouping (classes AB). Fine Gael supplies a sharp contrast, doing much better with middle-class voters than working-class ones. Fianna Fáil manifests a cross-class profile and Labour—unusually for a social democratic party—did a little better among middle-class voters. Others as a whole showed little sign of a class profile. However, looking within this group, and bearing in mind that numbers are quite small for some of the minor parties, suggests independents won fewer votes from the better off. AAA–PBP did not, perhaps surprisingly, show a distinctive class profile while the Greens, on the other hand, look distinctively middle class. This is hardly classic class politics, although it has to be said that in most of Europe the class basis of party systems probably passed a peak more than half a century ago.[6] Taking the difference between middle-class (ABC1) and working-class (C2DE) voters as a simple marker, the 'hard left'—here defined as Sinn Féin and AAA–PBP—as a whole are working-class parties (−12) while the soft left—Labour/Social Democrats/Greens—are certainly not, with more middle-class voters casting a ballot for them (+5) than working-class voters. Fianna Fáil (−4) is effectively catch-all, as usual, but Fine Gael (+12) looks more like a middle-class party than it has done since 1987.

Table 7.5 looks just at Dublin, and here we see that the class profiles are a little sharper for Sinn Féin and AAA–PBP, which won a combined 13 per cent from middle-class voters but a full 38 per cent from working-class ones. That is more working-class votes than won by Fine Gael, Fianna Fáil and Labour combined. Sinn Féin's support *outside* Dublin is not quite so distinctive: a difference between working- and middle-class voters of 12 points rather than 19. Sinn Féin actually was almost *four* times as popular in Dublin among working-class voters than it was among middle-class ones and AAA–PBP twice as popular. Looking at urban areas more generally, class differences in the main are twice as pronounced in such areas as they are in rural ones: Sinn Féin −14 as against −7 and Fine Gael +14 as against +8. There are, then, signs of class voting, but it is much stronger in some areas than others, and it is more obvious in some parties than it is in others. Taken as a whole, supporters of the parties of the centre-right (Fianna Fáil, Fine Gael and Renua) are more middle class than those who vote for parties that are left of centre, but the difference is largely down to Fine Gael and Sinn Féin support bases. The centre-right (ignoring independents) won 48 per cent of the vote among the middle classes of Dublin as against 31 per cent of the working-class votes, a difference of 17 percentage points. A comparable figure for Scandinavian countries nationally as late as 1980—after a period when class politics became less distinct—was around 50 per cent.[7] Even in the most recent Swedish election of 2014, only a third of middle-class voters supported left-wing parties (here defined as the Social Democrats and Left Party) compared with 51 per cent of working-class voters.[8] Ireland is still a long way away nationally from class politics on that model. Closer to home, at the last election in the UK, the Conservative party won about 13 per cent more support among the middle class than the working class, while Labour's profile was the reverse of this.[9] This muted class voting is similar to that seen in Dublin, but still stronger than that seen in the country as a whole.

Class politics can show itself not simply in the profiles of party supporters but sometimes, more strikingly, in the patterns of change, with the middle-class voters leaving a party going to different parties than leavers who are working class. If we consider this measure of class politics, we find that Fine Gael's losses were much less pronounced in the higher middle-class categories than they were in that party's 2011 working-class ones and Sinn Féin's gains were much greater among less well-off working-class voters than the higher middle-class ones. Fianna Fáil's gains were relatively larger among working-class voters. It is these underlying patterns that give rise to the stronger class profile of voting in 2016 than in 2011.

Table 7.5 Class and vote in Dublin	Middle class	Working class
Fine Gael	29	16
Fianna Fáil	15	12
Sinn Féin	7	26
Labour	11	7
Rest	38	39
Total	100	100
Independent	9	15
Independent Alliance	7	5
AAA–PBP	6	12
Social Democrats	5	2
Greens	6	1
Renua	4	3
Others	1	1

Source: RTÉ Exit poll. N = 1289

Note: Data weighted to conform to actual turnout and party support in 2016

What lies behind this emerging class polarisation? A popular explanation is the impact of the more than seven years of cutbacks following the economic crash in late 2008, in which the opposition, for the most part, claimed that government policies hurt the less well-off disproportionately hard. And the relative weakness of the major cross-class party, Fianna Fáil, meant that it was easier to mobilise the less well-off behind parties of the (opposition) left. For its part, the government put its faith in the 'recovery' (see Chapters 1 and 4), widely heralded abroad and evident at home at least in significant falls in unemployment figures and in the 2015 budget that started to cut some taxation and spend a little bit more money. In the next section, we explore the impact of the economy on voting behaviour.

THE ECONOMY

The 'economy' is widely seen to be a key feature in elections everywhere, with growth boosting the government performance at the polls and its absence hurting it.[10] Most of the focus tends to be on overall economic expansion or retraction, with parties maintaining or losing the attribute of being competent to run the economy. There has been less focus on the individual's own economic well-being. In essence, the argument has been that changes in individual circumstances may be down to a variety of circumstances in no way attributable to government activity, whereas the economy as a whole is something that the government often links itself to, with commentators and opposition parties reinforcing those links. However, the Irish experience tends to go against this trend. There is little doubt that the Irish economy improved over the course of the five years 2011–16. Externally, international agencies viewed Ireland as a much better bet to lend money to than they did in 2011, as debts as a proportion of national income fell, and budget deficits came down to levels prescribed by the European Union (EU). However, during the campaign, as well as before it, opposition forces argued that the benefits of the recovery were confined to the capital, and well-heeled areas of the capital at that. People in the real Ireland, opposition parties claimed, did not feel or see the recovery.

To explore this conundrum of overall national economic growth without personal economic progress, we can take advantage of the two questions in the Exit poll that asked voters about the state of the economy as a whole and also about their own family circumstances. In each case, they were asked to say whether things had got better, worse or stayed the same over the last year. Table 7.6 shows the results. The findings were much the same as shown in many polls in the run-up to the election.[11]

Table 7.6 Evaluations of the improvement in the state of the economy and personal financial situation over the last 12 months

	Personal situation			Total
	Better	Same	Worse	
Country				
Better off	23	18	5	46
The same	3	26	6	35
Worse off	1	4	14	19
Total	27	48	25	100

Source: RTÉ Exit poll. $N = 1436$

Note: Data weighted to conform to actual turnout and party support in 2016. Cell entries are percentages of the total

Looking at the row totals, we see that voters did tend to see the national economy as improving, with more than twice as many seeing things getting better as saw them getting worse. Better off exceeded worse off by 27 percentage points (46 to 19 per cent). However, when it came to their own pockets, opinion was much more balanced with a near majority saying that things had stayed the same and better off exceeding worse off by just two points (27 to 25 per cent). This is actually a rather large and, in a comparative context, quite unusual difference between these two indicators of economic well-being.[12] Typically evaluations of the national economy and personal economic well-being are more in line with each other. But it is not hard to find possible explanations for this divergence in the Irish case. The improvement in the national finances meant the country could pay its debts but did not mean there was money for significant tax cuts, or increased benefits; public sector pay remained well down on 2010 levels; and many people had large mortgages from the boom era, or were now paying very high rents. In the special circumstances of post-boom, post-crash Ireland, it would take some time for growth to be felt in the average person's pocket. Irish households remain the third most indebted in the EU (after the Netherlands and Denmark).[13]

The recovery was certainly not experienced evenly throughout the country, with some striking geographical and social differences. Comparing better off with worse off, we get a figure of +43 in Dublin, falling to +27 in Leinster, +28 in Munster and just +3 in Connacht–Ulster. In terms of personal circumstances, the differences are +7 in Dublin, +10 in Leinster, −1 in Munster and, a very striking, −17 in Connacht–Ulster. That is, significantly more people in Connacht–Ulster felt they were personally financially worse off than felt better off in 2016, compared with 2015. And in terms of social class, middle-class voters were far more inclined to see the national economy as getting better rather than worse (+47) compared with only +7 per cent of working-class voters. When it came to personal finances, the differences were even more stark; with the middle classes inclined to state their own personal situation was better off than worse off (+16) while the working classes felt their situation had grown worse (–14) over the course of the year.

Table 7.7 shows that those who did think the economy was in better shape, and who felt their own circumstances had improved were, unsurprisingly, more inclined to support government parties. The numbers here indicate the difference between those seeing things as better and those seeing them as worse. For instance, among those who voted for Fine Gael 37 per cent thought the economy was better and only 6 per cent thought it was worse, a difference of +31 percentage points. In contrast, among Sinn Fein supporters only 9 per cent thought things were better and 33 per cent thought them worse, a difference of –24 percentage points. The apparent effects of countrywide evaluations as against personal ones look pretty similar here. Again, this is unusual as research elsewhere finds that national evaluations tend to swamp personal ones, particularly when the effects of each are considered controlling for the effects of the other one.[14] When this is done here, each evaluation shows a strong and significant effect. Fine Gael and Labour did very much better among those who saw improvements, particularly in the general economy, and very poorly among those who thought things were worse. In contrast, Sinn Féin won support disproportionately among those who felt things were getting worse. Independent support was particularly strong among those who saw no recovery. Fianna Fáil voters were less distinctive, as the party won a fifth of the vote among those who saw personal or national improvements. This finding might be explained by the fact that the party itself accepted that there was an improvement in the economy but gave the government little credit for it, as, it claimed, the policies that brought about the recovery were established by the previous Fianna Fáil-led administration, and it additionally argued that the costs and benefits of recovery were not spread fairly.[15] In fact, the final Ipsos MRBI poll for the *Irish Times* found only 24 per cent of those polled credited the government with responsibility for the recovery.

Some researchers have expressed reservations about the inference of any causal connection on the basis of the clear relationship between these sets of evaluations, and in particular the national ones.[16] They argue

Table 7.7 Economic evaluations and vote choice	Better–worse national	Better–worse personal
Fine Gael	+31	+30
Fianna Fáil	–5	–6
Sinn Féin	–24	–18
Labour	+8	+5
Rest	–24	–9

Source: RTÉ Exit poll. N = 1436

Note: Cell entries show differences in levels of party support between those seeing improvement and those seeing things getting worse

that respondents tailor evaluations to coincide with their vote choice, so the evaluation reflects a bias rather than determines a choice. After all, however well the economy is doing there will be those who give a negative evaluation—as many Fine Gael voters did at the height of the boom in 2002. It is very difficult to disentangle these relationships, but one approach is to control for partisanship in some way. If we do so by allowing for 2011 vote, and include both personal and national evaluations, the results still indicate that both sets of evaluations do matter, and have a significant effect on vote choice, particularly for the government and main opposition parties.

This finding is reinforced by results from campaign opinion polls. A Millward Brown/*Sunday Independent* poll published near the end of the campaign found that Fine Gael was the party most trusted to manage the economy, with 32 per cent nominating it as against 17 per cent for Fianna Fáil and 15 per cent for Sinn Féin. (Sinn Féin easily led the 'most distrusted on the economy' stakes, with 42 per cent seeing it as most untrustworthy.) But among those giving Fine Gael top position on the economy, only 70 per cent intended to vote for that party, with another 5 per cent voting Labour. But 8 per cent said they would vote independent, and 8 per cent for Fianna Fáil. For these people, it would seem that some other factor was more important when it came to voting. The next section explores in some detail the issues that mattered to voters in 2016.

ISSUES: WHAT WERE PEOPLE VOTING FOR?

The economy and its management were central to the campaign of the government parties and while Fine Gael won the argument on that, vis-à-vis any other party, it would seem that for many voters 'the economy' was far from being the only issue. The Exit poll, as always, asked voters what was the most important issue for them in making their decision. The question was open-ended, but interviewers coded the answers into the pre-established categories shown in Table 7.8. Each respondent was asked for the most important issue, and the next most important. Most of these issues amount to general areas of concern, such as Health or Housing policy, and do not in themselves indicate a position that a voter might take on the matter. Some, such as 'Stable government' echo campaign slogans, and may do little more than indicate what party a voter supports, being at best a rationalisation rather than a basis for choice. The table shows for each issue the differences in support for each party or group between those mentioning the issues as a factor in their choice and those not doing so. So, for instance, those mentioning Health as a critical issue were six percentage points less likely to vote for Fine Gael than those were who did not mention that issue.

The issue of health was most widely mentioned and although no party seemed to gain or lose strongly among those who were concerned about it, the fact that over a third of voters expressed concern about the issue meant even small effects (if they can be seen as effects) could have been important for the outcome. The biggest party differences however were in the categories of Economic management, Stable government and Water charges. The first two worked to the benefit of Fine Gael, which won well on those issues, but they seemed to have proved of little help to Labour.

'Water charges' was an important issue for 16 per cent of voters—7 per cent said it was the most important and a further 9 per cent made it their second choice—and those voicing this concern were much more likely to support Sinn Féin (and AAA–PBP).[17] Sinn Féin was three times as likely to win the support of someone who thought water charges a major issue as it was to win the support of someone who did not (and AAA–PBP were almost four times more likely to do so). This issue was also more clearly differentiated by class, being mentioned by just 12 per cent of middle-class voters as against 23 per cent of working-class ones. For all its determination in the post-election negotiations to suspend water charges (see Chapter 11), Fianna Fáil actually did better among voters who did not think this was an issue! No other issue comes close to this one in its apparent impact. The only other issue to have much impact was homelessness. Again this worked to the benefit of Sinn Féin and AAA–PBP in particular. The fact that only 16 per cent mentioned unemployment is probably testament to the fact that the government did a good job in bringing it down so far, but those

Table 7.8 Differences in party choice according to issue mentioned as critical to their vote

	Health	Economy	Water	Stable government	Unemployment	Homelessness	Tax	Crime	Local issues
Fine Gael	−6	+13	−18	+28	−1	−14	+4	0	−8
Fianna Fáil	+2	−7	−5	−6	−2	+3	+3	+6	+14
Sinn Féin	0	−5	+15	−10	+5	+6	−5	−5	−5
Labour	0	+1	−4	+1	0	−2	+2	0	+2
Rest	+3	−5	+11	−15	−4	+8	−5	−2	−3
% Mentioned	36	31	16	16	16	14	12	10	10

Source: RTÉ Exit poll. *N* = 1418

Note: Cell entries show difference in each party's support between those mentioning and those not mentioning a particular issue as critical. Respondents were asked to provide up to two issues that were critical in deciding their vote. Other concerns mentioned were Education (7 per cent), Abortion (4 per cent), Childcare (4 per cent) and Housing/Mortgages (4 per cent). The response categories were set in advance and answers coded into them by the interviewers

who did mention it clearly thought it was still much too high and favoured Sinn Féin rather than any other party.

A very striking result here concerns 'local' issues, voiced by 14 per cent. Oddly, the big winner here was not independents, but Fianna Fáil. Almost 40 per cent of those with local concerns voted for that party. This is very different from the pattern in the past when Fianna Fáil was the natural party of government and thus seen as good/bad on the economy or health, but it may be one reason for the party's surge in the last few weeks of the campaign.

In general, though, what we see here is that the government parties, and most notably Fine Gael, gained from those who saw the economy and stable government as most important, and lost when people saw public services as key. A Millward Brown poll for the *Sunday Independent* confirms this general pattern. The survey put two statements to respondents and asked them to agree/disagree using a 5-point scale. The first statement was: 'A change of Government would put Ireland's economic stability at risk'. The second was: 'A change of Government would help create a fairer society'. On balance, people disagreed with the first statement (50 as against 35 per cent) and agreed with the second, 58 to 23 per cent. Taking the two together, 38 per cent thought a change would not endanger stability and would promote fairness, as opposed to just 13 per cent who thought the reverse. Even among those who did fear that a change would endanger stability, only three in five voted for the government parties, a figure that goes up to three out of four among the relatively small group who also disagree that a change would bring more fairness. In the following section, we explore this question of how the concept of 'fairness' impacted the vote.

TAXING AND SPENDING

This apparent concern with public services reflected the campaign of most of the parties with only Fine Gael making at least as much noise about reducing the burden of taxation. The Exit poll sought to establish how voters balanced the desire for better public services with the desire to reduce taxation. Respondents were asked to place themselves on an 11-point scale (0 to 10) where the end points were defined as 'Government should cut taxes a lot and spend much less on health and social services' and 'Government should increase taxes a lot and spend much more on health and social services'. The overall distribution of voters was skewed towards more spending on public services, as it has been whenever this question has been asked in the years 2002–16, more so than in 2011 but similar to 2002 and 2007. While 21 per cent favoured tax cuts, 47 per cent wanted more spent on public services, with 32 per cent placing themselves in the middle. It should be noted that voters of all parties tend to the spending end of the distribution. However, those on the tax-cutting side are more likely to vote Fianna Fáil or Fine Gael (and independents) than are those on the more spending side, who are more likely to favour Sinn Féin, AAA–PBP and the Greens. This is a question that tends to distinguish supporters of left and right parties quite effectively in other countries but barely does so in Ireland. While it reflects a desire by voters to spend more, it does little to account for the choice made by most Irish voters in 2016. There also seems to be some ambivalence here about the increase in taxation to pay for better services, with parties on the left certainly against most voters paying more tax.

Another indicator of a voter's broad policy preference is an item from the Exit poll asking voters to place themselves on an 11-point scale whose end points are 'The government should act to reduce differences in income and wealth' and 'The government should not act to reduce differences in income and wealth'. Forty-five per cent would like the government to act in this way as opposed to 33 per cent who would not. Again, while we would expect to see voters of left-wing parties much more inclined to support redistribution, this is not the case. While Fine Gael support in particular is stronger among those opposed to such action, those who favour such action are not very much more disposed to support Sinn Féin, AAA–PBP, Social Democrats or Labour.

Voters were also asked to place themselves on a scale of left to right where left was 0 and right was 10. The average voter placed himself or herself at 5.0. Fianna Fáil and Fine Gael voters were to the right of this at 5.7 and 5.8, respectively. Independents as a whole were at 4.9, Social Democrats were at 4.6 and Labour at 4.5, with Sinn Féin at 3.7 and AAA–PBP at 3.3. Voters as a whole are certainly left of where they have been in recent elections when the mean has been just below 6. In all parties, there is quite a spread of opinion, particularly within Sinn Féin, but there is a much clearer link with vote choice than there seems to be on issues that would generally be seen as providing the underlying meaning of left and right.[18] There is also not much difference in left–right self-placement across the social classes with both middle- and working-class voters placing themselves close to 5, at 5.1 and 4.7, respectively.

We have seen that there were some distinctive patterns of class voting even if the larger groupings, and Fianna Fáil in particular, still show a very strong cross-class character, and it might be expected that we would see equivalently strong signs of an economic left–right policy divide among voters. However, this is hardly the case. While the electorate is broadly left-leaning on government spending, and favours more redistribution of income and wealth, this holds across the parties and does not do much to separate the voters of one party from another. This is of course the 'old' politics, when the lack of clear policy differences between parties over time inhibited the development of a politics revolving around clear policy alternatives. As yet, reports of the death of the old politics seem to be premature on this evidence.

When it came to a change of government, there was very little clarity offered by parties about eventual outcomes over the course of the campaign. While Fine Gael and Labour asked the electorate to return them to power together, most of the other parties ran to get that government out, and offered little clarity over what might replace it. The Exit poll asked respondents to choose from a number of options, indicating what government they would prefer (figures presented in Table 7.9). The choice perhaps reflects a combination of idealism and realism on part of the respondents. However, 36 per cent opted for a Fine Gael-led government and 20 per cent for a Fianna Fáil-led government, with a further 13 per cent opting for Fine Gael and Fianna Fáil together.

Most voters wanted their party in government (in contrast to the positions of most parties!), although they varied on how that might best be done. Most Fine Gael and Labour voters wanted a return of the current government. Sinn Féin voters too wanted their party in government. Fianna Fáil voters were divided between government with Fine Gael and a Fianna Fáil-led coalition. And, as can be seen from Table 7.9, 'Other' voters had a variety of preferences which of course reflects the heterogeneity of this grouping. 32 per cent of independents rejected any of the alternatives put before them with 54 per cent preferring one of the options that included independents, although the Independent Alliance voters seemed better disposed to a Fine Gael-led party government. The apparent preference for a Fine Gael-led government may reflect the expectations going into the election that Fine Gael would be comfortably the largest party, even if few expected the government to be returned without help from other parties or independents. The eventual emergence of a Fine Gael-led government including several independents was not unexpected—the first choice

Table 7.9 Preference for government, by party choice

Preference for government:	Fianna Fáil	Fine Gael	Labour	SF	Others	Total
Fine Gael single party	2	16	3	0	3	6
Fine Gael and Labour	5	50	62	2	10	21
Fine Gael and Fianna Fáil	24	12	3	4	11	13
Fianna Fáil and Sinn Féin	9	1	0	13	2	4
Fianna Fáil and other parties/independents	44	2	5	2	13	16
Fine Gael and other parties/independents	2	12	8	0	16	9
Sinn Féin and other parties/independents	0	1	0	66	15	13
Other	4	2	7	1	11	5
Don't know	9	6	12	10	21	12
Total	100	100	100	100	100	100

Source: RTÉ Exit poll. *N* = 1418. Respondents were supplied with these options

of just 9 per cent—but the decision of Fianna Fáil to make a 'confidence and supply' deal with Fine Gael rather than form a grand coalition was more of a surprise. Yet it is clear that these two parties had relatively widespread support.

As a further illustration of how much broad support there is for Fianna Fáil and Fine Gael, one can examine how people filled in the mock ballot part of the Exit poll to see how far voters for each party were willing to support the other one. Fine Gael won 26 per cent of first preferences and gathered another 14 per cent of overall second preferences; that is, from those who voted for a second party after the first one. Fianna Fáil won 24 per cent of first preferences, and second preferences pushed that support up to 36 per cent. Two-thirds of all voters gave one or other of these two parties a first or second preference and 10 per cent of all voters supported both of them before any other party—just 1 per cent less than the equivalent support for Fine Gael and Labour, and well above any other party combination.

LEADERS

Much is made in media coverage of the importance of the various party leaders to voting behaviour. This is understandable as campaigns do tend to focus on party leaders, not least because the parties themselves organise their activities around their leaders. However, political science research has generally downplayed the impact of the leader, at least as a factor having much direct impact on choice, although leaders can have a more significant impact through the way they direct the behaviour and policy placement of their parties.[19] In 2016, the Fianna Fáil leader, Micheál Martin, did seem to enjoy a good campaign, and was also responsible for giving his party a slightly left-of-centre focus (see Chapter 4). Martin certainly 'won' the TV debates, with 40 per cent saying he came out best compared with 9 per cent for the next most popular choice (Gerry Adams) and only 8 per cent who thought Enda Kenny's performance was the best one.[20] Fewer voters in 2016 gave 'choosing a leader' as the most important aspect of their choice than did so in previous years, a change that may reflect both Kenny's weakness and the growth of smaller parties and independents. Some polling companies include a question on leaders, asking for each leader whether he or she is doing a good job as leader of their party, although in the case of the Fine Gael leader the question is asked about their role in running the country. While this is typically misinterpreted as a question about leader popularity, it is far from being so. Indeed, rating of each leader on a 0–10 like–dislike scale can give a very different picture.[21] Subject to this warning, Behaviour & Attitudes' polls did show more voters were satisfied with Martin (45 per cent) in 2016 than with Kenny (38 per cent). Much was also made of Gerry Adams's negative impact on Sinn Féin's electoral performance. The satisfaction ratings suggest Adams is viewed no differently from Kenny or Martin, but again that is to misinterpret the question asked. As leader of a party rising in the polls since 2016, arguably he was doing a decent job, but that does not mean he is popular. For these, we need popularity ratings and these are not currently available.

A Floating Electorate: Candidates versus Parties

The particular appeal of independent candidates in this election, coupled with the huge instability of choice since 2007, underscores the weakness of partisan loyalties in Ireland, although some voters are still willing to admit that they identify with a particular party. The RTÉ Exit poll used the conventional question, asking people if they feel close to a political party, and just 27 per cent did so. This is a very low figure by European standards, and while it is higher than the figure of 22 per cent amongst voters in 2011, it is below the 31 per cent in 2002.[22] Much of this decline since 2002 is down to the disappearance of Fianna Fáil partisans—down to 11 per cent from 17 per cent in 2002, but the number of Sinn Féin and Fine Gael partisans has increased.

Voters have also been asked whether their support was driven more by candidates or party labels. In 2016, leaving aside those who voted independent, only 44 per cent said their first preference vote was motivated by party considerations while 53 per cent said it was driven by the candidate on offer. This is similar to 2007, but much less party-centred than 2011, when 55 per cent said party. However, if we factor in the vote for independents, which by definition is a candidate vote, then that party figure effectively drops to 37 per cent, compared to 46 per cent in 2011, 40 per cent in 2007 and 38 per cent in 2002. In terms of party versus candidate on this evidence, 2016 looks like a normal election: 2011 was the exception, as managing the national crisis seemed to take priority over local concerns. The big difference with 2002 and 2007 is that then there was a large party, Fianna Fáil, whose support was based on partisanship. That is no longer the case, as Fianna Fáil support in 2016 was, according to its supporters, based more on candidate than party motivations. Only Sinn Féin and Fine Gael supporters gave party as the major factor in their choice. The importance of candidate is almost universal. One exception is that party seems to have more importance for AB voters (55 per cent, against 44 per cent for DE voters) and for those in Dublin (51 per cent) and least importance for those in Munster where only 38 per cent of non-independent voters gave party as the strongest factor in their vote. While it might have been expected that older voters might be more party-centred, there are actually no clear trends with respect to age.

A further question asked voters to consider whether they would have voted for the same candidate had that candidate run for a different party. 41 per cent said they would, with 43 per cent saying they would not and 17 per cent said it would depend on which party the candidate ran for. Only AAA–PBP and Green Party voters tended to say no, they would not have, with Sinn Féin voters very close behind. We can combine these two questions to get a more broadly based measure of party- versus candidate-based voting, taking those who said 'Party' was most important and who would not follow their candidate to a different party as party-centred and those who said 'Candidate' and would follow their candidate to a different party as candidate-centred. The rest can be classified as voters of mixed loyalties. In 2016, leaving aside those who voted independent, 28 per cent were party-centred and 29 per cent candidate-centred, while 43 per cent had more mixed feelings. These figures show little change in party-centred voting from 2002 to 2016, but do show an increase in candidate-centred voting, up from just 20 per cent in 2011 to 29 per cent this time.[23] Adding in those who voted independent, party-centred voting characterises less than a quarter of all voters, and this is lower than in any past year for which data is available.

It would be easy to read too much into these assessments by voters of their motivations, but it is the differences over time, and to some degree across parties, that are most interesting. It would be misleading to put the big losses by Fianna Fáil in 2011, and those of Fine Gael and Labour in 2016, down to 'candidate' factors: it was the performance by those parties in government that was critical. But it is reasonable to argue that one reason why Fine Gael and Labour did so poorly, despite signs of economic recovery, is because neither party had a large reservoir of committed *party* support to draw on. Only around one in three of Fine Gael voters in 2011 felt close to that party, and no more than one in four of Labour's supporters did so. Many would never previously have voted in the way that they did in 2011, and did not do so again this time. Partisanship helps parties by giving them leeway, providing a positive filter that can discount and explain away bad news. Neither Fine Gael nor Labour had that leeway.

CONCLUSION

One of the main puzzles of the 2016 election, particularly for international observers, is explaining why the governing parties did so poorly when they had overseen a reduction in unemployment from almost 15 per cent to below 9 per cent and, relatedly, witnessed economic growth rates of close to 7 per cent. But as we have demonstrated in this chapter, for Irish voters, it is not necessarily a case of 'it's the economy, stupid'; other issues, particularly those related to the quality of public services, trump economic considerations. Furthermore, Irish voters have experienced an economic recovery that has not lifted all boats. There is an unusually large divergence in perceptions of personal economic well-being compared with the overall health of the national economy.

The patterns of voting behaviour we observe in 2016 are not significantly out of kilter with those of previous elections, though some trends are worth noting. First, there does appear to be an emerging class divide, particularly evident in the greater Dublin region. Second, the voter volatility we witnessed in 2011 was clearly not a one-off; it is here to stay. Irish people are less attached to particular parties than their European counterparts and the levels of attachment are experiencing a downwards trend over time.[24] Third, Irish voters are still very candidate-focussed; the 2011 focus on party was an aberration. Fourth, there is no clear ideological patterning to vote choice; it is simply not the case that voters for parties on the left are systematically more in favour of increasing taxation to improve public services than those on the right. Fifth, voting patterns suggest that a significant portion of the public is quite comfortable with jointly supporting both Fianna Fáil and Fine Gael candidates, and indeed this combination of preferences remains one of the most popular. Finally, voters did not go to the polls with a clear preference for a government outcome.[25] The voters 'did not speak'; the most popular option was a return of the incumbent government, and even here barely more than one in five voters favoured this possibility.

NOTES

1. The RTÉ Exit poll was conducted by Behaviour & Attitudes for RTÉ in partnership with the School of Politics and International Relations of University College Dublin, the Department of Government in University College Cork, The School of Politics, International Studies and Philosophy in Queen's University Belfast, and Trinity College, Dublin. The poll was conducted on election day among a sample of 4283 voters nationwide at 223 polling stations across all of the 40 Dáil constituencies.

2. The Irish National Election Study 2002–07 (www.tcd.ie/ines) found using a panel survey that when asked in 2006 to say how they voted in 2002 fewer than 70 per cent of respondents recalled correctly, even if we discount those who claimed to have voted when they did not do so. On recall error, see also Ragner Waldahl and Bernt Aardal, 'The accuracy of recalled previous voting: evidence from Norwegian Election Study panels', *Scandinavian Political Studies* 23:4 (2000), pp. 373–389; Claire Durand, Melanie Deslauriers and Isabel Valois, 'Should recall of previous votes be used to adjust estimates of voting intention?', *Survey Insights: Methods from the Field, Weighting: Practical Issues and 'How to' Approach*. Retrieved from http://surveyinsights.org/?p=3543 (15 May 2016).

3. Both RED C and Behaviour & Attitudes ask respondents to recall their vote from 2011 and their polls conducted in February 2015 had more voters admitting to having voted Labour in 2011 than actually voted Labour in that election, and consequently more defecting, with no more than a quarter of Labour 2011 voters intending to remain with the party in 2015.

4. The age pattern of turnout was much as it was in the 2014 elections, suggesting that the same-sex marriage referendum of May 2015 that supposedly brought out a much younger vote did not have lasting consequences.

5. Note this particular classification of voters into social classes is quite rudimentary and may significantly understate the extent of class based voting. See Richard Sinnott, 'Patterns of party support: A. Social class' in Michael Laver, Peter Mair and Richard Sinnott eds, *How Ireland Voted* (Dublin: Poolbeg, 1987), pp. 101–112; Michael Marsh, Richard Sinnott, John Garry and Fiachra Kennedy, *The Irish Voter: the nature of electoral competition in the Republic of*

Ireland (Manchester: Manchester University Press, 2008). The six social classes are used widely in market research in the United Kingdom and Ireland and are based on the occupation of the Head of Household. ABC1 are regularly collapsed into one middle-class category, while C2DE are taken as working class. For an extensive review of class voting, see Geoffrey Evans, 'The continued significance of class voting', *Annual Review of Political Science* 3 (2000), pp. 401–417.

6. Mark Franklin, Thomas Mackie and Henry Valen, *Electoral change: responses to evolving social and attitudinal structures in Western countries* (ECPR Press, 2009).

7. See Torben Worre, 'Class parties and class voting in the Scandinavian countries', *Scandinavian Political Studies* 3:4 (1980), pp. 299–320.

8. Henrik Oscarsson and Sören Holmberg, *Swedish Voting Behaviour, Report 2015:05*. Swedish National Election Studies Program, 2015.

9. See IPSOS MORI, *How Britain Voted 2015*. https://www.ipsos-mori.com/researchpublications/researcharchive/3575/How-Britain-voted-in-2015.aspx. Accessed 23/5/2016.

10. On economic voting, see Raymond M. Duch and Randy Stevenson, 'Assessing the magnitude of the economic vote over time and across nations', *Electoral Studies* 25 (2006), pp. 528–547; Michael S. Lewis-Beck and Mary Stegmaier, 'Economic determinants of electoral outcomes', *Annual Review of Political Science* 3 (2000), pp. 183–219; Christopher J. Anderson, 'The end of economic voting? Contingency dilemmas and the limits of democratic accountability', *Annual Review of Political Science* 10 (2007), pp. 271–296.

11. See Michael Marsh, 'After 2011: continuing the revolution', in David Farrell, Gail McElroy and Michael Marsh (eds), *A Conservative Revolution* (Oxford University Press, 2016), Chapter 11.

12. Marsh, 'After 2011'. The classic case against the importance of evaluations of individual well-being is Donald R. Kinder and D. Roderick Kiewiet, 'Economic discontent and political behavior: the role of personal grievances and collective economic judgements in Congressional voting', *American Journal of Political Science* 23 (1979), pp. 495–527. See also D. Roderick Kiewiet and Michael S. Lewis-Beck , 'No man is an island: self-interest, the public interest, and sociotropic voting', *Critical Review* 23 (2011), pp. 303–319.

13. Irish Central Bank figures, 4th quarter Report 2015. Disposable incomes while rising also remain below the 2008 peak (CSO figures March 2016).

14. Christopher J. Anderson 'Economic voting and political context: a comparative perspective', *Electoral Studies* 19 (2000), pp. 151–170.

15. On the importance of attribution, see Michael Marsh and James Tilley, 'The attribution of credit and blame to governments and its impact on vote choice', *British Journal of Political Science* 40 (2010), 115–134.

16. Gerald H Kramer, 'The ecological fallacy revisited: aggregate versus individual-level findings on economics and elections, and sociotropic voting', *American Political Science Review* 77 (1983), pp. 92–111.

17. The pattern in these results is much the same if we look only at the first issue mentioned.

18. For more discussion of this point, see Michael Marsh and Slava Mikhaylov, 'A conservative revolution: the electoral response to economic crisis in Ireland', *Journal of Elections, Public Opinion and Parties* 24:2 (2014), pp. 160–179.

19. Kees Aarts, André Blais, Hermann Schmitt (eds), *Political Leaders and Democratic Elections* (Oxford: Oxford University Press, 2013).

20. It should be said that Martin also won in 2011, and the Fine Gael leader won in 1997 and 2002: in all those cases the debate winner went on to 'lose' the election.

21. Marsh et al., *The Irish Voter*, Chapter 6.

22. Marsh et al., *The Irish Voter*, Chapter 4.

23. For a wider discussion of this measure, see Michael Marsh and Laura Schwirz, 'Exploring the non-alignment of party and candidate assessments in Ireland: do voters really follow candidates?' in J.A. Elkink and David M. Farrell (eds), *The Act of Voting: identities, institutions and local* (London: Routledge, 2015), pp. 178–191.

24. On party attachment, see Russell J. Dalton and Steven Weldon, 'Partisanship and party system institutionalization', *Party Politics* 13:2 (2007), pp. 179–196.

25. The low salience of government alternatives beyond the inclusion of a favoured party is discussed in Michael Marsh, 'Voting for government coalitions in Ireland under single transferable vote', *Electoral Studies* 29:3 (2010), pp. 229–238.

CHAPTER 8

Women and the Election: Assessing the Impact of Gender Quotas

Fiona Buckley, Yvonne Galligan, and Claire McGing

This chapter analyses the impact of gender quotas on the selection and election of women in the 2016 general election. It begins by reviewing the gendered recruitment and candidate selection plans of political parties as they implemented gender quotas. This is followed by a review of women's candidate selection, identifying the challenges and controversies that emerged as parties set about reaching the 30 per cent gender threshold. Attention then turns to the election campaign to identify the presence, if any, of a gendered dimension to campaign issues before examining women's electoral performance to assess the impact of gender quotas on the electoral prospects of women. The chapter concludes by assessing the current status of women in political decision-making in Ireland and profiling the women elected.

F. Buckley (✉)
University College Cork, Cork, Ireland

Y. Galligan
Queen's University Belfast, Belfast, UK

C. McGing
Maynooth University, Maynooth, Ireland

© The Author(s) 2016
M. Gallagher, M. Marsh (eds.), *How Ireland Voted 2016*,
DOI 10.1007/978-3-319-40889-7_8

GENDER QUOTAS AND CANDIDATE SELECTION

A constellation of pressures combined to facilitate the introduction of candidate gender quotas in Ireland, notably demands for institutional change and political reform following the 2008 economic crash.[1] A draft bill was published in December 2011 by Minister Phil Hogan and it was enacted in July 2012 with the support of all political parties. The Electoral (Amendment) (Political Funding) Act 2012 incentivises political parties to select at least 30 per cent female candidates and at least 30 per cent male candidates. Non-compliant parties surrender half of the state funding they receive on an annual basis to run their operations, a potential loss of millions of euros for larger parties. The gender quota threshold rises to 40 per cent from 2023 onwards.[2]

In anticipation of the impending introduction of gender quotas at the 2016 general election, many political parties used the opportunity of the 2014 local elections to recruit and run women candidates. However, wide variations existed in terms of female candidacy rates across the political parties, providing an indication of the challenges that lay ahead for the roll-out of gender quotas at the upcoming general election. Legislative gender quotas do not apply at the local level but parties such as Sinn Féin, Labour, the Green Party, People Before Profit (PBP) and the AAA actively recruited female candidates and came close to or exceeded the 30 per cent threshold. However, Fine Gael and Fianna Fáil failed to reach their self-imposed gender targets of 25 and 33 per cent, respectively, running just under 23 per cent and 17 per cent women candidates.

Fianna Fáil was criticised by media commentators and party members alike for a perceived problem with women. In April 2014, then Fianna Fáil senator Averil Power wrote a hard-hitting piece in a newspaper criticising the party leadership's lack of commitment and progress in recruiting and supporting women's candidacy.[3] To counteract this perception and to prepare for the implementation of gender quotas at the 2016 general election, the party established the 'Markievicz Commission' in July 2014. Its report, issued in January 2015, recommended that women candidates should be selected to contest half of the constituencies where the party had no incumbent TD and half of the constituencies where the party held one seat and wished to run a second candidate.[4] The party's national constituency committee reserved the right to direct constituencies to select women at selection conventions. Fine Gael established a national strategy committee in September 2014 chaired by Minister for Justice Frances Fitzgerald. The committee identified a number of constituencies where directives on the gender composition of the candidate ticket would be issued as well as others where women would be added to the ticket. Facing a tough election, the Labour Party ran just one candidate in most constituencies it contested. However, in accordance with its constitution, the party aimed for gender balance where more than one candidate was selected.[5] Similarly Sinn Féin undertook to run gender-balanced tickets,[6] while other parties actively recruited women candidates to ensure they met the 30 per cent gender quota threshold.

IMPLEMENTING THE GENDER QUOTA: CHALLENGES AND CONTROVERSIES

With a reduced number of Dáil seats on offer (reduced from 166 to 158) and at least one incumbent TD in every constituency, many predicted that Fine Gael would face a greater challenge in implementing the gender quota than Fianna Fáil. This certainly seemed to be the case in early selection conventions. In Dublin Bay North (DBN) in April 2015, four candidates contested the Fine Gael selection convention, two men and two women. A directive from Fine Gael headquarters stated that two candidates were to be selected, one woman and one man. It was widely anticipated that the sitting TD and Minister for Jobs, Enterprise and Innovation Richard Bruton would come through the selection convention with ease. However, it was Cllr Naoise Ó Muirí and Stephanie Regan who were selected. Richard Bruton and the second female candidate Aoibhinn Tormey were not. Reports suggested disquiet among the constituency party over the gender quota; others claimed it was due to the number of candidates to be selected, with some in the constituency wanting three candidates for geographical reasons. Whatever the case, it was widely accepted that the DBN selectorate had engaged in tactical voting to undermine the directive from Fine Gael party headquarters. Bruton was quickly added to the ticket the following morning. The event was a cautionary reminder to Fine Gael headquarters that meeting the 30 per cent gender quota would need to be carefully managed. The party issued gender directives to four other constituencies: Dublin West, Dublin Rathdown, Kildare South and Longford–Westmeath. Similar to DBN, these directives were issued where a dual candidate strategy was planned—one woman, one man. In Kildare South, local party members chafed at the gender directive, describing it as being akin to North Korean-style rule but complied in the end. Ironically, at the time of the selection convention, Ireland and North Korea were jointly ranked in 111th position for women's political representation worldwide.

In total, Fine Gael selected 88 candidates including 27 women (31 per cent), a marked increase on the number of women the party selected in 2011 (see Table 8.1). Of the 27 women selected, 13 were selected at convention without a gender directive, 5 were selected via a gender directive and 9 were added to the ticket (as were 6 men). The female add-ons were largely seen as an exercise 'to balance the books'[7] and meet the gender quota following the completion of selection conventions.

From the outset, many predicted that Fianna Fáil would have an easier experience in implementing the gender quota than Fine Gael. After all, it had many open constituencies (referred to as 'green-field sites') across the country that had no incumbent TDs. However, selection patterns at the 2014 local election demonstrated the persistence of a masculinised culture within the party, with women's political candidacy receiving minimal encouragement. Early selection conventions were relatively uneventful but as autumn 2015 approached and the prospects of an early election in November 2015 loomed, Fianna Fáil headquarters indicated, as specified in

Table 8.1 Women candidates and TDs in the 2011 and 2016 general elections

	2011			*2016*		*Difference 2011–2016*
Party	*Women candidates*	*Women TDs*	*Party*	*Women candidates*	*Women TDs*	*Women's candidacy difference*
	N (%)			*N (%)*		
FF	11 (14.7)	0	FF	22 (31.0)	6 (13.6)	+16.3
FG	16 (15.4)	11 (14.5)	FG	27 (30.7)	11 (22.0)	+15.3
Labour	18 (26.5)	8 (21.6)	Labour	13 (36.1)	2 (28.6)	+9.6
SF	8 (19.5)	2 (14.3)	SF	18 (36.0)	6 (26.0)	+16.5
Greens	8 (18.6)	0	Greens	14 (35.0)	1 (50.0)	+16.4
ULA	5 (25.0)	2 (50.0)	AAA–PBP	13 (42.0)	2 (33.3)	–
–	–	–	Renua	8 (30.8)	0	–
–	–	–	SD	6 (42.9)	2 (66.6)	–
Inds	19 (9.6)	2 (11.8)	Inds	33 (20.0)	5 (21.7)	+10.4
Others	1 (5.9)	0	Others	9 (30.0)	0	+24.1
Total	86 (15.2)	25 (15)	Total	163 (29.6)	35 (22.2)	+14.4

the Markievicz Commission report, that it would issue gender directives to meet the 30 per cent gender quota. In September 2015, Fianna Fáil headquarters issued directives to its members in the Dublin Central and Dublin South-Central constituencies stipulating that a single candidate strategy and gender directive would apply. Prospective male candidates at these conventions, Brian Mohan and Cllr Daithí de Róiste, issued statements and took to social media to indicate their disappointment with the decision. Mohan described the gender quota as 'undemocratic and discriminative' while de Róiste tweeted 'Officially the first candidate for a General Election to be prevented to run because of my Gender'. Cllr Catherine Ardagh was selected unopposed in the Dublin South-Central constituency. However, chaotic scenes took hold at the Dublin Central convention as one of the female candidates, Denise McMorrow, read out a statement at the start of the convention, protesting against the directive and announcing that she was withdrawing her candidacy as she felt gender quotas 'had diminished her'. Mary Fitzpatrick was selected unopposed. In November 2015, Brian Mohan announced he was taking a constitutional challenge against gender quotas. The case was heard in the High Court in January 2016 but was dismissed as Justice David Keane adjudged that the plaintiff did not have locus standi to take such a challenge, the court deciding that the law did not adversely affect him personally or affect his rights to stand as a candidate. Mohan subsequently appealed the decision. In a third Dublin constituency, Dún Laoghaire, it was largely expected that a single candidate strategy and gender directive would be issued resulting in the selection of former TD and minister Cllr Mary Hanafin. However, in what was considered a climb down, Fianna Fáil headquarters did not issue a gender directive following the threat of legal action by Cllr Cormac Devlin. Devlin went on to win the convention but Hanafin was promptly added to the ticket.

Gender directives were not confined to Dublin constituencies. In Galway East and Louth, gender directives were issued to Fianna Fáil party members to select gender-balanced tickets, one woman and one man. In the Longford–Westmeath constituency, separate selection conventions took place across the two counties. Sitting TD Robert Troy was selected unopposed in Westmeath. In Longford, Fianna Fáil headquarters issued a gender directive stating that one candidate was to be selected and that the candidate must be a woman. Connie Gerety-Quinn was automatically selected. This led to uproar in the constituency party as members believed their democratic right to select a candidate of their own choosing was undermined. A motion of no confidence in Gerety-Quinn was passed and there were calls to reconvene the selection convention through an appeal to the Fianna Fáil national executive, but these were dismissed. Plans to nominate an unofficial Fianna Fáil candidate to challenge Gerety-Quinn eventually abated but many constituency party members refused to campaign for the selected candidate. In total, Fianna Fáil selected 71 candidates including 22 women (31 per cent) (Table 8.1), twice the number it had selected in 2011. Of the 22 women selected, 8 were selected at convention without a gender directive, 5 were selected via a gender directive and 9 were added to the ticket (as were 7 men).

In most other parties, the selection of women candidates took place without much controversy. Sinn Féin implemented a national strategy to meet the 30 per cent quota.[8] Based on particular constituency characteristics, such as whether or not there was an incumbent TD or obvious candidate in place, particular selection criteria and rules were applied. This included open conventions, second conventions, the application of gender directives (such as Mayo), and the addition of candidates by party headquarters. Party strategists emphasised that flexibility was key to this strategy. In Cork East, though, tensions emerged between potential candidates and the sitting TD Sandra McLellan before, in October 2015, she announced her intention to not seek re-election. In total, the party selected 50 candidates of whom 18 were women (36 per cent), more than twice the number it selected in 2011. Of the 18 women selected, 15 were selected at convention without a gender directive, 1 was selected via a gender directive and 2 were added to the ticket (as was 1 man).

The Impact of Gender Quotas on Women's Candidacy[9]

Overall a total of 551 candidates contested the election—388 men (70 per cent) and 163 women (30 per cent). This was the highest number and proportion of women ever to contest a general election in Ireland and represented a 90 per cent increase in the number of women candidates who had contested the previous general election in 2011. Despite reservations about where they would 'find' women candidates, all parties surpassed the 30 per cent threshold. Across the four main political parties of Fine Gael,

Fianna Fáil, Sinn Féin and Labour, a total of 155 selection conventions were held, of which 54 were contested. A total of 80 women were selected including 11 selected via a gender directive and 20 added by party headquarters (as were 14 men).

As the data demonstrates, the majority of female party candidates came through convention without the use of a gender directive. This signifies that the main achievement of gender quotas was to instil a cultural change within political parties whereby party strategists embraced gender-aware recruitment processes, encouraging, equipping and seeking women to run for election. Dedicated capacity training and mentoring for prospective women candidates was provided by political parties and all parties worked with the non-partisan organisation Women for Election, which offered tailored training and support for women candidates. These practices would seem to have aided the 'supply' of potential women candidates. However left-leaning parties were more likely to run higher proportions of women candidates than those on the right, in line with international patterns. Perhaps unsurprisingly, it was the two historically dominant political parties, Fianna Fáil and Fine Gael, that encountered the most difficulties in implementing the gender quota, especially Fine Gael as it had so many, mainly male, incumbents. Political parties are institutions and, like all institutions, they have their own distinct ideologies, cultures and norms.[10] Long-term institutional legacies and masculinised cultures within political parties can serve to undermine women's contributions, discouraging their political ambitions.[11] Newer political parties such as the Social Democrats and AAA–PBP recorded the highest rates of female candidacy indicating that new parties, free of the gendered legacies of more established ones, are more facilitating of women's candidacy. This finding is tempered somewhat by the fact that the new right-wing party Renua seemed to have had some initial difficulty in getting women to run. Also noteworthy is the increase in the number and proportion of female independent candidates suggesting that the discourse surrounding gender quotas and women in politics may have had a diffusion effect, encouraging women from outside the party fold to put themselves forward as independent candidates (Table 8.1).

As outlined in the previous section, the nature of candidate selection in Ireland saw tensions emerge between central party headquarters and the constituency level party over the implementation of gender directives (see also Chapter 3). Tensions of this nature are not new in Irish elections. Party headquarters and their constituency units are regularly at odds over informal candidate selection requirements such as the geographical spread of candidates and the number of candidates to be selected. But what the formal gender provision exposed is the masculinised nature of local party democracy. Research demonstrates how decentralised selection processes tend to favour well-networked and resourced (male) candidates.[12] The application of gender quotas essentially saw tensions emerge between the 'favoured local son' and the so-called 'quota woman'.[13]

Claims that women were selected on the basis of gender rather than merit were raised, yet male meritocracy and experience was rarely questioned.[14] If merit is measured solely by electoral experience, then the quality of women candidates in this election compares favourably to men. Eighty-four (52 per cent) women candidates were current office-holders at the time of the election in comparison to 235 (61 per cent) male candidates. Disaggregating these figures along (larger) party lines, 74 per cent of Fine Gael women candidates were office-holders at the time of the election in comparison to 97 per cent of male candidates. In Fianna Fáil, 73 per cent of women candidates were office-holders in comparison to 86 per cent of male candidates. The figures for female and male office-holding in the Labour Party were 92 and 100 per cent respectively, while in Sinn Féin the data shows that 72 per cent of female candidates were office-holders at the time of the election in comparison to 88 per cent of male candidates. In addition, all bar two of the women selected through a gender directive were office-holders and of the 20 women added to the ticket by party headquarters, 14 (70 per cent) had prior electoral experience. Therefore, the vast majority of party women candidates, like their male counterparts, were not electoral novices.

THE GENDERED NATURE OF THE CAMPAIGN

The gendered nature of political campaigns highlights how the media presents candidates through a gendered prism,[15] how gender influences campaign strategy,[16] the extent to which both male and female politicians use masculinised 'credentials' to burnish their electability,[17] and the role played by gender stereotypes in determining support for male or female candidates.[18] In this section, an exploration of the gendered nature of the campaign will focus on two areas, the representation of female candidates in the media and the extent to which party manifestos and individual candidates were influenced by an awareness of gender issues.

Female Candidates and the Media

Unlike previous general elections, 2016 was one in which women played a prominent role. Labour Party leader Joan Burton was the consistent communicator of her party's achievements in office and plans for the future; two of the Social Democrats' three joint leaders Róisín Shortall and Catherine Murphy, as well as Renua party leader Lucinda Creighton, were everyday articulators of their new parties' visions; Fine Gael Minister for Justice Frances Fitzgerald responded strongly to the organised crime murders during the second week of the campaign; Sinn Féin vice president Mary Lou McDonald was a constant media presence; while Ruth Coppinger (AAA), Clare Daly and Joan Collins (both standing for the Independents 4 Change) enjoyed high media visibility. However, the set-piece media debates, of which there were six, included just four (21 per cent) women from among the nineteen participating politicians.[19] The premier current affairs programme, RTÉ's *Prime Time*, broadcast on nine occasions during the election campaign. Six of these programmes, excluding the leaders' debate, included panel discussions with politicians. Female politicians accounted for seven (37 per cent) of the nineteen appearances. However, taking into account the double appearance of Fine Gael's Frances Fitzgerald and Mary Lou McDonald from Sinn Féin, the actual representation of women politicians was just five (26 per cent).

Three leaders' debates (11, 15 and 23 February) punctuated a pedestrian campaign. In these media set pieces, party leaders sought to differentiate themselves from one another, shore up their core support, and attract new voters. Marking her credentials as a tough politician, Joan Burton joined Enda Kenny and Micheál Martin in the first leaders' debate in strongly criticising Sinn Féin leader Gerry Adams's position on national security issues—the abolition of the Special Criminal Court and the protection of jury members in organised crime and terrorism trials. She also led in defending the outgoing government's record on economic recovery and social protection, in particular attacking the Sinn Féin leader on the party's economic analysis. In the second debate, which comprised seven party leaders, Burton again challenged Adams on his housing strategy and defended the government's record in office while criticising Martin for his party's collapse of the economy. Her combative style, sporadic in the early debates, was more assured in the final debate, as she reinforced the government's track record on the economy, defended her own portfolio of social protection including contentious changes to housing supports, and once again criticised the opposition leaders' policies on the economy, justice and social affairs. There was, however, an element of sexism directed at Burton from the public. Her emphatic hand gestures during the television debates were subject to online comment, though Burton dismissed the comments as sexist, noting that 'lots of male politicians have peculiarities when speaking that are not picked up on'.[20]

Awareness of Gender Issues in Manifestos

Election manifestos offer voters a package of policies that together articulate the priorities and ideological disposition of the individual parties. They represent a significant investment of time and effort on behalf of each party or grouping, and are designed to win voter support. Given that manifestos, then, are central documents for communicating party platforms to the electorate, the manner in which they shape and present a gendered view of society is of significance.

A major theme of the 2011 election was political and policy reform, of which gender equality was an important aspect. The ensuing years kept gender equality on the political agenda, and the manifestos reflect this continued relevance. However, awareness of the gendered nature of policies and issues varied in party manifestos. Of the nine party manifestos examined, a gender-aware narrative was distinctively present in the manifestos of Fine Gael, Labour, Sinn Féin and the Social Democrats, suggesting that this was one of the policy perspectives that framed the drafters' thinking. The Fianna Fáil manifesto contained specific policy measures relating to gender equality, and presented a stronger tone on these aspects than the Green Party manifesto. In the relatively brief manifestos of PBP and AAA, recognition was accorded to some important woman-specific issues generally addressed by parties, such as reproductive choice, low/unequal pay, affordable childcare and ending violence against women. The Renua manifesto placed rewarding merit as a core principle, yet gave scant recognition to the gendered nature of implementing this principle.

The National Women's Council of Ireland (NWCI) engaged in a consultative exercise among its members from which it developed a 10-point *Breakthrough Manifesto for Women*.[21] The points included a mix of gender-sensitive public policy and classic feminist issues: effective measures to eliminate violence against women, repeal of the eighth amendment to the Constitution (inserted in 1983 with the intention of preventing the legalisation of abortion), provision of early years education and affordable childcare, an increase of women's participation in decision-making, closing the gender pay gap, and equality-proofed budgeting. It sought support from party leaders and individual candidates for this policy platform. There was cross-party consensus on some of these issues: addressing violence against women (point 1), prioritising early years education and affordable childcare (point 2), ending the gender pay gap (point 3), strengthening women's employment supports (point 7), and advancing women's participation in decision-making (point 8). This shared agreement on a gender-sensitive issue platform indicates a consciousness by parties of the need to be responsive to women voters. It seems somewhat more than coincidental that parties' heightened awareness of, and responsiveness to, female-gendered priorities took place in the context of candidate gender quota implementation. It is worth noting, though, that the issues on which there was cross-party manifesto consensus are not ones that unsettle the gender regime of twenty-first-century Ireland.

Looking at the responses in more detail, Labour, Sinn Féin and the Social Democrats leaders supported all nine points of the NWCI 10-point plan, compared with the seven and five points, respectively, to which Fine Gael and Fianna Fáil committed. In addition to having separate sticking points, both of these last two parties shared a reluctance to 'make sure every budget delivers on equality' (point 5), 'support reproductive rights and repeal the 8th amendment' (point 6), and 'protect and invest in public services and ensure they serve the needs of all women' (point 9).

Of the 551 election candidates, 144 (26 per cent) endorsed the NWCI manifesto—66 women and 78 men. A total of 121 candidates from left-leaning parties and independents pledged their support. Of the six Fine Gael and seven Fianna Fáil candidates endorsing the platform, all were non-incumbents, and the majority were first-time candidates. This suggests that for these candidates, supporting a woman-centred manifesto was one way to differentiate themselves from their running mates and other constituency competitors. It also shows how little support there is among the two traditional parties for a woman-oriented policy platform, suggesting a woman-empowering agenda will not be high on the list of government priorities in the Fine Gael-led minority government.

The Outcome

A total of 35 women were elected in the 2016 general election, 16 incumbents and 19 new female TDs. This is 40 per cent up on the number of women elected in 2011 (25) and means that 22 per cent of TDs are women, the highest proportion of women deputies in the history of the state, though still far from gender parity. In addition, 19 new women TDs is the highest number of non-incumbent women ever elected in a single Dáil election. In recent elections, the general pattern has been for male and female candidates to have similar success rates in seat winning. However, this was not the case in 2016 where over 31 per cent of males were successful compared to just under 22 per cent of females. This may be partly due to so many women being first-time national candidates.

Despite winning 26 fewer seats than in 2011, Fine Gael elected 11 women TDs in this election (Table 8.1). While this was not a numerical increase, it brought the proportion of women TDs in the party from 15 per cent to 22 per cent. Minister Heather Humphreys (Cavan–Monaghan) won the tenth highest vote in the country—the highest of any female candidate—and the second highest in Fine Gael after the Taoiseach. Three Fine Gael women incumbents lost their seats, but this was offset by the election of four new female non-incumbents. Just one woman selected via a gender directive, Cllr Josepha Madigan in Dublin Rathdown, was elected.

The election was disastrous for the Labour Party, which returned only seven TDs, all incumbents. Of the party's 13 women candidates, only Tánaiste and party leader Joan Burton and cabinet minister Jan O'Sullivan were elected. As for Fianna Fáil, given that none of its incumbents was a woman, the election of six female TDs in 2016 must be considered a huge success, particularly in light of internal controversies surrounding the implementation of gender quotas. Women now comprise 14 per cent of Fianna Fáil TDs. First-time TDs Mary Butler and Margaret Murphy-O'Mahony both topped the poll in their constituencies. In the Taoiseach's constituency of Mayo, Lisa Chambers won a second seat for the party at the expense of Michelle Mulherin, a Fine Gael incumbent candidate. However, Fianna Fáil still has no female representation in Dublin. Just one woman selected via a gender directive, Anne Rabbitte in Galway East, was elected.

The election was a good day for Sinn Féin women, who trebled their representation from two to six. Women now account for 26 per cent of Sinn Féin TDs. Incumbent TD and party vice president Mary Lou McDonald topped the poll in Dublin Central. After losing all of its seats in 2011, the Green Party elected one female and one male TD in this election. In Dublin Rathdown, the party's deputy leader Cllr Catherine Martin won the final seat at the expense of Alan Shatter, a Fine Gael TD and former cabinet minister. Interestingly, transfers from Fianna Fáil's Senator Mary White were key to Martin's electoral success.

There were mixed fortunes for women in the new political parties. The Social Democrats re-elected their three incumbent TDs and co-leaders, two women and one man. By contrast, Renua, led by Lucinda Creighton TD, failed to win any seats in this election. Two of the six AAA–PBP TDs are women: Bríd Smith and incumbent TD Ruth Coppinger. Finally, five of the twenty-three independent deputies in the 32nd Dáil are women. Incumbents Clare Daly, Joan Collins and Maureen O'Sullivan were all returned as were Senator Katherine Zappone and Cllr Catherine Connolly. No female Independent Alliance candidate was elected.

As seen in previous elections, an interesting geography of female representation emerged, with urban and commuter belt constituencies more gender-balanced than rural areas. Of the 35 women TDs, 26 represent a constituency in either Dublin or the rest of Leinster. In addition, eight of the ten constituencies with more than one woman deputy are in these regions. For the first time in election history, every Dublin constituency has female representation, and in two Dublin constituencies (Dublin South-Central and Dun Laoghaire) women received a majority of the votes. Also notable is the geographical spread in the female vote with women winning 39 per cent of the first preference vote (FPV) in the Dublin region, followed by the rest of Leinster (25 per cent), Connacht–Ulster (24 per cent) and Munster (15 per cent).[22] The data indicates the continuing presence of an urban–rural divide in terms of women's candidacy, election and support levels.

There were a number of local 'firsts' for women in this election. History was made in Louth where Imelda Munster (Sinn Féin) became the first woman TD ever elected in the county. Margaret Murphy-O'Mahony (Fianna Fáil) was the first female TD ever elected in the Cork South-West constituency as was Fiona O'Loughlin (Fianna Fáil) in Kildare South.

An analysis of the FPV shows that female candidates won over half a million votes (25 per cent of the total votes cast) for the first time. This represents an increase of almost 200,000 in the number of first preferences won by women candidates in the 2011 election. The increased support levels for women candidates is largely attributable to the higher number of women contesting this election. However, despite the increase in female support levels, male candidates won on average 830 more votes than female candidates (Table 8.2). This reflects the lower success rate for women candidates. The 2016 picture stands in contrast to the 2011 election where women candidates received slightly more FPVs on average than men.[23] Men outpolled women in all parties and groupings—apart from the Social Democrats, and there the relationship is reversed when we control for incumbency. The largest gender gap emerged in Fianna Fáil, with male candidates winning 3161 more votes on average than their female counterparts. Given that research consistently shows the electoral benefit of incumbency, this factor is likely to explain the vote difference. Just under 5 per cent of all candidates were female incumbents in comparison to 22 per cent of candidates who were male incumbents. Among female candidates, 85 per cent were challengers. A review of the vote share among incumbent and non-incumbent candidates show incumbents received an average vote of 7249 in comparison to 2665 for non-incumbents (Table 8.2). However, male incumbents outpoll their female counterparts by around 1100 votes, probably reflecting the fact that some of the male incumbents had very high personal votes. Among the 15 top vote-getters in the country, 14 were male incumbents. Among non-incumbents, women outpolled men by almost 100 votes on average, but female non-incumbents did relatively less well in Fianna Fáil and Fine Gael in particular.

Table 8.2 Analysis of first preference vote disaggregated according to party/ grouping, incumbency and gender

	All candidates		Incumbent TDs		Non-incumbents	
	Male	*Female*	*Male*	*Female*	*Male*	*Female*
Fianna Fáil	8294	5133	10,552	–	6983	5133
Fine Gael	6628	5182	6847	7650	5512	3730
Labour	4239	3337	4601	3833	2522	2759
Sinn Féin	6629	4622	8302	5770	5752	4554
Green Party	1531	1300	–	–	1531	1300
Social Dems	4087	5233	14,348	10,824	2622	2437
AAA–PBP	3188	2060	9390	6520	2413	1688
Renua	2091	1115	4358	4229	1807	670
Ind/Others	2031	1646	8263	5888	1309	1311
All	4115	3285	7433	6367	2635	2723
N	389	162	120	25	269	137

Much of the academic literature states that women are more likely to be elected in larger constituencies.[24] However, evidence of this in Irish general elections tends to be mixed, particularly in recent elections.[25] In 2016, over 33 per cent of TDs elected from three-seat constituencies were women, compared with 22 per cent of those elected from four-seaters and 15 per cent of those elected in five-seaters.[26] The increase in the number of Fianna Fáil and Fine Gael women candidates, particularly in three-seaters, appears to be an important factor in this outcome.

WOMEN TDS AND CABINET MINISTERS

Teaching remains the most common occupational background for women deputies in the 32nd Dáil but the employment histories of women TDs are varied (Table 8.3).[27] The average age of a female TD is 48.8 years and women deputies have an average of two children each. Over 70 per cent of female deputies have a third-level qualification.

Of the 35 women TDs elected, all bar one had previous office-holding experience: 16 were incumbent TDs, two were members of the outgoing Seanad, and 16 held council seats prior to their election as a TD. Most (83 per cent) of the 35 were councillors at some stage in their political careers. This election confirms the importance of local government experience in the political career development of women politicians in Ireland.[28]

Traditionally, women TDs benefited from the so-called 'widows and daughters inheritance' where family Dáil connections proved electorally advantageous to women candidates. This phenomenon disappeared in 2011 when, for the first time in history, none of the women TDs was related to a former TD.[29] In 2016, two women TDs have links to previous TDs: Fine Gael's Helen McEntee retained the seat she won in a 2013 by-election following the death of her father while the grand-uncle of Fianna Fáil's Niamh Smyth represented the Cavan constituency between 1923 and 1977.

Nowhere is the historical dominance of men in public life more evident than at ministerial level. Of the 190 people who served in government prior to the formation of the 30th government, only 15 were women. In December 2015, Enda Kenny reiterated an aspiration he stated previously to appoint an equal number of women and men to cabinet.[30] However, when the new government was eventually formed, it consisted of four women, the same number as in the outgoing cabinet. Frances Fitzgerald retained her position as Minister for Justice and Equality and also assumed the portfolio of Tánaiste, the fourth woman to hold this position

Table 8.3 Occupational backgrounds of women TDs in 32nd Dáil

Occupation	Number
Teacher	10
Trade union worker	5
Law	3
Administration (secretarial, clerical)	3
Accounting and finance	2
Business owner	2
Lecturer	1
Social worker	1
Credit union manager	1
Airline ground staff	1
Parliamentary assistant	1
Chef	1
Retail	1
Research and consultancy	1
Company director	1
Optician shop assistant	1
Total	35

following Mary Harney, Mary Coughlan and Joan Burton. Katherine Zappone, Minister for Children and Youth Affairs, is the second independent woman TD to hold a cabinet ministry following Mary Harney (2009–11) and the sixth person to hold a ministry as a first-time TD. Heather Humphreys was reappointed to Arts and Culture and the portfolio was expanded to include Rural Affairs and Regional Development. Mary Mitchell O'Connor was appointed Minister for Jobs, Enterprise and Innovation. With Regina Doherty appointed Government chief whip, the second woman to hold this position following Mary Hanafin between 2002 and 2004, and Máire Whelan retaining her position as Attorney General, six women now attend cabinet meetings, the highest number in the history of the state. When the full list of 18 ministers of state was announced two weeks later, only 4 of these were women (for full list, see Appendix 3). It would not have been easy to appoint more, though, because only one of the independent TDs supporting the government was a woman (Katherine Zappone, who was in the cabinet), while among Fine Gael TDs the only women now without a ministerial position are the four newly elected first-term TDs.

CONCLUSION

Without doubt, gender quotas contributed to an increase in women's candidate selection and election in the 2016 general election. They helped create a cultural shift in political parties whereby women party members and their electoral ambitions were no longer overlooked. Instead female candidacies were actively sought and facilitated by party strategists and more women than ever put themselves forward for selection. However an urban–rural divide remains in terms of women's candidacy, election and support levels. It is likely to take a few electoral cycles before the gender quota is fully embedded into the political system and these variations are moderated.

Gender quotas have generated a debate on the requisite and desired qualities of political candidacies, which is a positive development. However, this debate tends to focus on women only; male meritocracy and qualifications are rarely questioned or interrogated. The data on women's previous political experience illustrates that the majority of women selected and elected in the 2016 general election possessed very similar credentials to those of their male counterparts, dispelling any suggestion that they were in some way unqualified candidates relying solely on their gender.

The data also demonstrates the importance of local government experience in the political career development of women politicians in Ireland. Given the importance of local government experience to electoral success in Dáil elections, it is imperative that the gender quota is extended to local government elections. The recruitment and development of women politicians at the local level is essential if more are to be encouraged to run for national office.

Gender quotas, despite difficulties, have worked. In one electoral cycle between 2011 and 2016, women's political representation in Dáil Éireann has risen to 22 per cent, a six percentage point increase. This compares favourably to the five percentage point increase achieved across five electoral cycles between 1992 and 2011. Furthermore, women candidates won a higher share of the vote than ever before. But it is a case of 'a lot done; more to do'. Political parties must continue to encourage and support women's political candidacies if the number of women TDs is to increase further and gender parity in political representation is achieved.

Notes

1. Fiona Buckley, 'Women and politics in Ireland: the road to sex quotas', *Irish Political Studies* 28:3 (2013), pp. 341–359.
2. To be in receipt of state funding, parties must be registered and achieve at least 2 per cent of the first preference vote at the preceding general election.
3. Averil Power, 'Why Fianna Fáil isn't meeting local election target on female candidates', *Irish Times* 2 April 2014; http://www.irish-times.com/news/politics/why-fianna-f%C3%A1il-isn-t-meeting-local-election-target-on-female-candidates-1.1746169 (accessed 10 April 2016).
4. Fianna Fáil, *Markievicz Commission Report: Gender Equality Document,* 2015, pp. 4, 9; https://www.fiannafail.ie/download/Markievicz%20DL%20Bleedless.pdf. The commission was chaired by Professor Yvonne Galligan, Queen's University Belfast, one of the authors of this chapter (accessed 10 April 2016).
5. The Labour Party constitution states 'Where more than one candidate is to be selected, the Organisation Committee may also prescribe outcomes with regard to the gender balance of the panel of candidates selected'; https://www.labour.ie/party/constitution/ (accessed 11 April 2016).
6. Donegal was exempt from this rule as two male incumbent TDs contested the election. In October 2015, Sinn Féin added a third male candidate to the ticket. The addition proved a risky strategy that resulted in a split in the Sinn Féin vote and sitting TD Pádraig MacLochlainn losing his seat (see p. 145 above).
7. Quote from a Fine Gael regional organiser interviewed for this chapter.
8. Information sourced from interview with a party strategist.
9. Aspects of this section were previously published online. See Fiona Buckley, 'The 2016 Irish election demonstrated how gender quotas can shift the balance on female representation', *LSE EUROPP blog* http://blogs.lse.ac.uk/europpblog/2016/03/16/the-2016-irish-election-demonstrated-how-gender-quotas-can-shift-the-balance-on-female-representation/ 16 March 2016 (accessed 18 May 2016) and Fiona Buckley and Claire McGing, 'Analysis of the women selected and elected by quota in Ireland dispel the myth that they were under-qualified', *Democratic Audit blog*

http://www.democraticaudit.com/?p=20454 17 March 2016 (accessed 18 May 2016)

10. Sarah Childs and Paul Webb, *Sex, Gender and the Conservative Party: from iron lady to kitten heels* (Basingstoke: Palgrave Macmillan, 2012).

11. Childs and Webb, *Sex, Gender and the Conservative Party.*

12. Elin Bjarnegård, *Gender, Informal Institutions and Political Recruitment: explaining male dominance in parliamentary representation* (London: Palgrave Macmillan, 2013); Meryl Kenny, *Gender and Political Recruitment: theorizing institutional change* (Basingstoke: Palgrave Macmillan, 2013).

13. Bjarnegård, *Gender, Informal Institutions and Political Recruitment*; Kenny, *Gender and Political Recruitment.*

14. See comments by Derek Byrne and Mary O'Rourke on RTÉ's *Claire Byrne Live*, 23 November 2015—http://www.rte.ie/news/player/claire-byrne-live-web/2015/1124/#page=3 (accessed 5 May 2016).

15. Lesley Lavery, 'Gender bias in the media? An examination of local television news coverage of male and female House candidates', *Politics & Policy* 41:2 (2013), pp. 877–910.

16. Kelly Dittmar, *Navigating Gendered Terrain: Stereotypes and Strategy in Political Campaigns* (Philadelphia: Temple University Press, 2015).

17. Emily Harmer, *The right man for the job: the gendered campaign*, 2015—http://www.electionanalysis.uk/uk-election-analysis-2015/section-1-media-reporting/the-right-man-for-the-job-the-gendered-campaign/ (accessed 27 March 2016); Sylvia Shaw 'Winning and losing the "Battle for Number 10": A linguistic analysis of the Paxman vs Cameron/Miliband election interviews', p. 22 in Daniel Jackson and Einar Thornsen (eds) *UK Election Analysis 2015: Media, Voters and the Campaign* (Poole: Bournemouth University/ Political Studies Association, 2015); Deborah Cameron and Sylvia Shaw, *Gender, Power and Political Speech: women and language in the 2015 UK general election* (Basingstoke: Palgrave Macmillan, 2016).

18. Kathleen Dolan, 'Gender stereotypes, candidate evaluations, and voting for women candidates: what really matters?', *Political Research Quarterly* 67 (2014), pp. 96–107; Tessa Ditonto, Allison Hamilton and David Redlawsk, 'Gender stereotypes, information

search, and voting behavior in political campaigns', *Political Behavior* 36:2 (2013), pp. 335–358; Nichole Bauer, 'Emotional, sensitive and unfit for office? Gender stereotype activation and support for female candidates', *Political Psychology* 36:2 (2015), pp. 691–708.

19. Joan Burton, Labour leader; Lucinda Creighton, Renua leader; Mary Lou McDonald, Sinn Fein Deputy Leader and Kathleen Lynch, Labour Health spokesperson.
20. https://www.newstalk.com/election2016/Joan-Burton-debates-scrutinised-hand-gestures-GE16-general-election (accessed 27 March 2016).
21. National Women's Council of Ireland, 'Election 2016', at https://www.nwci.ie/index.php/election2016/ (accessed 27 March 2016).
22. Adrian Kavanagh, 'Female candidates at the 2016 general election', Irish Elections: Geography, Facts and Analyses, https://adriankavanaghelections.org/2016/02/29/female-candidates-at-the-2016-general-election/ (accessed 5 April 2016).
23. Fiona Buckley and Claire McGing, 'Women and the election', pp. 222–239 in Michael Gallagher and Michael Marsh (eds) *How Ireland Voted 2011* (London: Palgrave Macmillan, 2011), p. 235.
24. Richard Matland, 'Institutional variables affecting female representation in national legislatures: the case of Norway', *The Journal of Politics* 55:3 (1993), pp. 737–755.
25. For an overview of the literature, see Claire McGing, 'The single transferable vote and women's representation in Ireland', *Irish Political Studies* 28:3 (2013), pp. 322–340.
26. Dun Laoghaire is treated as a three-seat constituency as the Ceann Comhairle, Seán Barrett, was automatically re-elected.
27. Average age is calculated on the basis of 29 women TDs (six missing cases).
28. The gendered local-to-national 'pipeline' has been demonstrated by research on previous Dáil elections; see Fiona Buckley, Mack Mariani, Claire McGing and Timothy J. White, 'Is local office a springboard for women to Dáil Éireann?', *Journal of Women, Politics & Policy* 36:3 (2015) pp. 311–335.
29. Buckley and McGing, 'Women and the election', p. 231.
30. 'Taoiseach wants equal number of men and women in next cabinet', *Irish Times* 26 December 2015; http://www.irishtimes.

com/news/politics/taoiseach-wants-equal-number-of-men-and-women-in-next-cabinet-1.2477506; 'Enda Kenny pledges to appoint women to half of cabinet posts', *Irish Times* 19 December 2014; http://www.irishtimes.com/news/politics/enda-kenny-pledges-to-appoint-women-to-half-of-cabinet-posts-1.2043269 (accessed 1 May 2016).

CHAPTER 9

Independents and the Election: The Party Crashers

Liam Weeks

Few books on elections make any reference to independents, let alone have a whole chapter devoted to them. That it should be the case in this volume of *How Ireland Voted* is testimony to the performance of independents at the February 2016 Dáil election. A record 23 independent candidates were elected, beating the previous high of 16 in June 1927. This was not just a national record but also one of international standing, as it was proportionally the most independents elected to any national parliament in a mainstream democracy since 1950. It is not surprising then that 'Independents' Day' was one of the more common newspaper headlines dominating post-election coverage. As is detailed in Chapter 11, independents also had an extensive role to play in the formation of government, following which three independents were appointed to cabinet and another three became ministers of state. Although non-party technocrats are a feature of some Mediterranean democracies, it is highly unusual from a comparative perspective for an independent member of parliament (MP) to be a member of cabinet.

Detailing and explaining the election outcome for independents is the aim of this chapter, as well as placing it in both a national and an international context. The year 2016 was not the first time that independents had

L. Weeks (✉)
University College Cork, Cork, Ireland

© The Author(s) 2016   207
M. Gallagher, M. Marsh (eds.), *How Ireland Voted 2016*,
DOI 10.1007/978-3-319-40889-7_9

an electoral impact in Ireland, and understanding their presence in the Irish political system is a necessary precursor to an analysis of their fate in 2016. To achieve this, what follows is an examination of who or what we mean by independents and the reasons for their presence in Ireland. This precedes a scrutiny of independents' electoral performance in 2016, and the consequences this poses for the functioning of the Irish political system.

WHAT IS AN INDEPENDENT?

Independents are sometimes erroneously spoken of in the collective sense as if they are a unitary grouping. In the early decades of the Irish state, there was an element of truth to this because of the relative homogeneity of the independents in parliament. Most of them came from a conservative, constitutional stock and were anti-Fianna Fáil. They were also referred to in the Dáil as the 'Independent party', and reaped the benefits of such a status, having a party room in parliament buildings and being allocated places on parliamentary committees in accordance with their collective strength.[1] This homogeneity did not last, as more diverse independents began to emerge, and today independents comprise a heterogeneous residual group of politicians standing for office on a non-party label.[2]

It is not always clear what they are independent of, because some identify with a political party, even running on an 'Independent Fianna Fáil' or 'Independent Labour' ticket, while others are chosen to represent an interest group. Consequently, while the adjective 'independent' implies a lack of bias, politicians who adopt this label are not necessarily either neutral or non-partisan. It is in this context that many party politicians resent independents' use of this title because it implies that they (independents) are somewhat more virtuous than their party counterparts. This explains why, when party labels were first included on ballot papers in Ireland in the 1960s, party TDs were united in their opposition to independents being able to identify themselves as such on the ballot paper. This proviso remains in place in 2016, as the only label independents are able to use to describe their candidacy on the ballot is 'non-party'. This is the simplest means of defining an independent—a candidate not running for a party.

HISTORICAL FORTUNES OF INDEPENDENTS

Very few independents are elected to national parliament in most democracies. Of the 18 European Union (EU) democracies that currently permit independent candidacies at lower house elections, there were just 19 independents elected at the first set of general elections held in these countries in the 2010s. One was to the British House of Commons, three to the unicameral Lithuanian Seimas, with the remaining 15 independents to the Dáil in 2011. Widening our gaze to all 37 industrial democracies,[3] there were a further ten independents elected in the states outside of the EU. This means that more than half of all 29 elected independents in established democracies in the early 2010s sat in the Dáil. This Irish exceptionalism is not unique to the 2010s. Since 1990, only 8 of these 37 countries have had independents elected to national parliament. In the other regimes, there are either no independents elected, or independent candidacies are not permitted. In some parliaments, MPs occasionally leave their party to sit out the remaining parliamentary session as an independent, but very few, if any, of these are re-elected as independents.

Expanding beyond cases of elected independents to overall patterns of electoral support for independents, significant examples of this are also limited to a few countries. In an analysis of independents' performance at national elections in EU member states since 1945, it was found that in two-thirds of all elections support for independents is less than 1 per cent of the national vote.[4] There are just 20 cases where the national vote for independents has exceeded 5 per cent—11 in Ireland and 9 in Japan. Further, the 2011 Dáil election was the first time independents won more than 10 per cent of votes at a national parliamentary election in any mainstream democracy since 1950.

While independents' presence in the Dáil is of international significance, they were not always a feature of the Irish political landscape. For almost 100 years up until the establishment of the Irish Free State in 1922, the non-aligned or independent MP in Ireland was believed to be dormant, if not extinct. The first elections in the new jurisdiction in 1922 saw the entry of nine independents into the Dáil, a presence they have maintained continuously since. This is indicated in Fig. 9.1, which details the number of independents elected to parliament at each Dáil election since 1922, including 2016. As can be seen, they have experienced mixed fortunes. For the first few decades of the state, independents were a considerable electoral force, winning an average 12 seats per election. They represented minority interests not catered for by the political parties, including independent unionists standing for the Protestant community, independent nationalists for supporters of the defunct Irish Parliamentary Party, as well as independent business and independent farming candidates. It was not just the case that there was a core group of independents consistently re-elected over this period. Certainly there were some, such as Alfie Byrne

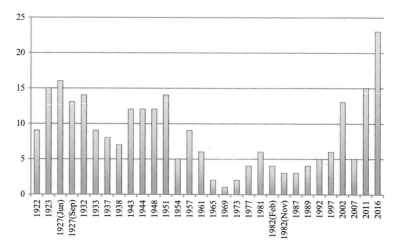

Fig. 9.1   Number of independents elected per Dáil, 1922–2016

in Dublin, elected on 12 consecutive occasions from 1922 until his death in 1956.[5] However, there was also a new crop of independents returned at every election and this continued into the 1950s. In 1923, nine new independents were elected to a Dáil of 153; in June 1927, the number was eight; there were four in 1932, 1937 (to a Dáil reduced in capacity to 138) and 1943; five in 1948 (to a Dáil of 147); and six in 1951. The exceptions were the 'snap' elections called less than a year into the Dáil's lifetime: September 1927 (one new independent TD), 1933 (no new independent) and 1938 (one new independent).

The success of independents at elections in the early years of a new party system is not an experience unique to Ireland. Because it takes time for a party system to settle on an established pattern of competition, for parties to establish identities, and for voters to forge concrete attachments to parties, the infant period of most party systems witnesses volatile electoral behaviour, a pattern that suits non-partisans such as independents. Once the political climate settles, and voters decide which party best suits their interests, parties gain a stranglehold on the political system and independents fall by the wayside. It took until the late 1950s for the parties to squeeze out independents in Ireland, as independents entered a period of decline in the subsequent two decades, with just two new independent TDs elected between 1961 and 1981.

Independents slowly re-emerged in the 1980s, beginning with an increase in the number of independent candidates. While the average number of independents contesting Dáil elections between 1922 and 1977 was 26, this doubled to 52 in 1977, and since 1997 the mean figure has doubled once again, to more than 100. Independents were thrust back into the limelight in the early 1980s, as first, several of them contributed to the defeat of the Fine Gael–Labour minority coalition's budget of January 1982, followed second, by the infamous Gregory Deal after the resultant election, when newly elected independent Tony Gregory held the balance of power in the Dáil, and negotiated an extensive agreement in exchange for his voting for Charlie Haughey of Fianna Fáil as Taoiseach.[6] Since then, apart from a hiccup in 2007, support for independents has been steadily on the rise, with more independents elected at almost every Dáil election since the 1980s. At the ten Dáil elections between 1961 and 1997, just eight new independent TDs were elected. At the six elections between 1997 and 2016, however, 31 new independent TDs were elected, including five in 1997, nine in 2002, nine in 2011 and eight in 2016.[7]

WHY THE INDEPENDENTS?

A number of factors explain the presence of independents in the Irish political system.[8] Perhaps the most commonly cited is the electoral system, proportional representation by the single transferable vote (PR-STV). Under PR-STV, the use of multi-seat constituencies in a small population ensures a relatively low electoral threshold. Any individual who can hope to attract five or six thousand first preferences has a reasonable chance of winning a seat to the Dáil. Ordinal voting, that is, the ability of voters to rank-order candidates, facilitates independents, as it can be easier for non-partisan candidates to attract lower preferences than those running for a party.[9] Preferential systems should also encourage sincere voting, lessening the likelihood that voters will fear wasting their vote on an independent, in contrast to what happens under plurality systems, where strategic voting militates against casting a vote for minor candidates such as independents. Being one of the more, if not the most, candidate-centred of voting systems,[10] STV encourages a form of political competition centred on candidates, which means that those without a party label (independents) are at less of a disadvantage than they would be under more party-centred systems. This works in tandem with the second factor, which is the presence of a candidate-centred political culture, where personalism and localism are to the fore.[11] These features contribute to an emphasis being placed on the personality and locality of candidates, again ensuring that those without a party brand are not at a disadvantage. The nature of this political competition is also a product of a party system with weak social bases, and where ideological competition is not to the fore.[12] In other European party systems, competition has traditionally been structured around social cleavages, which makes it difficult for independents running on individual platforms to compete. In contrast, the localistic and personalistic nature of competition in Ireland, where 'choosing a candidate to look after the needs of the constituency', is the most important priority of voters,[13] facilitates independents.

Another, related, behavioural feature is the level of detachment from political parties. Since it was first measured in the 1970s, Irish voters have historically had the lowest levels of closeness to a party compared to voters in most other industrial democracies.[14] The year 2016 proved no different, as 73 per cent stated they did not feel close to any party (cf p. 179 above).[15] This matters for independents because it indicates a political environment conducive to their emergence. It is also relatively easy to run in Ireland as an independent, certainly compared to other systems that prohibit independents, or that require a large monetary deposit. In Ireland, the requirement for an independent candidacy is €500 or 30 signatures, which makes it one of the least cartelised systems for aspirant candidates,[16] and more conducive to the emergence of independents.

A final factor to consider is the influence independents can exert on the government formation process.[17] Minority administrations are a frequent occurrence in Ireland, and these generally look to independents for support. Of the 11 governments formed after elections between 1980 and 2016, 7 ultimately relied on independents, while in another 2 cases (2002 and 2011) independents had some bargaining power and were an option for a hypothetical single-party minority government. The support provided by independents historically tends to be outside of cabinet, and up to 2016 there had been only two cases of independent ministers, James Dillon (1948–51) and Mary Harney (2009–11). This external position provides independents with a buffer to absolve themselves of blame for governmental mishaps, and makes it easier for them to withdraw their support. Rather than a cabinet post, the cost of an independent TD's vote in parliament tends to comprise patronage for the TD's constituency. The rulebook changed somewhat in 2016, as the main concession extracted by independents in return for their supporting a Fine Gael minority government was influence at the national level in the form of ministerial posts, rather than the traditional model of local influence via patronage deals, although the latter were by no means absent (see Chapter 11). Whatever their impact, independents' role in the formation of governments gives them a relevance and increases the rationality of a vote for independents.

THE CAMPAIGN

Support for independents grew in the lifetime of the 31st Dáil, and by mid-2014, independents and others were the most popular political grouping according to opinion polls. This rise of independents was confirmed in the May local elections of that year, when they won a combined 23 per cent first preference vote, just one percentage point behind Fine Gael, and two behind Fianna Fáil. While many expected independents' support levels to decline in the run-up to the general election, when voters focus on more national issues, such a fall never materialised, and the only significant changes were that some of the 'others' formed parties and alliances, increasing their share of this vote vis-à-vis independents.

The high levels of support for independents was undoubtedly a factor in the emergence of many new independent candidates in 2016. The year 2011 had witnessed a record 173 independents contesting a Dáil election, but this was in part due to the economic and political instability of the time. While it was not clear to what extent the latter had abated in 2016, the former seemed to have, and with a reduction in Dáil seats and constituencies, and increased competition from newly emergent parties, a significant decline in the number of independent candidates would not have been unexpected. That it fell by just ten, with the proportion of total candidates comprising independents narrowly declining from 31 per cent in 2011 to 30 per cent in 2016, indicates the persistent attractiveness of an independent candidacy.

Of the 163 independent candidates running in 2016, 44 were sitting local councillors, 19 were TDs and three were senators. In total, almost 40 per cent of independent candidates held political office at the time of the election. Fifty-nine (36 per cent) had previously contested Dáil elections, and 100 (61 per cent) had run for local office. In total, 119 of the 163 had experience either of elections or of holding political office.

Cognisant of the increased spotlight brought on by their rise in support, and hoping both to allay fears concerning potential instability and to maximise their opportunities if elected, a number of independents formed alliances with each other. For some, this comprised full-blown parties, in the form of Renua and the Social Democrats (see Chapters 1 and 4). A different initiative was an Independent Alliance of five independent TDs (Michael Fitzmaurice, Tom Fleming,[18] John Halligan, Finian McGrath and Shane Ross) and two senators (Feargal Quinn and Gerard Craughwell), which launched in 2015. Keen from the outset to emphasise that it was not a party, the Independent Alliance nevertheless promised to provide united support to a government on financial legislation and confidence issues provided it agreed with the Alliance's ten key demands, as outlined in a 'charter for change' (see p. 87). The Independent Alliance ultimately ran 21 candidates, including a number of local councillors and former Green TD, Paul Gogarty. Another, less high-profile and primarily left-wing, group of independents was Independents 4 Change. This included four TDs—Mick Wallace in Wexford, Clare Daly in Dublin Fingal, Joan Collins in Dublin South-Central and former Labour TD Tommy Broughan in Dublin Bay North. All four had signed up to the principles of the anti-water charge movement Right2Change. Although all members of the group maintained independence of each other, the group was officially registered as a political party, both to highlight the Right2Change campaign and to get their independent banner on the ballot paper. A 'rural alliance' of five independent TDs also formed after the 2016 election, initially comprising Denis Naughten from Roscommon–Galway, Mattie McGrath from Tipperary, Michael Harty from Clare, Michael Collins from Cork South-West and Noel Grealish from Galway West.

THE RESULTS

The support for independents that had been evident in the polls materialised on election day. They won 17 per cent of first preference votes, the most ever for independents in any national parliamentary election in an established democracy since 1950. They also won 23 seats, including four for Independents 4 Change and six for the Independent Alliance. The four sitting Independents 4 Change TDs were all re-elected, as were the four outgoing members of the Independent Alliance, which added councillors Kevin 'Boxer' Moran in Longford–Westmeath and Sean Canney in Galway East to its ranks.

Mean support for an independent was just over 4 per cent of the constituency vote, but this low figure is due to the considerable number attracting a very low tally. Sixty-five (40 per cent) of independent candidates won less than 1 per cent of votes, and a further 54 (33 per cent) won between 1 and 5 per cent. Outside of these candidates, the mean vote won by the remaining 44 independents was 11 per cent. Twenty-two independents won more than 10 per cent of first preferences in their constituency, and 16 of these won a seat. The mean vote won by incumbent independent TDs was 13 per cent, and 16 (84 per cent) of them were re-elected, in line with historical re-election rates of 80 per cent for independent TDs. The three independents who failed to hold onto their seats were Éamonn Maloney, Peter Mathews and Seán Conlan, all of whom were elected on a party ticket in 2011, and were running as an independent for the first time. Not surprisingly, political experience had a significant effect on the vote accrued by independents. The mean first preference for sitting councillors (five of whom, and 11 per cent of all independent councillors running, were elected) was 6 per cent, while the vote for those with no political office (98 independents) was just over 1 per cent. Independents with no experience of either running for, or of holding, political office won less than 2 per cent. Only one of them was elected, Michael Harty in Clare, a general practitioner who stood on a 'no doctor, no village' platform.

In 18, almost half of all, constituencies, the total vote for independents was at least 18 per cent, a large enough proportion of the Droop quota (see Appendix 4) to get elected in four- and five-seat constituencies, and in some cases a three-seat constituency. Independents won seats in all bar three of these 18 constituencies, missing out in Offaly (in spite of independents winning almost one in four first preferences), Limerick City and Cork North-West, all three-seaters. The only constituency outside of these 18 where independents won a seat was Wexford, where Mick Wallace won one of the five seats with a first preference total down over 5000 votes on 2011, when he had been the sixth highest vote-getter in the country.

In some constituencies, the increase in support for independents was substantial, by more than 20 percentage points in Cork South-West, Dublin Fingal (primarily just due to a change in the status of sitting socialist TD, Clare Daly), Kerry and Roscommon–Galway, while in another five constituencies it increased by between 10 and 20 percentage points. The national swing to independents was not universal, however, as their vote declined in 15 constituencies, although in six cases this change was less than two percentage points. The biggest swings against independents were in Kildare North and Wicklow, due to the switch in allegiance of Catherine Murphy and Stephen Donnelly, the respective independents elected in these constituencies in 2011, who helped found the Social Democrats party in 2015.

In terms of the constituencies that proved very fertile territory for independents, a number of them saw multiple independents returned. Two independents were elected in the five-seat constituencies of Galway West (Noel Grealish and Catherine Connolly), Kerry (Danny and Michael Healy-Rae) and Dublin Bay North (Tommy Broughan and Finian McGrath), and in the three-seat constituency of Roscommon–Galway (Michael Fitzmaurice and Denis Naughten), where a majority of voters supported independent candidates. For the first time ever, three independents were returned from a single constituency,[19] as Séamus Healy, Michael Lowry and Mattie McGrath all held their seats in the new five-seat constituency of Tipperary.

Of all these cases of multiple independents elected, Catherine Connolly and Danny Healy-Rae were the only non-incumbent TDs. The feat achieved by the latter and his brother in Kerry was unprecedented, becoming the first set of siblings elected from the same constituency at the same time.[20] Although a last-minute nomination, Danny built on his success at the 2014 local elections, when he had won the second largest number of first preferences (almost 4500; more than two quotas) of any candidate in the country. In 2016, the two Healy-Raes topped the poll in Kerry after the first preference count. Michael won 20,378 votes, the most in the country, and the fifth highest first preference ever at a Dáil election. Sibling loyalty was not as high as might have been expected as just over 50 per cent of his surplus transferred to his brother, but this was enough to elect Danny on the second count.

Although there were eight more independents elected than in 2011, the number of new independent TDs fell from nine to seven.[21] Despite the increased independent vote, there were few surprises in terms of the elected independents. Six of the eight new independents were serving county councillors with a strong electoral base, the two exceptions being Michael Harty and Senator Katherine Zappone in Dublin South-West. One independent who seemed unlikely to win a seat when the first preference votes were counted was Maureen O'Sullivan, a TD for Dublin Central since 2009. She attracted just 1990 first preferences but, demonstrating the advantage of PR-STV for independents, picked up transfers from all candidates, before overtaking Gary Gannon of the Social Democrats by 178 votes for the last seat on the 11th and final count (see her account in Chapter 5).

In terms of regional representation, independents seemed to do well in rural areas, capitalising on the perception that the economic recovery had not reached beyond the Dublin region. Apart from gaps in Mayo and Sligo–Leitrim, Independents were represented along the western seaboard from the most northerly point in the country of Malin Head in Donegal (with Thomas Pringle) to the most southerly point of Mizen Head in Cork South-West (with Michael Collins). They did not fare as well in the commuter belt counties around Dublin, failing to win a combined vote of more than 10 per cent in Carlow–Kilkenny, Louth, Wicklow and the two constituencies in Kildare and Meath. Independents had more success in Dublin, although these were primarily left-wing candidates, with the exception of Shane Ross in Dublin Rathdown.

ANALYSIS

Explaining the basis of support for independents is fraught with difficulties because of the heterogeneity of the candidates. Evidence from exit polls and previous election studies indicate little to no social bases to the independent vote, as regional differences tend to be averaged out in a national aggregate.[22] However, there is some distinctive attitudinal sentiment motivating support for independents, which echoes the aforementioned importance of anti-party sentiment, personalism and localism.

Independent voters were asked in May 2015 why they would prefer to vote for an independent, and the most popular answer given (by 31 per cent) was because the independents focused on local issues. Twenty-six per cent said it was because they do not trust or like the parties, 16 per cent because the candidates were independent of parties, 14 per cent because they agreed with their policies, 14 per cent because the candidate was known to them personally, and 10 per cent said because they believe independents are reforming and have new ideas.[23] Indeed, independent voters were almost twice as likely to cite the latter incentive as those voting for the main parties.[24]

Independent voters were not asked similar questions in an exit poll after the February election, making direct comparison difficult. However, stressing the new significance given to the independent label, 29 per cent of those voting independent said they did so because the candidate was an independent. They also had a greater constituency focus and less of a national and policy focus than party voters. When asked to rank the most important incentive in deciding their vote, 55 per cent of independent voters said choosing a candidate to look after the needs of the constituency was their main priority, compared to 38 per cent of voters for the main parties. Choosing between the policies as set out by the parties was important for 20 per cent of independent voters, compared to 32 per cent of main party voters.[25]

In terms of the specific issues that were the greatest influence on their first preference, there were clear differences between those voting for independents and those for the government parties. However, such differences were not as significant between independent and opposition party voters. Independent voters were less likely to cite management of the economy (12 per cent) than Fine Gael (28 per cent) or Labour voters (23 per cent), but were closer in sentiment to Fianna Fáil voters (15 per cent cited this issue) and Sinn Féin voters (11 per cent). Likewise, 5 per cent of independent voters cited stable government as an incentive, compared to 21 per cent of Fine Gael voters and 12 per cent of Labour voters, but just 6 per cent and 2 per cent of Fianna Fáil and Sinn Féin voters, respectively. There was an element of economic grievance to the independent vote, as just 27 per cent of those voting for independents said the economy was better off than in 2015, compared to the national mean of 46 per cent. Again, independents were closer in sentiment to opposition than government party voters (cf Table 7.7, and associated discussion, above). Twenty-eight per cent of independent voters said the economy was worse off than in 2015, compared to 5 per cent of government party voters, but 20 per cent and 41 per cent of those voting for Fianna Fáil and Sinn Féin. In terms of their personal financial situation, 13 per cent of independent voters felt better off than in 2015, compared to 40 per cent of government party voters, 22 per cent of Fianna Fáil voters and 14 per cent of Sinn Féin voters.

CONSEQUENCES OF INDEPENDENTS FOR THE IRISH POLITICAL SYSTEM

The conventional wisdom among many commentators, political scientists and, not surprisingly, political parties is that independents are bad for parliamentary democracy. They see independents as free riders, who avoid the responsibility of governing, but at the same time wish to extract patronage from governments. They see independents as shirking responsibility by prioritising local over national interests, and adopting populist mantras that they know can never be adopted, but for which they will never be in a position to have to make a decision. Such critics of independents believe that the latter contribute to instability, by making the formation and maintenance of government more difficult. Independents are also reproached for negotiating secret arrangements with party leaders when they hold the balance of power, the cost of which can involve the redistribution of state resources in favour of their respective constituencies. For these various reasons, former Labour minister Barry Desmond once described independents as 'like perfume: lovely to smell but dangerous to swallow'.[26] Given such criticisms, what are the consequences of this presence of independents for the Irish political system? This is addressed by an analysis of four of the key arguments made against independents.

Independents Make It Difficult to Form a Government

The first criticism is that independents occupying seats in parliament deprive parties of an overall majority, reducing the possibilities concerning government formation and rendering the process more difficult. Certainly it is true that whenever a single party fails to win an overall majority, government formation is that bit more difficult. But it is not wholly clear why more independents would necessarily make the process more arduous, since it is negotiations between parties that tend to be lengthier, as was evident in 2016. Indeed, there is quite a weak relationship between the numbers of independents in the Dáil and the length of time taken to form a government. If anything, independents can make the process of government formation somewhat easier, as they do not have to consult a parliamentary party or grass-roots members, which can sometimes be a stumbling block for inter-party discussions. Independents also do not wish to be responsible for the failure to form a government and the calling of a sudden election, at which they historically have tended to lose seats. This is one of the reasons why independents tend to be more than willing to negotiate agreements with minority governments.

Independents Cause Instability

The fear here concerns the level of instability that can ensue when minority governments look to independents rather than parties for external support. In the absence of a whip, independents are free to withdraw their support at any stage, and they can be under significant pressure from their local constituency to do so if the government introduces unpopular initiatives with local repercussions. The consequence is that such a government might always be teetering on the edge, one step away from collapsing, with significant effects for its ability to function and for the external perception of the stability of the national economy. Those who express such fears highlight the early 1980s as an example, when there were three general elections in 18 months, as two minority governments reliant on independents both survived less than one year.

Certainly, this threat of instability is a pressing issue that minority administrations have to face, and one that can undermine their ability to implement long-term strategies. It might also have the consequence that much of their time is spent in the form of day-to-day conflict management, the main aim of which is survival. Such a government might be likely to avoid the hard issues, those that most need resolution but that are particularly likely to contribute to its defeat.

In terms of a government's longevity, administrations looking to the support of independents have lasted an average of two years and eight months, shorter than the average majority government (three years and five months), but not short from an international perspective. This does not necessarily imply that such governments were not unstable, but one measure of stability is the support independents provide to governments in the Dáil. Considering all governments back to 1937, independents propping up a minority administration support them in 84 per cent of Dáil votes, compared to 22 per cent support from independents in opposition.[27] This suggests that independents can provide a level of stability, or at least support, to a government, and that it need not be short-lived nor regularly defeated. Whether such governments survive because they are strong enough to almost compel independent support, or because their weakness means they avoid potential conflict with independents, is another issue.

Independents Skew the Allocation of National Resources

The cost of the support independents provide to minority governments tends to be patronage for their respective constituencies, the details of which are sometimes part of an undisclosed agreement, such as those negotiated by independent TD Jackie Healy-Rae with Fianna Fáil party leader Bertie Ahern in 1997 and 2007. The democratic validity, and disproportionate nature, of this power, especially in relation to independents' influence on distributive policy, has been the source of some criticism, as it is claimed that this skews the allocation of national resources, without regard to priorities and needs.[28]

It is difficult to determine the true nature of independents' influence. Some of them in the past claimed responsibility for a lot of infrastructural expenditure.[29] However, an unknown quantity of this could already have been destined for the independent's constituency, irrespective of their influence. Independents may simply have been given advance notice by the government in order to allow them to claim credit for this expenditure. It could well be that independents' influence is exaggerated and is a quasi-charade tolerated by the government because it ensures the independents and their voters remain on side. Former Taoiseach Bertie Ahern, who negotiated agreements with four independents in two of his three administrations, admitted 'it was all a game'.[30] The independents issued threats, but so long as the government appeased them, they were kept on side. The ambiguous nature of this relationship is compounded by the secret nature of some of the independents' agreements with party leaders. This lack of transparency has been criticised, yet if such deals had to be published, independents might be under significant local pressure to demand more. Somewhat ironically, making such deals public might therefore result in a greater skew of the distribution of resources. The independents negotiating with Fianna Fáil and Fine Gael in 2016 to form a government were conscious of these accusations, and so both the Independent Alliance and the rural alliance were keen to stress that local deals would not be the cost of their vote. Nevertheless, there were claims after the formation of the government that projects in the constituencies of the independents supporting it would be prioritised.[31]

Independents Reduce the Efficiency and Accountability of Parliament

There are a number of concerns here. The first is that nothing will get done in parliament if there are too many independents, with a minority government needing their support, but unable to enforce it via a whip. In such a scenario, it could be difficult to secure parliamentary majorities to pass legislation, making the government a lame duck administration. Another concern is that it could be difficult for any government to form a coherent national policy if it had to pander to a large number of independents, each with their own concerns. The consequence could be that such policies are simply a mishmash aggregate of local interests. Of course, this does not necessarily imply that policies made by party governments in an environment where independents have no influence are always coherent. It would also be naïve to imagine that when formulating policy, Irish governments do not take account of local concerns, regardless of the presence or otherwise of independents.

In terms of accountability, independents cannot be held to account nationally as they contest only their local constituency. If independents were determining policy it would be difficult for voters to know whom to hold to account and how. The presence of parties also facilitates parliamentarians interpreting the nature of their mandate, and whether parties' policies are supported by voters. The argument here is that without a party running candidates in most constituencies, parliamentarians would not know what policies were preferred by voters.[32] These criticisms of independents concerning efficiency and accountability are really only relevant in a system where independents constitute a sizeable proportion, if not a majority, of parliament.[33] This is not the case in the Dáil, and in addition, such a defence of parties is based on a number of questionable and idealistic assumptions, namely whether voters cast preferences based on policy, are aware of party platforms, the nature of the mandate they give to parties, and whether they are capable of crediting or blaming parties for past performance.[34]

CONCLUSION

The Irish political system has always been friendly to independents, but in 2016 it reached unprecedented levels of affection. If independents are treated as a single grouping, they now seem to be one of the main pillars of the political system, but whether the foundations on which the independent bloc stand are more quicksand than granite remains to be seen. The disaffection with parties and the historical presence of independents suggests that they are not going anywhere just yet, but whether independents retain such sizeable levels of support is another matter. When they were elected in considerable numbers in the past, independents were often enticed into parties, but this is unlikely to happen now, given how unpalatable such a switch would be to their respective electorates. Indeed, any independent TD contemplating such a move would do well to pay heed to the electoral record of independents joining parties. Since 1937, of the nineteen independent TDs who have joined one of the three main parties while in parliament, only seven were re-elected.

The resurgence of independents in Ireland can perhaps be seen as part of a wider international rise of independents. They have been elected to both Houses of Congress and several governorships in the USA, and to parliament in Australia, Canada and the UK. However, it is stretching the comparative evidence too far to call it a rise, as these independent victories remain rather isolated cases, and what is happening in Ireland is far greater than all these other countries combined. It may be more appropriate to view the presence of independents in Ireland as part of the increasing personalisation of politics, which is manifested in different guises in other countries. This includes weakening partisanship, and the increased importance of individual candidates over party brand.[35] Another possible angle is that the resurgence of independents in Ireland is part of the wider phenomenon of the rise of populism. While in other countries electorally this has taken the form of parties, it could be that independents are one Irish variant of populism. Certainly, independents tap into the anti-party sentiment that has fuelled support for populist parties such as the Five Star Movement in Italy and Podemos in Spain, and for populist candidates in the USA such as Donald Trump and Bernie Sanders. The economic grievances and desire for reform of independent voters in Ireland reflects the mood of populist voters elsewhere.

Just as the rise of populist parties led some to fear the consequences for the stability of their respective polities, so too the presence of independents in Ireland stimulated much discussion about their ability to undermine the functioning of the political system. Measures of good governance, such as the Worldwide Governance Indicators produced by the World Bank since 1996, are one means of examining such consequences. These indicators measure perceptions of governance such as accountability, political stability, government effectiveness and control of corruption.[36] Periods of minority government rule reliant on independents had little effect on these variables, with the exception of the 2007–11 administration, when the decline in the quality of governance was the product of an economic recession, not necessarily independents' influence. Rather than weakening the political system, it was suggested in the aftermath of the 2016 election that a minority government reliant on independents might actually strengthen parliamentary democracy, by making the government more accountable.[37] Whether this materialises will no doubt be a topic of discussion for the next volume of this series.

NOTES

1. Basil Chubb, 'The independent member in Ireland', *Political Studies* 5 (1957), pp. 131–142, at p. 137.
2. Liam Weeks, 'We don't like to party: a typology of independents in Irish political life, 1922–2007', *Irish Political Studies* 24:1 (2009), pp. 1–27.

3. These are the 28 EU member states plus Australia, Canada, Iceland, Israel, Japan, New Zealand, Norway, Switzerland and the USA.

4. Piret Ehin, Ülle Madise, Mihkel Solvak, Rein Taagepera, Kristjan Vassil and Priit Vinkel, *Independent Candidates in National and European Elections* (Brussels: Policy Department, European Parliament, 2013), p. 29.

5. Three of his sons were also elected independent TDs: Alfie 'Fred' Jr. (1937–1952), Thomas (1952–1961), and Patrick (1956–1969), who later joined Fine Gael.

6. See Robbie Gilligan, *Tony Gregory* (Dublin: O'Brien Press, 2011), pp. 73–105.

7. Nine of the 39 new independent TDs since 1961 had previously been elected to the Dáil for a party: Seán Dunne in 1961, Neil Blaney in 1973, John O'Connell in 1981, Seán Treacy in 1987, Michael Lowry in 1997, Beverley Flynn in 2007, Noel Grealish and Mattie McGrath in 2011, and Denis Naughten in 2016.

8. See, for example, Liam Weeks, 'Why are there independents in Ireland?', *Government and Opposition*, published online 30 March 2015; Liam Weeks, 'Crashing the party: does STV help independents?'. *Party Politics* 20:4 (2014), pp. 604–616; Nicole Bolleyer and Liam Weeks, 'The puzzle of non-party actors in party democracy: independents in Ireland', *Comparative European Politics* 7:3 (2009), pp. 299–324.

9. Dawn Brancati, 'Winning alone: the electoral fate of independent candidates worldwide', *The Journal of Politics* 70:3 (2008), pp. 648–662, at p. 656.

10. Irish STV was ranked as the most candidate-centred electoral system in the Comparative Study of Electoral Systems (CSES) dataset of 29 democracies. David Farrell and Ian McAllister, *The Australian Electoral System: Origins, Variations, and Consequences* (Sydney: University of New South Wales Press, 2006), p. 154.

11. For more on the reasons motivating an independent vote, see Liam Weeks, 'Rage against the machine: who is the independent voter?', *Irish Political Studies* 26:1 (2011), pp. 19–43.

12. Liam Weeks, 'Parties and the party system', pp. 137–167 in John Coakley and Michael Gallagher (eds), *Politics in the Republic of Ireland,* 5th ed (London: Routledge, 2010), pp. 137–140.

13. Richard Sinnott, *Irish voters decide: voting behaviour in elections and referendums since 1918* (Manchester: Manchester University Press, 1995), p. 169.

14. Weeks, 'Rage against the machine', p. 34. See also Eurobarometer surveys 1978–1994; CSES database 1996–2015 @www.cses.org

15. RTÉ/Behaviour & Attitudes, *General election exit poll report*, 26 February 2016.

16. In a comparative analysis of ballot access, countries were ranked by their ease of access for potential candidates, which considered the electoral deposit, the number of petitioned electors required for a nomination, and the proportion of votes needed for a deposit refund. Ireland was ranked second after Luxembourg, making it one of the least cartelised systems. See Amir Abedi, *Anti-Political Establishment Parties: a comparative analysis* (London: Routledge, 2004), pp. 93–94.

17. For more, see Liam Weeks, 'Independents in government: a sui generis model?', pp. 137–156 in Kris Deschouwer (ed), *New parties in government: in power for the first time* (London: Routledge, 2008).

18. Tom Fleming later decided not to contest the election.

19. Excluding the Dublin University constituency, whose three seats were always occupied by independents up until the removal of university representation in 1937.

20. There are five other sets of siblings who represented the same constituency during the lifetime of the same Dáil, but not at the same time. Each case involved one sibling being elected at a by-election caused by the death of the other: Thomas Byrne replaced Alfie Byrne Jr. in Dublin NW in 1952; Patrick Belton replaced Jack Belton in Dublin NE in 1963; Cathal Coughlan replaced Clement Coughlan in Donegal SW in 1983; Mary Upton replaced Pat Upton in Dublin SC in 1999; and Gabrielle McFadden replaced Nicky McFadden in Longford–Westmeath in 2014.

21. This figure includes Denis Naughten, a TD for Fine Gael from 1997 to July 2011, when he lost the party whip for voting against cuts to health services in his constituency. He is classified as a new independent TD in 2016 as it was the first time he was elected on an independent platform.

22. Weeks, 'Rage against the machine'.

23. These questions were not asked of party voters.

24. Ipsos MRBI poll, *The Irish Times,* 14 May 2015.

25. RTÉ/Behaviour & Attitudes, *General election exit poll report,* 26 February 2016.

26. Stephen Collins, 'The rise and rise of independents', *The Irish Times* 1 November 2014.
27. Thanks to Martin Hansen for providing this roll-call data. See Martin E. Hansen, 'The parliamentary behaviour of minor parties and independents in Dáil Éireann', *Irish Political Studies* 25:4 (2010), pp. 643–660.
28. See, for example, former Taoiseach Garret FitzGerald, 'Gregory deal a precursor to destructive localism of politics', *The Irish Times* 19 August 2000.
29. For examples of such claims, see a series of newspaper interviews in 2000 with the four independent TDs supporting the Fianna Fáil–Progressive Democrat minority coalition in *The Irish Times* 7–10 August 2000.
30. Donal Hickey, *The Healy-Raes. A Twenty-Four Seven Political Legacy* (Killarney: Rushy Mountain Books, 2015), p. 69.
31. Pat Leahy, 'Independents playing both sides of political fence', *The Irish Times* 14 May 2016.
32. John Aldrich, *Why Parties: the origin and transformation of political parties in America* (Chicago: Chicago University Press, 1995), p. 23.
33. For more on how parliaments operate in the absence of parties see Liam Weeks, 'Parliaments without parties', *Australasian Parliamentary Review* 30:2 (2015), pp. 61–71.
34. Kaare Strøm, Wolfgang C. Müller, Torbjörn Bergman and Benjamin Nyblade, 'Dimensions of citizen control', pp. 651–706 in Kaare Strøm, Wolfgang C. Müller, and Torbjörn Bergman (eds), *Delegation and Accountability in Parliamentary Democracies* (Oxford: Oxford University Press, 2003), pp. 652–654.
35. Lauri Karvonen, *The Personalisation of Politics: A Study of Parliamentary Democracies* (Colchester: ECPR Press, 2010), pp. 21–22.
36. See govindicators.org
37. Eoin O'Malley, 'Minority government could be the best outcome', *The Irish Times* 27 February 2016; Ciaran Cannon, 'Why minority governments are the best way forward in the national interest', *Irish Independent* 2 March 2016.

CHAPTER 10

The Seanad Election: Second Chamber, Second Chance

Mary C. Murphy

The backdrop to the 2016 elections to Seanad Éireann was unlike that of any previous election. The prolonged and protracted process of forming a government following elections to Dáil Éireann in March meant that the election to the 25th Seanad took place in something of a political vacuum. With no government in place and ambiguity in relation to the possibility of a government being formed, the likelihood of a newly elected Seanad lasting no more than a few days seemed at various points to be a real prospect. It was also unclear if membership of the 25th Seanad would be complete given that it is the responsibility of the incoming Taoiseach, and not the caretaker Taoiseach, to nominate 11 Seanad members (Article 18.3 of the constitution). Eventual agreement on the formation of a minority government 10 weeks after the Dáil elections led to the nomination of the remaining 11 members by the Taoiseach a further three weeks later on 27 May.

The absence of a government was not the only factor that impacted on the 25th Seanad. During the lifetime of the 24th Seanad (2011–16), plans to abolish the institution were actively pursued. In 2009, Fine Gael leader Enda Kenny had proposed abolition of the Seanad, a position that was later included in the 2011 Fine Gael general election manifesto. There

M.C. Murphy (✉)
University College Cork, Cork, Ireland

© The Author(s) 2016
M. Gallagher, M. Marsh (eds.), *How Ireland Voted 2016*,
DOI 10.1007/978-3-319-40889-7_10

was some expectation that the 24th Seanad might have been the final Seanad.[1] The Seanad abolition referendum was held on 4 October 2013 and recorded a narrow win for those who favoured retention of the institution. On a turnout of 39 per cent, 52 per cent of voters chose to maintain Ireland's bicameral parliamentary system.[2] The result was surprising as opinion polls had suggested a victory for those who supported abolition. Instead, a vocal and ultimately effective Seanad reform campaign persuaded voters to not just save the institution, but to push for its substantial reform. In response to the vote, the government committed to a reform agenda and appointed an independent Seanad Reform Working Group (SRWG). The report of the SRWG was published in April 2015, but none of its recommendations was implemented before the dissolution of Seanad Éireann a year later. This effectively meant that the 25th Seanad election was conducted along the very same lines as had always been the case.

For all the similarities to previous elections, however, there were some novel features. Despite the resilience of the partisan vote, the 2016 Seanad election produced a more diverse membership recording gains for Independent candidates, Sinn Féin and the Green Party. The election also mirrored the outcome of the Dáil election by failing to produce a government majority. This chapter considers the election of the 43 panel members—their nomination, campaigns and election, and their broader political impact. Later it examines the election of the six university senators and the appointment of the Taoiseach's 11 nominees.

SEANAD ÉIREANN

The Inter-Parliamentary Union notes that of 192 national political systems worldwide, 77 are bicameral, that is, composed of a legislative institution with two chambers.[3] This represents a growth in the number of bicameral systems since the end of the twentieth century when there were 66 second parliamentary chambers. Not all bicameral systems are central to the legislative function and in some countries calls for reform or abolition of the second chamber have been persistent. New Zealand, Denmark and Sweden have all switched from a bicameral to a unicameral system, while in the UK and Canada, reform of the upper house has been undertaken. In Ireland, support for institutional reform has trumped attempts to abolish Seanad Éireann.

As an institution, the upper house has had a chequered history in Irish politics. The Irish Free State Seanad was similar in size, although it experimented with various electoral systems and for a time, it was largely non-party political. Focused predominantly on its legislative role, the institution flexed its political muscles by rejecting two major government bills in the 1930s. This move antagonised a Fianna Fáil party already intent on abolishing or downgrading the upper house. In 1936, a bill to abolish the institution was passed and the Free State Seanad ceased to exist.

Seanad Éireann, as created and defined by the 1937 constitution, was a weaker institution than its Free State equivalent.[4] The Seanad is politically subservient to the Dáil and its powers are largely limited to delaying legislation when there is a disagreement with the lower house. This suspensory power over ordinary bills amounts to a 90-day delaying tactic. When it comes to money bills, the Seanad has no right of initiative and can only delay a bill for up to 21 days. The Seanad has only rejected two bills, in 1959 and 1963.[5] The limited powers afforded the Seanad were intended by its creator, Éamon de Valera. He was of the view that the Seanad should not obstruct or mirror the work of the Dáil but should instead be a forum for independent critical input. In theory, the novel arrangements enshrined in the constitution for electing members of Seanad Éireann provide some basis for fostering this vision.

Seanad Éireann is more distinctive than its predecessor in that it emphasises *vocational representation* in the upper house. This concept was popular in the 1930s. It was closely linked to Catholic social thinking and found an audience among the drafters of the 1937 constitution. Parliamentary institutions that emphasise vocational representation are unusual, and in this respect at least, the Seanad differs considerably from other second chambers. In contrast to upper houses elsewhere, such as the Senate in the US and the Senate in Australia, which represent populations or territories, the composition of the Seanad is intended to represent functional and vocational interests. Seanad Éireann engineers this form of representation by means of an unusual electoral system that is based on a combination of indirectly elected members and appointees. Article 18 of the Irish constitution outlines the three components of the Seanad:

- 43 members elected from panels of candidates.
- Three members elected by graduates of the National University of Ireland (NUI) and three elected by graduates of the University of Dublin (Trinity College).
- 11 members nominated by the Taoiseach.

In practice, the manner in which senators are elected has ensured that Seanad Éireann is not vocational in its orientation. The institution has been dominated by political parties and arguably their influence has quelled the extent to which the Seanad has been enabled to fulfil its representative function as implied by the constitution.

The detailed rules for Seanad elections are contained in law and not in the constitution, meaning that they can be changed by parliament like any other piece of legislation. However, the timing of all Seanad elections is constitutionally decreed and is directly linked to the schedule of Dáil elections. Article 18.8 states: 'A general election for Seanad Éireann shall take place not later than ninety days after a dissolution of Dáil Éireann'. In 2016, Dáil Éireann was dissolved on 3 February and two days later, the relevant minister moved two Seanad General Election Orders: one for university members and one for panel members. The orders detailed the timing of arrangements for the nomination of candidates, the issuing of ballot papers and the closing of the polls. The poll for panel members was to close at 11 am on 25 April, while that for university members would close a day later. The counting of votes commenced as soon as the polls closed and concluded on 28 April.

The Panel Seats

A majority of Seanad members—43—are indirectly elected from panels representing specific vocational interests. The five panels are detailed in Article 18.7 of the 1937 constitution and were designed to reflect the interests of Irish society:

1. National Language and Culture, Literature, Art, Education and such professional interests as may be defined by law for the purpose of this panel;
2. Agriculture and allied interests, and Fisheries;
3. Labour, whether organised or unorganised;
4. Industry and Commerce, including banking, finance, accountancy, engineering and architecture; and
5. Public Administration and social services, including voluntary social activities.

Article 18.7 also notes that each panel may return between 5 and 11 members, and those members must have 'knowledge and practical experience' of the interests and services of each panel.

The Panel Nominations

The process of nominating Seanad candidates is more complex and restrictive than is the case for members of the lower house. Nominations are filtered through the five vocational panels, each of which is divided into two sub-panels. One sub-panel—the 'outside' sub-panel—is composed of nominating bodies that are registered and approved annually by the Clerk of the Seanad. There are currently 106 registered bodies across all panels.[6] These bodies represent vocational interests and enjoy privileged access to the Seanad electoral process by virtue of being registered as entitled to nominate Seanad candidates. On the second sub-panel, known as the 'inside' sub-panel, Seanad candidates must be proposed by four members of the Oireachtas. A minimum number of senators must come from each sub-panel (see Table 10.1).

There are variations in terms of how many candidates a nominating body can propose; broadly, the greater the number of nominating bodies entitled to put forward names, the lower the number of candidates each one can propose. For the Agriculture panel and the Labour panel, nominating bodies can put forward more than one candidate. Nominating bodies on the Agriculture panel can nominate two candidates each, and on this occasion, eight of the ten bodies did so.

Table 10.1   Seanad candidate nominations by panel and sub-panel, 2016

Panel	Nominating bodies sub-panel (outside)		Oireachtas sub-panel (inside)	Total candidates	Total senators to be elected	
	No. of bodies	No. of candidates	No. of candidates		Min. per sub-panel	Total
Culture & Educ	34	18	6	24	2	5
Agriculture	10	15	9	24	4	11
Labour	2	12	11	23	4	11
Ind and Commerce	44	28	9	37	3	9
Administration	16	7	10	17	3	7
Total	**106**	**80**	**45**	**125**		**43**

Source: Calculated from http://www.seanadcount.ie

All of those nominated were public representatives. Six were incumbent senators and nine were local councillors. Political balance has tended to be a hallmark of the Agriculture panel nomination process. Nominating bodies typically propose candidates from two different parties. In 2016, six nominating bodies proposed one Fianna Fáil and one Fine Gael candidate each. The Irish Greyhound Owners and Breeders Federation proposed one Fianna Fáil and one Labour candidate, and in an exception to the political balance convention, the Agricultural Science Association nominated two Fianna Fáil local councillors.

There are just two nominating bodies on the Labour panel and each can nominate seven candidates. The Irish Conference of Professional and Service Associations put forward seven nominees; four from Fianna Fáil, two from Fine Gael and one Independent. The Irish Congress of Trade Unions (ICTU) nominated five candidates with more diverse political affiliations: two Independent candidates, and one each representing Fine Gael, the Labour Party and Sinn Féin. Ten of the 12 candidates nominated on the Labour panel were (or had recently been) public representatives in either the Seanad, Dáil Éireann or local government. Of the remaining two candidates, Siptu official Paul Gavan fought the election on the Sinn Féin ticket and registered nurse Madeline Spiers declared as an Independent.[7]

Article 18.7.1 of the constitution states that candidates must have 'knowledge and practical experience of the interests and services' of the panel on which they are standing. In practice this requirement is quite nebulous and disqualification on these grounds is rare, though the issue arose in the controversial 'McNulty affair' of September 2014 (see p. 20 above). The Report of the SRWG recommended strengthening the Seanad nomination sequence by defining in legislation the level of knowledge and practical experience required by the constitution.[8]

The strength of political party influence remains strong, particularly in both the Agriculture and Labour panels. The profile of candidates here demonstrates how political party affiliation and/or experience of elected office are typically the norm for panel nominees. This practice serves to undermine the link between nominees and the vocational representation principle, though this was partially redressed by the nomination choices proffered by the other three panels. For these panels, the number of nominating bodies is more numerous and as such, they are restricted to nominating a single candidate each. Not all bodies, however, choose to nominate Seanad candidates. In 2016, just 19 of the 34 Culture and Education panel bodies put forward 18 nominees, and 32 of the 44 Industry and Commerce panel bodies nominated 28 candidates. All of the Administrative panel bodies proposed nominees. Multiple nominations for 3 candidates meant that 7 nominees were proposed in total by the 16 bodies represented in this panel. In the Administrative panel, two of the seven nominees were each nominated by five panel bodies. Interestingly, neither of these nominees were public representatives or affiliated to a political party. In 2016, of the 80 candidates nominated by panel bodies, 20 were not serving public representatives and this marks a contrast with earlier Seanad elections. In 2011, 71 of 78 nominating body candidates were either associated with the then largest three parties or were currently or formerly politically active in local councils or Dáil Éireann.[9] Although partisanship remains much in evidence in terms of those who secured election, 2016 suggests some move towards a greater embrace of the vocational representation principle of the Seanad.

An alternative means of being nominated to a panel is to capture the support of four members of the Oireachtas, also known as 'inside sub-panels'. This process of nomination is dominated by the political parties, although Independents did infiltrate it to a greater extent in 2016. Independents contested all five panels with the largest concentration of nine candidates in the Industrial and Commercial panel.

The number of inside sub-panel candidates is always less than the number nominated by the nominating bodies. Parties make strategic choices about not just which candidates they field, but also how many candidates. In 2016, Fianna Fáil had 47 candidates nominated in total to the vocational panels—the highest number of any party (see Table 10.2). The move was designed to build on the support the party had garnered in the Dáil election. In contrast, the Labour Party acknowledged

Table 10.2 Vocational panel candidates put forward by affiliation 2016

		Fianna Fáil	Fine Gael	Labour Party	Sinn Féin	Green Party	AAA–PBP	Social Democrats	Independents	Total
All	N	36	25	2	2	0	0	0	15	80
Panels	O	11	16	2	5	1	1	1	8	45
Total		47	41	4	7	1	1	1	23	125

Note: N denotes candidates nominated by a nominating body and O denotes candidates nominated by Oireachtas members

its reduced likelihood of winning seats and did not defend four of the Seanad seats the party had won in 2011.

Different parties employed different methods to select Seanad candidates. In Sinn Féin, the national executive chose the candidates. The party initially chose five candidates and then added two more following the Dáil election. Fianna Fáil relied on party headquarters to choose the party's nominees. Similar to previous years, Fianna Fáil had a 'preferred list' of candidates and encouraged voters to give preferential treatment to those on the list. On the Culture and Education panel, for example, the party was pushing two of the 13 Fianna Fáil candidates. Fine Gael does not employ this approach. The party's Executive Council selected Seanad candidates from nominations submitted by individual constituencies. The Labour's Party central council and parliamentary party decided their nominees through a postal vote. The view that an inside nomination is a better route to securing election is not universal among candidates. Other factors are seen as more decisive in the battle to be elected, including the support of a party, the strength of an individual's public profile, the ability to appeal to a wide selection of voters, and intense campaigning.

The Panel Electorate

The electorate for the Seanad panel elections comprises all members of the incoming Dáil, members of the outgoing Seanad, and members of county councils and city councils. In 2016, this electorate numbered 1160: 949 councillors, 53 outgoing senators and 158 incoming TDs. All voters may vote on all five panels and voting is by post but some parties, including Sinn Féin and Fine Gael, bring representatives together to vote on a designated day in different councils or in Leinster House (the seat of parliament). The electoral system, as at Dáil elections, is proportional representation by the single transferable vote (see Appendix 4).[10] Although the electoral process for Seanad elections is quite convoluted, the outcome is reasonably predictable. The party affiliation of voters provides a fairly accurate picture of voting intentions (see Table 10.3).

In 2016, Fianna Fáil had the largest number of votes in the electorate, but it was less dominant than it had been in the years prior to 2007.[11] The main difference in this regard between 2016 and previous elections is the strength of the Independents. In the period from 1977 to 2007, approximately 10 per cent of the electorate were Independents.[12] This share has grown since then and by 2016 Independents made up almost 20 per cent

Table 10.3   Composition of Seanad electorate 2016

Component	Fianna Fáil	Fine Gael	Labour Party	Sinn Féin	Green Party	AAA– PBP	Others	Independent	Total
Councillors	267	235	51	159	12	28	4	193	949
TDs	44	50	7	23	2	6	3	23	158
Senators	9	16	11	2	0	0	2	13	53
Total	320	301	69	184	14	34	9	229	1160

Source: Aodh Quinlivan, 'The 2014 local elections in the Republic of Ireland', *Irish Political Studies* 30(1): pp. 132–142

Note: The 'others' category for Dáil deputies and senators includes Renua Ireland and the Social Democrats. The 'others' category for local councillors includes South Kerry Independent, United Left, Workers and Unemployed Action Group, and the Workers' Party

of the electorate. Sinn Féin's share of the electorate has also grown significantly, from 2 per cent in 2002 to 16 per cent in 2016. This has impacted on the traditional dominance of the larger parties. In 2002, 84 per cent of the electorate was composed of Fianna Fáil, Fine Gael and Labour voters; mirroring these parties' decline in the popular vote at Dáil elections (see Fig. 12.1), the equivalent figure for 2016 is 59 per cent. The rise of the Independents and Sinn Féin combined with other smaller parties such as the Green Party and the AAA–PBP is diversifying the Seanad electorate and potentially diversifying the election outcome too. A key effect of this altered voting landscape is that the electoral contest is getting even more intense as candidates are increasingly required to seek support across party lines.

The Seanad election campaign is often described as a 'subterranean' election.[13] Although it takes place away from the public eye, it is an exceptionally challenging and gruelling election for candidates, even for those who have the backing of a large party and electorate. Candidates spend their time canvassing local councillors and public representatives. This invariably involves travelling to councils around the country and arranging to meet with councillors from across the political divide. When this is not practical, candidates connect with voters by telephone, online or via social media.[14] Some form of direct contact with voters is deemed to be important, particularly when voter discipline is not assured and when there is a growing number of Independent votes up for grabs. Candidates from smaller parties may have something of an advantage here. This is because small parties can mobilise fully behind an individual candidate as they typically field just one candidate per panel. In 2016, the Green Party candidate, the Labour Party candidates and, on three panels, the Sinn Féin candidates, did not face internal party competition and so could draw heavily on the support of party headquarters, in addition to their own canvassing efforts.

One factor that altered the engagement between local councillors and Fine Gael Seanad candidates was the implementation of the Local Government Reform Act 2014. The act led to much disgruntlement among councillors who felt that their pay and terms and conditions of employment had been adversely impacted.[15] Fine Gael candidates bore the brunt of this dissatisfaction on the doorsteps. They were seen as the lead governing party that had sponsored the legislation, and serving senators in particular were viewed as having not sufficiently defended the interests of local government during the lifetime of the 24th Seanad.

The Panel Results

The 2016 Seanad Éireann panel elections confirmed trends established in the Dáil election. Fianna Fáil overtook Fine Gael as the largest party among elected senators, despite not adding to its 2011 seat total (see Table 10.4). The composition of the electorate suggested that Fianna Fáil might have fared better, possibly securing up to 17 seats, but mistakes in electoral strategy cost it seats (see below). Fine Gael lost five seats, as did the Labour Party, although its losses were less devastating than at the Dáil election. In contrast, the 2016 Seanad election was a breakthrough one for Independents, and Sinn Féin also recorded gains.

The overall features of the Seanad vocational panel elections remain largely static. The proportion of successful candidates emerging from the Oireachtas and nominating bodies sub-panels is in keeping with recent patterns. In 2016, 19 senators were nominated by Oireachtas members and 24 by nominating bodies.[16] The most marked distinctions between 2016

Table 10.4 Party affiliation of 49 elected senators (panel and university seats)

Party	No of senators	Change since 2011
Fianna Fáil	14	0
Fine Gael	13	−5
Labour	5	−4
Sinn Féin	7	+4
Green Party	1	+1
Independents	9	+4

and previous Seanad elections are the elevated number of Independents returned to Seanad Éireann and the increasing diversity of the institution's membership.

Independents were elected on four of the vocational panels. Only the Culture and Education panel did not return an Independent, but even here, Independent councillor Joe Conway came close to winning a seat.[17] Returning Independent senator Gerard Craughwell played an important role in encouraging Independent councillors to support Independent Seanad candidates and the strategy paid off. Having been (unexpectedly) elected to Seanad Éireann at the 2014 by-election that saw Fine Gael lose out due to the 'McNulty affair' (see p. 20 above), Craughwell proactively engaged with local councillors. In addition to agitating for improved pay, terms and conditions for councillors, he communicated regularly with them and requested their input on matters coming before the Seanad. Using email, Facebook, YouTube and Twitter, local councillors, and particularly Independent councillors, were encouraged to support Independent candidates for Seanad Éireann. The non-party organisation of local councillors, *Independents Together*, also played a role in mobilising the Independent vote. Members organised caucus-style meetings across the country where Craughwell and other members of *Independents Together* encouraged councillors to support Independent election candidates. Voting patterns in 2016 suggest their efforts were successful in that there was a greater propensity among Independents to vote for their own, both with first preferences and with lower preferences. Across all panels, support for Independents was up relative to 2011. The most striking example is the Industry and Commerce panel where the vote for independent candidates amounted to 99 per cent of the number of Independent voters. The comparable figure for 2011 was 25 per cent. In 2011 overall, on no panel did Independents achieve more than 28 per cent of the available Independent vote; in 2016, the lowest vote proportion was 59 per cent.

Craughwell is joined by three new Independent Seanad members. Frances Black is a singer and anti-addiction campaigner. In addition to the support of Independents, she also enjoyed backing from Sinn Féin which endorsed her candidacy, although she was not an official party candidate. John Dolan, a disability advocate, and Victor Boyhan, a former member of Dún Laoghaire–Rathdown County Council, were also elected. These three candidates were the first Independent candidates to be elected in a Seanad vocational panel contest (not including by-elections) since the 1973 election. Greater Independent representation in Seanad Éireann goes some way to challenging the traditionally partisan nature of Seanad election contests. It also offers the promise of a greater vocational dimension to Seanad business as envisaged in the constitution.

Fianna Fáil secured more seats than any other party contesting the panel seats, but expected seat gains did not materialise. Given improved electoral fortunes at the previous local and general elections, it was surprising that the party's seat tally did not change from 2011 to 2016. Evidently, there was some squandering of opportunities to increase its Seanad representation. This was most marked in the Agriculture and Administration panels. In order to meet the requirements of the 'inside/outside' rule, as explained above, the final seat in the Agriculture panel went to 'inside' Green Party candidate, Grace O'Sullivan, despite a higher vote for 'outside' Fianna Fáil candidate, Michael Smith. Smith had been named on a list of candidates whom local Fianna Fáil councillors were asked to support in the Seanad elections by Seanad Director of Elections, Timmy Dooley TD. The move angered some of the Fianna Fáil electorate, and may actually have undermined the party's final seat tally as poor vote management and discipline on the part of the electorate was instrumental in sealing the fate of Smith's unsuccessful candidacy. Being on Fianna Fáil's preferred list of candidates was not necessarily advantageous. In addition to Smith, a number of other preferred Fianna Fáil candidates including Jennifer Cuffe, Mary Fitzpatrick, Connie Gerety-Quinn and Paul McAuliffe were unsuccessful in securing a Seanad seat. Similar to 2011, the Fianna Fáil strategy was of limited success.[18] In a rather telling response to the debacle, Dooley stated: 'Anyone identified and who is on the list is of course happy to be on it; there are others who, naturally enough, are not happy about it. But we as a party have a duty to pick people who can win *Dáil* seats' (emphasis added).[19] The majority of Fianna Fáil senators have political experience. Six are returning senators and six were local councillors. Keith Swanwick, a GP, and Lorraine Clifford-Lee, a solicitor, are the only two Fianna Fáil senators with no previous experience of political office, though Clifford-Lee, along with Fianna Fáil senator Jennifer Murnane-O'Connor, did unsuccessfully contest the 2016 Dáil election.

The 2016 Seanad election was not a good election for Fine Gael. Prior to the election, there was some expectation that the party might secure up to 16 seats but in the event it dropped from 18 to 13 of the panel senators. Fifteen incumbent Fine Gael senators contested the 2016 Seanad election,[20] but only five were successful. This is an unusually high number of unsuccessful incumbents and it included high profile casualties such as outgoing Fine Gael Seanad Leader, Maurice Cummins.

The poor showing of incumbent senators may be linked to internal party disquiet around the Local Government Reform Act 2014. While on the campaign trail, Fine Gael senator Colm Burke noted that there was 'huge anger out there among councillors'.[21] Privately, some senators acknowledged that some incumbents may have suffered as a consequence of the councillors' disgruntlement.[22] The Fine Gael casualty list also included outgoing junior minister Paudie Coffey, who lost his Dáil seat and then lost out on a Seanad seat, though he was later named as one of the Taoiseach's 11 nominees. Other former TDs who failed to win Seanad seats included Ray Butler, Noel Coonan and Anthony Lawlor. Former Fine Gael TD, Jerry Buttimer, however, won a Seanad seat after a disappointing Dáil election. He is one of four new Fine Gael senators to have lost their Dáil seats in 2016. Except for Maura Hopkins, all of the other newcomers had political experience at local government level.[23] It appears that Fine Gael councillors may have been more supportive of fellow councillors than sitting senators. The party's poor showing in the Seanad election is problematic in the context of a Fine Gael minority government. There are few assurances that the passage of legislation through the Seanad will be smooth given the limited representation the party now has in the upper house.

Sinn Féin's electoral appeal has been growing steadily in recent years, and the 2016 Seanad election continues that trend. The party ran seven candidates across all five panels and remarkably all seven were elected. Moreover, each was elected on the first or second counts in all five vocational panel contests. Sinn Féin voters appear to have been the most committed in supporting their party's candidates. In addition to mining the obvious party vote available from an elevated number of party members following the 2014 local elections and the 2016 Dáil election, Seanad candidates benefited from support from others too. Fintan Warfield is a particular case in point here. He was elected to the Culture and Education panel on the first count winning 200 votes, approximately 184 of which were available from Sinn Féin voters (see Table 10.5). There is a strong likelihood that Warfield also enjoyed support from his fellow councillors on South Dublin County Council[24] and other Independent councillors around the country. Warfield won the most first preference votes of any candidate contesting the five vocational panel elections. The extent to which the party needed transfers was minimised by strong Sinn Féin voter discipline and the election of party candidates early in the panel contests.

The election of outgoing TD, Pádraig MacLochlainn, was an important victory for Sinn Féin. Disastrous vote management in the Dáil election

Table 10.5   Results of Seanad panel elections by party 2016

Panel	Fianna Fáil	Fine Gael	Labour Party	Sinn Féin	Green Party	AAA– PBP	Other	Total
Cultural and Education	389	365	0	200	0	0	169	1123
(candidates-seats)	(12–2)	(7–2)	(0–0)	(1–1)	(0–0)	(0–0)	(4–0)	(24–5)
Agriculture	367	316	72	188	48	0	133	1124
(candidates-seats)	(9–3)	(9–3)	(1–1)	(2–2)	(1–1)	(0–0)	(2–1)	(24–11)
Labour	357	307	74	188	0	52	146	1124
(candidates–seats)	(8–4)	(7–3)	(1–1)	(2–2)	(0–0)	(1–0)	(4–1)	(23–11)
Ind and Commerce	351	336	88	114	0	0	235	1124
(candidates–seats)	(13–3)	(13–3)	(1–1)	(1–1)	(0–0)	(0–0)	(9–1)	(37–9)
Administration	387	331	99	150	0	0	157	1124
(candidates–seats)	(5–2)	(5–2)	(1–1)	(1–1)	(0–0)	(0–0)	(5–1)	(17–7)
Electorate	320	301	69	184	14	34	238	1160
(total candidates–seats)	(47–14)	(41–13)	(4–4)	(7–7)	(1–1)	(1–0)	(24–4)	(125–43)

Source: Collated from www.seanadcount.ie

had lost Sinn Féin a seat in the Donegal constituency (see p. 145 above). MacLochlainn's Seanad nomination, however, came at the expense of outgoing Sinn Féin senator, Kathryn Reilly, an unsuccessful Dáil candidate in Cavan–Monaghan. MacLochlainn, new senator Rose Conway-Walsh and returning senator Trevor Ó Clochartaigh unsuccessfully contested the 2016 Dáil election. Other Sinn Féin senators include those with experience of local government and two are former mayors. In 2011, Niall Ó Donnghaile became the youngest ever Lord Mayor of Belfast at the age of 25, while Fintan Warfield was previously Mayor of South County Dublin.[25]

In addition to backing Independent candidate Frances Black, Sinn Féin also supported the nomination of Independent candidate, Ciarán Staunton, as 'a voice for the diaspora', to the Industrial and Commercial panel. Staunton is Chair of the Irish Lobby for Immigration Reform and is based in Queen's, New York. He was eliminated on the 31st count. Overall, Sinn Féin's Seanad tally is impressive. The party more than doubled its representation from 2011 and returned senators from each of the vocational panels. These Seanad members—along with Independent senators—will likely be a strong voice for opposition in a more fragmented upper house.

Similar to the Dáil election, the Seanad election saw Labour lose seats. It secured four panel seats, down four on its 2011 tally. There was some solace for the party in that three former junior ministers—Aodhán Ó Ríordáin, Ged Nash and Kevin Humphreys—having lost their Dáil seats, returned to the Oireachtas through this route. Interestingly, these former TDs and new senators had been supporters of plans to abolish the Seanad in 2013. The party's nominee on the Agriculture panel, Denis Landy, also won a seat. An informal pact between Fine Gael and Labour helped Labour candidates, who benefited from Fine Gael transfers. Labour's outgoing senator Lorraine Higgins was unsuccessful in securing a Seanad nomination, while another Labour incumbent, Aideen Hayden, contested the NUI panel but did not win a seat. The poor showing of Labour in the general election effectively meant that the party seemed likely to struggle to secure the election of even three senators. In the event, strong voter discipline and the relatively high profile of Labour nominees ensured that they were able to rely on more than just Labour voters. All four Labour Party panel senators have, at some point, contested a general election and failed to win a seat. This senatorial profile does little to challenge the traditional image of the Irish Seanad as a 'crèche' or a 'holding bay' for would-be TDs.

This was a good election for the Green Party, which scored its first ever elected Seanad seat. Grace O'Sullivan was elected to the Agriculture panel of the 25th Seanad, taking a seat at the expense of Fianna Fáil. The Greens marshalled support for O'Sullivan from other parties and candidates by agreeing in return to support specific candidates on other panels. In addition, O'Sullivan canvassed heavily, in person and by phone, and enjoyed strong support from Green headquarters (see her account in Chapter 5). Given that she was their only candidate, the Greens could invest time and effort in aiding her campaign efforts. The emphasis was on securing high preferences for the party candidate and this materialised. The count figures show that O'Sullivan received a sizeable boost in transfers on the elimination of the Social Democrats' candidate Jennifer Whitmore, a clear sign of one particular inter-party agreement.

THE UNIVERSITY SEATS

A further six members of Seanad Éireann are elected by graduates of the University of Dublin (Trinity College) and of the NUI. This arrangement is a historical overhang and one that has been strongly and persistently criticised for its perceived elitist character (a charge that it is difficult to deny). Its roots are located in the pre-independence era when Trinity College Dublin returned representatives to the old Irish House of Commons and after 1800 to the UK House of Commons. This entitlement was extended to the NUI in 1918, and after 1922 both university constituencies were represented in Dáil Éireann. The arrangement ended in 1936 following a constitutional amendment, but was compensated for by the provision in the 1937 constitution that allocated three Seanad members each to both Trinity College Dublin and the NUI. The inclusion of the university constituencies was not wholly elitist; it was also politically motivated and intended to ensure representation for Unionists through the three Trinity seats. The electorate for the university Seanad seats is therefore confined to those who are graduates of the two oldest universities in the state. Candidates for election do not have to be graduates of either institution.

In 1979, a referendum supported the extension of the university franchise for Seanad elections. The Seventh Amendment of the Constitution (Election of Members of Seanad Éireann by Institutions of Higher Education) Act, 1979 provided that the procedure for the election of six senators by university graduates could be altered by legislation. This effectively allows for the university senators to be elected by the graduates of any of Ireland's third-level institutions once so legislated for by the Oireachtas. In the decades since 1979 no government introduced the necessary legislation. The result of the 2013 referendum, however, placed the issue of Seanad reform firmly back on the political agenda. In early 2014, the Fine Gael–Labour government published the General Scheme of the Seanad Electoral (University Members) (Amendment) Bill, which would create a single six-seat university constituency and an extension of the franchise to include graduates from all third-level educational institutions.

In 2011, there were approximately 151,000 voters on the combined registers for the two university constituencies. In 2016, the figure was almost 161,000. According to the General Scheme of the Seanad Electoral (University Members) (Amendment) Bill, the proposed legislative change to alter the franchise would increase the number of those entitled to vote to approximately 800,000.[26] In its 2015 report, the Seanad Reform Working Group noted and welcomed the government's plans to implement the seventh constitutional amendment. The necessary legislation however was not implemented in advance of the dissolution of Dáil Éireann and so the election of university senators in 2016 was based on the existing legislative provisions.

The complete disenfranchisement of non-graduates and the continu-ation of the selective privileging of graduates of only some of Ireland's third-level institutions are objectionable to many, but this process pro-duces other anomalies too in that it skews the electorate. Although the NUI electorate broadly reflects the distribution of the Irish population with a slight Dublin bias, the Trinity College electorate has a much stron-ger Dublin orientation and a higher proportion of graduates based outside Ireland.[27] The reliability of the electoral register is also open to question. In 2016, the total electorate of the Trinity College constituency was 57,732 graduates and the NUI electorate was 103,131.[28] However, in the days before the election, nearly 10,000 voting papers were sent back to Trinity College and 13,000 to the NUI. Voters had either not been home to sign for the ballot paper, which is sent by registered letter, or papers were sent to old addresses. This effectively disenfranchised one in six of the Trinity electorate and 12 per cent of NUI voters.

Despite expectations to the contrary, then, the 2016 election of univer-sity senators proceeded in the traditional manner. Turnout was low: 35 per cent of NUI graduates and 28 per cent of Trinity College graduates cast a vote. This fits with the norm in that turnout for the university constituen-cies does not generally exceed 40 per cent. Thirty candidates contested the NUI seats and 16 contested the Trinity seats; these were among the highest ever numbers of nominations for both constituencies.

Two sitting NUI senators, John Crown and Feargal Quinn, did not con-test the 2016 election, so Rónán Mullen was the only incumbent seeking re-election in 2016. In contrast, all three Trinity incumbents stood again. Most university candidates are Independents and the 2016 Trinity and NUI election candidates fit this profile. Just one Trinity candidate had a party affiliation: Ivana Bacik fought the election with the support of the Labour Party. Likewise only one NUI candidate declared a party affiliation: Pearce Flannery for Fine Gael. Even so, the genuineness of the supposedly inde-pendent status of several candidates was questioned. Fine Gael headquarters wrote to voters advising them to favour certain Independent candidates with Fine Gael leanings. In the letter, a number of Independent candidates were variously described as 'Fine Gael activist' (John Higgins), 'Fine Gael mem-ber' (Deirdre Burke) and 'Fine Gael affiliated' (Professor Anthony Staines).

Many Independent candidates tended to be closely associated with particular ideological positions, or specific causes and issues. Mullen is socially conservative, while Bacik has a liberal profile. Bacik is associated with women's rights, as is Alice-Mary Higgins. Trinity senator Lynn

Ruane is an active social justice campaigner and her Trinity senatorial colleague David Norris is well known for his work in support of the LGBT community. Equality was a theme that pervaded the campaigns of both successful and unsuccessful university candidates. In addition to Bacik, Higgins and Ruane, unsuccessful candidates Laura Harmon, Rory Hearne and Tom Clonan focused their campaigns around an equality agenda. A focus on health issues also featured as a key priority for a number of candidates including NUI candidates Eddie Murphy and Martin Daly.

In the NUI constituency, Rónán Mullen was comfortably returned. The second seat was won by former Tánaiste, Minister for Justice, Attorney General and leader of the now-defunct Progressive Democrats, Michael McDowell, who ran as an Independent. McDowell campaigned vigorously for the retention and reform of the Seanad during the 2013 referendum. He is joined by equality advocate, Alice-Mary Higgins, who also ran as an Independent and took the third NUI seat. She is the daughter of President of Ireland, Michael D. Higgins, and his wife Sabina. She benefited from strong transfers from former president of the Union of Students of Ireland, Laura Harmon, and this proved to be decisive in ensuring her eventual election. She is the first female since 1977 (when Gemma Hussey was elected) to win a seat in the NUI constituency. Higgins beat the founder of Aer Arann Express, Pádraig Ó Céidigh, on the final count. Former general secretary of the ICTU, David Begg, and former CEO of the Dublin Rape Crisis Centre, Ellen O'Malley-Dunlop, also contested this constituency, but each secured fewer than 5 per cent of the first preferences.

The election of the Trinity senators threw up two predictable results—incumbent senators David Norris and Ivana Bacik were re-elected at the head of the poll—and one surprise. This was the unseating of sitting senator Seán Barrett, who lost his seat to newcomer Lynn Ruane by just 115 votes. Indeed during the latter stages of the count, Ruane, Barrett and Averil Power were neck and neck. Ruane, however, benefited from the elimination of Power and took a substantial number of her transfers, enough to unseat Barrett. Lynn Ruane has an interesting personal story. A single parent from Tallaght, a largely working-class suburb of Dublin, she was 30 years old when she gained a place at Trinity College and went on to become president of the university's Students' Union, a position she held at the time of the election. She has spent many years committed to community and campaign work. Her election to the Seanad is further evidence of the strong showing of Independents in 2016 and the appeal of non-traditional and increasingly diverse candidates.

The traditional pattern whereby university seats do not throw up surprises has been challenged twice in the last three Seanad elections. In 2007, incumbent NUI senator Brendan Ryan was defeated by Rónán Mullen. Nevertheless, it is unusual for a Trinity incumbent to lose their seat. Barrett had been an active member of Seanad Éireann and had served on the Joint Oireachtas Committee of Inquiry into the Banking Crisis (see pp. 22–3 above). Outgoing vocational senator and former Fianna Fáil member, Averil Power, also contested the Trinity constituency as an Independent candidate. With a strong public profile (and perhaps surprisingly, the support of Fine Gael minister Leo Varadkar), she was expected to poll well, but was unable to match the vote of either Ruane or Barrett and came in fifth.

For all the criticism of the manner of their election, Seanad Éireann's university members play an important role in the institution. More than other elected members, university senators meet the vocational representation aspiration of Seanad Éireann's founders. Unencumbered by a party whip, NUI and Trinity senators represent strong independent voices in the upper house and they are typically among the more vocal and visible of Seanad members. The profiles of the 2016 intake of university senators suggest the newest cohort will be no different.

THE TAOISEACH'S NOMINEES

In 2016, the Taoiseach's 11 nominees were not announced until 27 May and were strongly influenced by political arithmetic. A strong government majority in 2011 had allowed the Taoiseach to choose senators who did not have political affiliations, but this approach was abandoned in 2016 as the Taoiseach sought to shore up the government's position by using the Seanad nomination process to bolster the Fine Gael presence in the upper house. He chose a significant number of former TDs and party supporters, although not all 11 choices fit this profile. In an interesting (and unexpected) political twist, the Taoiseach's Seanad nominees include three senators chosen by Fianna Fáil leader, Micheál Martin, apparently as part of the broader government agreement between the two parties (for which, see Chapter 11). In a further break with traditional political practice, Fianna Fáil was also involved in the selection of the Cathaoirleach (Chair) of the Seanad.

Of the eight senators chosen by the Taoiseach, six were former TDs; five had been defeated in the earlier Dáil election, while one had not contested it. The most high-profile of these was the party's former deputy leader, James Reilly, who had had a high media profile during his controversial time as Minister for Health. Along with other Fine Gael nominees, he had been a strong advocate for Seanad abolition in 2013. Of the other two appointments made by Kenny, Marie-Louise O'Donnell was an incumbent senator who had been a strong supporter of the government in the previous Seanad. The second independent senator appointed by the Taoiseach was a surprise choice. Billy Lawless is a Chicago-based advocate for Irish immigrants in the USA. Little known in Ireland, he had contested the 1991 local elections as a Fine Gael candidate before emigrating. The question of how frequently Lawless would sit in the Seanad chamber given that his home is in the USA, and the related issue of travel expenses, generated much discussion following his nomination.

Fianna Fáil leader Micheál Martin chose three Independents. Businessman Pádraig Ó Céidigh had unsuccessfully contested the NUI panel a few weeks earlier. He was joined by Joan Freeman, the founder of suicide awareness and support charity, Pieta House, and Colette Kelleher, CEO of the Alzheimer Society of Ireland. Four of the Taoiseach's 11 nominees were female, bringing the total number of female senators to 18 (30 per cent), the same as in 2011. None of the 2016 appointees was linked to Northern Ireland political interests, as had been the practice until 2002. Northern Ireland representation is addressed in the SRWG report which includes a recommendation to allow Irish citizens there to vote in Seanad elections.

In 2011, five of the Taoiseach's 11 nominees took the government whip. In 2016, at least six (and probably eight) of the nominees will support the government in the upper house. The party, however, is still in a minority position with only 19 of the 60 Seanad seats (see Table 10.6), around the same proportion as it has in the Dáil, and will require the support of others to avoid the defeat of legislation. This support is likely to come from some of the 14 Independent senators and, on occasion, from the 14 Fianna Fáil representatives in the Seanad.

The installation of a minority government and a broader emphasis on 'new politics' signals a challenging period ahead for the Oireachtas. The Taoiseach's Seanad nominees do not entirely fit with the 'new politics' agenda. Instead, they are linked to the established practice whereby a Taoiseach privileges party attachment over vocational expertise in an express attempt to engineer a government majority in the Seanad. Although the panel elections produced a more diverse Seanad member-

Table 10.6   Overall result of Seanad election, 2016

Group	Fianna Fáil	Fine Gael	Labour Party	Sinn Féin	Others[a]	Total (women)	
Panels							
Culture and Education	2	2	0	1	0	5	(2)
Agriculture	3	3	1	2	2	11	(3)
Labour	4	3	1	2	1	11	(2)
Ind and Commerce	3	3	1	1	1	9	(3)
Administration	2	2	1	1	1	7	(1)
Universities							
Nat Univ of Ireland	0	0	0	0	3	3	(1)
University of Dublin	0	0	1	0	2	3	(2)
Taoiseach's nominees	0	6	0	0	5	11	(4)
Total	14	19	5	7	15	60	(18)

[a]The Others category includes Green Party senator, Grace O'Sullivan, elected on the Agriculture panel

ship in 2016, it appears that this may have been partly diluted by the Taoiseach's nominations.

THE FUTURE OF THE SEANAD

Following the outcome of the 2013 referendum on Seanad abolition, the government committed itself to responding to the electorate's apparent desire for Seanad reform as opposed to Seanad abolition. In late 2014, the Taoiseach appointed the Seanad Reform Working Group. The group was chaired by Dr Maurice Manning, a Fine Gael TD in the 1980s and a former leader of Seanad Éireann. Other members included four former senior figures in the Seanad[29] and three independent experts.[30] The SRWG contained no serving senators and there was some disquiet about their absence among members of the 24th Seanad.

The terms of reference for the SRWG tasked the group with exploring ways of reforming Seanad Éireann, and the manner in which the institution carries out its business.[31] Importantly, all proposals for change produced by the group had to be within the framework of the constitution. This not only limited the ambition of the proposals, but also potentially heightened the prospect for their introduction as any reforms would require only legislative action and not constitutional amendment (and hence a referendum).

Over the course of four months in late 2014 and early 2015, the group met on seven occasions and sub-sets of the group also met with other individuals to gather information and advice. The SRWG also received 69 written submissions.[32] The work of the group was heavily informed by three fundamental principles, namely: addressing the popular legitimacy of the Seanad; ensuring the Seanad has adequate powers and functions; and creating an institution with a distinct composition.[33]

The group was mindful of the failure of successive governments to implement the recommendations outlined in previous reports on Seanad reform.[34] It drew on the content and spirit of earlier reform proposals, but the final recommendations of the SRWG, published as the *Report of the Seanad Reform Working Group 2015*, included a number of radical proposals. These included extending the principle of one person one vote to all citizens on the island of Ireland and overseas, for the majority of Seanad seats—specifically for 36 senators, including the six university senators. The report also proposes the maintenance of an element of indirect election by Oireachtas members and local councillors, but this would be reduced to 13 seats rather than the current 43. The principle of vocational representation is emphasised via the nominating bodies, which the group proposes be better monitored and publicised in the context of the extension of the franchise to all voters. In line with constitutional provisions, the Taoiseach maintains the right to nominate 11 Seanad members (see Figure 10.1).

Among the more novel proposals are recommendations to modernise the entire electoral process by moving to online registration and receipt of

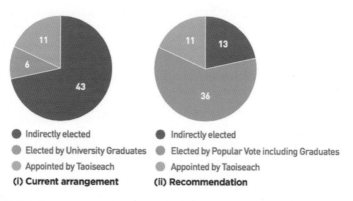

(i) Current arrangement

● Indirectly elected
● Elected by University Graduates
● Appointed by Taoiseach

(ii) Recommendation

● Indirectly elected
● Elected by Popular Vote including Graduates
● Appointed by Taoiseach

Fig. 10.1 Current composition and SRWG recommended composition of Seanad Éireann *Source: Report of the Seanad Reform Working Group 2015*, p. 30

ballot papers. In terms of the roles and powers of the Seanad, the group advised that the Seanad better marshal its capacity, particularly in the context of an altered electoral process diversifying the membership of the institution. Among the areas where the Seanad might make a distinctive contribution, the report suggests a more robust role for the institution in revising, reviewing and consolidating legislation; scrutinising EU business; considering North–South Ministerial Council proposals; and investigating and reporting on matters of public interest.

The SRWG sought to maximise the chances of the report being implemented by proposing an implementation process, and by drafting the accompanying necessary legislation. The Taoiseach welcomed the report and committed to a 'public and political discussion and consultation' on the report's recommendations. Members of the SRWG actively engaged with the Seanad after the publication of the report and agitated for full implementation. The 2015 report, however, went the way of earlier reports and its recommendations were not implemented during the lifetimes of the 31st Dáil and 24th Seanad. A lack of political will and more pressing policy challenges distracted from the government's stated commitment to pursue reforms. The subject of Seanad reform does, however, receive an airing in the 'Programme for a Partnership Government' agreed in May 2016 between Fine Gael, the Independent Alliance and Independent TDs. In the section on 'Political and Constitutional Reform', the minority government notes that 'significant reform of the Seanad itself is now long overdue' and commits to the implementation of the Manning Report 'as a priority'.[35]

The SRWG did not view its reform proposals as being intended to challenge the primacy of the Dáil in the parliamentary system; rather it viewed them as a way of strengthening and legitimising the broader parliamentary system. Nevertheless, the political will to pursue reforms was wanting in advance of the 2016 general and Seanad elections. Intriguingly, the political resolve to pursue reforms may now be stronger given that the (minority) government of the day does not stand to lose a majority position in the upper house as a consequence of a reformed electoral process.

Eventual agreement on the creation of a minority government and programme for government signals a challenging period ahead for the Oireachtas. This new reality has prompted talk of 'new politics', a term that was ubiquitous in the aftermath of the Dáil election. In truth, however, the (possible) embrace of 'new politics' is not just applicable to how the lower house might function, it also has application in a more diverse upper house. How, indeed if, new politics emerges is down to the leadership and membership of both houses.

CONCLUSION

Although it is the upper house of the Oireachtas, Seanad Éireann has the lower profile. Being less powerful than the Dáil, it is often contended that little of consequence happens in Seanad Éireann. This view is strongly held by both supporters of Seanad abolition and advocates of Seanad reform. Even in the absence of reforms to date, it is conceivable that in the aftermath of the 2016 Seanad election, the operation of the Seanad, and by extension the traditional (negative) characterisation of the institution, may be challenged. A commitment to future Seanad reform appears to be more robust than earlier promises. Rather unusually, the outcome of the 2016 election may have addressed some of the institutional deficiencies that Seanad reform is designed to rectify. The election of this more diverse membership and a more independent oriented institutional character may alter the dynamic of the institution. The absence of a government majority in the upper house will arguably require greater engagement and interaction between the Dáil and Seanad in order to facilitate the passing of legislation (see p. 286 below). Fianna Fáil TD Dara Calleary suggests that the Seanad will play a very important role during the current Oireachtas.[36] Although it remains to be seen how prophetic his views might be, it is possible that the 25th Seanad might be a slightly more interesting institution than its predecessors.

NOTES

1. See John Coakley, 'The final Seanad election?', pp. 240–263 in Michael Gallagher and Michael Marsh (eds), *How Ireland Voted 2011: the full story of Ireland's earthquake election* (Basingstoke: Palgrave, 2011).
2. For further information on the Seanad abolition referendum, see Muiris MacCarthaigh and Shane Martin, 'Bicameralism in the Republic of Ireland: the Seanad abolition referendum', *Irish Political Studies* 30:1 (2015), pp. 121–131.
3. Inter-Parliamentary Union, *Parliaments at a Glance: Structure*, http://www.ipu.org/parline-e/ParliamentsStructure.asp? REGION=All&LANG=ENG

4. See John Coakley, *Reforming Political Institutions: Ireland in comparative perspective* (Dublin: Institute of Public Administration, 2013), pp. 110–112.
5. For further detail see Maurice Manning, 'The Senate', pp. 153–166 in Muiris MacCarthaigh and Maurice Manning (eds.), *The Houses of the Oireachtas: Parliament in Ireland* (Dublin: Institute of Public Administration), p. 160. In late 2014, the Seanad came close to defeating a third bill, the *Water Services Bill 2014*, which established Irish Water. The Fine Gael–Labour Party coalition had a minority in the Seanad and so relied on the support of Independent senators to ensure the legislation was passed. Following a heated debate that continued into the early hours of the morning, the Seanad voted 28–25 in favour of the bill. Of particular curiosity is the fact that the Seanad did not even reject the bill to abolish itself in 2013!
6. For further information on nominating bodies, see Coakley, *Reforming political Institutions*, p. 116.
7. Spiers had previously fought the 2014 local elections as a Fine Gael candidate, but failed to win a seat.
8. *Report of the Seanad Reform Working Group 2015*, p. 32, available at: http://www.merrionstreet.ie/en/ImageLibrary/20150413Se anadReformFinal1.pdf
9. Coakley, 'The final Seanad election?', p. 246.
10. See Coakley, *Reforming Political Institutions*, pp. 117–118, for a detailed account of how Seanad votes are counted.
11. Ibid., table 4.1, p. 119.
12. Ibid., figure 4.1, p. 120.
13. Michael Gallagher and Liam Weeks, 'The subterranean election of the Seanad', pp. 197–213 in Michael Gallagher and Michael Marsh (eds), *How Ireland Voted 2002* (Basingstoke: Palgrave, 2002).
14. For a detailed and first-hand account of the Seanad election campaign trail from a candidate's perspective, see Averil Power, 'On the campaign trail', pp. 134–138 in Gallagher and Marsh, *How Ireland Voted 2011*, as well as Grace O'Sullivan's account in Chapter 5 of this volume.
15. The Association of Municipal Authorities of Ireland (AMAI), which represents the town and borough councils abolished under the act, initially objected to the bill.
16. See Coakley, *Reforming Political Institutions*, p. 118 for trends since 1938.

17. Having secured the second highest number of first preferences votes of the Culture and Education panel, Conway was pipped near the finish. He was eliminated following the 22nd and penultimate count.

18. Coakley, 'The final Seanad election?', p. 252.

19. Daniel McConnell, 'Seanad candidates angry as Fianna Fáil runs "preferred" list', *Irish Examiner*, 20 April 2016.

20. This figure includes two Fine Gael senators—Eamonn Coghlan and Jim D'Arcy—who had been nominated by the Taoiseach in 2011, but had not previously contested a vocational panel election.

21. Marie O'Halloran, 'O'Ríordáin elected to Seanad despite calling for its abolition', *Irish Times*, 28 April 2016.

22. Niall O'Connor, 'Fine Gael revolt threatens seats of senators', *Irish Independent*, 13 April 2016.

23. Hopkins had unsuccessfully contested the 2014 Roscommon–South Leitrim by-election.

24. South Dublin County Council has 40 members, approximately one-third of whom are non-party, AAA, PBP or Green Party.

25. Ó Donnghaile also contested the 2016 Northern Ireland Assembly elections less than two weeks after the Seanad poll closed but was unsuccessful.

26. See Seanad Electoral (University Members) (Amendment) Bill 2014, published 14 February, available at: http://www.environ. ie/sites/default/files/migrated-files/en//Legislation/ LocalGovernment/Voting/FileDownLoad%2C35464%2Cen.pdf

27. Coakley, 'The final Seanad election?', pp. 254–255.

28. Marie O'Halloran, 'Thousands of Seanad ballots for university panels undelivered', *Irish Times*, 7 April 2016.

29. Mary O'Rourke, former minister and former Leader of Seanad Éireann; Joe O'Toole former leader, independent group in Seanad Éireann; Dr Maurice Hayes, former senator, former Northern Ireland Ombudsman and former chairman of the National Forum on Europe; and Pat Magner, former Labour leader in Seanad Éireann.

30. Dr Elaine Byrne, commentator and author on public policy; Tom Arnold, former chairman of the Constitutional Convention; and the current author.

31. For a full outline of the terms of reference of the SRWG, see *Report of the Seanad Reform Working Group 2015*, Appendix 1.

32. Just four current senators sent submissions. All were Independents and three were from university panels. An additional submission from senator Ivana Bacik represented the views of Labour senators.
33. Ibid., p. 12.
34. The Report of the SRWG makes reference to 'eleven separate reports [that] have been published on Senate reform, focusing mainly on its composition and electoral system. Many of the early reports were technical in nature but in recent times there have been two significant reports' (p. 17). Coakley suggests (*Reforming Political Institutions*, p. 127) that the figure of 11 is based on a misunderstanding as not all of these reports were advocating Seanad reform.
35. *A Programme for a Partnership Government*, May 2016, p. 148, available at: http://www.merrionstreet.ie/MerrionStreet/en/ImageLibrary/Programme_for_Partnership_Government.pdf
36. Dara Calleary TD speaking on *The Week in Politics*, RTE1 television, 8 May 2016.

CHAPTER 11

70 Days: Government Formation in 2016

Eoin O'Malley

Though elections often feature a debate about government formation, that debate is sometimes rendered obsolete when the election results come in. The Irish election did not feature much debate on government formation but what debate did occur was quickly forgotten. The eventual government formed was predicted by very few commentators, except in the final days of the election as it became increasingly clear that the outgoing government would not be returned. The final election result showed the outgoing government roundly defeated, as we saw in Chapter 6. Yet no obvious alternative government emerged. The election produced the most fragmented Dáil in the country's history, making government formation much trickier.

It was 70 days between election day and the formation of the government, which was composed of Fine Gael and a number of independents, with the expressed willingness of Fianna Fáil to support it or abstain on key votes. It was not the country's first minority government, but it is by some way the government with the smallest level of support locked in to a coalition deal. It was the first time there was an

This chapter was written using interviews with six protagonists in the formation of government, on the basis of confidentiality.

E. O'Malley (✉)
Dublin City University, Dublin, Ireland

© The Author(s) 2016
M. Gallagher, M. Marsh (eds.), *How Ireland Voted 2016*,
DOI 10.1007/978-3-319-40889-7_11

express 'confidence and supply' deal with another party that stayed out of government.[1] It was also the first time Fine Gael formed a government without the support of Labour. The length of time it took to form a government was to some extent a function of the fact that so few parties were actively interested in forming one. If this was the election that nobody won, it was also the government that nobody wanted to be in.

This may have been because most parties saw themselves in a growth or regrowth phase and participation in government has been viewed as deleterious to a party's subsequent electoral performance. Though it had a bad election, as the largest party and incumbent in government Fine Gael felt it had a duty to lead the government formation negotiations. Added to this was the personal ambition of Enda Kenny to be the first Fine Gael leader returned as Taoiseach.

With most of the other parties evidently uninterested in forming a government, some of the record number of independent TDs were called upon to support a minority government. Their willingness to do so may have been in part driven by a fear of a second election—something that hung like a pall over all politicians in the long interregnum—but some also identified an unusual opportunity for independent TDs to serve in government.

Despite having lost so many seats Fine Gael now dominates the government, but its minority position means that government is much less powerful than its predecessors. It may also be less durable than other governments. Though formed under an agreement that ran at least until late 2018, there was little confidence that it would last this long. Most politicians seemed to be on election footing from 6 May, the day Enda Kenny was nominated as Taoiseach and appointed by the President.

EXTENT OF THE DEBATE IN THE ELECTION

The outgoing government, which essentially served its full five-year term, went to the country seeking re-election. While Fine Gael could in theory have been returned as a single-party majority government (it had 88 candidates, where 80 TDs are needed for a majority), unlike in 2011 this was never mooted as remotely likely. Labour and Fine Gael in government had had major disagreements on some issues over that time (see Chapter 1). However, ministers reported that they worked well together, and it was a part of the two parties' electoral strategy to seek the re-election of the government. Both sought to emphasise the stability that would come only from the government's return and suggested that no other government was obviously feasible. This assertion was helped by the fact that no other alliance or party, including Fianna Fáil, had sufficient candidates to form a majority government even if all were elected.

The available data showed some form of Fine Gael and Labour coalition to be the most popular options (see Table 11.1). However, as an issue for voters, government formation did not loom large. Just 15 per cent of voters cited 'stable government' as a strong determinant of their vote, though this was much higher for Fine Gael-Fine Gael voters, at 33 per cent (see also discussion on pp. 172–4 above). As in 2011, but in contrast to 2007, few cited the Taoiseach or the set of ministers forming the government as important (see Chapter 7). This was perhaps because there were no alternatives on offer. As a result, the campaign did not focus greatly on government formation or government preferences, something that possibly did not suit the government parties.

Much of what did feature in the campaign on government formation related to who would not coalesce with whom. At Sinn Féin's ard-fheis (party conference) in March 2015 the party unanimously passed a motion ruling out supporting a Fianna Fáil or Fine Gael-led government, which essentially meant it would only form a government if it were the lead party (see p. 83–4 above). Though completely rejecting Fine Gael, Adams refused to rule out working with Fianna Fáil. And while it was critical of Labour in government Sinn Féin also left open the possibility of working with Labour in a left-led government. Sinn Féin structured its campaign around its being an alternative to the establishment parties, but there was no sense that it was expecting to lead an alternative government. Part of its

Table 11.1 Stated coalition preferences in opinion polls

Coalition	December 2015	10 February 2016	22 February 2016	26 February 2016
	Red C	Red C[a]	tnsMRBI[a]	B&A RTÉ exit poll
FG, Labour (and others)	43	44	28	30
FG and FF	19	18	20	13
FF and SF	15	16	na	5
SF and others	9	9	17	15
None/other	10	11	21	24
Don't know	4	3	15	13

[a]Totals add to more than 100 due to rounding. Different questions and options, rather than real change, might account for the differences over time

problem is that there is a *conventio ad excludendum* with relation to Sinn Féin's that extends to most parties. There is the possibility that, like the Italian Communist Party, Sinn Féin's could be a reasonably large party in the long term but never take part in government.

Labour's Joan Burton had ruled out working with Sinn Féin's in any way in the party's leadership election of summer 2014, and she reiterated this as leader during the election campaign. Fine Gael had similarly ruled this out, though it would be unlikely Sinn Féin would be interested in working with Fine Gael. Given its nationalism and that Fianna Fáil places itself on the centre-left, a Fianna Fáil–Sinn Féin government might be considered politically feasible and could actually have sufficient numbers. This option was suggested by Fianna Fáil's former deputy leader, Éamon Ó Cuív in 2012 though it was rejected by party leader, Micheál Martin. Martin saw Sinn Féin as a primary threat to Fianna Fáil's recovery after the 2011 election and directed a good deal of criticism at Sinn Féin up to and during the election. Martin, like others, cites Sinn Féin's association with violence as a key factor preventing Fianna Fáil working with Sinn Féin. He also highlighted issues such as the treatment of Máiría Cahill (see p. 82 above) as an ongoing example of problems with the party. Most mention Adams as a problem, especially his denial that he was ever a member of the Provisional IRA. This raises the possibility that Sinn Féin would be 'rehabilitated' and hence coalitionable if it were led by one of the new generation of Sinn Féin politicians.

As with Sinn Féin and Labour, Fianna Fáil now requires the approval of an extraordinary party conference to enter a coalition government. Both Fianna Fáil and Fine Gael leaders were asked during the campaign about whether they would enter government with the other, and both rejected it on a number of occasions. Micheál Martin ruled out a coalition with Fine Gael, but the parliamentary party was split on the issue. Some, such as finance spokesperson Michael McGrath, were open to the possibility of working with Fine Gael. Others, such as Éamon Ó Cuív, were implacably opposed to it. Micheál Martin argued against it on the basis that Fine Gael had moved too far to the right.[2] In any case there was a widespread view that Fianna Fáil members would reject a coalition with Fine Gael. On 15 February at a press conference Kenny refused to rule out dealing with Fianna Fáil, saying that he did not contemplate such a deal. This caused annoyance in Labour, which asked for clarification, which Kenny gave stating that he had ruled out working with Fianna Fáil on at least ten occasions during the campaign. Labour was willing to use the prospect of a Fine Gael–Fianna Fáil coalition for its own purpose when on the last day of the campaign it warned voters of the 'danger' of a 'conservative' government if sufficient numbers of Labour TD were not returned.

THE RESULTS AND CONTEXT

The results when they came through showed that people had not listened to Labour's message in sufficient numbers. The government parties' loss of seats was larger than most had expected, but it was not clear that any specific alternative had been chosen. There were over 4000 permutations that are 'winning' coalitions (see Table 11.2 for the configuration of parties and groups). Fine Gael was critical in over half these situations, which might indicate its bargaining strength, and the likelihood that it would be part of a government. But we also know that Sinn Féin was 'critical' in over 40 per cent of coalitions[3] yet this figure carried no predictive power for the likelihood of Sinn Féin taking part in government. This is because these power indices are insensitive to policy or other relevant dynamics, such as opinion polls, party system and personal relations.

In the end none of these 'winning coalitions' was formed. That there was a failure to form a majority government relates to some aspects of the Irish party system that such mathematical calculations cannot take into account. The intelligent visitor might have noted that both Fianna Fáil and Fine Gael, being centrist parties, would be natural collaborators for coalition, but this would fail to take into account the historical and social differences that are evidently important to some in both parties.[4] More important than those historical and social differences might have been the strategic impact such a government might have on the Irish party system. Party systems are possibly more a function of government formation than is acknowledged. By forming coalitions parties often move closer to each other in policy terms, and opposition parties move to exploit policy spaces left open. Fianna Fáil's decision to reject a possible 'Grand Coalition' with Fine Gael was a result of the party's unwillingness to leave Sinn Féin as the main opposition party. Were the two centre-right parties to have come together in government, this might have allowed Sinn Féin to dominate the opposition and realigned the party system on a more left–right basis. Sinn Féin had used the campaign to try to align what it branded as establishment parties and contrast itself with those parties.

Though there were many coalition possibilities, there were few obviously feasible ones on offer. This was reflected in the length of time it took to form the government. The previous average length for government formation in Ireland was 20 days, and this might be an over-estimate

Table 11.2 Dáil strengths after the 2016 election

Party/group	Seats	
Fine Gael	50	
Fianna Fáil	43[a]	
Sinn Féin	23	
Labour	7	
AAA–PBP	6	
Social Democrats	3	
Green Party	2	
Independents	23	*of which*
Independent Alliance[b]		6
'Rural five'		5
Healy-Raes (FF gene-pool)[c]		2
Independents 4 Change		4
Other radical left[d]		3
Moderate left[e]		2
M. Lowry (FG gene-pool)		1

[a]This reflects Fianna Fáil's loss of one seat from its voting strength on the election of one of its TDs as Ceann Comhairle

[b]The Independent Alliance lost one of its 6 TDs after the government formation process

[c]'Gene-pool' independents are those TDs who have strong ties to a particular party. Many failed to secure the nomination of the party to which they belonged and on winning a seat often vote with the party

[d]Connolly, Healy, Pringle

[e]O'Sullivan and Zappone

as it includes the time between an election and the first meeting of the new Dáil. At 70 days, this government formation was closer to the Dutch or Austrian averages.[5] A reason the government formation took so long was because of the exceptionally fragmented structure of the Dáil after the February 2016 election (see Fig. 12.3, p. 282). At 4.93 the effective number of parliamentary parties (ENP) was by some distance the largest in recent Irish electoral history.[6] One would have to go back to June 1927 (when another technically minority government was formed) to see as fragmented a configuration in the Dáil.[7] The other factor making government formation difficult was the size of the largest party. Fine Gael held just under a third of the seats in the Dáil, compared to 45 per cent of the seats in 2011. We can derive a measure of how hard it can be to form a government on the basis of these two variables.[8] The logic is that where there are more parties there are more coalition options available and therefore negotiating an agreement is more difficult. Linked to this is the size of the largest party. The larger the largest party is the clearer is it for small parties whom it 'should' deal with to form a stable government and the easier it is for that party to achieve majority support in parliament. Here I develop an 'Index of Coalition Difficulty' which is calculated as:

$$= ENP \times \sqrt{(50 - \text{Largest party})}$$

Table 11.3 shows values on the index, which has no intrinsic meaning, for the last nine Irish general elections and recent examples from Belgium, Netherlands and Austria for comparison. The Belgian comparison is the now famous occasion when it took over 500 days to form a government. We can see that the Irish result in 2016 created a situation in which was by some way 'harder' to form a coalition government than before. It was twice as 'hard' as in 1992, which also featured a highly unusual government in Irish political history, and three times as hard as in 2011. The Irish figure is close to that after the 2013 Austrian election. The relatively long time it took to form a government might then not be as surprising.

That it was so difficult to form a government in 2016 was also because so few parties wanted to enter government. Smaller parties were naturally sus-

Table 11.3   Index of coalition difficulty in Ireland

Year	Effective number of parties in parliament	% of seats held by largest party	Index of coalition difficulty
1982	2.52	45.2	5.52
1987	2.89	48.7	3.30
1989	2.94	46.4	5.58
1992	3.46	41.0	10.38
1997	3.00	46.4	5.69
2002	3.38	48.8	3.70
2007	3.03	46.9	5.33
2011	3.52	45.7	7.30
2016	4.93	31.6	21.15
Belgium 2010–12	8.42	18.0	47.63
Netherlands 2012	5.70	20.5	30.96
Austria 2013	4.59	29.3	20.88

picious of doing so because of the evidence that small parties are damaged by being part of government.[9] The PDs, the Greens and then Labour had all suffered near-death experiences after taking part in government. When the results came in there was an immediate agreement that with just seven seats Labour could not risk returning to government. The Social Democrats indicated they would not take part in government formation talks. The decision of Sinn Féin to enter government only as the larger party might similarly be thought to be in the interest of the party's longer-term growth.

The constitutional context was also important.[10] Article 13.1.1 of the Irish Constitution states 'The President shall, on the nomination of Dáil Éireann, appoint the Taoiseach, that is, the head of the Government or Prime Minister'. The standing orders of the Dáil are completely silent on the mechanism of the investiture vote. Unlike in other countries where formateurs (designated prime ministers) or informateurs (honest brokers to facilitate a deal) are appointed, Ireland allows for different groups to compete for election to the post of Taoiseach at the same time. Nor is there any time limit on the process. The president's role is limited to refusing to dissolve a Dáil if such a dissolution is requested by a Taoiseach who has lost the confidence of the Dáil. There was nothing, however, to stop the president from getting involved if he so wished. President Hillery had informally sounded out Garret FitzGerald to perform the role of informateur in 1987 when no party had achieved a majority.[11] A presidential intervention in the event of deadlock in government formation remained a possibility in 2016.

The crucial factor in the constitution was that to be elected a Taoiseach needs only a simple majority rather than an absolute one—in other words, a majority among those voting rather than a majority of all TDs, which would require 79 votes. This makes it possible for a Taoiseach to be elected with the abstention of a number of TDs. The numbers were such that if Fianna Fáil or Fine Gael TDs were to abstain, Enda Kenny or Micheál Martin could be elected Taoiseach with 58 and 54 votes respectively. That meant Kenny needed the support of at least eight other TDs and Martin at least 11 more.

THE NEGOTIATIONS

In the immediate aftermath of the election both Enda Kenny and Micheál Martin were seen as potential candidates for Taoiseach, though the possibility of a second election remained very real. Given Fine Gael's performance it did not seem utterly unlikely that Kenny would have resigned or been removed from office. Kenny indicated that he would seek re-election as Taoiseach and the uncertainty of the outcome of a leadership contest and the logistical difficulty of holding one while their attempts to form a government were ongoing meant that Kenny was reasonably safe.[12] Enda Kenny sought a mandate from his party's cabinet ministers to seek to form a government, which he received. In the days immediately after the election a number of seats were still being decided—the last was not filled until 3 March—which made the options open to the parties and independent TDs more uncertain.

Micheál Martin left open the possibility of his becoming Taoiseach, but in a statement released on 29 February he sent a clear signal that Fianna Fáil saw its role as being in opposition. The statement called for meaningful political reform to be agreed before a new government took office, rather than left to that new government to introduce. His specific proposals would see the opposition become much more powerful in the new Dáil. There was, however, already open talk about the necessity of doing some form of a deal with Fine Gael, and the future of Irish Water was identified as a clear issue of contention. Simon Coveney caused controversy on 1 March by announcing on the RTÉ *Prime Time* programme that Fine Gael would be willing to discuss the future of Irish Water. A deal between these two parties was thought likely to involve one party enabling the other to form a government, thus avoiding an election. To achieve that Fianna Fáil made contact with some smaller parties and a number of independents on the issue of political reform, for which there was broad support. Martin hoped to secure their support in the vote for Taoiseach scheduled to take place on 10 March, at the first meeting of the 32nd Dáil.

If there was a 'race' to see who could get more support in that vote, there was no expectation that either Martin or Kenny would actually be elected Taoiseach on that occasion. Senior Fine Gael figures met with independents, outlining political reform proposals. Kenny had the express support of the seven Labour TDs, but this was only for that initial vote and did not amount to any commitment to ongoing support. When the Dáil met that day the most productive business was the election of the Ceann Comhairle, which for the first time was by secret ballot. For this reason, and because the largest party was so far from a majority, it was the first time the Ceann Comhairle was not in the gift of the incoming Taoiseach. The position has often been used in the government formation process—as a way of taking out an opposition party TD or letting down a ministerial aspirant gently—and the decision of Fine Gael to allow multiple nominations from within its party was in part motivated by the desire that none of its TDs would actually win. Seán Ó Fearghaíl, a Fianna Fáil TD, won, reducing the number of Fianna Fáil TDs to 43.

In the subsequent vote on Taoiseach four people were nominated: Enda Kenny, Micheál Martin, Gerry Adams and Richard Boyd Barrett of the AAA–PBP. Each was rejected by a sizeable margin (see Table 11.4). The Taoiseach went to Áras an Uachtaráin to tender his resignation to the President, though he and all his ministers continued in office in a care-taker role—a role that has no distinct legal status. Kenny had, however, announced that his government would not take any major decisions or make public appointments. This was a departure from past practice.

Because of St Patrick's Day (17 March) events many senior political fig-ures were out of the country. The Dáil resumed on 22 March but no vote was taken on electing a Taoiseach, which was scheduled for 6 April. Easter, which was especially important in 2016 because of the centenary of the Easter Rising, also delayed negotiations; but there was no apparent rush to start any formal talks. Fine Gael and Fianna Fáil continued attempts to woo indepen-dents and small parties, though of the small parties only the Greens indicated a willingness to engage in government formation. Both sides accepted that any deal would require the agreement of the other party to abstain.

Formal business only got under way on Tuesday 29 March when Fine Gael arranged meetings with independents in Government Buildings. These meetings were large roundtable discussions chaired by an indepen-dent facilitator and assisted by a rapporteur whose job was to summarise the proceedings and eventually produce an agreed programme for govern-ment. The meetings were attended by about eight TDs from Fine Gael including Enda Kenny and senior ministers as well as two backbenchers, and these were supported by a number of advisers. They were joined by

Table 11.4 Votes on the election of a Taoiseach

	10 March	6 April	14 April	6 May
Enda Kenny (FG)	57 for / 94 against	51 / 81	52 / 77	59 / 49
Micheál Martin (FF)	43 / 108	43 / 95	43 / 91	–
Gerry Adams (SF)	24 / 116	–	–	–
AAA–PBP	9 / 111	10 / 108	–	–

Sinn Féin and some of AAA–PBP, Independents 4 Change and other independents took a decision to abstain on the votes for each other's nomination for Taoiseach. Labour supported Kenny in the first vote, abstained in the second and third and opposed Kenny in the final vote. Some of the independents who were then engaged in talks with Fine Gael abstained on votes taken from 6 April onward. The Green Party abstained on all votes for Taoiseach taken after 10 March. In the final vote Fianna Fáil and a number of independents also abstained. Some other abstentions in the first three votes were due to absences rather than explicit decisions to abstain

2 Green TDs and 15 independents. Those comprised the so-called 'Rural Five', the six TDs in the Independent Alliance, the two Healy-Rae brothers, Maureen O'Sullivan and Katherine Zappone. The talks took place in sessions on different policy areas.

The sessions and formal negotiations changed the mood of some independents. They went from demanding concessions from government to a realisation that they could be part of that government. It is thought this awareness was reinforced by the fact that that the meetings took place in Government Buildings, and that civil servants gave separate briefings. The Taoiseach was involved in a majority of the roundtable discussions, but the presence of Michael Noonan was thought to be crucial. He was seen as authoritative in giving background to policy choices that the independents saw as sub-optimal but that Fine Gael insisted were necessary.

The Greens were open to entering government if there was a critical mass of centre-left TDs involved. Because only Zappone and O'Sullivan could be categorised as centre-left this made it difficult for the party to stay on in the talks. The talks on housing caused the Greens concern, and the absence of a number of independents from the session on climate change led them to believe they would receive no support from those TDs.[13] They made further attempts to persuade Labour and the Social Democrats to join the talks, but having failed took the decision that joining government would not be in the Green Party's interest.

Meanwhile Fine Gael opened discussions with Labour. After the initial decision that any involvement in government would be too damaging, some, including the leadership, felt that the party might also suffer in opposition, especially when it could hardly oppose policies it supported in government. That internal discussion was ongoing but there was a sense that the party was just too damaged to re-enter government. As with Fianna Fáil, there was a recognition that the leadership would not be able to secure support from a party conference. There were also some in Fine Gael who were concerned that a return of the Fine Gael–Labour government would alienate voters by failing to deliver the change that the electorate apparently wanted.

About 60 hours of roundtable talks with independents produced a 120-page 'foundation' document, which was at that stage more akin to a list of issues raised than a programme for government. Not enough progress was made to qualitatively change the support for either Enda Kenny or Micheál Martin in the vote for Taoiseach that took place on 6 April. Kenny lost the support of Labour, which chose to abstain (see Table 11.4).

That night Enda Kenny released a statement stating that he had made an offer of 'full partnership government' to Micheál Martin after the vote.

This would have included an equal number of cabinet positions for the two parties, with the support of some independents, and moreover the idea of a 'rotating Taoiseach' (each party leader would hold the role for a time, with a handover at the halfway point) was not ruled out. Though this apparently took Fianna Fáil by surprise there had been back-channel communications between the parties in the previous weeks. Some of the independent TDs involved in talks with both Fine Gael and Fianna Fáil indicated that they would prefer a full coalition with a built-in majority. It is not clear whether there was a miscommunication or Machiavellian manoeuvring, but the offer was either unexpected or regarded as a trap. Some in Fine Gael suggest that they were told Fianna Fáil would be willing to consider such a deal. Fianna Fáil sources say that they said no such thing, and had firmly and continually ruled it out over the previous month. Some in Fianna Fáil saw this as Fine Gael making an offer that it knew Fianna Fáil would refuse in order to put the blame for any ensuing election on Fianna Fáil. Fine Gael must have known that even if the leadership was minded to favour such an arrangement it was extremely unlikely that a Fianna Fáil ard-fheis would pass a motion to sanction it.

On 7 April the 'roundtable' talks with the independents were paused. Both Fianna Fáil and Fine Gael parliamentary parties met to consider Kenny's offer of a 'full partnership'. Fine Gael was broadly positive sanctioning further talks. Fianna Fáil's reaction was predictably negative. The meeting agreed that it preferred to pursue the possibility of a Fianna Fáil-led minority government and rejected the coalition deal outright. The two party leaders met for a short and testy meeting, after which there was disagreement about what was conveyed.[14] For Fine Gael this was typical Fianna Fáil; rejecting an historic opportunity for party political gain.

Despite this both sides knew that a new government had to involve some form of a deal between the two parties. The independents also recognised this and said that this agreement should come before continued negotiations with Fine Gael. On Saturday 9 April, Leo Varadkar, the Minister for Health, and Kenny's policy adviser, Andrew McDowell, met with newly elected Fianna Fáil TD Jim O'Callaghan and Martin's *chef de cabinet*, Deirdre Gillane, to set up negotiations between the parties. They agreed that the two parties would meet on Monday to set out how a minority government would work.

On the evening of Monday 11 April talks started between Fine Gael and Fianna Fáil. Each side was represented by four TDs. They agreed a media blackout and issued similarly worded statements that the talks were 'constructive' and 'cordial'. The Fianna Fáil negotiators were given instructions to agree a deal that did not look like a programme for government. It did, however, feel it had to emerge with some clear policy 'wins'. Fianna Fáil went through a list of policy principles, and made some progress, though some issues were parked. An important issue Fianna Fáil had to settle was Irish Water. It had been an important issue in Irish politics since 2014, mobilising large protests. Fianna Fáil was aware that Sinn Féin would introduce a Bill to abolish Irish Water, and/or motions calling on the government to get rid of water charges. It was open to allowing the Dáil decide these matters but warned Fine Gael that it might lose these votes. Both parties wanted a deal on water.

Fianna Fáil envisaged a 'confidence and supply' arrangement that would allow the party influence government policy in the Dáil while undertaking to abstain on key confidence votes including the vote on the budget. In return it wanted revisions in how budgets would be introduced, giving the Dáil more ability to scrutinise and amend budgets. This was agreed relatively quickly, and was never a sticking point. Fianna Fáil also insisted that Fine Gael must be open to the possibility of supporting a Fianna Fáil-led minority, something that was not really settled until 14 April.

On that day there was another vote for Taoiseach, which produced a race between the two parties to get more independents to support their leader. In a way this was as much a psychological game as a numbers game. Had Martin made more progress than Kenny, even if he were still well behind him in support, it would have given Martin the impetus to win further support. Martin declared an ultimatum. He said that this vote was the last chance to vote for him. Though this could be seen as cheap talk, when in that vote he had made no progress in getting any other TDs to support him he immediately ruled Fianna Fáil out of participating in any government.[15] This settled the issue about Fine Gael being open to facilitating a Fianna Fáil-led minority government, and may indicate that Fianna Fáil was never really that interested in forming a government. Kenny managed just one extra vote, that of Katherine Zappone.

The negotiations between Fianna Fáil and Fine Gael continued, though they switched venue. On Monday 18 April the negotiators met in the Provost's Library in Trinity College. Fianna Fáil wanted a neutral venue, and one away from the Leinster House complex, to which journalists (and of course backbenchers) had full access. Other venues were either unavailable or too expensive. In what became known as the 'Trinity Talks' Irish Water was to the foreground. Fine Gael was insistent that Irish Water remain a utility. This seemingly arcane issue mattered because Fine Gael was concerned that by ceasing to be a utility Irish Water would not be able to borrow money for infrastructural investment off the state's balance sheet, though given that a decision by Eurostat the previous year had insisted that Irish Water's debts should be classified as state debt that may have been moot. Fianna Fáil suggested a referendum on privatisation, which was considered, but the corporate structure of Irish Water was not so much an issue as the charging regime.

On 21 April the two parties appeared close to an agreement on water charges. It would have involved a generous water allowance system, but when officials produced details of how it would work this was rejected by Fianna Fáil. That agreement then unravelled, with the talks reportedly close to collapse on the weekend of 23–24 April, and once again there was a sense that Ireland might see a fresh election on the Irish Water issue. Fine Gael conceded to many of Fianna Fáil's demands, including the suspension of water charges, which Fine Gael saw as being motivated by party political rather than policy concerns. Fianna Fáil wanted charges suspended for the lifetime of the Dáil. The two parties agreed to suspend them for nine months, but Fianna Fáil made no commitment to supporting their reintroduction, and so it looked unlikely they would be reintroduced as Fine Gael had earlier conceded that it would be the Dáil and not the government that would make that decision. There was also an agreement to send the issue to an independent expert commission to report back to a special Oireachtas committee, further reducing the likelihood that water charges would re-emerge as an issue.

Fine Gael was in the position that it did not want to go to the country, especially on the issue of water. An election would also signal the end of Enda Kenny's career. Many in his party were unhappy about facing into another election with Kenny as leader—indeed he himself said he did not intend to lead his party into another election[16]—but there was no certainty as to who would succeed him and whether it could elect a leader in a timely manner. As noted above, the Fine Gael constitution allows for up to 20 days to change the leader, and if Kenny were to resist being forced out it could have taken longer. As a result Fine Gael's negotiating hand was particularly weak. Fine Gael however did manage to get Fianna Fáil to agree to two sections on economic policy and public sector pay, though Fianna Fáil added some details here. While most of the document is deliberately vague, Fianna Fáil secured some specific policy commitments, for instance regarding mortgage interest relief and rent supplement.

The two sides had managed to keep a lid on disagreements for much of the talks, but by the end of April comments by Leo Varadkar that the insistence by Fianna Fáil that water charges be suspended was 'ridiculous' caused 'outrage'—whether real or affected—within Fianna Fáil. It in turn condemned Fine Gael as having no sense of ordinary people. These were as much about playing to internal party audiences as a sign of a genuine inability to work with each other.

On 3 May, the 1800-word agreement (see Box 11.1) was approved unanimously by the two parliamentary parties. Fianna Fáil insisted it was

---

Box 11.1 Main points of agreement between Fianna Fáil and Fine Gael
Fianna Fáil agrees to:

- abstain in the election of Taoiseach, nomination of Ministers and also the reshuffling of Ministers;
- facilitate Budgets consistent with the agreed policy principles attached to this document;
- vote against or abstain on any motions of no confidence in the Government, Ministers and financial measures (e.g. money bills) recognised as confidence measures; and
- pairing arrangements for EU Council meetings, North–South meetings and other Government business as agreed.

The Fine Gael-led Minority Government agrees to:

- accept that Fianna Fáil is an independent party in opposition and is not a party to the Programme for Government;
- recognise Fianna Fáil's right to bring forward policy proposals and bills to implement commitments in its own manifesto;
- publish all agreements with Independent Deputies and other political parties in full.
- allow any opposition Bills (that are not money bills) that pass 2nd stage, proceed to Committee stage within 10 working weeks;
- Implement the agreed policy principles attached to this document over a full term of Government;
- have an open approach to avoiding policy surprises; and
- introduce a reformed budgetary process in accordance with the OECD review of the Oireachtas along with the agreed Dáil reform process

not a programme for government, rather the parameters around which Fianna Fáil could 'facilitate' the formation of a government and the budgetary process. It is a political agreement, signed by the party leaders, and to be reviewed at the end of 2018. It was not the 'Grand Coalition' that many predicted, but it was an historic accord between two parties that had formed out of a split in Sinn Féin over 90 years earlier.

That agreement was not enough, however. Fine Gael still needed to get independents to sign off on that deal and to agree a programme for government. Those talks had been left in abeyance during the talks with Fianna Fáil. During this time some independents responded to the foundation document with proposed inclusions or amendments. Progress was made, but a deal not finalised. Items were added to it as necessary, and given the different interests of the independents it led to a not wholly consistent document. The independents were very keen that they were not seen to extract local deals, and that their policy demands were nationally focussed. This position could be sustained to some extent, but some items, in particular those agreed with John Halligan, were constituency demands. There were few ideological concerns in the negotiations; instead it was a matter of what it was felt the exchequer could afford. While there had been ongoing communications formal talks recommenced on 2 May, though they were parallel meetings with less involvement of Enda Kenny.

On Thursday 5 May, the government chief whip placed a vote on the nomination of the Taoiseach on the order paper for the following day. While this annoyed the independents, there was a sense in Fine Gael that some could have continued talking without ever deciding whether to sign up. There was also concern that independent TDs would be lobbied in their constituencies over the weekend with resultant inflation of their demands when negotiations resumed. Even without the weekend some TDs did fall away. A side deal with Katherine Zappone would see the government send the issue of abortion—specifically, whether the eighth amendment to the constitution (added to the constitution in 1983 with the aim of preventing any future legalisation of abortion) should be retained, amended or deleted—to a citizens' assembly. Some pro-life TDs refused to support this and on the morning of 6 May, with a vote scheduled at noon, four independent TDs indicated they could not support Enda Kenny in that vote. Fine Gael felt that for some this was a useful excuse for Fianna Fáil-gene pool TDs to pull out of a deal they were unwilling to sign up to unless they received ministerial appointment.

Though the Independent Alliance had agreed ministerial positions with Kenny on the previous night, there was more anxiety on Friday morning as the Alliance, which throughout the talks was as cohesive as a party, had a problem. One member, Michael Fitzmaurice, had an issue with turf-cutting rights (the government has been under pressure from the EU Commission for a number of years to protect Ireland's bogs, but any attempts to prevent the cutting of turf from these bogs has encountered fierce local resistance, a factor in Fitzmaurice's victory in a by-election in October 2014), though this was probably used to mask his broader reservations about going into government. Fine Gael refused to make further concessions. The debate had started at noon on the nomination of Taoiseach but remarkably the negotiations were still ongoing. Those Fine Gael TDs speaking in the Dáil were told to pad out their speeches as much as they could to give those talks time, and there was a real sense that the whole deal could fall apart if the Dáil debate were to end abruptly. It was acknowledged that had Enda Kenny lost this vote he would have had to seek a dissolution of the Dáil from the president. In the end the only presidential involvement in the entire process was limited to accepting Kenny's resignation on 10 March and appointing the Taoiseach on 6 May. The Independent Alliance members came into the chamber to the visible relief of Fine Gael TDs. Fitzmaurice abstained, but the other five TDs of the Independent Alliance filed through the lobby to join Fine Gael and four other independent TDs to re-elect Kenny as Taoiseach by 59 votes to 49. Though the majority was comfortable because of abstentions other than Fianna Fáil's, Fianna Fáil had made it clear that Kenny had to have the support of eight independents for the deal to stand.

Cabinet Composition

With just 59 supporting votes the new Taoiseach had the smallest ever pool from which to choose his new cabinet. Though constitutionally a Taoiseach can select members of the Seanad for cabinet, this has scarcely ever been done.[17] One of the conventional explanations is simply the time lapse between forming a government and the election of a new Seanad. This was not an issue on this occasion, though, as the Seanad elections were finished by 27 April (see Chapter 10), suggesting that more important reasons are the political cultural expectation that ministers be popularly elected and that government TDs would be resentful, and possibly more inclined to rebel in Dáil votes, if people who had not been elected were promoted over them. Despite the small pool all 15 constitutionally allowed cabinet positions were filled. Fine Gael received 12 positions and 3 went to independent TDs (2 of whom, Denis Naughten and Shane Ross, had previously been members of Fine Gael). Kenny did deals with Naughten, who managed to bring only one other TD with him, and Katherine Zappone, who became only the sixth first-time TD appointed to cabinet. His deal with the Independent Alliance gave that group a senior ministry, which the Alliance itself chose to award to Shane Ross as its de facto leader.

Kenny's cabinet selection was cautious. He retained all the outgoing Fine Gael ministers who had been re-elected. Noonan's experience and authority meant he was kept on despite his poor health. Kenny gave the post of Tánaiste to a loyalist, Frances Fitzgerald. By selecting her for this position he possibly aimed to postpone the leadership challenges of Simon Coveney and Leo Varadkar. Neither man received an obvious boost from their new appointments to the renamed Department of Housing, Planning and Local Government, and the Department of Social Protection respectively, though Coveney claimed to have asked for that position.[18] By leaving others in cabinet he created no enemies that might have hastened his removal as leader.

During the election he announced that half the ministers he would appoint would be women. Problematically only 11 of the 50 Fine Gael TDs were women, and there was only one woman among the eight independents he did deals with. Four women were appointed to cabinet (see pp. 199–200 above). In announcing his cabinet he was obviously conscious of the issue, as when announcing the identities of ministers he named the women first rather than listing the ministers in order of seniority as is established practice. He also retained Máire Whelan as Attorney General and appointed Regina Doherty as chief whip, bringing to six the number of women sitting at the cabinet table. The cabinet is slightly younger than the last one, with one minister, Simon Harris, still in his twenties. His elevation was expected given what was regarded as his impressive performance in a junior ministry. Though 7 of the 15 ministers are from Dublin, this is less than the 9 Dublin-based ministers in the cabinet formed in 2011.

Striking a deal evidently put pressure on his available patronage. In 1994, the position of 'minister of state attending government' was invented (colloquially known as 'super junior'). It was designed to allow small parties in government with only one cabinet minister, and no expectation of a second cabinet minister on a proportionality criterion, to be supported by a second member at cabinet. The number of 'super juniors' was increased to two, to allow him to promote a loyalist, Paul Kehoe and accommodate a second Independent Alliance TD, Finian McGrath, to sit at cabinet.

The number of junior ministers was also increased from 15 to 18 (including the 'super juniors'). It meant that the number of ministers was greater than the number of government backbenchers. The independents got three of these junior posts, formally termed Ministers of State, and would probably have had four had all six of the Independent Alliance TDs voted for Kenny as Taoiseach. Though many claim geography is an important determinant of ministerial selection it is difficult to see how the ministers could possibly not be geographically broadly distributed given that the members of the pool from which they are chosen are broadly distributed. There was no sense that the allocation of ministries was done with an eye to the future of the party; rather it was probably designed to minimise threats to Kenny's leadership.

How Will It Work?

The very long *Programme for Partnership Government*[19] was criticised as being too aspirational, and given the government's legislative position it might be thought more as a manifesto than a programme whose implementation can be expected. Unlike previous Irish governments, the Fine Gael-led minority government has no automatic expectation to pass legislation in the Oireachtas. Given the ideological position of the government and how far it is from a Dáil majority, it will have to take account of Fianna Fáil positions. Except in a number of specific areas, such as abortion, it will not really be possible for the government to secure enough support from other parties to secure a majority if Fianna Fáil opposes a policy. Fianna Fáil wishes to be seen to 'facilitate' a government rather than support one. It will wish to ensure it can vote against the government regularly. Thus, we can expect that the government will suffer more defeats than any previous government, but the agreement with Fianna Fáil (see Box 11.1) should mean that these will not lead to the fall of the government. It could mean that ministers will be more selective in the amount of legislation they propose, leading to a reduction in government-sponsored bills.

Fianna Fáil indicated its intention to introduce private member bills and its expectation that these will not be vetoed by government—according to the constitution government can veto Money Bills, but the Standing Orders of the Oireachtas further restrict this, disallowing opposition amendments to government bills that could incur a charge. Within two weeks of the government's formation ministers were forced to take into account the positions of Fianna Fáil, allowing its Bill on variable mortgage interest rates to pass its first legislative hurdles despite expressing its opposition to the measure. The Oireachtas has agreed significant changes to the standing orders that will restrict the powers of government, including its use of the guillotine, and control of budgetary process. A new Business Committee chaired by the Ceann Comhairle will further restrict government control of Dáil time.

Predictions of the durability of the government were pessimistic. Most parties remained on election footing even as the new government took office. Some suggested that the main source of instability would be the independents.[20] Independents in government have in the past shown themselves to be reliable, and this might be further helped by their having positions they will be reluctant to give up easily (see Chapter 9). In government making a series of small concessions is often easier than making one big decision to leave government. We can expect that the dynamic between Fine Gael and Fianna Fáil is as likely to be important. Micheál Martin and Enda Kenny will have regular private meetings[21] though whether these lead to 'new politics' might not be helped by the reported fact that the two men do not get on personally.[22] The agreement that Fianna Fáil will facilitate the government until the end of 2018 might not be worth much if opinion polls were to shift to give one (or both) of the main parties an advantage.

The leadership of Enda Kenny will also influence the success and durability of the government. Kenny indicated that he did not wish to lead Fine Gael into another election but that he intended to serve the full term as Taoiseach.[23] Fine Gael TDs will have been spooked by the precarious nature of the government's formation. How that leadership change is managed, its timing and the identity of the new leader will influence Fianna Fáil's decision on how long to allow the government to last. Whatever the outcome, the formation of the government demonstrated Enda Kenny's remarkable political skill and resilience.

Notes

1. The Fianna Fáil minority government between 1987 and 1989 relied on the agreement of Fine Gael to abstain on key votes provided the government was acting in what it saw as the national interest. The so-called 'Tallaght Strategy' was a unilateral decision by Fine Gael. See Brian Girvin, 'The campaign', pp. 5–22 in

Michael Gallagher and Richard Sinnott (eds), *How Ireland Voted 1989* (Galway: PSAI Press, 1990), pp. 7, 11.

2. See Kevin Doyle, 'Micheál Martin: "We won't humiliate Labour like Fine Gael did" ', *Irish Independent* 25 February 2016.

3. These do not add to 100 per cent because more than one party can be critical for a winning coalition.

4. See Kevin Byrne and Eoin O'Malley, 'Politics with hidden bases: unearthing the deep roots of party systems', *British Journal of Politics and International Relations* 14 (2012) pp. 613–629.

5. See Alejandro Ecker and Thomas M. Meyer, 'The duration of government formation processes in Europe', *Research & Politics* (2015), doi: 10.1177/2053168015622796.

6. The 'effective number of parties' is a measure developed by Laakso and Taagepera that is based on the number of political parties in a country's party system weighted by the parties' relative strength. For Irish data see Michael Gallagher 2016. 'Election indices dataset' at http://www.tcd.ie/Political_Science/staff/michael_gallagher/ElSystems/index.php, accessed 5 May 2016.

7. In June 1927, the Cumann na nGaedheal government secured election because the newly established Fianna Fáil refused to take its seats in Dáil Éireann. An election was called soon after Fianna Fáil entered the Dáil in August 1927.

8. This is adapted from Paul Chaisty, Nic Cheeseman and Timothy Power, 'Rethinking the "presidentialism debate": conceptualizing coalitional politics in cross-regional perspective', *Democratization* 21:1 (2012), pp. 72–94.

9. See Eoin O'Malley, 'Punchbags for heavyweights? Minor parties in Irish government' *Irish Political Studies* 25:4 (2010), pp. 539–561.

10. For an overview see Shane Martin, 'Government formation in Ireland: learning to live without a majority party', pp. 121–135 in Bjørn Erik Rasch, Shane Martin, and José Antonio Cheibub (eds.) *Parliaments and Government Formation: Unpacking Investiture Rules* (Oxford: Oxford University Press, 2015).

11. See Garret FitzGerald, *All in a Life* (London: Macmillan, 1991), pp. 644–645.

12. If Fine Gael does not form part of the government, the leader must submit himself to a vote of confidence of the parliamentary party within two months. The rules allow for up to 20 days' campaigning

in a leadership election, though some suggested it could be compressed to about a week.

13. The number of people in talks varied, possibly because of interest, but also because parallel briefings by officials occurred in some areas. There was always at least one representative from the Independent Alliance or the Rural Five there.

14. See Stephen Collins, Sarah Bardon and Fiach Kelly, 'Recriminations as Fine Gael–Fianna Fáil talks collapse', *The Irish Times* 8 April 2016.

15. See Eoin O'Malley, 'Fianna Fáil leader seems content to rebuild in opposition', *Sunday Independent* 17 April 2016.

16. See Sarah Bardon and Mary Minihan, 'Election 2016: Enda Kenny says Friday's poll will be his last as Taoiseach', *The Irish Times* 24 February 2016.

17. See Eoin O'Malley, 'Ministerial selection in Ireland: limited choice in a political village', *Irish Political Studies* 21 (2006) pp. 319–336.

18. See https://twitter.com/NeilRedFM/status/729585236271566849

19. At 42,000 words it was the longest ever Irish programme for government. The next longest was in 2007 at 33,000 words. Available from http://www.merrionstreet.ie/MerrionStreet/en/ImageLibrary/Programme_for_Partnership_Government.pdf (accessed 11 May, 2016).

20. See Stephen Collins, 'Fine Gael and Fianna Fáil have incentive to deliver political stability', *The Irish Times* 7 May 2016.

21. Micheál Martin speaking to RTÉ radio's 'Today with Seán O'Rourke' broadcast on 10 May 2016.

22. See Pat Leahy, 'Enda and Micheál: best of enemies', *The Irish Times* 16 April 2016.

23. See Sarah Bardon, 'Enda Kenny says he will serve full term as Taoiseach', *The Irish Times* 16 May 2016.

CHAPTER 12

The Election in Context

David M. Farrell and Jane Suiter

In his assessment of the 2011 election, the late Peter Mair observed that while undoubtedly it had marked 'enormous change', nevertheless it had done little 'to disturb the fundamentals'.[1] The 2011 election outcome may at first blush have appeared dramatic, but, if anything, it represented a 'conservative revolution'.[2] The result was cataclysmic for Fianna Fáil and the Greens and it saw further electoral gains by Sinn Féin and micro-parties and independents on the left of the spectrum, but the major electoral beneficiaries were Fine Gael and Labour. Just like in all previous elections, the baton of government was passed between the traditional parties. Relative party positions may have been seriously disrupted, but the hold of the traditional parties of government (Fianna Fáil, Fine Gael and Labour) remained intact; for the most part the political system remained unscathed. As of 2011 Mair's view was that Ireland was 'becoming a democracy … in

We are grateful to James McBride for his assistance with some of the Figures used in this chapter.

D.M. Farrell (✉)
University College Dublin, Dublin, Ireland

J. Suiter
Dublin City University, Dublin, Ireland

© The Author(s) 2016
M. Gallagher, M. Marsh (eds.), *How Ireland Voted 2016*,
DOI 10.1007/978-3-319-40889-7_12

277

which elections might continue to be full of drama, sound and fury, but in which the outcomes might signify little'.[3]

In both respects 2016 was very different. This was an election whose campaign was light on drama, sound and fury (as discussed further in Chapter 4 and the Chronology), but whose outcome signified a lot. The outgoing government parties were routed in the polls, giving Fine Gael its worst electoral outcome since its disastrous 2002 campaign, and Labour the second worst result in the party's history. Fianna Fáil may have benefited at the others' expense, but with just 24 per cent of the vote this was a bad election for that party too—the second worst result in its history. In short, this election outcome marked an historic low point in support for the traditional parties, symbolising a party system possibly at the advanced stages of fragmentation. This chapter starts with an assessment of this significance of this development.

The impact of the election outcome on established Irish political institutions and norms is the focus of the second part of the chapter. This election had a collateral impact on the Irish political system speeding up a process of Dáil reform that had been initiated by the last government, and revitalising the Seanad (a chamber that was almost abolished several years earlier). The combination of a more uncertain electoral climate and large-scale institutional reforms has important ramifications for the nature of Irish democracy with, in particular, a potential to move away from Westminster-style majoritarianism.

A Fragmenting Party System

It used to be all so simple: in election after election Ireland's two-and-a-half party system of Fianna Fáil, Fine Gael and Labour won the lion's share of votes and seats, with a combined vote support generally over 80 per cent, and in their heyday (1960s–1970s) over 90 per cent. As Fig. 12.1 shows that proportion has been trending downwards since the early 1980s: in the 1990s and 2000s the three parties were attracting about three-quarters of the vote; in 2016 this plummeted to just 56 per cent. This is mirrored in the trends for the two main civil war parties, which in 2016 attracted less than half of the total vote, a big drop from their combined 85 per cent score in the early 1980s. There is no other way of putting this: 2016 was the worst electoral outcome for these three parties in the history of the state; this was the election that nobody (at least among the establishment) won.

Fig. 12.1 The decline of the traditional party system.
Source: https://irishvotersdecide.wordpress.com

To an extent we could see this coming. There has been a consistent decline in the attachment Irish voters feel towards political parties, placing Ireland at the lower end of international trends.[4] This has coincided with growing levels of voter volatility (total electoral volatility, which is a measure of net party system change), which reached record levels in 2011 of just short of 30 per cent.[5] At that time, Mair observed that that election was the third most volatile election among Europe's established democracies since the Second World War. The two instances of higher volatility—Italy in 1994 and the Netherlands in 2002—were in large part due to the emergence of new parties; not so in Ireland in 2011, which had no new parties of any significance in the mix, making the high volatility in that election even more exceptional.

As Fig. 12.2 reveals the 2011 election was also the most volatile election in the history of the state. In 2016, the level of volatility may have dropped a little (to just short of 24 per cent), but this was still second only to the previous election as the most volatile election in Irish history, and it once again placed Ireland in the top 10 of Western Europe's most volatile

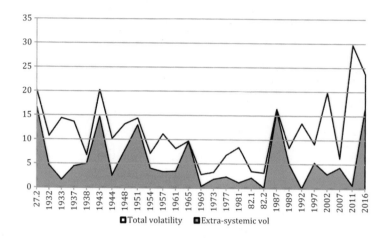

Fig. 12.2   Total and extra-systemic voter volatility in Irish elections.
Note: Total volatility is the standard Pedersen measure of aggregate change in party support. Extra-systemic volatility is the change in the combined vote for Fianna Fáil, Fine Gael and Labour from one election to the next

postwar elections (Table 12.1). This election, therefore, is just the latest in a series of highly volatile elections: with the exceptions of 1992 and 2007 every Irish election since 1987 has had volatility scores of the order of about 10 per cent or more, and three of the last four have seen volatility bordering on 20 per cent or more.

The measure of overall voter volatility tells only part of the story. Also of interest is the form that volatility takes. Over the past three decades, the bulk of the electoral volatility in Ireland has reflected vote-switching between the traditional parties: Fianna Fáil, Fine Gael, and Labour—the three parties that have formed the core of the party system throughout much of the history of the state. The tendency over this period has been for only a small proportion of voters to switch to either one or other of the new parties or independents. In fact, until this election, the one exception to this trend was in 1987 when the arrival of the Progressive Democrats (PDs) drove voter volatility to over 16 per cent. Almost all of this was due to voters switching their vote to the new party, albeit a party that was formed out of two existing parties—Fianna Fáil, and Fine Gael—and therefore one whose status as entirely 'new' was qualified at best. The PDs

Table 12.1   Europe's most volatile elections since 1945

	Country	Year	Level of volatility (%)
1	Italy	1994	36.7
2	Netherlands	2002	30.7
3	Ireland	2011	29.6
4. =	France	1958	26.7
4. =	Denmark	2011	26.7
6	France	2012	25.5
7	Austria	2013	25.3
8	Ireland	2016	23.6
9	Italy	1948	23.0
10	Netherlands	2010	22.5
11	Sweden	2010	22.3
12	Italy	2001	22.0
13	Austria	2009	21.9
14	Netherlands	1994	21.5
15	Denmark	2015	21.4
16. =	Denmark	1973	21.2
16. =	Germany	1953	21.2
18	Austria	2002	21.1

Note: All elections with a level of volatility greater than 20.0 per cent. These data refer only to the long-established European democracies

were more of the establishment than against it. Allowing for the unusual circumstances of 1987, the 2016 result stands out in sharp relief.

Figure 12.2 distinguishes between the total measure of volatility and 'extra-systemic' volatility—that portion of votes that transfer away from (or on occasions back to) the three main established parties in the political system (Fianna Fáil, Fine Gael and Labour).[6] In 2016, extra-systemic volatility was more than 16 per cent, accounting for over two-thirds of total volatility in this election. As the Figure shows there have been other elections with high proportions of extra-systemic volatility. Of particular interest are those elections that have seen high levels of both overall and extra-systemic volatility: this is generally indicative of a large shift away from the established parties. Once again taking 20 per cent as a measure of high volatility this results in three cases of interest: the second election of 1927 (when extra-systemic volatility accounted for over four-fifths of the volatility measure of 20.3 percent in that election), 1943 (almost three-quarters of a volatility of 20.2 per cent) and 2016. The high scores of 1927 and 1943 reflect a party system in the process of consolidation in the first instance and wartime electoral instability in the second; the 2016 result suggests something else entirely. This is the only Irish postwar election to manifest such an outcome.

Ireland's 2016 election follows in the wake of uncertain electoral outcomes in Greece, Portugal and Spain—all countries that share in common the trait of being particularly badly affected by the impact of the Great Recession. In their recent analysis of the cross-national evidence, Hernández and Kriesi focus on extra-systemic volatility trends to show how this particularly 'deep crisis' has served to accelerate the destabilisation of Western Europe's party systems, with voters punishing established parties and rewarding the populist parties of opposition. The impact has been felt the most in those countries that have been in receipt of IMF aid, and it has become stronger over time (as shown by vote trends in those elections occurring later in the period of economic crisis).[7]

Hernández and Kriesi's research pre-dated Ireland's 2016 election, but there is no doubt that this recent election fits their analysis perfectly: the traditional parties have had their worst electoral outcome in the history of this state (Fig. 12.1), and parties and independents ped-

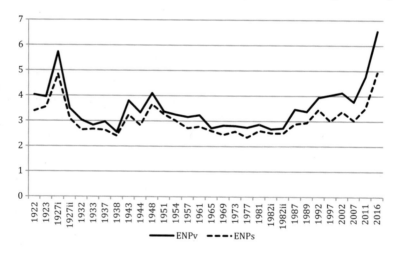

Fig. 12.3 A changing Irish party system. *Note*: ENP (effective number of parties) is a weighted index of the numbers and respective sizes of parties and independents competing for votes (v) and being elected (s). *Source*: http://www.tcd.ie/Political_Science/staff/michael_gallagher/ElSystems/Docts/ElectionIndices.pdf, https://www.tcd.ie/Political_Science/staff/michael_gallagher/Election2016.php

dling a populist line have seen their vote rise. One result is that the Irish party system has never been so fractionalised. As Fig. 12.3 shows, never before have there been so many parties and independents competing for votes and being elected to the Dáil. The 'effective number of parties'[8]— a weighted measure of the number of parties, groups and individuals (taking account of their respective sizes) running for election and being elected to the Dáil—shows just how crowded the Irish party space has become: as discussed in more detail in Chapter 6, the traditional two-and-a-half party system that stood the test of time through to the end of the 1970s has transformed into a fully-fledged multi-party system more akin to the sort of crowded party systems of countries such as Israel, Italy or the Netherlands.

It is, of course, too early to draw definitive conclusions—we need to see how things develop in future elections—but the trends over time and their culmination in showing such an extent of dramatic change in 2016 are indicative of a party system that is unstable and 'inchoate',[9] a party system that, in Chiaramonte and Emanuele's terms, is becoming 'de-institutionalised'.[10]

New Politics?

Only time will tell how this electoral uncertainty plays out, but, as we shall see, it is already having important implications for the balance of power between parliament and government in Ireland. Dáil Éireann has been famously described as a 'puny parliament', a legislature that is very much in a subordinate position to the executive.[11] In part this is the consequence of a Westminster tradition inherited from the British, in part it reflects a lack of serious engagement with the need for institutional reform over time. In the light of the 2016 election outcome, Dáil reform has been propelled to the top of the political agenda in a way not seen before, and re-igniting a political reform agenda that had featured in the 31st Dáil but with mixed success.

In 2011, the programme for government of the newly elected Fine Gael–Labour coalition promised a 'democratic revolution'[12] that was widespread in its coverage but varying in its ambitions.[13] Among the more significant reforms were two key developments: the introduction of candidate gender quotas, which had a significant impact on increasing the number of women TDs elected in 2016 (as discussed in Chapter 8), and steps to make government more open and transparent. This latter move, reflecting a reforming zeal by the relevant minister in charge of this brief, Brendan Howlin, the Minister for Public Expenditure and Reform, was to see the reinstatement of freedom of information legislation that had been pared back severely in 2003 by the Bertie Ahern administration (revised legislation was passed in 2014).[14] It was also reflected in the passing of legislation to protect whistle-blowers (Protected Disclosures Act, 2014) and to regulate lobbying (Regulation of Lobbying Act, 2015)—which meant that Ireland now joined a small but growing band of countries requiring the registration of lobbyists.[15]

The government's reform record on the theme of government accountability (relating to the balance of power between the executive and the parliament) was more mixed. A series of proposals was made relating to the role and powers of the Dáil and its committees, but in the event what transpired was, for the most part, window dressing, amounting to such measures as more regular meetings of the Dáil, a rejigging of Oireachtas committees and a slight reduction in the number of TDs. The only change of any great significance was the introduction of a 'pre-legislative' stage, giving TDs the right to have an input at an earlier stage in the process of drafting legislation. An effort was made to remove a constitutional block on Oireachtas committee inquiries, but the referendum in October 2011 was defeated, with 53 per cent of the public voting against (see p. 8 above). As the term of the 31st Dáil drew to a close it was clear that little of significance had changed: the agenda and order of business of the Dáil remained firmly in the hands of the government; the position of Ceann Comhairle (Speaker) remained effectively the gift of the Taoiseach of the day, as did the allocation of committee chairs (for all but the Public Accounts Committee).[16]

The rationale behind many of the Dáil reform moves was supposedly to increase the status of the Oireachtas. A separate initiative, that had an entirely different rationale, was a proposed referendum to abolish the Seanad. This was a pet project of the Taoiseach, Enda Kenny, who promoted it as part of a package of reforms (other proposals included a smaller Dáil, abolition of most state-provided ministerial cars and reduced ministerial salaries) aimed at stemming public anger with the political class during the Great Recession. The Seanad abolition referendum was held in October 2013. While it may well be argued that as a small, unitary democracy Ireland is somewhat out of place in having a second parliamentary chamber,[17] this was not the principal focus of the government's referendum; instead, the campaign centred on populist messages focused on reducing the numbers of politicians in the country and saving taxpayers' money. Contrary to opinion poll trends the referendum was narrowly defeated. Subsequent research showed that a factor in the public's decision was concerns over government control over the legislative process: the view was that Seanad abolition would serve to further weaken the accountability of government to the Oireachtas.[18] In the light of the referendum result the Taoiseach turned full circle, establishing a Working Group on Seanad Reform (chaired by former Fine Gael TD and academic Maurice Manning), with promises to respond in timely fashion to its proposals. The Working Group worked quickly to deliver its report in early 2015 in which, among other measures, it proposed a radical overhaul of Seanad elections including enfranchisement of the whole population (see pp. 248–9 above); but by then public and political attention had moved on, the long countdown to the general election had started, and the government took the opportunity to shelve the report.

There was a final flurry of government interest in Dáil reform on the eve of the 2016 election, with last-moment moves to institute changes to Dáil standing orders to arrange that the Ceann Comhairle of the 32nd Dáil would be elected by secret ballot and that committee chair positions would be allocated by a D'Hondt proportional formula—both significant steps that had been called for by political reform proponents and that represent a shift in the power balance in favour of the Dáil. Exactly what prompted this late initiative is unclear; some speculated that it was part of a wider effort by Fine Gael to remove potential targets for public criticism before the election.[19] But it served as a precursor to the Dáil reform debate that would start with some urgency after the 2016 election.

In the wake of the election result Micheál Martin, the leader of Fianna Fáil, called for a debate over Dáil reform, a call that received widespread support from all parties. The newly elected Ceann Comhairle, Seán Ó Fearghaíl (elected by secret ballot), and unusually by Dáil standards a member of the second largest party, was put in charge of a revitalised Dáil reform sub-committee with a brief to consider widespread changes to standing orders. At the time of writing this process is still ongoing, but in its first interim report to the Dáil (on 6 April 2016) the sub-committee proposed a suite of reforms including: the establishment of a business committee to set the Dáil agenda (which up till now has been determined by the government chief whip), a move to dedicated committee times to avoid clashes with Dáil plenary debates, a more efficient system for taking Dáil votes, relaxing rules relating to parliamentary group status (clearly needed given the plethora of new minor parties and independents in the Dáil chamber),[20] and further standing order changes to give the Ceann Comhairle the power to challenge the adequacy of ministerial replies to parliamentary questions. Among the other reforms that are being considered by the sub-committee are plans to institute a more formal scheduling system for processing legislation (including a more prominent role for committees in the legislative process), and giving the Dáil a greater scrutiny role over the budgetary process through the creation of a powerful new Budget and Finance Committee resourced by an independent Parliamentary Budget Office.

These Dáil reforms will undoubtedly have an impact on the Seanad (not least because senators are also members of Oireachtas committees). That plus the fact that (as discussed in Chapter 10) the government does not have a majority in the upper house (the first time this has happened since 1994) means that senators will be seeking to flex their muscles in a way not seen before. At the very least the government is likely to face legislative delays as the passage of bills becomes subject to consensus-building and negotiation between both houses. We can also expect fresh moves to institute large-scale Seanad reform: the new government has committed to implementing the Manning working group proposals. Among other things this will mean the introduction of mass suffrage for future Seanad elections rather than the current highly politicised electorate of 1000 councillors, TDs and senators each with five votes. The upshot is likely to be an upper house of parliament with far more status in the political system than heretofore—a long way from the unicameral parliamentary system envisaged by Enda Kenny.

In the months leading up to government formation (detailed in Chapter 11), there was a lot of rhetoric about 'new politics', with some suggesting that the 2016 election outcome had spelled the death knell of majority government, so that from now on minority governments would have to learn to work in a more co-operative arrangement with parliament. This brings to the fore the nature of Irish democracy today. In his classic study of *Patterns of Democracy*,[21] the Dutch political scientist Arend Lijphart sets out two very different forms of democracy: the majoritarian model (often referred to as the Westminster model) and a consensus model. It is worth reminding ourselves of some of the main features of both models. The main traits of the majoritarian model include: single-party governments; cabinet dominance over parliament; a two-party system; a non-proportional electoral system; a unicameral or weakly bicameral parliament; and a flexible (or uncodified) constitution. The consensus model differs in all respects: broad coalitions (including minority governments); a more balanced power relationship between cabinet and parliament; multi-party politics; a proportional representation electoral system; strong bicameralism; and a rigid constitution.

The Irish political system has tended to fall in between these two models: the constitution has always been fixed (making it difficult to amend), and the country has always used a proportional representation electoral system. Recent developments, such as the emergence over time of multiparty politics and coalition government combined with other institutional developments that are part of the Lijphart framework, would suggest that Irish politics has been shifting towards greater consensualism. Certainly this was the view of Bulsara and Kissane in their detailed examination of the evidence.[22] But one major exception to this trend has been the relationship between government and parliament, which has remained stubbornly majoritarian. In his assessment, MacCarthaigh observes that 'Ireland aligns itself most closely with the majoritarian systems of France, Greece and the UK ... [whose] parliamentary systems are characterised by power centralisation and considerable imbalances in agenda-setting power between government and opposition'.[23]

Is all of this about to change? Three important developments are in the process of unfolding. First, the Dáil reform process looks set to give that chamber much greater say over controlling its own agenda, and its committees much greater status in the legislative process. Governments are to be held accountable to parliament in a way not seen before in Ireland. Furthermore, it is proposed that the parties' whips will be relaxed[24] and that the Ceann Comhairle will come to have greater control over who gets to speak in the Dáil. All of this amounts to a more equal balance of power between executive and legislature, something more akin to a consensual style of politics.

The newly elected minority government represents a second important feature of a shift in a consensual direction. There have been minority governments in Ireland before, and this is not the first time that one of the established parties has provided 'supply and confidence' support for the other—the Fine Gael 'Tallaght strategy' that supported the 1987 Fianna Fáil minority administration was a similar scenario. But the current situation is different in a number of respects: the distance in number of seats that the government is from a Dáil majority; the wide range of political opponents it faces in the Dáil; the new power relationship between government and Dáil; and the likelihood that this sort of electoral outcome may be the way of the future. Regardless of how stable and long term the current government may end up being, the potential that minority governments of this type may become the norm marks an important step towards the governmental power-sharing feature that is at the heart of Lijphart's consensus model.

Finally, the Seanad is likely to be far more assertive than heretofore. Seanad reform is promised by the new government, including at its heart giving all citizens voting rights for future Seanad elections. This will make it all the more difficult for future governments to secure a majority in the upper chamber. While the Irish parliament will still be a long way from the 'symmetric bicameralism' of countries such as Australia or the USA—after all, the Seanad will still have very limited delaying powers—there is little doubt that there will be a significant rebalancing of the power relations between both chambers.

These three features—the power balance between cabinet and parliament, the emergence of minority governments, and a more assertive Seanad—represent the final vestiges of majoritarianism in Ireland. While it would be stretching things to suggest that Irish politics is about to witness 'consensualism in our time', some faltering, but important, steps are being made in that direction.

CONCLUSION

In this centenary year we are witnessing a party system that is changed utterly. The old shibboleths of Irish party politics have been ruptured: it is no longer Fianna Fáil versus the rest; the mainstream parties no longer hold sway over government nor do they over the opposition; the left may still be weak and divided, but it is no longer the Cinderella figure of Irish politics. All of this speaks of a political system that has experienced major change. There are also, as we have seen, significant ramifications for how government and parliament may operate in the future. The Dáil reform process will change the dynamic and power balance between the two main branches of government. The Seanad is likely to play a more assertive role (even if, strictly speaking, its constitutionally prescribed legislative powers remain weak). The precarious position that the minority government finds itself in means that the process of governing will be slower certainly, and possibly also more inclusive.

This election marked important changes to Irish party politics, and its uncertain outcome to the nature of government in Ireland. Ireland's political institutions may now be more akin to the consensual form of government set out by Lijphart, but whether the political system will operate in a more consensual manner will be reliant on how the politicians work under this new dispensation. Government ministers will have to learn a politics of accommodation, but so too will their opponents. Consensus politics is not a one-way street: politicians of all parties and none face a steep learning curve in the months and years ahead. In an age of 'new politics', the electorate may not be forgiving of those who seek to play an old politics of punch-and-judy adversarialism. The government members have to learn how to operate this new politics, but so too do the members of the opposition.

NOTES

1. Peter Mair, 'The election in context', pp. 283–297 in Michael Gallagher and Michael Marsh (eds), *How Ireland Voted 2011: The Full Story of Ireland's Earthquake Election* (Basingstoke: Palgrave Macmillan, 2011), p. 283.
2. Michael Marsh, David Farrell and Gail McElroy (eds), *A Conservative Revolution? Electoral Change in Twenty-First Century Ireland* (Oxford: Oxford University Press, 2017).
3. Mair, 'The election in context', p. 296.
4. For analysis of Irish party identification trends over time, see Michael Marsh, Richard Sinnott, John Garry and Fiachra Kennedy, *The Irish Voter: The Nature of Electoral Competition in the Republic of Ireland* (Manchester: Manchester University Press, 2008), ch. 4. See also Chapter 7 of this volume. For international comparisons, see Rudy Andeweg and David Farrell, 'Legitimacy decline and party decline', in Carolien van Ham, Jacques Thomassen, Kees Aarts and Rudy Andeweg (eds), *Myth and Reality of the Legitimacy Crisis: Explaining Trends and Cross-National Differences in Established Democracies* (Oxford: Oxford University Press, in press).
5. Total electoral volatility (the 'Pedersen index') is a simple measure of aggregate electoral change that takes account of the vote gains and losses of all parties from one election to the next.
6. By 'extra-systemic' we mean a shift in votes away from (or towards) those parties that are seen as core to the established system of par-

ties. This is the term used by Omar Sanchez in his 'Party non-systems: a conceptual innovation', *Party Politics* 15:4 (2009), pp. 487–520.

7. Enrique Hernández and Hanspeter Kriesi, 'The electoral consequences of the financial and economic crisis in Europe', *European Journal of Political Research* (published online, 2015; accessed on 28 April 2016).

8. Markku Laakso and Rein Taagepera, ' "Effective" number of parties: a measure with application to west Europe', *Comparative Political Studies* 12:1 (1979), pp. 3–27.

9. Sanchez, 'Party non-systems', p. 493.

10. Alessandro Chiaramonte and Vincenzo Emanuele, 'Party system volatility, regeneration and de-institutionalization in Western Europe (1945–2015)', *Party Politics* (published online, 2015; accessed on April 28 2016).

11. Basil Chubb, *The Government and Politics of Ireland,* 3rd ed (Harlow: Longman, 1992), p. 189.

12. *The Programme for Government, 2011–2016,* Department of the Taoiseach. http://www.taoiseach.gov.ie/eng/Work_Of_The_Department/Programme_for_Government/Programme_for_Government_2011–2016.pdf

13. For more on political reform developments in 2011–15, see David Farrell, 'Political reform in a time of crisis', in Bill Roche, Philip O'Connell and Andy Prothero (eds), *Austerity and Recovery in Ireland: Europe's Poster Child and the Great Recession* (Oxford: Oxford University Press, in press).

14. Maura Adshead and Tom Felle (eds), *Ireland and the Freedom of Information Act* (Manchester: Manchester University Press, 2015).

15. Gary Murphy, John Hogan, Raj Chari, 'Lobbying regulation in Ireland', *Journal of Public Affairs* 11:2 (2011), pp. 111–119.

16. The lack of serious Dáil reform was a key factor in the decision of the Convention on the Constitution to devote one of its two final sessions to this issue. The Convention, established by the government in late 2012, consisted of a random selection of 66 citizens and 33 members of the Oireachtas and the Northern Ireland Assembly. It was tasked with considering a number of topics for constitutional and political reform. Its recommendations on Dáil

reform (https://www.constitution.ie/AttachmentDownload.ashx? mid=bd05f391-a9b8-e311-a7ce-005056a32ee4), which were for the most past dismissed at the time by the government, are now in the process of being adopted by the Dáil sub-committee on Dáil reform as we discuss below. For more on the Convention, see Jane Suiter, David Farrell and Clodagh Harris, 'The Irish Constitutional Convention: a case of "high legitimacy"?', in Min Reuchamps and Jane Suiter (eds), *Constitutional Deliberative Democracy in Europe* (Colchester, Essex: ECPR Press, 2016).

17. John Coakley, *Reforming Political Institutions: Ireland in comparative perspective* (Dublin: Institute of Public Administration, 2013), ch. 4.

18. Muiris MacCarthaigh and Shane Martin, 'Bicameralism in the Republic of Ireland: the Seanad abolition referendum', *Irish Political Studies* 30:1 (2015), pp. 121–131.

19. Noel Whelan, 'Government had no option but to embrace Dáil reforms, *Irish Times* 30 April 2016. http://www.irishtimes.com/opinion/noel-whelan-government-had-no-option-but-to-embrace-dáil-reforms-1.2488637. The current authors were among those calling for Dáil reforms. See www.smaointe.org

20. The rule had been that parties needed at least seven TDs to be officially recognised in the Dáil. There was provision for the formation of a technical group of non-party TDs, providing this had at least seven members; and just one technical group was allowed. Under the new rules, party group status is achieved with just five TDs, and there are no limits on the number of technical groups that can be formed.

21. Arend Lijphart, *Patterns of Democracy: Government Forms and Performance in Thirty-Six Countries*, 2nd ed (New Haven, CT: Yale University Press, 2012).

22. Hament Bulsara and Bill Kissane, 'Arend Lijphart and the transformation of Irish democracy', *West European Politics* 32:1 (2009), pp. 172–195. See also Michael Gallagher, 'The Oireachtas: parliament and president', in John Coakley and Michael Gallagher (eds), *Politics in the Republic of Ireland*, 5th ed (London: Routledge, 2010), pp. 201–202.

23. Muiris MacCarthaigh, 'The role of the Houses of the Oireachtas: theory and practice', in Muiris MacCarthaigh and Maurice Manning (eds), *The Houses of the Oireachtas: Parliament in Ireland* (Dublin: Institute of Public Administration, 2010), p. 37.

24. The proposal to relax the parliamentary whip is included in the programme for government of the new government. Given that rules on party whips are a matter for the political parties rather than the Oireachtas it is a curious proposal. No doubt its inclusion was at the insistence of the Independent Alliance (which stressed the need to relax the whip in its election programme), but whether it will be implemented will be a matter ultimately for each of the political parties.

Appendices

David Barrett

Appendix 1: Results of the General Election, 26 February 2016

© The Author(s) 2016
M. Gallagher, M. Marsh (eds.), *How Ireland Voted 2016*,
DOI 10.1007/978-3-319-40889-7

Table A1.1 Electorate, valid votes and votes for each party

Constituency	Electorate	Valid votes	Fine Gael	Fianna Fáil	Sinn Féin	Labour	AAA–PBP	Green Party	Others
Carlow–Kilkenny	107,023	70,009	19,147	28,267	8,700	4,391	2,702	2,621	4,181
Cavan–Monaghan	90,618	59,650	18,957	17,952	16,126	–	–	1,251	5,364
Clare	83,660	57,000	14,707	17,580	4,216	4,472	–	1,700	14,325
Cork East	83,236	52,806	15,038	12,858	5,358	6,949	1,999	806	9,798
Cork North-Central	81,609	51,174	9,105	14,286	10,004	3,723	8,041	1,693	4,322
Cork North-West	67,589	46,958	15,106	16,256	3,238	–	–	1,354	11,004
Cork South-Central	84,482	55,682	14,384	23,141	6,986	2,417	1,732	2,064	4,958
Cork South-West	63,583	43,258	13,803	8,482	3,656	3,035	–	752	13,530
Donegal	117,675	73,303	11,243	22,731	20,178	–	–	428	18,723
Dublin Bay North	109,516	73,625	14,517	11,367	8,566	5,675	6,645	1,024	25,831
Dublin Bay South	74,326	39,703	11,966	4,575	3,774	4,205	1,728	4,529	8,926
Dublin Central	46,028	23,686	3,226	2,508	5,770	2,092	721	644	8,725
Dublin Fingal	93,486	60,388	12,180	14,185	5,228	6,009	2,067	2,783	17,936
Dublin Mid-West	69,388	43,104	11,365	6,971	9,782	2,146	4,629	388	7,823
Dublin North-West	60,406	37,009	4,642	4,750	10,008	2,750	1,434	915	12,510
Dublin Rathdown	62,340	41,099	12,573	4,220	2,858	4,048	–	4,122	13,278
Dublin South-Central	74,666	42,857	6,130	5,441	9,971	3,297	4,374	1,410	12,234
Dublin South-West	105,420	67,271	14,746	9,647	9,590	4,378	12,246	1,297	15,367
Dublin West	64,639	41,952	9,321	6,917	6,034	6,445	6,520	1,730	4,985
Dún Laoghaire	92,248	59,238	21,306	11,143	3,167	5,192	9,775	3,478	5,177
Galway East	68,432	45,238	13,597	12,364	2,683	4,531	–	769	11,294
Galway West	103,704	64,271	15,437	15,629	5,755	3,220	1,017	1,588	21,625
Kerry	112,751	79,273	16,939	12,504	9,458	4,813	981	1,011	33,567
Kildare North	77,609	48,935	11,553	13,802	3,205	4,087	781	1,485	14,022
Kildare South	59,162	36,786	11,101	13,375	4,267	4,277	–	836	2,930
Laois	63,295	38,868	12,603	13,626	8,242	2,856	–	1,541	–

Limerick City	75,568	46,761	13,341	12,999	5,894	5,227	4,584	964	3,752
Limerick County	67,633	44,412	16,492	12,276	3,347	–	–	311	11,986
Longford–Westmeath	89,241	55,246	13,156	15,596	5,270	4,817	506	1,102	14,799
Louth	104,696	67,529	13,222	12,521	19,490	6,143	3,462	3,187	9,504
Mayo	92,958	63,646	32,434	17,633	6,414	–	576	629	5,960
Meath East	65,588	41,388	14,386	10,818	5,780	2,270	–	766	7,368
Meath West	64,600	38,605	12,555	10,585	9,442	1,166	–	1,421	3,436
Offaly	65,636	44,034	6,838	15,760	4,804	–	–	525	16,107
Roscommon–Galway	64,235	45,680	6,812	8,819	3,075	1,211	982	286	24,495
Sligo–Leitrim	95,911	62,335	17,247	20,177	11,103	1,829	1,768	603	9,608
Tipperary	112,615	77,948	12,542	18,604	5,724	7,746	–	1,341	31,991
Waterford	81,819	51,703	14,850	10,603	9,739	2,268	1,646	2,237	10,360
Wexford	109,861	71,661	16,708	19,106	7,260	10,574	1,472	1,056	15,485
Wicklow	97,858	68,804	18,955	9,279	11,151	2,634	1,780	1,350	23,655
Dublin	852,463	529,932	121,972	81,724	74,748	46,237	50,139	22,320	132,792
Rest of Leinster	904,569	581,865	150,224	162,735	87,611	43,215	10,703	15,890	111,487
Munster	914,545	606,975	156,307	159,589	67,620	40,650	18,983	14,233	149,593
Connacht–Ulster	633,533	414,123	115,727	115,305	65,334	10,791	4,343	5,554	97,069
Total	3,305,110	2,132,895	544,230	519,353	295,313	140,893	84,168	57,997	490,941

Notes: The number of votes obtained refers to first preference figures. A further 18,398 votes were deemed invalid
In this and all other tables 'Others' includes the Social Democrats (64,094), Renua (46,552), Independents 4 Change (31,365), Direct Democracy Ireland (6481), Workers' Party (3242), Catholic Democrats (2013), Fís Nua (1224), Irish Democratic Party (971), Postmasters' Union (930), the Communist Party (185) and independents (333,884), which includes the Independent Alliance (89,828)

Table A1.2 Turnout and percentage votes for each party

Constituency	Turnout	Fine Gael	Fianna Fáil	Sinn Féin	Labour	AAA–PBP	Green Party	Others
Carlow–Kilkenny	65.4	27.3	40.4	12.4	6.3	3.9	3.7	6.0
Cavan–Monaghan	65.8	31.8	30.1	27.0	0.0	0.0	2.1	9.0
Clare	68.1	25.8	30.8	7.4	7.8	0.0	3.0	25.1
Cork East	63.4	28.5	24.3	10.1	13.2	3.8	1.5	18.6
Cork North-Central	62.7	17.8	27.9	19.5	7.3	15.7	3.3	8.4
Cork North-West	69.5	32.2	34.6	6.9	0.0	0.0	2.9	23.4
Cork South-Central	65.9	25.8	41.6	12.5	4.3	3.1	3.7	8.9
Cork South-West	68.0	31.9	19.6	8.5	7.0	0.0	1.7	31.3
Donegal	62.3	15.3	31.0	27.5	0.0	0.0	0.6	25.5
Dublin Bay North	67.2	19.7	15.4	11.6	7.7	9.0	1.4	35.1
Dublin Bay South	53.4	30.1	11.5	9.5	10.6	4.4	11.4	22.5
Dublin Central	51.5	13.6	10.6	24.4	8.8	3.0	2.7	36.8
Dublin Fingal	64.6	20.2	23.5	8.7	10.0	3.4	4.6	29.7
Dublin Mid-West	62.1	26.4	16.2	22.7	5.0	10.7	0.9	18.1
Dublin North West	61.3	12.5	12.8	27.0	7.4	3.9	2.5	33.8
Dublin Rathdown	65.9	30.6	10.3	7.0	9.8	0.0	10.0	32.3
Dublin South-Central	57.4	14.3	12.7	23.3	7.7	10.2	3.3	28.5
Dublin South-West	63.8	21.9	14.3	14.3	6.5	18.2	1.9	22.8
Dublin West	64.9	22.2	16.5	14.4	15.4	15.5	4.1	11.9
Dún Laoghaire	64.2	36.0	18.8	5.3	8.8	16.5	5.9	8.7
Galway East	66.1	30.1	27.3	5.9	10.0	0.0	1.7	25.0
Galway West	62.0	24.0	24.3	9.0	5.0	1.6	2.5	33.6
Kerry	70.3	21.4	15.8	11.9	6.1	1.2	1.3	42.3
Kildare North	63.1	23.6	28.2	6.5	8.4	1.6	3.0	28.7
Kildare South	62.2	30.2	36.4	11.6	11.6	0.0	2.3	8.0
Laois	61.4	32.4	35.1	21.2	7.3	0.0	4.0	0.0
Limerick City	61.9	28.5	27.8	12.6	11.2	9.8	2.1	8.0

Limerick County	65.7	37.1	27.6	7.5	0.0	0.0	0.7	27.0
Longford–Westmeath	61.9	23.8	28.2	9.5	8.7	0.9	2.0	26.8
Louth	64.5	19.6	18.5	28.9	9.1	5.1	4.7	14.1
Mayo	68.5	51.0	27.7	10.1	0.0	0.9	1.0	9.4
Meath East	63.1	34.8	26.1	14.0	5.5	0.0	1.9	17.8
Meath West	59.8	32.5	27.4	24.5	3.0	0.0	3.7	8.9
Offaly	67.1	15.5	35.8	10.9	0.0	0.0	1.2	36.6
Roscommon–Galway	71.1	14.9	19.3	6.7	2.7	2.1	0.6	53.6
Sligo–Leitrim	65.0	27.7	32.4	17.8	2.9	2.8	1.0	15.4
Tipperary	69.2	16.1	23.9	7.3	9.9	0.0	1.7	41.0
Waterford	63.2	28.7	20.5	18.8	4.4	3.2	4.3	20.0
Wexford	65.2	23.3	26.7	10.1	14.8	2.1	1.5	21.6
Wicklow	70.3	27.5	13.5	16.2	3.8	2.6	2.0	34.4
Dublin	62.2	23.0	15.4	14.1	8.7	9.5	4.2	25.1
Rest of Leinster	64.3	25.8	28.0	15.1	7.4	1.8	2.7	19.2
Munster	66.4	25.8	26.3	11.1	6.7	3.1	2.3	24.6
Connacht–Ulster	65.4	27.9	27.8	15.8	2.6	1.0	1.3	23.4
Total	64.5	25.5	24.3	13.8	6.6	3.9	2.7	23.0

Notes: Others include the Social Democrats (3.0 %), Renua (2.2 %), Independents 4 Change (1.5 %), Direct Democracy Ireland (0.3 %), Workers' Party (0.2 %), Catholic Democrats (0.1 %), Fís Nua (0.1 %), Irish Democratic Party (0.05 %), Postmasters' Union (0.04 %), the Communist Party of Ireland (0.01 %) and independents (15.7 %), which includes the Independent Alliance (4.2 %)

Table A1.3 Seats and candidates by party

Constituency	Total	Fine Gael	Fianna Fáil	Sinn Féin	Labour	AAA–PBP	Green Party	Others
Carlow–Kilkenny	5–15	2–3	2–3	1–1	0–1	0–2	0–1	0–4
Cavan–Monaghan	4–15	1–2	2–3	1–2			0–1	0–7
Clare	4–16	2–3	1–3	0–1	0–1		0–1	1–7
Cork East	4–15	1–3	1–2	1–1	1–1	0–1	0–1	0–6
Cork North-Central	4–14	1–2	1–1	1–2	0–1	1–1	0–1	0–6
Cork North-West	3–13	1–2	2–2	0–1			0–1	0–7
Cork South-Central	4–15	1–2	2–2	1–1	0–1	0–2	0–1	0–6
Cork South-West	3–11	1–2	1–1	0–1	0–1		0–1	1–5
Donegal	5–16	1–2	2–2	1–3			0–1	1–8
Dublin Bay North	5–20	1–3	1–2	1–2	0–1	0–2	0–1	2–9
Dublin Bay South	4–14	2–2	1–1	0–1	0–1	0–1	1–1	0–7
Dublin Central	3–15	1–1	0–1	1–1	0–1	0–1	0–1	1–9
Dublin Fingal	5–15	1–2	1–2	1–1	1–1	0–1	0–1	1–7
Dublin Mid-West	4–15	1–2	1–1	1–1	0–1	1–1	0–1	0–8
Dublin North West	3–11	1–1	0–1	1–2	0–1	1–1	0–1	1–4
Dublin Rathdown	3–9	1–2	0–1	0–1	0–1		1–1	1–3
Dublin South-Central	4–13	1–1	0–1	1–2	0–1	1–1	0–1	1–6
Dublin South-West	5–21	1–3	1–1	1–2	0–2	1–2	0–1	1–10
Dublin West	4–11	1–2	1–1	0–1	1–1	1–1	0–1	0–4
Dún Laoghaire	4–12	3–3	0–2	0–1	0–1	1–1	0–1	0–3
Galway East	3–10	1–2	1–2	0–1	0–1		0–1	1–3
Galway West	5–20	2–3	1–3	0–1	0–1		0–1	2–10
Kerry	5–16	1–3	1–2	1–1	0–1	0–1	0–1	2–7
Kildare North	4–14	1–2	2–2	0–1	0–1	0–1	0–1	1–6
Kildare South	3–9	1–2	2–2	0–1	0–1	0–1	0–1	1–6
Laois	3–6	1–2	1–1	1–1	0–1		0–1	0–2

Limerick City	4–11	1–2	1–1	1–1			0–1	0–4
Limerick County	3–10	2–2	1–1	0–1			0–1	0–5
Longford–Westmeath	4–18	1–3	1–2	0–1			0–1	1–9
Louth	5–16	2–2	1–2	2–2	0–2		0–1	0–6
Mayo	4–16	2–3	2–2	0–1			0–1	0–8
Meath East	3–12	2–2	1–1	0–1	0–1		0–1	0–6
Meath West	3–9	1–2	1–1	0–1	0–1		0–1	0–3
Offaly	3–11	1–1	1–2	1–1			0–1	0–6
Roscommon–Galway	3–12	0–1	1–2	0–1	0–1		0–1	2–5
Sligo–Leitrim	4–18	1–3	2–3	1–2	0–1		0–1	0–7
Tipperary	5–13	0–3	1–3	0–1	1–1		0–1	3–4
Waterford	4–12	1–2	1–1	1–1	0–1		0–1	1–5
Wexford	5–17	2–3	1–3	0–1	1–1		0–1	1–7
Wicklow	5–16	2–3	1–2	1–1	0–1		0–2	1–6
Dublin	44–156	14–22	6–14	7–15	2–12	5–12	2–11	8–70
Rest of Leinster	43–143	16–25	14–21	7–12	2–11	0–8	0–11	4–55
Munster	43–146	12–26	13–19	6–12	3–9	1–7	0–11	8–62
Connacht–Ulster	28–107	8–16	11–17	3–11	0–4	0–4	0–7	6–48
Total	158–552	50–89	44–71	23–50	7–36	6–31	2–40	26–235

Figures include outgoing Ceann Comhairle Seán Barrett (FG), automatically re-elected in Dun Laoghaire. They also include two candidates (one DDI, one independent) who each stood in two constituencies.

Notes: Others includes 14 Social Democrats (three elected), 26 Renua (none elected), five Independents 4 Change (four elected), 19 Direct Democracy Ireland (none elected), five Workers' Party (none elected), three Catholic Democrats (none elected), two Fís Nua (none elected), one Irish Democratic Party (none elected), one Irish Postmasters' Union (none elected), one Communist Party of Ireland (none elected) and independents consisting of 21 Independent Alliance (six elected), and 137 other independents (13 elected)

APPENDIX 2: MEMBERS OF THE 32ND DÁIL

TD (constituency)	Party	Occupation	Date of birth	First elected	Times elected	First pref votes in 2016
Gerry Adams (Louth)	SF	Barman	Oct-48	2011	2	10,661
Bobby Aylward (Carlow–Kilkenny)	FF	Farmer	Apr-55	2007	3	9,366
Maria Bailey (Dun Laoghaire)	FG	Aer Lingus ground staff	Nov-75	2016	1	10,489
Seán Barrett (Dun Laoghaire)	FG	Insurance broker	Aug-44	1981	10	—
Mick Barry (Cork North Central)	AAA–PBP	Journalist	Aug-63	2016	1	8,041
Richard Boyd Barrett (Dun Laoghaire)	AAA–PBP	Teacher	Nov-67	2011	2	9,775
John Brady (Wicklow)	SF	Carpenter	Jul-73	2016	1	11,151
John Brassil (Kerry)	FF	Pharmacist	Mar-63	2016	1	8,156
Declan Breathnach (Louth)	FF	School principal	Jun-58	2016	1	9,099
Pat Breen (Clare)	FG	Farmer, architect	Mar-57	2002	4	6,583
Colm Brophy (Dublin South-West)	FG	Company director	Jun-66	2016	1	7,195
Tommy Broughan (Dublin Bay North)	I4C	Teacher	Aug-47	1992	6	5,361
James Browne (Wexford)	FF	Barrister	Oct-75	2016	1	9,827
Richard Bruton (Dublin Bay North)	FG	Economist	Mar-53	F1982	10	9,792
Pat Buckley (Cork East)	SF	Builder	Feb-69	2016	1	5,358
Peter Burke (Longford–Westmeath)	FG	Accountant	Oct-82	2016	1	5,681
Joan Burton (Dublin West)	Lab	Accountant	Feb-49	1992	5	6,445
Mary Butler (Waterford)	FF	Retailer	Sep-66	2016	1	10,603
Catherine Byrne (Dublin SC)	FG	Homemaker, chef	Feb-56	2007	3	6,130
Thomas Byrne (Meath East)	FF	Solicitor	Jun-77	2007	2	10,818
Jackie Cahill (Tipperary)	FF	Farmer	May-62	2016	1	7,414
Dara Calleary (Mayo)	FF	Employee of Chambers Ireland	May-73	2007	3	9,402
Seán Canney (Galway East)	IA	Lecturer	Dec-57	2016	1	8,447
Ciarán Cannon (Galway East)	FG	Publican	Sep-65	2011	2	7,123
Joe Carey (Clare)	FG	Accountant	Jun-75	2007	3	6,071

(continued)

(continued)

TD (constituency)	Party	Occupation	Date of birth	First elected	Times elected	First pref votes in 2016
Pat Casey (Wicklow)	FF	Hotelier	Mar-61	2016	1	6,289
Shane Cassells (Meath West)	FF	Journalist	Apr-78	2016	1	10,585
Jack Chambers (Dublin West)	FF	Medical student	Nov-90	2016	1	6,917
Lisa Chambers (Mayo)	FF	Barrister	Aug-86	2016	1	8,231
Joan Collins (Dublin SC)	I4C	An Post clerk	Jun-61	2011	2	6,195
Michael Collins (Cork South West)	Ind	Farmer	Feb-58	2016	1	6,765
Niall Collins (Limerick County)	FF	Lecturer, accountant	Mar-73	2007	3	12,276
Catherine Connolly (Galway West)	Ind	Barrister	Nov-55	2016	1	4,877
Ruth Coppinger (Dublin West)	AAA–PBP	Teacher	Apr-67	B-2014	2	6,520
Marcella Corcoran-Kennedy (Offaly)	FG	Company director	Jan-63	2011	2	6,838
Simon Coveney (Cork SC)	FG	Manager of family business	Jun-72	B-1998	5	7,965
Barry Cowen (Offaly)	FF	Auctioneer	Aug-67	2011	2	12,366
Michael Creed (Cork North-West)	FG	Farmer	Jun-63	1989	6	8,869
Seán Crowe (Dublin South-West)	SF	Printing operative	Mar-57	2002	3	6,974
David Cullinane (Waterford)	SF	Car parts manager	Jul-74	2016	1	9,739
John Curran (Dublin Mid-West)	FF	Company director	Jun-60	2002	3	6,971
Clare Daly (Dublin Fingal)	I4C	Trade unionist	Apr-68	2011	2	9,480
Jim Daly (Cork South-West)	FG	Teacher	Dec-72	2011	2	7,370
Michael D'Arcy (Wexford)	FG	Farmer	Feb-70	2007	2	7,798
John Deasy (Waterford)	FG	US congressional aide	Oct-67	2002	4	7,641
Pat Deering (Carlow–Kilkenny)	FG	Farmer	Feb-67	2011	2	6,562
Pearse Doherty (Donegal)	SF	Civil engineer	Jul-77	B-2010	3	10,300
Regina Doherty (Meath East)	FG	Sales director	Jan-71	2011	2	6,830
Stephen Donnelly (Wicklow)	SD	Management consultant	Feb-75	2011	2	14,348
Paschal Donohoe (Dublin Central)	FG	Sales & marketing director	Sep-74	2011	2	3,226
Timmy Dooley (Clare)	FF	IT and publishing salesman	Feb-69	2007	3	10,215
Andrew Doyle (Wicklow)	FG	Farmer	Jul-60	2007	3	6,045

Bernard Durkan (Kildare North)	FG	Agricultural contractor	Mar-45	1981	10	6,147
Dessie Ellis (Dublin North-West)	SF	Television repairman	Oct-52	2011	2	7,571
Damien English (Meath West)	FG	Accountant	Feb-78	2002	4	8,123
Alan Farrell (Dublin Fingal)	FG	Estate agent	Dec-77	2011	2	7,514
Martin Ferris (Kerry)	SF	Fisherman	Mar-52	2002	4	9,458
Frances Fitzgerald (Dublin Mid-West)	FG	Social worker	Aug-50	1992	4	9,028
Michael Fitzmaurice (Roscommon–Galway)	IA	Contractor, farmer	n/a	B-2014	2	9,750
Peter Fitzpatrick (Louth)	FG	Regional business manager	May-62	2011	2	6,408
Charlie Flanagan (Laois)	FG	Solicitor	Nov-56	1987	7	8,370
Seán Fleming (Laois)	FF	Accountant	Feb-58	1997	5	13,626
Kathleen Funchion (Carlow–Kilkenny)	SF	Trade union organiser	Apr-81	2016	1	8,700
Pat 'the Cope' Gallagher (Donegal)	FF	Fish exporter	Mar-48	1981	9	10,198
Noel Grealish (Galway West)	Ind	Company director	Dec-65	2002	4	7,187
Brendan Griffin (Kerry)	FG	Publican	Mar-82	2011	2	9,674
John Halligan (Waterford)	IA	Radio operator	Jan-55	2011	2	8,306
Simon Harris (Wicklow)	FG	Political aide	Oct-86	2011	2	10,819
Michael Harty (Clare)	Ind	Medical doctor	Jul-52	2016	1	8,629
Seán Haughey (Dublin Bay North)	FF	Full-time public representative	Nov-61	1992	5	8,007
Séamus Healy (Tipperary)	Ind	Hospital administrator	Aug-50	B-2000	4	7,452
Danny Healy-Rae (Kerry)	Ind	Businessman, contractor	n/a	2016	1	9,991
Michael Healy-Rae (Kerry)	Ind	Shop and plant hire owner	Jan-67	2011	2	20,378
Martin Heydon (Kildare South)	FG	Farmer	Aug-78	2011	2	7,851
Brendan Howlin (Wexford)	Lab	Teacher	May-56	1987	8	10,574
Heather Humphreys (Cavan–Monaghan)	FG	Credit union manager	1963	2011	2	12,391
Paul Kehoe (Wexford)	FG	Sales representative	Jan-73	2002	4	7,696
Billy Kelleher (Cork North Central)	FF	Farmer	Jan-68	1997	5	14,286
Alan Kelly (Tipperary)	Lab	Semi-state e-business manager	Jul-75	2011	2	7,746
Enda Kenny (Mayo)	FG	Teacher	Apr-51	B-1975	13	13,318
Gino Kenny (Dublin Mid-West)	AAA–PBP	Care assistant	Jan-72	2016	1	4,629

(continued)

(continued)

TD (constituency)	Party	Occupation	Date of birth	First elected	Times elected	First pref votes in 2016
Martin Kenny (Sligo–Leitrim)	SF	Community project coordinator	Oct-69	2016	1	6,356
Seán Kyne (Galway West)	FG	Agri-environment consultant	May-75	2011	2	6,136
John Lahart (Dublin South-West)	FF	Psychotherapist	Nov-64	2016	1	9,647
James Lawless (Kildare North)	FF	Barrister	Aug-76	2016	1	7,461
Michael Lowry (Tipperary)	Ind	Company director	Mar-54	1987	8	13,064
Charlie McConalogue (Donegal)	FF	Farmer, political organiser	Oct-77	2011	2	12,533
Mary Lou McDonald (Dublin Central)	SF	Productivity consultant	May-69	2011	2	5,770
Helen McEntee (Meath East)	FG	Political aide, bank employee	Jun-86	B-2013	2	7,556
Finian McGrath (Dublin Bay North)	IA	School principal	Apr-53	2002	4	5,878
Mattie McGrath (Tipperary)	Ind	Plant hire contractor	Sep-58	2007	3	11,237
Michael McGrath (Cork South-Central)	FF	Accountant	Aug-76	2007	3	11,795
John McGuinness (Carlow–Kilkenny)	FF	Transport company director	Mar-55	1997	5	10,528
Joe McHugh (Donegal)	FG	Teacher	Jul-71	2007	3	8,412
Tony McLoughlin (Sligo–Leitrim)	FG	Sales representative	Jan-49	2011	2	6,172
Marc MacSharry (Sligo–Leitrim)	FF	Estate agent	Jul-73	2016	1	8,856
Josepha Madigan (Dublin Rathdown)	FG	Solicitor	May-69	2016	1	6,668
Catherine Martin (Dublin Rathdown)	Green	Teacher	Sep-72	2016	1	4,122
Micheál Martin (Cork South-Central)	FF	Teacher	Aug-60	1989	7	11,346
Denise Mitchell (Dublin Bay North)	SF	Assistant team leader	May-70	2016	1	5,039
Mary Mitchell O'Connor (Dun Laoghaire)	FG	School principal	Jun-59	2011	2	10,817
Kevin 'Boxer' Moran (Longford–Westmeath)	IA	Owner of taxi company	Apr-67	2016	1	7,586
Aindrias Moynihan (Cork North-West)	FF	Engineer	n/a	2016	1	8,924
Michael Moynihan (Cork North-West)	FF	Farmer	Jan-68	1997	5	7,332
Imelda Munster (Louth)	SF	Optician shop assistant	n/a	2016	1	8,829
Catherine Murphy (Kildare North)	SD	Clerical worker	Sep-53	B-2005	3	11,108
Dara Murphy (Cork North Central)	FG	Catering entrepreneur	Dec-69	2011	2	5,264

Name (Constituency)	Party	Occupation				
Eoghan Murphy (Dublin Bay South)	FG	Speechwriter	Apr-82	2011	2	4,529
Eugene Murphy (Roscommon–Galway)	FF	Radio presenter	Oct-58	2016	1	6,813
Paul Murphy (Dublin South West)	AAA-PBP	Political aide to MEP	Apr-83	B-2013	2	9,005
Margaret Murphy O'Mahony (Cork SW)	FF	Special needs assistant	Apr-67	2016	1	8,482
Denis Naughten (Roscommon–Galway)	Ind	Research scientist	Jun-73	1997	5	13,936
Hildegarde Naughton (Galway West)	FG	Teacher	May-77	2016	1	4,567
Tom Neville (Limerick County)	FG	Teacher, business consultant	Sep-75	2016	1	8,013
Carol Nolan (Offaly)	SF	School principal	n/a	2016	1	4,804
Michael Noonan (Limerick City)	FG	Teacher	May-43	1981	11	7,294
Darragh O'Brien (Dublin Fingal)	FF	Insurance firm manager	Jul-74	2007	2	10,826
Jonathan O'Brien (Cork North-Central)	SF	Community worker	Dec-71	2011	2	6,231
Eoin Ó Broin (Dublin Mid-West)	SF	Policy advisor	Jan-72	2016	1	9,782
Jim O'Callaghan (Dublin Bay South)	FF	Senior Counsel	Jan-68	2016	1	4,575
Caoimhghín Ó Caoláin (Cavan–Monaghan)	SF	Bank official	Sep-53	1997	5	10,060
Kate O'Connell (Dublin Bay South)	FG	Pharmacist	Jan-80	2016	1	5,399
Éamon Ó Cuív (Galway West)	FF	Cooperative manager	Jun-50	1996	6	9,539
Willie O'Dea (Limerick City)	FF	Accountant, barrister	Nov-52	F1982	10	12,999
Patrick O'Donovan (Limerick County)	FG	Teacher	Mar-77	2011	2	8,479
Fergus O'Dowd (Louth)	FG	Teacher	Sep-48	2002	4	6,814
Seán Ó Fearghaíl (Kildare South)	FF	Farmer	Apr-60	2002	4	6,469
Kevin O'Keeffe (Cork East)	FF	Farmer	Apr-64	2016	1	8,264
Donnchadh Ó Laoghaire (Cork SC)	SF	Political aide	Feb-89	2016	1	7,965
Fiona O'Loughlin (Kildare South)	FF	Primary school teacher	May-63	2016	1	6,906
Louise O'Reilly (Dublin Fingal)	SF	Trade unionist	Sep-73	2016	1	5,228
Frank O'Rourke (Kildare North)	FF	Company head of operations	May-57	2016	1	6,341
Aengus Ó Snodaigh (Dublin South-Central)	SF	Teacher	Aug-64	2002	5	6,639
Jan O'Sullivan (Limerick City)	Lab	Teacher	Dec-50	B-1998	5	5,227
Maureen O'Sullivan (Dublin Central)	Ind	Teacher	Mar-51	B-2009	3	1,990
Willie Penrose (Longford–Westmeath)	Lab	Barrister	Aug-56	1992	6	4,817
John Paul Phelan (Carlow–Kilkenny)	FG	Barrister	Sep-78	2011	2	7,568

(continued)

(continued)

TD (constituency)	Party	Occupation	Date of birth	First elected	Times elected	First pref votes in 2016
Thomas Pringle (Donegal)	Ind	Water treatment plant manager	Aug-68	2011	2	6,220
Maurice Quinlivan (Limerick City)	SF	Travel agency manager	Jan-67	2016	1	5,894
Anne Rabbitte (Galway East)	FF	Financial advisor	Oct-70	2016	1	6,928
Michael Ring (Mayo)	FG	Auctioneer	Dec-53	B-1994	6	11,275
Noel Rock (Dublin North-West)	FG	Political aide	Nov-87	2016	1	4,642
Shane Ross (Dublin Rathdown)	IA	Stockbroker, journalist	Jul-49	2011	2	10,202
Brendan Ryan (Dublin Fingal)	Lab	Food chemist	Feb-53	2011	2	6,009
Eamon Ryan (Dublin Bay South)	Green	Environmental consultant	Jul-63	2002	3	4,529
Éamon Scanlon (Sligo–Leitrim)	FF	Butcher, auctioneer	Jul-54	2007	2	5,874
Seán Sherlock (Cork East)	Lab	Political aide	Dec-72	2007	3	6,949
Róisín Shortall (Dublin North-West)	SD	Teacher of the deaf	Apr-54	1992	6	10,540
Brendan Smith (Cavan–Monaghan)	FF	Ministerial advisor	Jun-56	1992	6	8,775
Bríd Smith (Dublin South Central)	AAA–PBP	Trade unionist	n/a	2016	1	4,374
Niamh Smyth (Cavan–Monaghan)	FF	Arts and Education Officer	May-76	2016	1	6,268
Brian Stanley (Laois)	SF	Truck driver, builder	Jan-61	2011	2	8,242
David Stanton (Cork East)	FG	Teacher	Feb-57	1997	5	7,171
Peadar Tóibín (Meath West)	SF	Management consultant	Jun-74	2011	2	9,442
Robert Troy (Longford–Westmeath)	FF	Postmaster	Jan-82	2011	2	11,653
Leo Varadkar (Dublin West)	FG	Medical doctor	Jan-79	2007	3	8,247
Mick Wallace (Wexford)	I4C	Builder and property developer	Nov-55	2011	2	7,917
Katherine Zappone (Dublin South-West)	Ind	Lecturer	Nov-53	2016	1	4,463

Notes: Most TDs are full-time public representatives. For such TDs, the occupations given here are those previously followed
Seán Barrett was returned automatically as the outgoing Ceann Comhairle
There were two general elections in 1982, in February (F) and November (N). 'B-' indicates that deputy was first elected at a by-election

APPENDIX 3: THE GOVERNMENT AND MINISTERS OF STATE

A government was elected by the Dáil on 6 May 2016, 70 days after election day (see Chapter 11). It consisted of ministers of Fine Gael together with some independent deputies. Enda Kenny's nomination as Taoiseach was supported by 59 TDs; 50 Fine Gael deputies plus Seán Canney, John Halligan, Michael Harty, Michael Lowry, Finian McGrath, Kevin 'Boxer' Moran, Denis Naughten, Shane Ross and Katherine Zappone. It was opposed by 49 TDs. Fianna Fáil and the Green Party abstained on the vote. The cabinet consists of:

Enda Kenny	FG	Taoiseach and Minister for Defence
Frances Fitzgerald	FG	Tánaiste and Minister for Justice and Equality
Richard Bruton	FG	Minister for Education and Skills
Simon Coveney	FG	Minister for Housing, Planning and Local Government
Michael Creed	FG	Minister for Agriculture, Food and the Marine
Paschal Donohoe	FG	Minister for Public Expenditure and Reform
Charles Flanagan	FG	Minister for Foreign Affairs and Trade
Simon Harris	FG	Minister for Health
Heather Humphreys	FG	Minister for Regional Development, Rural Affairs, Arts and the Gaeltacht
Mary Mitchell O'Connor	FG	Minister for Jobs, Enterprise and Innovation
Denis Naughten	Ind	Minister for Communications, Climate Change and Natural Resources
Michael Noonan	FG	Minister for Finance
Shane Ross	Ind	Minister for Transport, Tourism and Sport
Leo Varadkar	FG	Minister for Social Protection
Katherine Zappone	Ind	Minister for Children and Youth Affairs
(Máire Whelan		Attorney General)

Ministers of state, their departments and areas of special responsibility

Regina Doherty	FG	Taoiseach (Government Chief Whip)
Pat Breen	FG	Jobs, Enterprise and Innovation (Employment and Small Business)
Catherine Byrne	FG	Regional Development, Rural Affairs, Arts and the Gaeltacht; Health (Communities and the National Drugs Strategy)
Seán Canney	Ind	Public Expenditure and Reform (The Office of Public Works and Flood Relief)
Marcella Corcoran Kennedy	FG	Health (Health Promotion)

(*continued*)

(continued)

Andrew Doyle	FG	Agriculture, Food and the Marine (Food, Forestry and Horticulture)
Damien English	FG	Housing, Planning and Local Government; (Housing and Urban Renewal)
John Halligan	Ind	Education and Skills; Jobs, Enterprise and Innovation (Training and Skills)
Paul Kehoe	FG	Taoiseach, Defence (Defence)
Seán Kyne	FG	Regional Development, Rural Affairs, Arts and the Gaeltacht; Communications, Climate Change and Natural Resources (Gaeltacht Affairs and Natural Resources)
Helen McEntee	FG	Health (Mental Health and Older People)
Finian McGrath	Ind	Health; Justice and Equality; Social Protection (Disability Issues)
Joe McHugh	FG	Taoiseach, Foreign Affairs and Trade (Diaspora and Overseas Development Aid)
Dara Murphy	FG	Taoiseach; Foreign Affairs and Trade; Justice (European Affairs, Data Protection and the EU Single Market)
Eoghan Murphy	FG	Finance; Public Expenditure and Reform (Financial Services, eGovernment and Public Procurement)
Patrick O'Donovan	FG	Transport, Tourism and Sport (Tourism and Sport)
Michael Ring	FG	Regional Development, Rural Affairs, Arts and the Gaeltacht (Regional Economic Development)
David Stanton	FG	Justice (Equality, Immigration and Integration)

Note: Regina Doherty, as chief whip, and Paul Kehoe and Finian McGrath, as 'super-junior' ministers, attend cabinet meetings

APPENDIX 4: THE ELECTORAL SYSTEM

Proportional representation by the single transferable vote (PR-STV) is the electoral system used in Ireland for Dáil elections, for Seanad elections, for local elections and for elections to the European Parliament. Internationally it is relatively rare; Malta is the only other country to employ it for elections for the lower house of a national parliament. It is also used for elections to the Australian Senate and for the Northern Ireland Assembly.

Ireland does not use a national constituency in order to elect parliamentary deputies (TDs). Rather the country is divided into 40 separate constituencies. The district magnitude of these districts in Dáil elections varies between three and five. There is a constitutional minimum constituency size of three. There is no maximum size, but since 1948 no constituency has returned more than five TDs. In 2016, there were 13 three-seat constituencies, 16 four-seat constituencies and 11 five-seat constituencies. In the 2016 election these 40 constituencies returned 157 deputies, with another—the Ceann Comhairle—being returned automatically. All Irish and British citizens, provided they are resident in Ireland, are entitled to vote.

Ballot papers are arranged in alphabetical order by the surname of the candidate. This will be accompanied by their photograph, a party label if applicable and usually an occupation (though this is often simply 'public representative') and address. Independents cannot describe themselves as such but may use the designation 'non-party' (see p. 208 above). Voters rank candidates in their order of preference, so they would write '1' next to the name of the candidate they would most like to win, '2' for their second choice and so on; only a first preference is required to render the vote valid, and after that the voter may rank as many or as few of the other candidates as they wish. There are no constraints as to what criteria voters may use in order to rank the candidates, so they are free to vote across party lines with their preferences if they wish. In most cases, polling stations are open from 7:00 AM to 10:00 PM. Voting before polling day is restricted to those living on offshore islands and those very few who are entitled to postal votes.

A candidate is deemed elected if they reach a number of votes equal to the Droop quota at any point in the election count. The Droop quota is calculated as follows: it is the smaller integer greater than the result of dividing the total number of votes cast by the number of seats in the constituency plus one. For example, if there were a five-seat constituency with 60,000 votes cast, the quota would be $((60,000/(5 + 1)) + 1) = 10,001$. This number has the property that it is the minimum number of votes that only five candidates can possibly attain.

Unlike in many countries, the counting of votes does not commence immediately after the closing of polls. Instead, the ballot boxes are taken to a counting centre and opened at 9 the following morning. At the end of each stage of the counting process, the constituency returning officer announces the result. If a candidate exceeds the quota on that count they are deemed elected. If all seats are not filled at the end of the first stage the count proceeds to a second stage, and so on. Assuming that no candidate reached the quota at the first stage the candidate with the lowest number of first preferences is eliminated and each of their votes is distributed according to the second preference marked on it. If a candidate exceeds the quota their surplus—the number of votes they had over and above the quota—is calculated and distributed according to the proportion of second preferences marked for each of the remaining candidates. (For a full explanation of exactly how the system works see 'Further reading' below.) This continues until all seats are filled by candidates reaching the quota, or until, even if the highest-placed remaining candidate is still below the quota, it is not mathematically possible for them to be overtaken even if they receive no votes from each remaining elimination. In 2016, the shortest count was Laois (three stages) and the longest was Dublin South West (16). Candidates whose vote total reaches a quarter of a quota at any point in the count may claim back expenses, to a maximum of €8700.

The transfer of votes is the distinctive feature of PR-STV. It allows voters to convey very detailed information as to what they really prefer—unconstrained by party or any other criteria. This allows us to assess many factors that are otherwise difficult to measure, such as how close parties stand to each other in the minds of voters and the importance of non-party-based candidate characteristics, such as geography or gender, for voters.

Further Reading

Department of the Environment, *Guide to Ireland's PR-STV Electoral System*, available at http://www.environ.ie/sites/default/files/migrated-files/en/Publications/LocalGovernment/Voting/FileDownLoad,1895,en.pdf

Gallagher, Michael, 'Ireland: the discreet charm of PR-STV', pp. 511–32 in Michael Gallagher and Paul Mitchell (eds), *The Politics of Electoral Systems* (Oxford: Oxford University Press, 2008).

Sinnott, Richard, 'The electoral system', pp. 111–36 in John Coakley and Michael Gallagher (eds), *Politics in the Republic of Ireland*, 5th ed (Abingdon: Routledge and PSAI Press, 2010).

APPENDIX 5: RETIREMENTS AND DEFEATED INCUMBENTS FROM THE 31ST DÁIL

Members of the 31st Dáil who did not contest the election to the 32nd Dáil

John Browne	Wexford	FF
Michael Colreavy	Sligo–Nth Leitrim	SF
Michael Conaghan	Dublin South-Central	Lab
Robert Dowds	Dublin Mid-West	Lab
Frank Feighan	Roscommon–Sth Leitrim	FG
Tom Fleming	Kerry South	Ind
Éamon Gilmore	Dun Laoghaire	Lab
Joe Higgins	Dublin West	AAA–PBP
Seán Kenny	Dublin North-East	Lab
Séamus Kirk	Louth	FF
Michael Kitt	Galway East	FF
Dinny McGinley	Donegal South-West	FG
Sandra McLellan	Cork East	SF
Olivia Mitchell	Dublin South	FG
Dan Neville	Limerick County	FG
Ruairí Quinn	Dublin South-East	Lab
Pat Rabbitte	Dublin South-West	Lab
Liam Twomey	Wexford	FG
Jack Wall	Kildare South	Lab
Brian Walsh[a]	Galway West	FG

[a]Walsh had resigned his seat in January 2016, and it was vacant at the time of the 2016 general election

Members of the 31st Dáil who were defeated at the 2016 election

James Bannon	Longford–Westmeath	FG
Tom Barry	Cork East	FG
Ray Butler	Meath West	FG
Jerry Buttimer	Cork South-Central	FG
Eric Byrne	Dublin South-Central	Lab
Paudie Coffey	Waterford	FG
Áine Collins	Cork North-West	FG
Seán Conlon	Cavan–Monaghan	Ind
Paul Connaughton	Galway East	FG
Ciara Conway	Waterford	Lab
Noel Coonan	Tipperary	FG
Joe Costello	Dublin Central	Lab
Lucinda Creighton	Dublin Bay South	Renua
Jimmy Deenihan	Kerry	FG
Anne Ferris	Wicklow	Lab

(*continued*)

(continued)

Terence Flanagan	Dublin Bay North	Renua
Dominic Hannigan	Meath East	Lab
Noel Harrington	Cork South-West	FG
Tom Hayes	Tipperary	FG
Kevin Humphreys	Dublin Bay South	Lab
Derek Keating	Dublin Mid-West	FG
Colm Keaveney	Galway East	FF
Anthony Lawlor	Kildare North	FG
Ciarán Lynch	Cork South-Central	Lab
Kathleen Lynch	Cork North-Central	Lab
John Lyons	Dublin North-West	Lab
Pádraig MacLochlainn	Donegal	SF
Éamonn Maloney	Dublin South-West	Ind
Peter Matthews	Dublin Rathdown	Ind
Michael McCarthy	Cork South-West	Lab
Gabrielle McFadden	Longford–Westmeath	FG
Michael McNamara	Clare	Lab
Michelle Mulherin	Mayo	FG
Ged Nash	Louth	Lab
Derek Nolan	Galway West	Lab
Kieran O'Donnell	Limerick City	FG
John O'Mahony	Galway West	FG
Joe O'Reilly	Cavan–Monaghan	FG
Aodhán Ó Ríordáin	Dublin Bay North	Lab
John Perry	Sligo–Leitrim	FG
Ann Phelan	Carlow–Kilkenny	Lab
James Reilly	Dublin Fingal	FG
Alan Shatter	Dublin Rathdown	FG
Arthur Spring	Kerry	Lab
Emmet Stagg	Kildare North	Lab
Billy Timmins	Wicklow	Renua
Joanna Tuffy	Dublin Mid-West	Lab
Alex White	Dublin Rathdown	Lab

INDEX

A

Aardal, Bernt, 182n2
Aarts, Kees, 184n19, 289n4
Abedi, Amir, 225n16
abortion, xxiii, 16, 18, 63, 87, 132,
    140, 141, 173, 195, 270, 273
Adams, Gerry, xxii, xxiii, 27, 82, 84,
    92, 178, 179, 193, 257, 258, 264
Adshead, Maura, 290n14
age
    of ministers, 272
    of TDs, 103, 132, 153–4, 199,
        204n27
    and voting behaviour, 164, 180,
        182n4
Agricultural Science Association, 232
Ahern, Bertie, 11, 121, 220, 221, 284
Aldrich, John, 226n32
Alternative für Deutschland, 86
Anderson, Christopher J., 183n10,
    184n14
Andeweg, Rudy, 289n4

Andrews, Chris, 151
Anglo–Irish Bank, 5, 23
Anti-Austerity Alliance–People Before
    Profit (AAA-PBP)
    background, 6, 18, 73, 84, 87–8
    in campaign, 104, 105, 132, 137,
        159, 165, 193, 194
    candidates, 52, 64–5, 68, 69, 72,
        186, 191
    and government formation, 264
    in party system, 148, 235
    support, 135, 138, 166, 172, 175,
        180
    TDs, 197
Áras an Uachtaráin, xxi, 1, 2, 90,
    264
Ardagh, Catherine, 149, 189
Arkins, Audrey, 24n9
Arnold, Tom, 252n30
Australia, 222, 229, 288, 308
Austria, 260, 261, 281
Aylward, Bobby, 20, 301

Note: Page number followed by "n" denote footnote.

© The Author(s) 2016
M. Gallagher, M. Marsh (eds.), *How Ireland Voted 2016*,
DOI 10.1007/978-3-319-40889-7

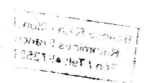